SO-AEV-531

FLORIDA STATE
UNIVERSITY LIBRARIES

JAN 27 2000

TALLAHASSEE, FLORIDA

Two Hamlets in Nam Bo

TWO HAMLETS IN NAM BO

*Memoirs of Life in Vietnam
Through Japanese Occupation,
the French and American Wars,
and Communist Rule, 1940–1986*

by
DAVID LAN PHAM

McFarland & Company, Inc., Publishers
Jefferson, North Carolina, and London

DS
556.83
.P42
A3
2000

Library of Congress Cataloguing-in-Publication Data

Pham, David Lan, 1940–
    Two Hamlets in Nam Bo : memoirs of life in Vietnam through
Japanese occupation, the French and American wars, and
communist rule, 1940–1986 / by David Lan Pham.
        p.   cm.
    Includes index.
    ISBN 0-7864-0646-1 (library binding : 50# alkaline paper) ∞
    1. Pham, David Lan.   2. Vietnam — History — 20th century.
I. Title.
DS556.83.P42A3   2000
959.704 — dc21   99-54797
                                                                    CIP

British Library Cataloguing-in-Publication data are available

©2000 David Lan Pham. All rights reserved

*No part of this book may be reproduced or transmitted in any form
or by any means, electronic or mechanical, including photocopying
or recording, or by any information storage and retrieval system,
without permission in writing from the publisher.*

Manufactured in the United States of America

*McFarland & Company, Inc., Publishers
    Box 611, Jefferson, North Carolina 28640
    www.mcfarlandpub.com*

This book is dedicated to all the freedom lovers

Contents

Preface

This book reflects what was going on in my Vietnam over the past fifty years. All the political, cultural, historical, social, and economical aspects of this period of time are found in this book.

Readers will see a social painting of Vietnam through the images of two small villages in Nam Bo (the southern part of Vietnam): Binh Chuan and Tuy An (An Phu). I was born and spent my childhood in these villages. They did not play important roles in history, but they witnessed historic and political events and were deeply modified by them. They serve as models for other Vietnamese villages during the French and Japanese occupations, the short-lived independence period, and two bloody Vietnamese wars after World War II.

Two Hamlets in Nam Bo faithfully records good and bad things in our society, both in feudal and colonial times and in the independence period. I have tried to write what I saw, what I heard and what I knew faithfully and impartially.

After reading this book, readers will understand why the Communists were successful in 1945, 1954, and 1975 and why the Nationalists failed bitterly, even though they were backed by France and the United States. Readers will get in touch with some Vietnamese leaders, such as Emperor Bao Dai, President Ho Chi Minh, President Ngo Dinh Diem, and President Nguyen Van Thieu, make friends with other Communist and Nationalist politicians, and hear different opinions on Communism-Nationalism, Ho Chi Minh–Bao Dai, Ho Chi Minh–Ngo Dinh Diem, leadership, foreign aid, dependence, and independence. Readers will see how public opinion changed endlessly. They will see how people respected Cu Ho (Old Ho) or Bac Ho (Uncle Ho) and how they ridiculed him after the fall of South Vietnam. They also will see the anti–American demonstrations in South Vietnam under French rule and during the Vietnam War and the hope of *qui ma* (slang for *qua My*, "going to America") or *ma qui* (slang for *My qua*, "the return of the Americans") under Communist rule.

In these memoirs, readers will have a good opportunity to encounter some ordinary people of noble character and to witness some singular acts.

1

They will become aware of the tragic diaspora of 2 million Vietnamese on the East Sea and on the Gulf of Thailand and of their tearful and horrible stories.

Two Hamlets in Nam Bo was written twelve years after I left Vietnam. I thank Sister Thomasa (Philippines), Jean Washington (Alabama, New Mexico), Michele Prockup (Alabama), Lynn Nettles (Alabama), Juanita Stele (Washington, D.C., Alabama), Sue Terrill (Ohio), Ms. Elsie Delaplane (Ohio), and Stephen Cottrell (Alabama, Mississippi) for encouraging me to write this book.

I thank Tammy Nguyen Pham, my wife; Albert Quoc Pham, my oldest son; Elizabeth Lan Pham, my daughter; Wellington Nguyen Pham, my son; An Quoc Pham, my son; and Victoria Chau Pham, my daughter, for their encouragement and technical assistance in finishing this book.

I thank Vietnam for giving me sacred love for the country; my father and mother for making me a good man; my teachers for saving me from darkness and ignorance; my grandfather and grandmother for caring about me in my childhood; my aunts, uncles, friends and former students for their concerns about me and my family; and my brothers and my sisters-in-law for encouraging me and helping me to study after my father's death.

I thank the *Médecins du Monde* for rescuing me on the East Sea; Dr. Dominique, vice chairman of the *Médecins du Monde*; Nguyen Huu, French general consul to the Philippines; and correspondents Philippe Theard and Pascal Deloche for their concerns about us in the refugee camp.

I am thankful to all the Vietnamese fallen for the cause of our country and all the American and allied troops for fighting for freedom in South Vietnam.

I thank the American government and people for their kindness and generosity. The United States has become my second homeland in which I have enjoyed freedom and human rights. I wrote *Two Hamlets in Nam Bo* and *Vietnam: The Past Memories* (poems) in the land of freedom. I enjoy true freedom, democracy, and happiness and will spend the rest of my life in this second homeland.

David Lan Pham
Toledo, Ohio
August 1999

1

Peaceful Life in Wartime

I was born as the Japanese troops were invading North Vietnam.

My family was wealthy and popular in the village. My great-grandfather was originally from South Central Vietnam. He recruited the villagers to go south and founded Tuy An village by the end of the reign of Tu Duc. After his death the villagers worshipped him in the village temple (*dinh*) as a local deity.

Tuy An village is an arid village without rivers, springs, mountains, or valleys. It was hard for the villagers to dig wells. They had to get water from the spring in Tan Phuoc about two miles from their village. The rich villagers kept rainwater in big jars or cement basins.

There were no rice fields in Tuy An. Its villagers weren't good farmers. They planted fruit trees, such as jack trees, mango trees, and grapefruit trees, around their houses for shade and for pure air. It was very dusty in Tuy An in the spring and summer.

Because the land was almost sterile, farming wasn't lucrative. The villagers had to study hard in the hope of having better lives. Many good students in Thudaumot province graduated from Tuy An school. Some students from Di An, Tan Ba, Tan Hiep, Bung, Laithieu, and Binh Nham studying there had to rent rooms in boardinghouses.

Tuy An was annexed to Vinh Phu to become An Phu Xa (*xa* means "village"). This village was famous for its numerous teachers, civil servants, and employees working for French firms in Saigon. Their incomes were pretty high and allowed them to have pretty houses. Some houses had big gates with signs: *Attention! Chien Méchant* (Beware of Dog). Others had nice hibiscus hedges.

Before 1945, Tuy An (An Phu Xa) had as residents a lawyer, a judge, a teacher of math at Lycée Sisovath in Phnom Penh, Cambodia, a civil servant working for the French general government in Hanoi, and a large number of *diplômés*. Under French rule, the *diplôme d'étude primaire supérieure* was a dream for the Vietnamese who wished to improve their lives. Most teachers graduated from the *Ecole Normale* (a school of pedagogy). Teaching was less lucrative, however, than other professions. The teachers' poverty was ridiculed in the following popular song:

> *The cucumbers must be soaked in salted trash fish.*
> *Poor students must study at the school of pedagogy.*

A few adventurous villagers went trading in Dau Giay, Xuan Loc, Bau Ca, Xa Cam, Xa Cat, and other towns. Some got wealthy by selling timber or rattan. Some took salt from the cities to the highland, sold it to the ethnic tribes, and bought their local products for sale in the cities.

One villager owned a bus and served passengers traveling to Loc Ninh and Hon Quan from Thudaumot. Most passengers were traders in charge of distributing goods to both urban and rural consumers. This triangular trade helped many villagers get rich quickly.

Some villagers had horse-drawn coaches and provided transportation to passengers from Tuy An to Bung, Laithieu, and Tan Ba. These coachmen were wealthy and had large brick houses in the village.

In the 1940s there was no bus in Tuy An. In order to go to Saigon, people had to get up early. They went to Laithieu, Thudaumot, Bung, or Di An by coach. There, they took the bus or train to get to Saigon. It took a day to make a twenty-mile trip. Only the civil servants, teachers, and merchants had bicycles, which they lovingly called "iron horses." Alcyon, Labor, and Peugeot were the then-famous bike brands. The Alcyon bikes were more comfortable than other bikes thanks to their solid bike forks and large tires. The old bikes had solid tires that caused constipation in the riders.

My paternal village was intellectually superior to the neighboring ones. The villagers were influenced by Western culture, which they learned from the local school, the *Lycée Petrus Ky* and the *Ecole Normale*. They developed their knowledge by reading books, magazines, and newspapers and by running businesses. Saigon, the Pearl of the Far East, wasn't strange to them. Neither were Da Lat, Cap St. Jacques (Vung Tau), My Tho (Dinh Tuong, Tien Giang), Hanoi, and even Phnom Penh. Most villagers could speak, write, and read French correctly. Some of them gave their children French names, such as *Jean, Jacques, Jacquot, Paul, Pierre, Jules,* or *Denis,* or Vietnamese names phoneticized from French, such as Oanh (*vingt*), On (*un*), Rang (*Jean*), Rac (*Jacques*), Bon (*point*), etc. My father named my oldest brother *Jules.* One of my uncle's children was named *François.*

My maternal village is Binh Chuan, a rich and populous area about three miles from my paternal village. Its villagers were farmers who worked hard from dawn until dark.

Compared to Tuy An, Binh Chuan was more rural. People lived scattered far away from their farmlands. Every house had its bamboo or cactus fence. Some villagers put dry bamboo branches around their houses to set the limit of their properties. Wealthy villagers were hard-working farmers, who owned fertile rice fields and had many strong children. Most of the fertile lands lay near a creek, which facilitated irrigation. They stretched along the creek leading to Bung. These lands are good for rice paddies, vegetables, and tobacco. The further the lands are from the creek, the drier they are. Farmers dig deep wells to get water. Such dry lands are good for peanuts, cassava, and jack trees.

In the first half of the twentieth century, farmers in Binh Chuan didn't plant fruit trees. They weren't familiar with some favorite Western vegetables, such as lettuce, potatoes, tomatoes, carrots, cabbages, and cauliflowers, or even with tropical fruit trees. Arid lands were good for jack trees, but most villagers didn't like to plant them for fear of ghosts. They believed that ghosts touched jack fruit and made them prematurely rotten. To prevent the fruit from being touched by ghosts, they hung torn cloths or something dirty on the jack trees.

The villagers had little faith, but they were highly superstitious. There was a Buddhist temple in the village at the boundary between Binh Chuan and Thuan Giao. It was called the Pagoda of Venerable Hue for the monk who founded it. The evening bell ringing and drum beats from the pagoda reminded the farmers of the end of the working day. Their matinal sounds helped them know the dawn. The bell ringing and the rooster's song became a sort of alarm clock for the villagers for none of them had a watch. The concept of time was based on the position of the sun in the sky. The concept of space was based on the number of lit incense sticks. If somebody asked, "How far is it from here?" the answer would be, "About a lit incense stick."

The Catholic church was the biggest brick building in the village. It was located on the interprovincial road linking Thudaumot and Bien Hoa. Because none of the villagers were Catholic, this priestless church was abandoned during the persistent wars. It existed in spite of the challenge of time, damp weather, and continual wars.

It is difficult to tell about religions in Binh Chuan, given that the villagers lived harmoniously in the community. They helped one another in house construction and repair, in farming, and in funerals and wedding ceremonies. The patriarchal regime was rigidly observed. The father was the real leader in the family. His wife and children executed his orders. The children had to be pious toward their parents. Every family commemorated their ancestors' death day annually by offering good food, rice alcohol, fruit, and tea. It seemed that the villagers didn't know a lot about Buddhist, Confucian, and Taoist philosophy. They tried to have good behavior and to be more humanistic. The village customs were severe. Unmarried pregnant women and those ladies committing adultery or running away to live with their boyfriends faced rude reactions from public opinion. Fortunately, these cases were rare. If they existed, the women in question had to leave the village.

Without really knowing much about it, a few villagers were followers of Hoa Hao Buddhism, a Vietnamese religion founded in 1939 by Huynh Phu So in the Mekong Delta. They called it *dao tuyet coc* because the followers didn't eat rice but ate cassava and sweet potatoes. Some people living at the intersection of the interprovincial and communal roads were Caodaists. Caodaism is a Vietnamese religion founded by a group of Cochinchinese civil servants in 1926. Its Holy See is in Tay Ninh province.

Unlike other villages, Binh Chuan didn't have a big *dinh* (village temple). It had a small temple. The villagers came there annually, bringing rice, pork, chickens, fruit, and flowers to offer to the local deity and to pray for good weather, good harvest, good luck, good health, and prosperity. They kept the temple clean and believed in the divine power of their local deity. Nobody dared say rude words at the temple, which also served as a sacred place where people came and swore to tell the truth when they were in dispute. The liars didn't dare to swear in the *dinh* for fear of being strangled by the local deity. It helped the villagers be more sincere and honest.

Binh Chuan was far away from Western culture, although it was about twenty-five miles from Saigon and five miles from Thudaumot.

The Catholic church, the elementary school, and the communal office were the three brick buildings in the village. The villagers called the communal office *nha hoi* (the assembly house) or *nha vuong* (square house) in accordance with its use and shape. The villagers lived in wooden houses. Wealthy farmers had large houses with red tile roofs, large front doors, and wooden walls. Poor people lived in cottages whose frames were made of bamboo. The walls were made from mud mixed with hay, and the roofs were covered with thatch. Usually, these cottages had neither door nor window.

My grandmother's house was large. It was composed of three compartments and two small rooms on each side. My grandmother was in widowhood in the 1930s, but her life remained cozy thanks to her rice fields. She was richer than other villagers. But she didn't have expensive furniture made of precious wood, like the rich families in the cities. She had two old-style pearly cabinets made in 1922 that she used as altars, and she had unfinished furniture in the living room, two cupboards and two large divans. The floor of the house was neither tiled nor cemented. It was clean, though.

Houses in Binh Chuan were simple. Their architecture was rudimentary, and their decoration was poor. There were neither pictures nor statues on the altars. One home had a piece of red paper with some Chinese characters written in ink with a paint brush. Nobody knew what they meant. There were no photos in Binh Chuan. People only had pictures taken when they entered the colonial army, went to jail, or applied for *laissez-passer* (ID). They didn't have any photos of their parents or grandparents. Many of them didn't know what their parents or grandparents looked like. They seemed not to pay much attention to that. Some superstitious people believed that they would lose their mind if they posed for a picture.

It was unusual to find a painting on the wall, even a simple picture of a mountain and river with the usual three colors: red, green, and blue. Red was for the dusty path and house roof, green for the trees and grass along the path, and blue for the sky and water. The painters took their inspiration from the four cardinal professions in society (student, farmer, craftsman, and merchant, or, fisherman, woodcutter, farmer, and student), from the four seasons, from Chinese stories, and from the natural landscape (mountains, rivers, streams, bamboo trees, clouds). They drew on glass and displayed their paintings at the market.

Binh Chuan didn't have any artists by the mid–twentieth century. Its villagers focused on farming and ignored the arts. At times, they went to the theater in Tan Khanh. They liked the *hat bo,* which was similar to the *noh* in Japan or to the *chanson de geste* in France in the Middle Ages. But they didn't say which actors and actresses they admired. In the early twentieth century, Phung Ha was the most beautiful actress, well known in Vietnam for her beauty and performance. However, our villagers didn't know her. Why? Because of their illiteracy? Because of their attachment to the Confucian concepts unfavorable to theatrical people? In olden times, Dao Duy Tu couldn't participate in the triennial contest because his father was an actor. He fled to the South and served Lord Nguyen as a strategist.

The village school had only three classrooms. They seemed to be big enough in comparison with the small number of students. Most children in Binh Chuan didn't have birth certificates, which were one of the enrollment requirements in school. Many parents didn't send their children to school because of this complication. On the other hand, farming needed manpower. If the children went to school, their parents would lose helpers. They helped their mother to take care of their siblings and their father to keep and to feed oxen. That is why Binh Chuan school didn't have any reputation. Almost none of the villagers had a third-grade certificate. Consequently, the villagers read neither books nor newspapers.

Because of illiteracy and poor health none of them could be chosen to bear arms. Chin Rua, who did have a third-grade certificate, knew some French words he had learned in *cours préparatoire* (second grade). His French helped him to become a *ma ta* (policeman). His two sons were named Rang and Rac, phoneticized from *Jean* and *Jacques.* That was one of the vestiges of French culture in my maternal village. Once in a while, Chin Rua, in a rusty uniform, came back to the village. Everybody listened to him telling about urban life and comforts. I was among his listeners and admirers.

After the Japanese overthrew the French in March 1945, Chin Rua fled to his home village and made his living by farming. He lived a simple life in the country during the two bloody wars.

Chin Rua's brother was Muoi Boi. Like his brother, Muoi Boi was cheerful and funny. He used to tell the farmers funny stories. He made them laugh and forget their hard work in the torrid sunlight and torrential rains. When a villager died, Muoi Boi recited Buddhist prayers to wipe out all the terrestrial sins of the dead so that Buddha would bring his soul to Nirvana. The children used to follow Muoi Boi when he prayed for the dead at the tomb on the third day after burial. He put offerings at the tombstone and recited prayers while beating a gong to introduce the dead to the officials of Hell. He let a small hen drink rice alcohol and helped it climb a ladder made from a banana leaf stem. The children watched him attentively. When he threw the hen, they competed with one another to catch it. Such a hen is believed to lay many eggs.

The villagers had busy and agreeable days during the harvest, at Tet (Lunar New Year), planting rice paddies, and participating in the annual assembly at the temple to offer food, fruit, and flowers to the local deity. Without these days, life would have been quiet and monotonous in this remote area.

I liked to take part in farming, although it wasn't my duty. I joined my aunt and her husband in catching crabs when they plowed and harrowed their rice fields. I enjoyed eating crab soup for lunch in the open air. On the day the farmers planted the paddies, I got up early, like my aunt, when I heard the horn sounding. I sowed seeds, cropped beans, and uprooted peanuts, and then we had a collective lunch in a shady place at noon. I didn't pick tobacco leaves. My aunt's husband sliced them in tiny pieces, and I trampled them down until they became thin sheets before they were dried in the sun.

My aunt was a typically successful farmer. Her diligence and patience determined her wealth. All of her children worked intensively. After the peanut crop came sweet potatoes, rice, tobacco, and vegetables. They worked all year round on their rice fields and arid lands. Every time I came to my aunt's house, I saw her cleaning and sorting rice, salting fish, cooking meals, slicing banana trees to feed the pigs, or drying beans and tobacco. She was busy all the time. Her daughters carried produce home from the rice fields or the dry farmlands. They worked endlessly without time to take care of their beauty. They didn't know what was going on outside the village, either.

The Americans dropped two A-bombs in Hiroshima and Nagasaki. My aunt's family didn't care. It wasn't their business. They had many things to do. My aunt's sons, whose skin was sunburned, sweated blood under the torrid heat of the sun. Their family income was much higher than that of other villagers, but they neither went to school nor knew delicious food and expensive clothes.

In my aunt's house, there were many jars of salted fish, which was served every day. Sometimes people ate steamed gourds or bamboo shoots with salted fish. Sometimes they ate grilled fish or boiled sweet potato browses with it. They rarely ate meat. They preferred chicken soup, but it wasn't served regularly. In general, the villagers only had delicious food during Tet and on the memorial days of their ancestors.

Needy villagers caught fish and crabs in the rice fields to improve their meals. Crystallized sugar was very expensive. Even rich farmers couldn't afford it. Many poor villagers ate brown sugar for breakfast, lunch, and dinner instead of meat. Usually, the villagers used brown sugar and molasses made by the local sugar mill. They liked salty and spicy food. They drank water and rice alcohol instead of tea and beer.

Malnutrition was the root of many illnesses. Many people had tuberculosis from working hard without having enough food. When they got sick, they used traditional ways of treatment. Coining and rubbing were for colds and headaches. In case of a serious headache, the patient went to see Ong Nam, a charlatan, who, with a sharp knife, slightly cut the patient's head skin to squeeze out some stagnant blood. When the villagers caught a cold, they collected various kinds of leaves for fumigation. They ate minty leaves and prepared a concoction of ginger roots, rock sugar, and sliced lemons when they coughed. In cases of chronic or deadly disease, they looked for a wizard, who offered some food to the spirits to ask them to leave the patient. The wizard gave the patient a voodoo. The patient burned it and took its ash as medicine. Sick children had to wear magic paper ties. When people had dropsy, they ate husked rice. Those who had mental health problems were sent to the Buddhist temple. For rabies, people boiled water that had been used by the blacksmith to cool down hot iron in the forge and drank it. When people had typhoid fever, they appealed to the charlatan for help. He would use a piece of porcelain sterilized by the heat of a lamp to cut the patient's back slightly and squeeze out some blood. Before the treatment, the charlatan would examine the patient's back with an oil lamp to locate the microbes that, according to him, looked like crabs. This simple treatment saved only some lucky patients.

In 1942, Japanese troops went down south. They paid attention to the importance of Dong Xoai. They occupied Phu Loi and repaired its airport to prepare for their expansion in continental Southeast Asia.

Binh Chuan wasn't ravaged by World War II, but the villagers' lives were visibly and deeply modified by the war. Whether people were interested in the outside world or not, the war brought them miseries. During World War II, Vietnam lacked commodities imported from France. Getting rice from the Mekong Delta to the eastern provinces of Nam Bo (the southern part of Vietnam) was very difficult. The villagers were in rags. They washed their clothes in the spring with sand. They had no thread to mend their torn clothes. Some people used pineapple leaf fibers instead of thread, but these fibers break when people breathed out strongly. Not all the villagers even had pineapple fibers. Many of them tied up their torn clothes with banana tree fibers instead of mending them.

Nutrition got worse during the war. Salt was rare, even though it was the least expensive and the most useful in cooking. Most villagers stopped salting fish except for some wealthy families like my aunt's. Her family still had abundant agricultural produce, which facilitated her regular trade in this critical period. Some rich farmers made fish sauce by cooking crabs, which they caught in the rice fields, with salt. There is no river in Binh Chuan. The spring isn't fishy because of its clear water. Farmers catch small fish in the rice fields, but fishing was absent in this remote village. The villagers raised poultry for protein. For lack of food, the chickens weren't fat. They died of cold when the weather changed. The villagers tried to save them by letting them eat pounded onions or by cutting their claws. From time to time, some villagers slaughtered a pig they had raised at home to sell pork to other villagers. There was no professional butcher in the village. Sometimes people trapped wild boars and sold the meat to other villagers. It was difficult to have good beef. Strong oxen and water buffaloes were used to draw carts, to plow, and to harrow the lands. As they got old or sick, they were slaughtered, but their meat was tough. Most villagers didn't eat either dog meat or water buffalo meat. That didn't mean they were influenced by Buddhism. (Buddhist followers deem that the water buffalo is the incarnation of Bodhisattva. They are advised to neither slaughter animals nor eat their meat.) Our farmers just observed what their ancestors did. The dog and water buffalo have been not only useful to them but also familiar to them. The former ensure their property's safety; the latter contribute to their prosperity.

In wartime children in the village caught chameleons with bamboo poles. They ground their meat to prepare soup with gourds. I made a bamboo pole with a long rope at its end and joined these children in hunting for reptiles. I hissed. The chameleons raised their heads. I moved the bamboo pole to catch them. People took advantage of the nocturnal rains to catch toads and frogs to enrich their diet. I joined them, although my grandmother prevented me from hunting these amphibians.

My grandfather owned a rice mill and many hectares of land before World War II. He was dead before I was born. I didn't know some of my aunts and uncles, who died before my birth, but I did know two aunts and three uncles. One of my aunts lived near my grandmother's house. The other lived in Hoa Thanh. Both of them were wealthy. The first was a rich farmer making her fortune by her hard work, diligence, and good management. The second got rich by running a restaurant in Phu Loi during the Japanese occupation. Two of my uncles lived in my grandmother's house. They were of different characters. One was pious and careful. The other was absentminded. He couldn't accomplish anything smoothly, but his image remains vivid in my mind.

He wasn't scared of anything. He could walk in the rain without catching a cold. He could be awake all night without getting tired. On the other hand, he could sleep anytime in daytime or nighttime in the noisiest place. He slept hungry for two or three consecutive days. He was clumsy. He had no skills. He couldn't live without my grandmother. He was married four times but remained childless until 1953, when he had his first baby, with his fifth wife. The baby boy had to wear earrings, as if he should have been a girl, and had an ugly name so that he wouldn't die young. All three of his children had ugly names, which they changed when they grew up.

His first wife got remarried to a Frenchman. She left Vietnam for Paris during the Franco-Vietnamese War. She sent him gifts and money, but he refused to receive them. His second wife slept so deeply that she crushed her baby to death. Scolded by my grandmother, she left my uncle. His third wife was lazy and greedy. She was able to eat thirty-seven eggs at one time. This excess was too "progressive" to an exemplary mother-in-law like my grandmother and to the conservative villagers. His fourth wife left him because of his uncertain future.

My careless uncle loved the wandering life. One day, my grandmother asked him to go to Hoa Thanh to tell my aunt some important things. He left and wandered in the neighboring villages all week long. My grandmother seemed to be used to his habits. When he came home, she didn't ask him any questions. As for him, he didn't remember what my grandmother had asked him to do!

This lovely uncle didn't spend money. He saved all the money he had. He seemed not to need anything. He had no hair cuts. He didn't drink either coffee or rice alcohol. He never complained about his fate. He ate any food he had without any complaint. He didn't have any words that displeased my grandmother. He had no concept of time, of the past, present, or future. He didn't have any high expectations. He asked me to educate his children. That was his hope. I made it come true. Perhaps he was very happy about that in the Yellow Spring (world of the dead).

In the eyes of the villagers, he was a nonranking citizen, poor in everything. I found in him many characteristics that were absent in most ordinary people. He was altruistic. He loved to bring pleasure to others. He used to give his money to needy cousins. He spent time visiting his friends and cousins in the distant villages. When he visited them, he brought them symbolic gifts, no matter what the cost.

My grandmother's sister lived in An Son on the left bank of the Saigon River. She had a large orchard of mangosteens, durians, and rambutans. Her fertile land was watered by the Saigon River and many canals. But this area has no fresh water. One day, my uncle went to An Son, twelve miles from Binh Chuan, to see his aunt. He carried two pails of fresh water to give to her. The cost of two pails of fresh water was almost negligible but walking twelve miles with two pails of fresh water on his shoulders was a real hardship. His altruism moved everybody. It was an unforgettable picture in the memory of his aunt.

This uncle never refused to help anybody when he was asked to do so. Because of his extraordinary behavior, he was deemed to be stupid, but he didn't care about such a superficial judgment.

My third uncle was a rich businessman. He had a large house near my grandmother's. Unlike my second uncle, this one was poor in love and filial piety. The war made many people suffer, but it gave him a good opportunity to make much money. At night his house was lit up by an incandescent mantle. He had costly china and glasses and a new phonograph, marks of Western civilization in Binh Chuan. His wife and children wore expensive clothes. From time to time, a coach came to his house to take his family to Thudaumot, Tuong Binh Hiep, to see his wife's parents. He never visited his own mother, sisters, or brothers. He wasn't friendly with anybody in the village. He dug an abyss that separated him from the villagers. The latter seized any good opportunities to bury him in this abyss.

My grandmother was a quiet person. She was born intelligent, but she had no chance to go to school. In her childhood, a woman's opportunity in society was almost nil. Many parents didn't send their daughters to school. They didn't teach them some secret vocational skills for fear that their husbands' family would steal them. My grandmother was well respected in the village. Her prestige arose from her personality, age, and good behavior more than from her wealth. She had a good memory. Her mental arithmetic was surprising. She remembered with accuracy how much a villager owed her, how much he had paid, and how many pennies were left in his debt. She would tell a story with details and precise dates. I learned a lot from her during my stay in her house. She taught me of God, who has absolute power. She taught me to avoid evil by telling me many stories in which good guys had blessings and bad guys underwent awful punishments. She also told me some stories about Hell to give me my first concepts of causality and finality.

My grandmother also paid attention to my nutrition. She didn't let me eat chicken guts or rotten eggs for fear that I would be stupid. But she did let me eat chicken liver, which was believed to strengthen my sight and courage. She didn't allow me to eat chicken legs for fear that my legs would shake. She taught me not to spill rice, not to eat during singing, and not to eat in darkness.

I pleased my grandmother very much. She was proud of me when somebody praised my bravery, intelligence, diligence, and helpfulness. The Japanese soldiers liked me too. Maybe I reminded them of their children. One day, they took me to their citadel in Phu Loi. My grandmother and youngest uncle were scared. They prayed until the soldiers brought me back home.

My youngest uncle usually gave me cakes. He liked to ask me about my daily activities because he thought I knew all the paths in the village and its daily news. I told him stories with accurate details. The night he died, I stood by his bed, looking at him leaving the world. I was present at his funeral and at the construction of his grave. His death made my grandmother suffer a lot. Fortunately, I was beside her to cheer her up in her solitude.

The Japanese soldiers in Phu Loi came to Binh Chuan. They cut down bamboo trees, stole chickens, beat up the villagers, and forced them to do *corvée*, digging trenches and repairing the airport. When they came, the villagers hid themselves in the clay pits. The villagers didn't get paid when doing *corvée*, and they were brutally beaten by the Japanese soldiers. After the war, they were accused of being "Japanese collaborators." My aunt's husband was badly beaten. He stayed in bed all year round and took the juice of pounded crabs as medicine.

Until 1945, no road in Binh Chuan was macadamized or asphalted. All the paths in the village were sandy. Ox carts were the best means of transportation. Those people who didn't have ox carts had to carry their agricultural produce to the market. After selling their produce, they got some necessities, put them in two big baskets, and carried them home. Binh Chuan dwellers had to go to Thudaumot, Tan Khanh, or Bung to exchange goods. In wartime it was difficult to move from one place to another because of the presence of different checkpoints controlled by the Japanese, the French, and the Viet Minh. People walked barefooted so that they could walk fast and keep their balance on the narrow and slippery dikes. How hard the country ladies struggled when carrying heavy baskets of agricultural produce on their shoulders with bamboo yokes and walking barefooted on the hot sandy paths at noon.

No villager could ride a bicycle. The motorcycle was something strange and monstrous.

Pajamas became formal clothes in ceremonies. Farmers were barefooted. They put on wooden clogs only when they attended a wedding ceremony or when they were sick. The charlatan advised them not to let their legs touch the ground.

Two symbols of the existence of French culture in Binh Chuan were my uncle's phonograph and the red sign inside a restaurant at the east gate of the village, which bore the yellow letters "R.A.," the abbreviation for *Régie d'Alcool.*

Binh Chuan and Tan Khanh were noted for martial arts. According to oral history, Mr. At and Mr. Giap killed tigers with their hands. It was also said that an old woman named Tra knocked down sixteen teenagers at one time. For that reason, the local martial arts were called "Old Tra's Martial Arts." These were the echoes of the past. But under the French and Japanese occupations, famous local boxers claimed not to remember their fighting techniques and closed their schools of martial arts. Otherwise, they would have had trouble with the foreign rulers. Such a line of conduct was taken from the Vietnamese saying

> *How smart you are! You must die.*
> *How stupid you are! You must die.*
> *Adapt to the circumstance! You survive.*

Many of my cousins were good at Vietnamese martial arts, but they claimed to have forgotten them. Old Gia, Old Anh, and Old Hien, who were famous martial arts teachers, got skinny for lack of food. They had scabies, which were very common in the whole country after the war. People were so itchy that they scratched their hands and legs until they were swollen. They boiled various kinds of leaves for their showers. The smell of sulfur wafted through the air.

There were a few landless farm laborers in the village. They lived in small thatched cottages. Their roofs were so leaky that they could see the sun in daytime and the moon at night. They had neither education nor skills. They had frugal meals, and they did hard labor to make their living. Unfortunately, they didn't have regular work to do. In the country, farmers used to work in rotation instead of hiring workers. Under this system, workers didn't get paid. They were served brunch and lunch only. Needy villagers gleaned rice, beans, and peanuts and gathered mushrooms to sell at the market. Pilferage usually occurred when the farmers were in the rice fields. The pilferers stole bamboo shoots, chickens, and rice. After a theft, the most suspected would be the poorest man in the hamlet.

Every rich family had spears to use against the burglars, and the local government did know the background of each wrongdoer. Usually the wrongdoer wasn't a village dweller. Professional thieves had their own principles: they didn't steal anything in their native villages, which served them as refuges.

When a burglar came into a house, the owner would beat an empty pail to alert the neighbors. Everybody would wake up, light the lamps and shout, "Burglar! Burglar! Capture him! Capture him!" Everybody would get excited. That sometimes scared the wrongdoers into trying to quit their risky "profession." Sooner or later, they would be caught, tortured, and dishonored. If the villagers caught a burglar, they cut off his big toes to minimize his effectiveness in his nocturnal activities. The sandy paths kept the footprints of the walkers. The four-toed footprints were made by the burglars. People followed them to find the wrongdoers.

What surprised me was that the villagers lived peacefully during World War II. Burglary was negligible. Social evils were almost absent except for fights at the open air casinos during Tet. Polygamy wasn't found in the village, although the patriarchal regime was rigorously observed. That was the red score (good grade) for the villagers with limited educations.

Binh Chuan rarely witnessed the common disputes in Vietnamese society about marital problems and land ownership, but some small things became subjects of quarrels. People quarreled with one another over things like bad relations between their children or chickens and pigs damaging their neighbors' gardens. Sometimes people cursed a neighbor whose oxen had injured their own. Irrigation in the dry season and flooding in the rainy season were also subjects of dispute.

However, the villagers showed a surprising amount of solidarity and mutuality. No villagers died of hunger, even if they were poor. Needy people would borrow rice from their neighbors to survive. When they died, the villagers took care of their funeral expenses without counting on the local government. They helped one another in roofing, building homes, planting and reaping paddies. They were active in helping their friends during their funerals or wedding ceremonies. They assembled twice a year at the temple to give offerings to the local deity, to discuss their common problems in the village, and to share their agricultural experiences.

I lived in my maternal village for a short time. I enjoyed a cozy life there even in wartime, but this happy life faced stormy challenges after 1945.

2

To the Paternal Land

After the coup d'état of March 9, 1945, Vietnam was at a historic turning point. All the schools were closed. My father was unemployed. My mother replaced him economically and made life smooth by exchanging goods. My parents decided to bring me back to Tuy An to prepare my education. But knowing that my grandmother loved and indulged me, my father was afraid that I would prefer rural games to school.

My father was interested in our education. He expected us to carry out his noble hopes. Like many Vietnamese influenced by Confucianism, Buddhism, and Taoism, my father used to remind us to avoid any inhuman acts. He encouraged us to do good things. His simple concept was that those people who have God's blessings are economically and morally happy. In his opinion, all occupations were good and useful. He kept on saying, "Every trade has its value. Only silly people are unworthy."

My father was severe. He seized any opportunity to educate us. He taught us how to speak politely, how to behave properly, how to clean the table, and how to handle a knife without injuring others. He said, "People could suffer from our negligence. Our carefulness will keep them away from sufferings."

I left Binh Chuan by bicycle one night. My grandmother saw me off with tears in her eyes. She said in a choked voice, "Be ready for school, my dear grandson. I will get there to see you some day." I didn't know what to say but "Yes, Grandmother." The bicycle rolled along slowly. I crossed an immense field and dark woods before arriving in Tuy An. That night I slept soundly. When I got up, I realized that I lived far away from my grandmother. I said good-bye to my grandmother and to her house and started a new life in my paternal village.

Tuy An was new to me. Everything was strange. I didn't hear the harmonious jingles from the bells on the oxen's necks anymore. I didn't hear the carters screaming angrily when their disobedient oxen refused to draw the carts. I didn't hear the bell ring twice a day from the pagoda, the sound of the horns, the rhythmic popular verses recited by the country ladies, or the country songs sung by the herdsmen. Tuy An was very "urban" to me. It was more cultural than Binh Chuan. It didn't have anything rural in my eyes.

I missed Binh Chuan. I missed my grandmother. I missed my aunt, who used to give me freshly baked cakes. I missed my extraordinary uncle. I missed poor Muoi with his rude words, poor Dung, a hooligan, and poor Cau and Ganh, two roguish children. I missed the green bamboo hedge in front of my grandmother's house, the natural fence of cactus in its backyard, and the thorny red bougainvillea near the gate. I missed some of our neighbors who asked me to give them some rice when my grandmother wasn't home. I had left Binh Chuan. If they knew it, they would be unhappy.

From the morning until the evening, I heard people singing and arguing stormily. Teenagers of both sexes assembled in one of my father's apartments. Some sang songs; some were in the meeting room. I didn't understand what they talked about. My brothers joined the children's groups.

My father stayed home while my mother was busy trading. The house was quiet and empty. My family had to feed five militia members. I didn't know where they were from. They left in the early morning and came home at dark. They behaved as members of my family. In reality, they represented a different world from that of my family. We didn't have the right to know anything about their activities, but they knew a lot about my family. My father was sick of this unwanted duty. My mother worked alone to feed many people. My brothers couldn't help her. They had to take part in the youth activities. They had a meeting every day to be aware of the policies of the newly independent government led by Ho Chi Minh. People talked about their leader, about independence, about the political and economic difficulties of Vietnam during the French and Japanese domination and after World War II, and about the famine in North Vietnam. They sang patriotic songs, such as "Our People," "Bac Son," "Missing the Jungles," and "The Break Day Clarion Sound." The teenagers sang so joyfully that they forgot their meals, the hot summer, and the misery of their families. They were happy and excited. If not, they would be severely criticized by the group.

My father was meditative. The Autumn Revolution had been successful. Nobody could be upset or skeptical. That was the argument of the Viet Minh cadres at the meeting. In my eyes, everybody looked serious and important. They saluted one another with their fists to say that they were ready to offer their minds and hearts to their homeland. They called one another *dong chi* (comrades). This word was both political and cultural. It was absent in Binh Chuan during my stay there. I heard many Sino-Vietnamese words, such as *phu nu* instead of *dan ba* (women), *ai quoc* instead of *yeu nuoc* (patriotism), and *nien ky* instead of *nam* or *tuoi* (years).

As a wandering child, I soon learned many things. The coachmen were cheered. An auto mechanic was considered a hero. It is normal in our time. But it wasn't in feudal and colonial Vietnam in the 1940s.

The auto mechanic spent time and energy fixing an old bus that took the Viet Minh to the Japanese military posts to steal their weapons. I was among the people who pushed the bus. My pure and simple hope was to make a tour around the village on the bus to enjoy the comfort of Western technology. What a naughty bus. The more we pushed it, the more it remained inert. I lost the opportunity to be on the bus even for a minute.

When I lived in Binh Chuan, I had what I wanted. In my paternal land, life was austere. I said to myself, "Food isn't abundant here." My father planted pineapples in the woods, but I didn't dare to pick them. There were many grapefruits in the orchard. They were expensive fruit, so I couldn't touch them. I couldn't eat other fruit in the garden because of insects and because of their sour taste. There were plenty of wild rambutans around my father's house. It was impossible for me to climb tall trees. Only Ly Quang climbed trees and picked wild rambutans in the village.

Ly Quang was the poorest man in Tuy An, but he was kind to me. He built a hut on my father's land. I often went to his hut to play with his children, but I didn't see his wife. Was she dead? Why did he take care of his children by himself? I didn't know. His three children were barebacked all year round. Quang made his living by climbing trees, picking fruit, and doing any kind of hard labor. The cries of Ly Quang's children sounded bizarre. When crying, they seemed to call, "Am binh! Am binh!" (soldiers in the ghost world). They cried all the time because they were always sick and hungry. Ly Quang worked hard to feed his children, but he had no time to take care of them.

Ly Quang always smiled. He was kind and helpful. His children were naturally good. They neither picked fruit nor stole anything from my family.

During the Franco-Vietnamese War, Ly Quang emigrated to Tri An Falls near the source of the Dong Nai. He had a simple life in the heart of the forest. After 1954, my oldest brother invited him to visit Saigon. It was his first trip to Saigon, and he stayed a couple of days. On this occasion he told us about his risky and adventurous life near Tri An Falls during the war. I was as happy to hear his story as I would have been to see Tarzan and Robinson Crusoe in Saigon. Ly Quang was a Vietnamese Tarzan in Bien Hoa province. He left us for the forest and waterfalls in Tri An, where his life was threatened by tigers, pythons, and wild boars. Since then, I haven't heard anything from him or his children.

I sat on the fence of Tuy An school and watched students building campfires, singing, and playing roles, trying to appeal to the villagers to contribute to the rescue of hungry North Vietnamese.

I climbed the mango trees to watch the farewell ceremony in honor of Tu But the Brave, who was going to Laithieu to kill our enemies. The brave man was laden with honor. His neck was covered with flowers. Everybody admired him and believed in the military exploits he was going to carry out. It moved him very much. People praised him with their best words.

Tu But the Brave was born in North Vietnam. He came to the South in the 1940s on the famous Chemin de Fer Trans-Indochinois (Trans-Indochinese Railway), which wound along the Vietnam coast. He worked for my aunt's husband in Tuy An and lived there. Sometimes he went to Xuan Loc and Tay Ninh with his employer to collect timber and rattan. My aunt's husband got rich by supplying the Japanese with rattan, which facilitated the movement of tanks in the muddy regions in Southeast Asia. Before being a rattan supplier, he had owned a joiner's workshop. Tu But was a joiner working in Tuy An.

Nobody knew if Tu But had belonged to the Communist party in Tonkin (in the northern part of Vietnam) or not. When the Viet Minh led the resistance, Tu But was chosen as Kinh Kha the Brave, who had failed to assassinate Shih Huang Tsi twenty centuries before. Maybe he was used as a scapegoat to excite people's hatred. If he was a scapegoat, he wouldn't have been a member of the Communist party.

Silently, Tu But the Brave set forth with his gun. He walked on a graveled rural road. Sometimes he stopped under a shady tree along the road. Sometimes he disappeared in the woods for fear of French aircraft and ambushes. The gun on his shoulders was too long for his height and weight. The longer he walked, the heavier it became. He left the east hamlet and entered Binh Hoa village. He went on walking to Councilman Thao's tomb and stopped at a road bifurcation, half a mile from Laithieu. He hid himself behind a bush. He felt hungry and thirsty. The sun moved to the west. Tu But felt lonely and chilly. Some coaches wheeled along wearily from Laithieu to Binh Nham. Road 13 was deserted. Some French military trucks rolled back and forth to ensure safety on the road. Tu But didn't want to remember his glorious minutes in Tuy An. He didn't know what to do with his long gun. Kill the French? How could he kill them when they didn't wander on the road? Attack their military posts? How could he do it by himself? He felt unable to kill even a military truck driver or any soldier on the road. Tu But knew how to saw, to plane and to chisel wood. He wasn't trained to use a gun. Who in Tuy An could train him to use weapons? Only Warrant Officer Kinh, a French collaborator, could. The more he thought, the more he was embarrassed. What would he say to the villagers to deserve the title "the brave"? Tu But blamed them for praising him too much. He had gooseflesh when he remembered their praise. If he left Tuy An forever, he would lose his job and shelter. What was to be done? He wondered.

A blast paralyzed him. His heart dropped to his feet. He was dripping with cold sweat. *Oh! My God! They see me!* Tu But thought. He sat on the ground and waited. He only regained his composure when nothing happened to him.

An old tire of a military truck had blown up. Curious people rushed to the road to watch the truck. Tu But said to himself, "I should leave this place. It is dangerous for me to be seen with a gun." He stood up, dusting his clothes. He looked carefully in all directions and walked away from the bush, leaving the gun there.

People looked forward to his triumphal return and the celebratation of a solemn ceremony in Tuy An. There was no news about him. The committee decided to commemorate him. Melancholic songs resounded in the air:

> *Leaning on the wind your soul comes here.*
> *As a hero, you lived for the future*
> *You fought courageously and enthusiastically*
> *Without fearing either rains or winds,*
> *Hoping that you saved your countrymen*

> *Here are the incense smoke and our sorrows*
> *In the memory of all heroic fallen, descendants of the Hong Bang.*

Everybody there burst into tears of regret for "the liberators," who went to the battlefields without thinking of their return.

Tu But was born to be famous. He was laden with honor on his departure day. He was commemorated because his fellow villagers didn't know that he had not accomplished his mission. In the city, he was considered a peace lover. After making his fortune in the city, Tu But felt that after all, he deserved these praises.

Next to my father's house was my great-grandmother's house, which was requisitioned by the Viet Minh to provide shelters for mobile "liberators." All of them were North Vietnamese recruited by the French to work for the plantations of rubber in Quan Loi, Phu Rieng, and Dau Tieng. They cooked our food and used the water we kept in brick basins. I didn't see their weapons. It was said they participated in the battles of Phu Nhuan and Cau Ben Phan in Gia Dinh province. Probably they were on the way to War Zone D through Tan Long, Ben San, and Tan Uyen. I didn't know exactly what they did. I saw them killing lice, splintering scabies with thorns, and arguing with one another. Sometimes they fought one another until they were bleeding. They were more brutal than the five young men in our house, and they struggled against poverty, oppression, and exploitation to improve their lives and social positions. Many of them were members of the Communist Party in the 1930s and 1940s. They had their clandestine activities in the rubber plantations, where, according to the Communist propaganda, "a drop of rubber resin is a drop of blood and each rubber tree grows on the dead body of a worker." On the basis of this exaggeration they "swore to cut the bodies of the enemies and to suck their blood" without any remorse. The men staying in our house were students struggling for their country's independence.

Teachers in Tuy An were divided into two groups. The first group was more professional than political. The second group was more revolutionary. They accused teachers of the first group of being pacifists, reactionary, and traitors to their country. Obviously, few teachers of that group deserved such labels. Most of them were purely professional. They didn't like politics. That didn't mean they sold out their country. They were scared of bloodshed, although they didn't know anything about Communism. They didn't know why proletarian illiterates held high positions they never dreamed of. The revolutionary teachers said that was "democracy." The nonpolitical teachers couldn't accept this sophisticated explanation. They believed that management by those without education would be unproductive. However, they kept their golden silence so they wouldn't be labeled *Viet Gian* (traitor) or *phan cach mang* (antirevolutionary) by their opponents.

My father was the leader of the first group.

My uncle belonged to the second group.

My grandfather remained quiet. He admired Phan Boi Chau, a revolutionary, and clandestinely read his books, which had been banned by the French rulers. He was a member of Thien Dia Hoi, a secret society led by Phan Xich Long, who, in 1916, had launched an attack on the Saigon prison. My grandfather couldn't applaud carnage and revenge blindly and mechanically. Politically, he was more experienced than my father.

Being a teacher imbued with Western democracy and Confucian ethics, my father thought that frankness was a virtue. It was right in ethics. But it was a real danger in politics.

My grandfather didn't let people read his thoughts. He was safe. On the contrary, my father had indescribable troubles. Once, one of his colleagues threatened to shoot him, accusing him of having reactionary thoughts. He gave my father a bamboo pole and ordered him to watch a French plane. My father asked him what to do when he saw it and how to react with the bamboo pole. My father's colleague didn't answer this naïve and funny question of my father. But he threatened to kill him. Their friendship ended after they argued with each other violently.

My father began to drink rice alcohol to lull himself to sleep in order to avoid any possible troubles.

The Viet Minh ordered the villagers to kill their dogs because the barking could unveil their movements. It was a tragic time for dogs. My father, Tu Sieng, Nam Phon, the auto mechanic, and many other villagers ate dog meat and drank rice alcohol almost every day. When they got drunk, they argued noisily. Nam Phon salted the dog meat he ate like barbecue. These drinkers made their lives peaceful in wartime, but they attracted the attention of the committee. The National Police of the Eastern Provinces watched this reactionary group. Strictly speaking, they didn't pay attention to Tu Sieng or Nam Phon but to my father. They seized any favorable opportunity to arrest him.

Tu Sieng was a skin-headed man. After drinking some glasses of rice alcohol, his eyes would be half closed and he would talk about Confucian teachings. Not a few people thought that he was a defrocked Buddhist monk and that he was linked to a Chinese monk, Lo Tri Tham, when he ate dog meat.

I was too young to know what he was doing to make his living. I saw him as a full-time drinker. If he didn't get drunk, he sat on a chair, looking at people going back and forth. At times, he smiled and clicked his tongue. The committee hadn't categorized him yet. His family situation showed that he was needy, but his way of life was that of a petite bourgeoisie. Our thoughts led our way of life. His thoughts were "I don't care." So was his way of life.

I heard this interpretation of Confucian thoughts from this sophisticated man: When you [lady] get married, you have to depend on your husband. When your husband dies, you depend on your children.

Tu Sieng interpreted it in his own way. He said, "When you get into a coach, you depend on the coachman. If the coachman dies, you cannot survive." (In Sino-Vietnamese *xuat gia* means "to get married" and "to get into a coach." *Phu* means coachman or husband. *Tu* means to die or children.)

That funny interpretation made Tu Sieng immortal in my mind. But his wife was tired of his idle lifestyle. She spent the rest of her life in the pagoda. Tu Sieng joined her there and had his head shaved like the other Buddhist monks in the pagoda. Unwittingly, he became a Buddhist without either being baptized or knowing Buddhist catechism. He said, sophisticatedly, that he observed the fifth Buddhist commandment by not drinking alcohol while sleeping. He died of dropsy during the nine-year war in a pagoda in Tan Phuoc.

While the villagers gave themselves up to ideological struggles and to carnage, the Chinese in the village ran their businesses as usual to make money. Chu Dung's restaurant was crowded with eaters. Chu Xay (*chu* means uncle, father's younger brother, or younger brother) made his fortune by roasting pork. Thay Phu, the Goiter, ran an oriental drugstore. The money stream flowed to their houses. Thay Phu, the Goiter, remained beefy. His complexion was rosy in comparison with the pale faces of the feverish villagers. From time to time, he fortified his health with a litter of puppies cooked with Chinese herbal medicine. Chu Xay bought hogs and carried them on his bicycle. He also made money by castrating pigs. In the twinkling of an eye, he took out the testicles of the animal and plugged the wound with some soot. Two or three days after the castration, the wound would be healed. When the animal got fat enough, Chu Xay bought it and brought it to his roasting spit. Before buying it, he threw the pig on the ground and opened its mouth with a piece of wood to see if it had tapeworm eggs. He kept his cool temper in spite of the loud yell of the animal. If he said, "Oh, no! There are eggs," the price of the pig would be negligible. It was a big loss for the pig's owner, who anxiously awaited his conclusion.

Pigs were the saving accounts of the rural people. The grunting of the pigs in the evening announced that somebody had just sold pigs. That night, there might be a robbery.

Unlike Binh Chuan, Tuy An witnessed many cases of robbery. Where were the thieves from? Even today, nobody knows. The robbers used rubber pistols to terrify their victims. Coming into the victim's house, they used five-inch nails to menace the house owner. If their victims didn't show them where they kept their jewelry and money, their ears would be nailed. The villagers were fearful after a robbery. They mentioned it briefly and tried to forget it as quickly as possible. It seemed they knew who the robbers were.

❖　❖　❖

I began to explore Tuy An. This was the woods. That was the village temple. I found trees everywhere. The prettiest house was Principal Diet's. He was my father's teacher. He was well respected by the villagers for bringing education to the village. His son, Nguyen Lam Sanh, was an experienced lawyer and chairman of the Asian Anti-Communist Alliance. His daughter was a billionaire in South Vietnam in the 1960s and 1970s.

The apartments along the communal road belonged to my father. They "promoted" my father to the rank of "landlord" although the renters never paid for the rent fairly. When a tile was broken, they called the landlord to replace it. That was the landlord's responsibility. The landlord had to pay taxes to the colonial government. If the apartments for rent collapsed, the owner had full responsibility for the renters' safety. These houses for rent taught my father how to look more deeply and to learn wisdom from the Vietnamese language. In plain Vietnamese, "market" is *cho bua* (*cho* means market; *bua* means hammer). "Apartment" or "house" was *pho xa* (*pho* means house or apartment; *xa* means to salute with clasped hands). The war destroyed all of my father's apartments, allowing him to say good-bye to them.

The village school was about 400 yards from my house. It was a big school surrounded by woods. This school was the cradle of many devoted teachers, patriots, good civil servants, and revolutionary *surveillants* working for the rubber plantations. It was the cultural, educational, and ethical center of the village. The villagers got in touch with Western culture and democracy from this school. Mr. Trinh, a patriotic teacher, cried when talking about the sorrowful situation of our country as a result of the French invasion. He got angry with the insolence of a French gun broker in Tonkin, Jean Dupuis. He insisted on the sovereignty of our country and was displeased with the impotence of the Nguyen dynasty. He told about the revolution of 1789 in France and made his students think about a similar revolution in Vietnam. The Autumn Revolution gave him an opportunity to participate in revolutionary activities. He died on the battlefield, but his name fell into oblivion like the names of other unknown heroes.

The Tuy An market was located around the crossroad linking Tuy An, Bung, Thudaumot, Tan Ba, and Di An. "Downtown," there were two restaurants, a grocery store, a ten-cent store, and an oriental drugstore. Near our house, there was a grocery store. These businesses were run by the Chinese. All of them were wealthy except for the Chinese man who owned the grocery store in my father's apartment. He had married a Vietnamese lady. They both were kind and joyful. They were tall and beefy. The husband was always shirtless, showing his heavy belly. He had an extraordinary appetite. One day, I saw him boiling eggs. Skinning ten eggs, he put them in a big bowl. Two other bowls contained wild vegetables and fish sauce prepared with red pepper, garlic, sugar, and vinegar. He soaked rice paper in water and one by one put sheets on a bamboo sieve to have a big, thick piece of rice paper. Then he put the ten peeled eggs and the wild vegetables on it and rolled them all together. He enjoyed eating this big roll with fish sauce. (The Chinese usually don't use fish sauce, but this man was used to it because his wife was Vietnamese.)

The fortune-teller couldn't tell this man's future with accuracy. He was beefy, rosy, and sweet. He was a faithful husband, a responsible father, and a helpful neighbor. But he was really poor. What a controversy! He gave his children Vietnamese names. His first son was named *Bu* (big), his daughter *To* (great, big), and his last child *So* (huge, mammoth). Poor *Bu* wasn't big but was tall and skinny. *To* was slender, while poor *So* was always sick, so he wasn't "huge" yet.

Tuy An became a war zone. It wasn't good for business. The Chinese man moved his family to Binh Nham, the home village of his wife. Shortly after they moved, I learned that he had passed away.

My father had a socioeconomic renovative spirit. Socially, he was progressive because he did not despise the poor, did not discriminate against his servants and refused to inherit his ancestral properties. He conceded his share to his brothers. He bought land with his own money. In his youth, he was interested in the lectures given by Phan Chu Trinh advocating reforms and democracy. He thought a lot about the Vietnamese economy, which was controlled by the French, Chinese, and Hindus. The Vietnamese were only servants, donkeys carrying all the burden of taxes, *corvée*, and long-life debts to these foreigners. As a teacher, however, my father disliked bloodshed and revenge. He accepted fair competition.

I didn't know why my father founded a plantation of kapok trees whose fibers floated in the air in the summer. The villagers complained very much. They blamed my father, who, in turn, worried a lot about the market for his kapok fibers after drying and cleaning them. The world was at war. All economic activities were paralyzed. My father couldn't find a market for his kapok fibers. He had a big loss of money. In addition to that, he faced the villagers' discontent. When the Cingalese came to Nam Bo with the British troops, my father planted turmeric. Once again, he had a big loss.

Sau Cu was a man from the village who owned a small restaurant and ran it in competition with Chu Dung's restaurant. He was the owner, waiter, and cashier. Rice noodles, coffee, and cakes were served in his restaurant. It wasn't enough for breakfast. Most customers had breakfast at Chu Dung's restaurant, which had plenty of delicious food. Sau Cu's restaurant attracted people who loved music, painting, planting flowers, and raising rare birds and golden fish.

Sau Cu's father was a powerful civil servant working for the French government in Hanoi. Sau Cu grew up in a wealthy and powerful family. His hair was well groomed. His clothes were clean and fashionable. He was a soft-spoken man. His words were literally refined. Sau Cu was good at drawing and narration. But these things couldn't ensure his restaurant's survival. Sau Cu shut down his restaurant to open a barber shop. When the village was completely ravaged by the war, he had to leave it to live a wandering life in Laithieu, Thu Duc, and Saigon. He died a bachelor in Laithieu a year after the end of the nine-year war.

Adventurous villagers making their fortune in the highland and in Cambodia were more successful than my father and Sau Cu. In the critical situation after the Autumn Revolution, my family survived by selling pineapples and firewood. My father owned many hectares of woods. We trimmed branches and cut down trees and sold firewood to the pottery kilns. In the woods, we planted pineapples and sold them to the farmers living at the interprovincial limit of Bien Hoa (Dong Nai province) and Thudaumot (Binh Duong, Song Be). They used them to prepare *mam nem*, salted small fish with sliced pineapples. *Mam nem* was served almost every day in the meals of the farmers living in this area.

Every family tried to make money to survive. People steamed *banh tet*, composed of sticky rice, bananas or mung beans, and fried *chuoi chien* (bananas coated with flour) and *banh cam* (flour, mung beans, sugar, and sesame), all dishes familiar to the villagers in this period of want.

Most villagers were broke, while a few people had their luxurious lives. Ironically, they were the ones who denounced the petite bourgeoisie with intolerance. They compared them to traitors selling out the country for the sake of their own happiness. They had important roles in the local government. They were in black but not in rags. They wore striped scarves, but they weren't peasants. In the name of independence, they smoked expensive Cotab cigarettes and drank coffee with milk that was rare and expensive, milk that could cost the monthly salary of an elementary school teacher! On behalf of the working and farming classes, they put on leather slippers. Their complexions were bright and rosy, unlike the sunburned faces of the peasants. They had fancy haircuts and wore expensive felt hats. They spit blazing words that incited bloodshed and hatred.

My paternal village had a big temple. There was neither pagoda nor Catholic church there. The villagers weren't superstitious because of their level of education, which made some of them more materialistic than spiritual. Nobody was Roman Catholic in Tuy An. Some were Caodaists. Most villagers were influenced by the three religions. Every family had its altars on which they put large pictures of their ancestors. Buddhism did not have a big influence in Tuy An for lack of a pagoda. However, many women practiced fasting once or twice a month on the first and fifteenth days of the lunar calendar. On the fifteenth day of the seventh month of the lunar calendar, they would give offerings to the wandering souls. They offered chickens, pork, eggs, steamed sticky rice, fruit, and flowers to the local deity in the spring and the autumn. The ceremony was solemn. People from neighboring villages came to the village temple with their offerings to pay respect to the divine power of the local deity who, when alive, was a scholar and physician. The Tuy An residents were believed to have education because of their intellectual local deity. Tuy An faced many challenges, but its villagers didn't kill one another bloodily for any reason. By the end of 1946 they had scattered throughout the country. They were economically and socially successful wherever they lived. The materialistic intellectuals didn't dare to deny their local deity's divine power.

Polygamy, social evils, and murders were rare in Tuy An.

During the war some villagers collaborated with the French, but most of them didn't endanger their countrymen. Power abuse didn't find a good environment in Tuy An where most villagers welcomed the democratic spirit *à l'occidentale* and maintained the essence of their culture. They had deep attachments to their arid land and to their lovely *dinh*. They were rich in common sense without being excessively materialistic. They were straightforward without being brutal. They were patriotic without being chauvinistic. They were progressive without getting rid of their ancestors' traditional heritage. They helped one another in hardship and forgave one another by forgetting their mistakes. In diaspora, they kept on worshipping their local deity. Every time they met with one another, they talked about their common wish: coming back to their village to reconstruct the temple. All that reminds me of the arid land of Israel. Tuy An is also on an arid highland. The promised land has its "milk and honey." Tuy An has its honey and sweet tropical fruit. The Israelis have their temple and their patriarch, Abraham. The Tuy An villagers have their *dinh* and their local deity, Pham Van Truc. They have attached their faith to their local deity and their own ancestors. At this point, we can't say that they are irreligious. The Israelis were in diaspora. After 1945 the Tuy An villagers became expatriates. Their village became a battlefield and an immense sea of fire. The war destroyed it and erased it from the map. The Israelis used to greet one another with "Next year in Jerusalem." The natives of Tuy An greeted one another with talk of the reconstruction of the *dinh* and the restoration of their village. The Israelis succeeded in giving birth to a new nation in the Middle East. The Tuy An villagers came back to their ancestral land and reconstructed their *dinh* and village in 1956 and in 1973. Rothschild, the most influential banker in Europe, made his fortune from empty hands. Mrs. Nguyen Thi Giau, the founder of one of the most well known textile companies in South Vietnam, built up her success from a few pieces of fabric. Many of the villagers were economically, socially, and culturally famous throughout the whole country. For these reasons I venture to find some similarities between Israel and my paternal land, which I call "Israel in miniature in the Far East."

When the French troops came to Tuy An, the villagers fled to the woods. My parents looked for refuge in Tan Uyen. The French burned down the communal office. Then they withdrew from the village after firing some shots of intimidation in the air.

Flames blazed at the communal office. The children seized this opportunity to find something usable in the ashes. One of my brothers was among them. That night the Viet Minh police came to our house. They said that my father was working with the French. The suspicion seemed to be confirmed when they didn't find my parents at home. They arrested my oldest brother, saying that he was responsible for the other brother who stole the people's property from the communal office. My oldest brother became the first in the village to serve as a scapegoat of the revolutionary government. He lost his freedom for a week for an unjust charge and underwent a terrible investigation with many arbitrary accusations.

My parents came home from Tan Uyen.

One day, my father was in a coffee shop. By chance, he saw one of his students, who was also his cousin. He waved to him to come and have coffee. His student came into the coffee shop with anxiety. In a low voice he said to my father, "Teacher, get out of here! I have the order to arrest you." My father was surprised. His student urged him to leave the coffee shop immediately to avoid arrest. My father hurried home to inform my mother of the bad news. Then, he ran for his life.

From Laithieu the French troops rushed to Tuy An again. This time they built military posts and recruited collaborators. They sowed terror by searching, arresting, and killing some villagers. Ba Moi served them as a cook. He was a single parent, and his only son had serious dropsy. Mai collaborated with the French and endangered the villagers a lot because of his poor French. One young man was shot dead for stealing a betel mortar (*mortier de bétel*) from an old woman. The translator didn't know what to call it in French, but he tried to explain it by using some gestures. The French thought that the young man had raped an old woman, so they shot him.

Poor Mot practiced speaking French with *oui* (yes) and *non* (no). He was badly beaten by the French because of his misuse of *oui* and *non*.

"Es tu Viet Minh?" (Are you Viet Minh?)

"Oui, monsieur." (Yes, sir.)

After he gave his wrong answer, they hit his head with their guns until he fainted in a pool of his own blood.

One day, Ba Moi invited a French soldier to visit his house. I saw my first Frenchman on this occasion and heard Ba Moi speaking French for the first time.

La me dong beo (*la maison est belle*) (the house is pretty). I understood nothing but I thought that French was easy. Ba Moi showed his son, Bi, and said to the Frenchman, "Mon garçon malade. Voyez! Jaune!" The Frenchman nodded his head to show that he understood what Ba Moi said.

The French soldier I saw was tall. His skin was white, his hair blond, his nose straight, and his eyes gray. Physiognomically speaking, there was nothing to indicate that he was mean. I didn't know why his companions and maybe he himself beat up the villagers with brutality, killed people, and burned down their houses without any remorse.

One evening, as the sun disappeared behind the tops of the trees, I heard a burst of gunfire, breaking the sunset tranquillity. An awful silence reigned after the burst of gunfire. Everybody wanted to know what had happened to their countrymen. Ba Moi ran home fearfully. He exclaimed, "Your uncle was shot! Seven persons were executed!"

My oldest brother burst into tears. My grandfather was panic-stricken. Seven teachers in the Viet Minh Front had been shot in my father's plantation of kapok trees about ninety feet from my grandfather's house. They were the first soldiers to fall in Tuy An. They died silently and were buried in a mass tomb without coffins, without any prayers, and without a funeral. Nobody saw them off and said *adieu* to them. They returned to the bowels of the earth. Time erased their names.

In the 1930s my uncles studied in Saigon. My father paid for all of their expenses there. After having their educational training, they found good jobs in Cambodia. The uncle just shot by the French was a teacher of math at Lycée Sisovath in Phnom Penh, Cambodia. He had returned to Vietnam after the Japanese capitulation and had become a member of the Viet Minh Front.

The Viet Minh didn't have well-trained armed forces, but it was undeniable that they had many supporters. The French officers looked down on untrained militia armed only with spears and sharpened bamboo sticks. These militia members were militarily weak but politically strong. These peasants were fighting for their country's independence, while the French were fighting for the reestablishment of their colonization of Vietnam. The cause of the former eclipsed the greediness of the latter. In the short term the French could win the battle, but in the long term they couldn't win the war. They occupied

Tuy An and built their military posts but they failed to take control of the village. After a short stay, they had to withdraw their troops. Before their withdrawal, they burned down all the houses in the village and captured some suspects. My paternal village was plunged into fire.

My father was arrested by the French and taken to Laithieu. My mother took me to Binh Chuan again, but she didn't live in my grandmother's house. My brothers ran away from the village. My father wasn't arrested by the Viet Minh but by the French. My mother was scared of being arrested by the Viet Minh, who labeled my father a "collaborator of the French." The war separated all the members of my family from one another. My father was in jail. My mother avoided the Viet Minh. Her shelter was uncertain, and my brothers were homeless.

❖ ❖ ❖

I was in Binh Chuan when the French bombarded the spring in Tan Phuoc. This was the source of fresh water for the Tuy An residents. One of my cousins was seriously wounded. Fortunately, that bombardment cost no lives.

My grandfather passed away in solitude. My father was imprisoned in Laithieu. My mother suffered from persecution. My uncle was killed. One of his children was wounded during the French raids. My brothers left Tuy An. I was in Binh Chuan. How sad my grandfather's funeral was! The woods of Tuy An were the target of the batteries of artillery from Phu Loi, Di An, and Thu Duc. The villagers were forced to leave their native land. They were in a hurry to bury my grandfather on his own land with a wooden tombstone before leaving the village for good.

My grandfather had loved me, but when he died, I neither saw him nor attended his funeral. My tears ran down every time I recalled this tragic event. Our country faced many challenges. So did my paternal village and my own family.

Binh Chuan had changed a lot in the past few months, during my absence. My uncle's house had become the office of the Administrative Committee. A big red flag with a yellow star hung on the wall. Some people assembled there every morning to salute the flag and to sing the national anthem, the famous "Tien Quan Ca" by Van Cao. Ms. Nhon, Ba Cha's daughter, worked for the committee. Her father was a Viet Minh policeman. He had a long gun, the symbol of authority. He changed his attitudes quickly. Ms. Nhon was proud of her beauty and her important role in the village. Her father liked to show who he was and what he was doing. In the past he had been friendly with my grandmother and called her "my dear aunt." When he became a Viet Minh policeman, he tried not to meet her. He began calling her *dia chu* (landowner). My grandmother also had a son-in-law (my father) who belonged to the "petite bourgeoisie intellectual and landowner" class, a daughter who was a wealthy farmer and landowner, and a "reactionary and pro-fascist" son.

My uncle was beheaded. His property was confiscated. The deep cause of his death was his cozy and luxurious life. Personally, he was unsociable. The villagers detested him and his family. He was charged with antirevolutionary ideas, pro-fascism, and espionage. During Tet of 1946, he decorated his house with green, white, blue, red, and yellow paper. The Viet Minh accused him of displaying the French tricolored flag. He was decapitated in Tan Long. His wife and children left Binh Chuan empty-handed.

I had only one uncle left. This is the one who adored the "I don't care" attitude. He wandered from one place to another, not knowing that the country was at war. Sometimes he wasn't home for a week. This time my grandmother had two grandsons at home: the son of my deceased aunt and myself. This aunt died when I was a year old. Her husband lived in widowhood and took care of his son. He earned his living by selling tobacco. One day, he left and never returned. Even today, nobody knows exactly why, when, and where he died. His commemoration has been celebrated every year on the last day he left. My cousin became an orphan. My grandmother became his mother, father, and grandmother all at the same time. In her sixties, she witnessed many tragic changes in the family. One of her beloved sons died in his twenties. A second son was killed by the Viet Minh. When alive, he wasn't a pious son, but his death made my grandmother suffer a lot. She worried about her daughter-in-law and her grandchildren as well. My father lost his freedom. My mother's safety wasn't ensured. My family was in separation. My deceased aunt's husband was missing. All of these sufferings and burdens weighed upon her. I loved my grandmother. She made me understand the moral and physical sufferings of the Vietnamese women and their noble sacrifices in wartime. She made duty her happiness and suffering a challenge to her patience.

One dark moonless night, as my grandmother turned off the lamp, I heard somebody whistling. A man with a hoarse voice yelled, "Catch him! Catch him!" This hoarse voice was very familiar to me. My grandmother lit the lamp. The man with the hoarse voice ordered, "Light off!" My grandmother turned off the lamp immediately. Some people knocked at the door, shouting, "Open the door! Open the door!" My grandmother staggered. As she reached the front door, they kicked it in and rushed into the house. "Search!" This was the order from the hoarse-voiced man. A flash shone out from a man in black. I recognized none of them. They all were in black. They hid their faces with black veils. That showed they weren't strangers. They lived in Binh Chuan. Maybe they were my grandmother's cousins. They could be her debtors. It was shameful for them to give trouble to the benefactor who had saved them from hunger. It was shameful to search the house of an elderly woman they had respected. The black veils helped them hide their shame.

"Where is your son-in-law?" the hoarse-voiced man asked.

"He isn't living here," my grandmother replied.

"What a lie! Where did you hide him?" the churl asked.

"If you don't believe me, search my house!" my grandmother replied .

They searched the house without finding my father. They asked my grandmother to empty the cupboard. I didn't know why they thought that my parents hid themselves in the cupboard. They looked covetously at the pretty plates, but none of them dared to take one. Finally, they blindfolded my grandmother and left the house, taking her with them. My cousin and I cried bitter tears. The hoarse-voiced man scolded loudly, "Shut up!" We went on crying and shouting, "Don't jail our grandmother! Grandmother! Don't go! Don't leave us!"

My grandmother didn't say a word. She was pulled out of the house and walked away in spite of our lamentable cries. About half an hour later, I heard three shots. I cried louder, thinking that they had killed my grandmother.

I was more attached to her than was my aunt's son. I had lived beside her for a long time. She was my mother and grandmother. I missed her very much when I was in my paternal village. When I came back to Binh Chuan, I had witnessed many tragic changes. The peaceful life of the past didn't exist anymore. Some lovely villagers had become redoubtable. Silence had replaced their innocent smiles. I neither saw people husking rice in the moonlight nor heard the familiar country songs.

My cousin and I couldn't sleep. We lay down on the divan to wait for dawn through the long dark night. Suddenly, I heard my grandmother calling us. I shouted with joy, "Grandmother has come home! Grandmother has come home!" I jumped off the divan and opened the door. I embraced her as I was crying.

"Uncle Can arrested you. I recognized his hoarse voice," I said.

"Keep silent," my grandmother said weakly.

Until the end of her life, twenty-seven years later, she never mentioned this arrest.

All the people who were sick seemed to be used to their chronic diseases. All the sufferings, although awful, either disappeared or were faced with immense containment. All the joys came to an end soon. The joy would be forgotten, but the suffering wouldn't be.

I was accustomed to sudden changes. Most villagers kept on doing their daily work. When the French troops came, the villagers hid themselves in the clay pits or in underground trenches beneath the bamboo hedges. Some fled to any safe areas in the village. When the village was shelled, they hid themselves in the trenches outside their houses. During the nine-year war, no villager was killed by French bombs or mortar shells.

The farmers attached their lives to the land. They didn't want to leave their vital lands, where they kept the memories of many generations. Their attachment to their native villages angered both the Viet Minh and the French. The

Viet Minh called for "no man's land." They wanted all the farmers to join them instead of attaching themselves to their property. The French wanted to isolate the Viet Minh from the farmers, who were deemed to support the resistance. The villagers captured by the French were badly tortured by them. They were believed to work for the Viet Minh. The investigators used brutal measures to force them to tell what they wanted them to tell even if it was nothing they had really done. How could an illiterate farmer answer thorny questions regarding politics and intelligence? The more they said, "I don't know," the more cruelly they were tortured. The investigators poured water in their mouths until they choked. They hit their chests with drumsticks until they were almost dying.

In the daytime, the villagers were persecuted by the French. In the nighttime, they faced difficult questions from the Viet Minh police. Those villagers released by the French were suspected by the Viet Minh.

The Binh Chuan villagers developed their knowledge of the outside world. They talked with one another about nuclear bombs and their terrible destruction. I didn't know how they knew these things since they read neither books nor newspapers.

On Commemoration Day, in the house of my grandmother's neighbor, I heard the host and his guests talking about current issues. One of them said that two Japanese cities were on fire, and their residents were reduced to ash. The bridges collapsed when the wind blew. Technically and financially, Vietnam couldn't make an A-bomb, he said.

Everybody clicked their tongues, showing mercy to the dead and admiration for the scientist who had given birth to this horrible weapon. Many guests hardly believed that deadly heat could have spread over the cities. They asked, "How can a small bomb have enough heat to kill all the residents of two cities? Suppose we boil a big jar of water. Then we pour all the hot water over a city. Will all the residents of the city be killed?"

Nobody there could give the right answer. The question sounded thorny because of its scientific characteristics. Another man added, "In my opinion, people died not because of the heat but because of the smell."

There were two different opinions on the destruction of the nuclear bomb, according to the reasoning of the peasants in Binh Chuan. The first opinion said that the A-bomb diffused deadly heat. The second opinion said that it produced stinking fumes.

One guest said, "I don't pay attention to the cause of A-bomb destruction. What pleases me is that the Japanese must leave our country. They forced us to do *corvée* and beat us up as if they were whipping water buffaloes. Poor Teo went mad because of their torture. Uncle Tien took the juice of pounded live crabs all year round."

Another guest sought to change the topic. He said, "Now we are independent. Old Ho is great."

His neighbor murmured, "The allies bombarded Saigon. It is said that the British and Hindu troops went there. They helped the French come back to their former colony. We must fight again."

At this, everybody looked anxious. Their fields would be bloody and full of bones and would smell of cannon powder. All the guests didn't say a word while they were thinking of this tragic possibility.

One day, some people sang as they were walking outside:

> *Dear companions! Let's get along on time!*
> *For the sake of our country let's walk and fight!*
> *Dear companions! Let's unite*
> *And vow to kill the cruel and mean-minded invaders.*
> *Dear companions! Let's get along on time!...*

Nobody knew where these people were from. They were called "new Vietnamese youngsters." Their hair was curly. Their complexions were dark brown. They were equipped with bows and scimitars. The villagers received an order from the committee to wave to them and to give them some dried food they had prepared many days earlier. The "new Vietnamese youngsters" left many footsteps on the sandy paths. They disappeared but their songs resounded in the distance.

> *Armed with spears*
> *And portable bamboo mosquito nets*
> *On our shoulders*
> *We never feel less imposing...*

❖ ❖ ❖

We vow to be in solidarity when praying to our forefathers.

Sau Truong wasn't a member of any political groups in the village. However, he seemed to know many things. He was one of my aunt's sons. He worked the land at the age of ten. He carried the plow as if he were lifting two baskets of hay although he was short. He had dark brown skin blackened by the torrid sunlight and oily rains. He had smoked tobacco since his childhood. He behaved like an adult by speaking slowly and by saving every half-smoked cigarette, which he stuck on the colonnade to be used when necessary. He used to cough and spit saliva because he smoked and talked too much. In the past he told me about the God of Life and the God of Death. Now, he liked to talk about local, national and international news. I preferred fairy tales to this news, which wasn't interesting to a boy of my age. Sau Truong taught me how to use jack-tree sap to trap birds, and how to dig holes to catch crickets, how to catch chameleons, crabs, and fish. He protected me when the other children tried to hurt me. He was good at using a slingshot and catching birds. When I was a child, I admired him very much.

Sau Truong told me about Viet Minh military exploits and about Hoang Tho's bravery. He described Hoang Tho as a perfect man. "Hoang Tho was an excellent scholar and an exceptional military man," he said. It was said that he had sunk a French boat on the Saigon River by himself. Sau Truong told me about the Viet Minh–controlled zones, such as Tan Long, Khanh Van, Bong Trang, Nha Do, Thanh Tuyen, and Ben Suc, and about the transcendent appearance and disappearance in Saigon of Mr. Thi, Mr. Trinh, Mr. Lo, Mr. Nghe, and Mr. Tra, who were legendary persons in history. In Tuy An, I had heard about Pham Thieu), Ca Van Thinh, and Dao Son Tay. Sau Truong gave me some new names. Some of them were well known, like Nguyen Van Thi, Tran Van Tra, and Huynh Van Nghe. He praised the boldness of the Thuan Giao militia, which fought the French, Captain Danh's back-up forces, and the Caodaist troops. He insisted on the importance of the growth of resistance in Binh Chuan and Tan Khanh.

I didn't know how he knew those things in such detail. He was really a farmer. He had never been to Saigon. He didn't finish the second grade. He was too busy farming. I never saw him at the village meetings but what he told me was true. It wasn't his imagination. How did he know it? Maybe somebody told it to him. I wondered how he could give me such a detailed historic narration with his low level of education. Until his death in the 1990s, he remained a farmer living from hand to mouth in the arid fields hollowed by the bombs.

The Viet Minh leaders held their meetings in my grandmother's house. Mr. Thi was their head. He had a good-looking appearance. It was said that his wife was a teacher in the city. Mr. Thi loved me. He called my grandmother "Mummy." Not long ago, this woman he was calling "Mummy" had been blindfolded and threatened with death on the brink of a clay pit because it was rumored that my father had surrendered to the French in Laithieu.

The Viet Minh leaders never spent a night in my grandmother's house. They left for an unspecified place after each meeting. My grandmother's house became a meeting room for the villagers and a rest area for the Viet Minh leaders in the Thu-Bien provinces (from *Thu*daumot and *Bien* Hoa).

Viet Minh cadres exaggerated the news and described imaginary espionage activities to terrorize the villagers. They killed a lady who was using a white handkerchief embroidered with red threads, charging her with drawing a map for the French. A Saigonese girl student trying to join the resistance was arrested and charged with infiltration. A Francophile partisan was captured and buried alive. A provincial businessman who came to Binh Chuan to buy agricultural produce was sentenced to death. He was charged with espionage and had his flesh hashed. We didn't know how many of the dead deserved their deaths. It was certain that many of them died because of the revolutionary infantilism and blind enthusiasm of the Viet Minh.

Those villagers who had 100-piastre bills issued by the Bank of Indochina had to give them to the local committee. It was unlawful to keep them home. The bank notes with the picture of Angkor Wat were confiscated. Nobody dared to ask why.

One evening, when I came home from the spring, I saw a crowd in my grandmother's house. Everybody was quiet and meditative. Four men armed with pistols and guns stood at the front door and looked outside. I saw a bloody man whose face was pale. He looked very tired and in great pain. He was Phan Cong Trieu, one of the Viet Minh leaders in Thu-Bien provinces. He had commanded a militia clash with the French and was seriously wounded on the outskirts of Binh Chuan and Thuan Giao. A man who seemed to be a superior looked at him and said, "His leg is wounded. It needs sawing."

I was curious to know how they sawed off a leg. A few minutes later, a man brought a saw borrowed from a woodcutter. He put Trieu's wounded leg on a pot and sawed it. Blood spilled in the pot. A man took the sawed-off part of the leg outside to bury it. It hadn't been buried yet when Phan Cong Trieu heaved his last sigh. He was buried near the Pagoda of Venerable Hue, some hundred yards from the battlefield, after a minute of silence and some shots in the air. His tombstone bore these plain words: "Comrade Phan Cong Trieu, dead in 1946."

After 1975, when I went back to Binh Chuan to visit my grandmother's grave, I passed his grave. What a surprise! The old tombstone had disappeared. It had been replaced by a new one with the gilded words "Thomas Phan Cong Trieu, dead in 1946."

My father was taken to Laithieu and jailed in a small room behind the communal office of Tan Thoi, next to the school. He was tortured by the French. The bridge of his nose was broken. At that time the French were antipathetic to the Tuy An natives. They had concluded that we all were Viet Minh.

Tuy An, in the eyes of the French in Thudaumot province, was as dangerous as Hoc Mon, Ba Diem and An Phu Dong. Many villagers had to falsify their backgrounds and birthplaces to avoid political troubles. Some decided not to deny their birthplace but lived as far from Laithieu and Thudaumot as possible.

Tuy An had neither significant revolts like Hoc Mon, Ba Diem, Can Long, Cao Lanh, and Cho Dem nor Communist movements like Hung Dinh, which was under the direction of Phan Van Hum between the two great wars. However, its geographic location was very important. The Viet Minh tried their best to make it an "untouchable" war zone like Bien Hoa, Thudaumot, and near Saigon. The French troops in Laithieu and Thudaumot tried to remove this thorn to narrow the Viet Minh sphere of activity.

Phan Van Hum was born in Bung, Laithieu district, Thudaumot province. When working in Hue, he visited the revolutionary Phan Boi Chau. After this visit, he decided to quit his job as a public works technician in Hue and become involved in revolutionary activities. He joined Nguyen An Ninh and was imprisoned in the Saigon prison, a Vietnamese Bastille under French rule. This prison inspired him to write the famous *Ngoi Tu Kham Lon* (In the Big Prison). Phan Van Hum was the author of many precious works. After being released he went to France and studied philosophy at the Sorbonne. After receiving his degree in philosophy, he returned to Vietnam to struggle against the French colonialists with Ta Thu Thau, Ho Huu Tuong, and Doan Van Truong, who were Trotskyites, and Duong Bach Mai and Nguyen Van Tao, who were Stalinists. He was considered a Trotskyite. After the Autumn Revolution, he was killed by the Viet Minh in Tan Uyen.

Some teachers in Tuy An admired Phan Van Hum's patriotism without knowing why the Stalinists (Third International) and Trotskyites (Fourth International) killed one another. Both the Viet Minh and the French disliked the intellectuals, the petite bourgeoisie, and the teachers in Tuy An. The latter used to belong to secret societies or revolutionary parties. In the Viet Nam Quoc Dan Dang and Dang Cong San Dong Duong (Indochinese Communist Party), there were many teachers who played important roles. Ho Chi Minh, Pham Van Dong, Vo Nguyen Giap, Tran Phu, and Dang Thai Mai were all teachers. Influenced by Confucianism, the Vietnamese people respected teachers who linked Western and Eastern cultures, the rich and the poor, the educated and the illiterate. The French watched them carefully. Later, so did the Communists.

My father was a teacher and a native of Tuy An. My uncle was killed by the French along with six other teachers for working for the Viet Minh Front. These factors led the French to conclude that my father was a Viet Minh. To be shot! That was the secret code in my father's file. He asked the French investigator, "What could I do when all the schools were closed? Where should I go when all of my property is in Tuy An? If you were in my situation, a man who has his wife, children, relatives, and property in his native village, what would you do?"

The French investigator was surprised by my father's questions. His conscience seemed to revive. He asked my father in a soft voice, "Would you like to teach again?"

"How can I teach? I am a prisoner," my father replied.

The French investigator looked at my father, smiling. "You are free. You will be a teacher tomorrow."

My father had a health screening and was given new clothes to prepare to return to school. The jail behind the communal office became the shelter of my family in Laithieu a few months later.

My father returned from the brink of death. He was a prisoner whose honor was rehabilitated and an unemployed person who found his old job again. He lived by himself in the small house that had been his prison.

My father tried to get in touch with my mother, my brothers, and myself. We had been separated from one another when Tuy An village was plunged into fire. Some unfavorable news had come to Binh Chuan and Tuy An. It was rumored that my father really had collaborated with the French. Some people said that he was happy. Others said that he sold out the country. Praising was less important than blaming and denouncing. Many of the people who blamed and denounced my father severely were jealous of his new situation. After they left the village for the cities, they apologized to my father and said that they had said those things to deceive the Viet Minh.

My brothers had an unstable life with the family of one of our cousins near Tuy An. My oldest brother was jailed in Phu Loi, where he saw Tam Tron, our grandmother's neighbor in Binh Chuan. In less than a year, this young student from the Lycée Petrus Ky was jailed by both the Viet Minh and the French. Thanks to his French name and his proficiency in French, he had a little favor at the French investigation office. After a month in prison, he was freed and came back to Tuy An, which had been almost ruined by fire.

In Binh Chuan, I faced grumbling from some villagers. They imitated the Viet Minh cadres by calling me *con cua dan bo sua* (the son of the buttermilk people), a disdainful term to call a six-year-old child. Few people dared to defend me. A tolerant villager tried to restrain them by saying, "He is a child. Why do we denounce an innocent child?"

My aunt asked, "What is he guilty of?"

"His father is a traitor," a man said.

"Are you saying that teaching is betraying our homeland? How about Mr. Thi's wife?" my aunt asked.

The man kept his mouth shut. He spit on the ground and left.

My mother contacted my father and joined him in Laithieu. My brothers in turn joined our parents in the city, but I was still in Binh Chuan. My father hired a villager to bring me to Laithieu, and my family was reunified. A family of seven persons then lived temporarily in a 12-by-12-foot room behind the Tan Thoi communal office.

3

To the City

Laithieu was a prosperous city, five miles from Tuy An. It was economically important in the southern part of Thudaumot province. It was surrounded by fertile farmlands. Binh Nham was well known for its orchards and vegetables. Nhi Binh, on the right bank of the Saigon River, had many orchards and sugar mills. Tan Thoi had many pottery kilns, joiners' workshops, and good restaurants. Phu Long and Vinh Phu had many plantations of sugar canes. Rice and vegetables were abundant there.

The Catholic churches of Binh Nham and Nhi Binh were the oldest ones in Gia Dinh and Thudaumot provinces. These two villages were mostly populated by Roman Catholics. They were the cradles of many Catholic priests in South Vietnam under French rule.

Laithieu was known for its paper mill and for delicious food, such as *nem* made from pounded pork mixed with shredded pork skin, salt, sugar, and black pepper wrapped in banana leaves and *keo hot dieu* made from fried cashew nuts and sugar. At one time, Laithieu served as a cockpit and fish-fighting place. It was the birthplace of boxer Dong Phuong Soc. Laithieu had a good soccer team, with Chin Bien as goalkeeper and Duc and Chac as fullbacks. The three of them were well known in the 1950s. Laithieu was enlivened by the Saigon–Loc Ninh railroad. Before 1945, its station was very busy. Many people went to Saigon, Thudaumot, or Loc Ninh by train.

The Laithieu River is an affluent of the Saigon River. It is navigable from its junction with the Saigon River to the market. The quay was busy with many sampans carrying agricultural produce from Nhi Binh, An Son, Thanh Loc, and Binh Nham to Laithieu. Some produce was sold in Laithieu. The rest was carried to Saigon.

The Laithieu market was pretty large. Almost all the stores there belonged to the Chinese. There were a dozen restaurants and five Oriental drugstores owned by Chinese who were originally from Tai Pou district, South China. Two Vietnamese practiced oriental medicine and ran two oriental drugstores in the city. In the 1940s there were two medical doctors in Laithieu. One had studied medicine in France. The other graduated from the Hanoi Medical School. Then, Western medicine was very expensive. Rural people couldn't afford it. Neither could needy urban residents. The patients were used to Chinese or Vietnamese medicine. The oriental physicians diagnosed the patients and sold them medicine. They also sold medicine for animals. The farmers came to their drugstores to get medicine if their pigs had round worms or to get elephant skin to feed them to accelerate their growth.

It was very noisy at the market. A Hindu shouted, hawking incense sticks. A Vietnamese salesman publicized his round worm medicine and its effectiveness. A Chinese beat a drum and advertised various kinds of oriental medicine prepared by the Dai Tu Bi Laboratory. People talked, laughed, and quarreled with one another, making a deafening noise. At noon the crowd melted away. A sweeper collected trash and put it in a wheelbarrow. In the afternoon some Chinese displayed bok choi, celery, lettuce, tomatoes, carrots and potatoes for sale. These vegetables were strange to the Vietnamese farmers at that time. Their customers were Chinese, French and a few Vietnamese urban residents.

All the hamlets around Laithieu remained rural with lateritic graves, peanut fields and rice fields. The residents were mostly farmers. At night there was no electricity. The insects groaned all night long, making a monotonous harmony.

Only the center of the city had electricity. Running water was absent. In the market area, there were many water carriers, who supplied the residents with water. People in the hamlets got water from the wells.

Laithieu had a big *dinh* (temple). In front of the *dinh*, there were many centennial trees and a big statue of a red horse. In 1947, the Viet Minh attacked Laithieu and burned down the *dinh* and the market as well. The statue of the red horse was demolished. After that, the French troops used this area as their military post. In 1967, this temple was reconstructed.

The Chinese had two temples in the city. They celebrated their religious festivals solemnly every year. They had their own community with a cemetery, school, basketball team, and a classical music band.

Tan Thoi was the district town of Laithieu. It had a massive communal office whose floor was covered with splendid tiles made in Marseilles. The district office building was located near the water tower. This building was requisitioned from a Chinese businessman who made peanut oil and fertilizers. The district office building was surrounded by a long defense line made from coconut or areca trees with a thick stratum of soil that couldn't be pierced by bullets.

Under French rule almost all the province and district chiefs were French. Usually they had graduated from the Ecole Nationale d'Administration (ENA). The School of Administration of Dalat, headed by Dr. Tran Cuu Chan, was a copy of the French ENA. This school moved to Saigon and became the National

Institute of Administration (NIA); it was headed by Dr. Vu Quoc Thong after the partition of Vietnam. In 1963, *Agrégé* (accredited teacher) Nguyen Van Bong returned to Vietnam and was appointed president of the NIA. Eight years later, he was assassinated.

The French chief of Laithieu district looked less like a soldier than the officers of the Deuxième Bureau. The latter had their investigation room behind the district government office. Mr. Kiem, a teacher, became the most redoubtable investigator and torturer. He wasn't famous for teaching, but he had a bad reputation for torturing suspected people. When he was a teacher, he used to slap and kick his students. When he was an investigator, he seemed to be happy to see people suffering from his brutal torture. His slogan was "torture the innocent until they are guilty."

Leaving the investigation room, all the victims were unconscious. They were almost dying. Some had been hung upside down; some had been beaten with drumsticks; some had been electrically shocked; some had been filled with water. The torturers then stood on their bellies and pressed with their feet to push water out through the victims' nostrils and mouths to make them suffocate. Their pain was indescribable. Kiem and some partisans were in charge of the torture under the supervision of a French officer. Every evening I saw a big military truck carrying prisoners to the bridge linking Phu Long, Thudaumot province, and Thanh Loc, Gia Dinh province, to be executed. They were shot and thrown in the Saigon River, which, during the Franco-Vietnamese War, was full of rotten dead bodies. Some of the bodies got caught at the quay of Laithieu after the reflux. That military truck brought the prisoners to their deaths. The familiar sounds of its engine became horrible. The desperate people on the truck saw their ephemeral lives on this planet about to end. They were conscious of their approaching deaths, the final step of human suffering caused by mankind. After their deaths, they served the aquatic animals with their bodies.

People could be victims of both the French and the Viet Minh. The latter decapitated or disemboweled any suspects they labeled *Viet Gian* (traitors). Innocent people lived under two strata of terrible persecution; it was difficult to conclude whether those who fled from the Viet Minh–controlled zones were traitors, whether those who joined them were really patriotic, or whether quiet folks were selfish and opportunistic. Hatred called hatred. Vengeance called vengeance. Continual bloodshed made human beings lose their humanity.

The rivers were polluted by dead bodies. As a result, fish and shrimp had good food. Consequently, at one time, people didn't eat catfish and shrimp. The then-slang *di mo tom* (to go catch shrimp) meant being shot or decapitated and thrown in the rivers.

The *fonctionnaires* (civil servants) working for the French were well dressed. They put on white shirts and shorts or pants. Usually they wore short-sleeved shirts. When they wore long-sleeved shirts, they used to roll both sleeves up to their elbows. Their hair was fancily combed in different styles. They used brilliantine to keep their hair stuck, wavy, and shiny. They put on sandals or rubber-soled shoes. Only their superior wore leather-soled shoes, which made a big noise when they walked. That gave the superior more authority and self-confidence. Rich people or petite bourgeoisie put on black, brown, or two-tone shoes.

The republican guards wore yellow khaki uniforms and heavy military boots. Most of them looked bony. Corporal Bo was in charge of training the new soldiers. They practiced marching and presenting arms according to Corporal Bo's instructions. Corporal Bo commanded them in French. It wasn't necessary for him to understand what he said. He just told them to do this or that as a habit. When he said, "En avant! Marche!" (forward march), they marched. When he said, "L'arme sur l'épaule" (shoulder arms), they put their guns on their shoulders. When he said, "Repos" (stand), they stood on the spot. When he said, "Un! Deux!" (one! two!), they marched, moving their feet at the rhythmic count "Un! Deux!" of their chief. I don't know how long they practiced firing at the shooting range. One afternoon, after coming off duty, a soldier was on the way back to his barracks with his gun. A dog barked at him, showing its sharp teeth as if it were ready to bite him. Our dear soldier pressed the trigger of his gun to shoot the dog. Bang! Bang! Two bullets hit the wall of Mr. Khinh's house. The dog ran fearfully. The French *délégué* (chief of the district) asked his staff what was going on. When he learned that the soldier shot at the dog, which was sound and safe, while the wall of Mr. Khinh's house was pierced by two bullets, he got very angry. He said rude words. Nobody knew why he got angry. Because the soldier was bad at shooting? Because he wanted to protect the dog? Or to ensure human life?

The civil servants had their comfortable lives. Their wives and children were well dressed. Their wives put on wooden clogs. Their children wore slippers and had some toys. They went to school to study French and *quoc ngu* (national language), that is, Vietnamese. Many civil servants' wives were progressive, using lipsticks and perfumes and having their hair curled. They usually wore Vietnamese suits. They only put on the *ao dai* (robe) during Tet or for Sunday mass.

The soldiers' salaries were low. Their lives weren't comfortable. Their wives kept their chignons with the lovely black *ao ba ba* (skirt), like the country ladies. Their children were feeble. Most of them didn't live in the city with their parents but in the country.

The sergeant of police was very authoritative. His family looked wealthy. His wife behaved like a ringleader. His children were impolite and insolent. People were scared of them. They took everything at the market without paying a penny. They raised four German shepherds and let them bite anybody freely. The sergeant of police abused his power by asking the butchers to give him beef to feed his dogs every day. After 1954, he was forced to retire. He lived in misery without having a small piece of beef to warm his hungry stomach.

After World War II, only wealthy families had phonographs and radio sets. There were no refrigerators in Laithieu, then. Nobody had a family car. Bicycles remained important. Then, in the 1950s, there appeared a Vélo Solex and a Mobylette (motorcycles) in the most prosperous district of Thudaumot province.

The soldiers' wives liked to sing classical songs. Most urban people loved "reformed music." I heard people singing everywhere in the city. On the street the children sang songs by Le Thuong, Pham Duy, Luu Huu Phuoc, and Phan Huynh Dieu. The songs "Ba Tu Ban Hang" (Old Mother Tu, the Peddler) and "Hon Vong Phu" (Mount Vong Phu) by Le Thuong were in vogue at that time. The former described Old Mother Tu, a peddler and her four children, who joined the resistance. The latter described the sufferings of a warrior's wife who, holding her baby, looked forward to her husband's homecoming. Both the mother and baby were petrified that the warrior would not return. The war went on persistently.

Everybody sang. The circus man advertising oriental medicine at the market sang a classical song about World War II that described German military operations in the Soviet Union. He finished his song: "The Germans were thirty-six kilometers from Moscow." A blind beggar sang sorrowful songs reflecting human ingratitude and betrayal. He recited "Luc Van Tien," a masterpiece by Do Chieu glorifying filial piety, loyalty, and virginity. He looked very angry when reciting verses describing how Trinh Ham endangered Luc Van Tien. At every bus stop tea, fruit, and bread were sold. The sellers shouted while a blind musician played mandolin and sang patriotic songs, such as "Bac Son," "Tam Vu," and "Tieu Doan 307" (Company 307). I wondered whether this man was from my maternal village. *How could he know these songs?* I asked myself.

The house we lived in temporarily was too small in comparison with my family's size. In Binh Chuan and Tuy An, I had lived in big houses with large front yards and back yards. There were many fruit trees around the houses. The house in Laithieu had neither front yard nor back yard.

A few days after our arrival in Laithieu, the Viet Minh attacked the city. French and Moroccan soldiers fired in the air as if shooting off fireworks. The market and the village temple were on fire. The Viet Minh blew a blast on a bugle. They opened the stables and shot in the air to frighten the horses, which ran noisily onto Road 13. The French soldiers felt horrible, thinking that the Viet Minh rode horses to command the battle. They were demoralized and shot without seeing the enemy. After the withdrawal of the Viet Minh, they shelled Binh Hoa and Tuy An.

The French ensured territorial security with difficulty. It took time to go to Thudaumot, seven miles from Laithieu, by bus. Armored cars had to clear Road 13 and escort the convoy every day. By 4:00 P.M. there were no vehicles on Road 13. The French and their partisans took control of their military post area only. Security in the suburban areas was uncertain. The Viet Minh intimidated the urban people by blasting grenades. Mr. Thiet, the secretary of the district chief, was assassinated in front of the Tan Thoi communal office. Mr. Ho, a tax collector, was shot dead near the Chinese school about seventy feet from the military post. Another tax collector, Mr. Phu, was stabbed to death. The collaborators' safety was uncertain if they lived far away from the military posts. They were ordered to spend nights in the military post. Each of them had a billet there. This billet was larger than the house we lived in behind the communal office. Our billet was next to writer Binh Nguyen Loc's. During his stay in Laithieu, he knew Old Tu Hoa Liem, who was believed to be talismanic and invulnerable; many real persons and interesting stories inspired his novels.

I began to go to school in Laithieu. Most of my classmates were four or five years older than I. Some were seven years older than I. I was a little afraid and shy. I was a rural boy in the city. Everything was new or strange to me. My friends were older, taller, and bigger than I. I didn't understand what they said. How could I compete with them?

I was good at Vietnamese, French, history and geography. I was bad at math and handicrafts. I read fast and learned the lessons by heart quickly. I didn't know anything about grammar and verbs' conjugation, but I wasn't shy about speaking French. I disliked some math vocabulary, such as "area," "perimeter," "gain," and "loss." I was scared of fractions.

I was never studious. My schedule opposed that of the school. I disliked what the teachers taught at school. I wanted to satisfy my curiosity, but I had to accept what the teacher taught me mechanically. I liked to answer the questions asked by the teacher. The teacher asked me to recite my lessons by heart without knowing whether I understood what I recited or not. He gave grades based on the speed of recitation. A friend of mine was very good at recitation. When called on by the teacher, he closed his eyes and stopped breathing to recite the lesson from the top to the end in a few seconds. When he recited the lesson, the teacher listened to him with half-closed eyes. When he finished his lesson, the teacher said, "Very good."

I was always whipped by the teacher for not knowing my lessons by heart and got zero in math. However, I didn't have any worries about that. Thursdays and Sundays were two weekly holidays. I took advantage of these days to go to Phu Long to catch paradise fish and to look for algae, duckweed, and hyacinth for my fish. I knew where to find paradise fish and how to distinguish the good from the bad ones. In class I thought about them. I took care of their food, lodging, and health. I protected the small ones from being eaten by their parents. I loved fish and spent a lot of time and energy taking care of them. On the contrary, big fish never loved their young. They ate as many small fish as possible. In my childhood, I had many plans in my mind. I didn't have enough time and money to carry them out. I spent all my time on paradise fish. How could I pay attention to my homework? to math and science? and to other subjects? I would have liked to have a big jar for my fish. I planned how to have it, where to put it, and what to say to my father so that he would let me do whatever I liked. It was difficult for me to convince my father because I was a bad student. That disappointed my father too much. But I didn't quit my plans. I assumed that everything would go smoothly. What should I put in the jar? What kind of fish should I multiply? How could I get enough mosquito larvas for many fish? To get enough mosquito larvas wasn't difficult. I put some megass (crushed sugar cane) in a pot of water to attract the mosquitoes to lay eggs. It was the best way to get mosquito larvas. The big problem was my father. He thougth it was stupid to attract mosquitoes and to facilitate their fecundation.

I wasn't satisfied with the paradise fish I caught in Phu Long. They were weak and bad in defense and offense. I hoped to have a pair of dark blue paradise fish. I was fond of watching them and studying how they lived and what they ate. I went to the fighting-fish amateurs to learn from their experiences. It wasn't easy to approach them. Tu Hoa Liem was old and difficult. He disliked children who were noisy and sought to steal his fish. When he heard a noise at the gate, he asked with a bitter voice, "Who is that? What are you standing there for?" I had no way to see him to reveal my dream. Mr. Sau Qua had different varieties of fighting fish. He was wealthy. He had a small bus. His wife sold fabrics. His age and financial situation showed that he disliked children. As a child, I felt that there was a thick wall separating adults from children. I thought that they never respected children's freedom and equality. At the table, children sat on their own side. The other side was for adults. When the children ate fish cheeks, the adults stopped them, saying, "It's for the adults," or "Don't eat it. It makes you stupid." When children wanted to eat chicken heads, they heard this: "My God! That's for the adults!" When they had haircuts, the barbers bent their necks until they cried. Therefore, they didn't like to go to the barber shop. I thought bad of the adults who prevented me from working on my dream. I never hid it. I told it to everybody. My sincerity got a positive response from one of my friends, Leo. He told me that his father had many dark blue fighting fish. Leo brought me to Phu Long to see his father. I greeted him politely. He was a sweet farmer in his fifties. He loved his son, Leo. So he was kind to me. Leo introduced me to him and told him about the purpose of my visit in Phu Long. With perfect comprehension he said, "No problem. You can have as many fish as you wish." He walked to the ditch and picked some impermeable leaves. He made them into a funnel into which he poured some water to keep the fish alive. His kindness and zeal gave me a big remorse for thinking ill of adults. Now I deemed that everybody loved their children. Through the images of their kids, they loved other children. I felt a little ashamed. In a short time, I had had two opposite thoughts.

I realized that our self-interest harmed our judgment and impartiality and that our society was a mixture of good and evil.

I was successful in steering a paradise fish movement in my family and in my neighborhood. My father liked paradise fish. My brothers liked them. Our neighbors had some at home. It was the favorable moment for me to put a big jar on the back porch. My father's silence seemed to be an approval.

The problem was how to get a big jar. I didn't have money to get one. Would the Chinese owner of the pottery give me one? I went to the pottery kiln, choosing my best words to convince him to give me what I wished to have.

"What are you doing here?" the Chinese man asked.

"Uncle, may I have this jar?" I asked, showing him a flawed jar.

"What for?" he asked.

"For my paradise fish. I think you can't sell it to anybody."

"Take it," he said.

I carried the heavy jar home. It took time for me to clean it, to fill it with water, and to put some hyacinth, duckweed, and algae in it. My dark blue paradise fish swam happily in the clear water. The next morning I got up very early. I went straight to the jar. How happy I was to see many tiny eggs on the white foam. I fished up the female with a spoon net to let the male hatch the eggs. A few days later, I had many small fish in the big jar. It was time to fish up the male. Otherwise, it would eat all the small fish I was proud of.

My studies got worse. My teacher informed my father of the bad news. I was whipped by the teacher. Sometimes he gave me some blows. I deserved such a punishment and took it without any complaints.

At that time all the students were barefooted. One student was badly whipped and cursed by his teacher because he put on wooden clogs. It was a sign of impoliteness, according to the intolerant teacher. She thought that her students wanted to be equal to her if they wore wooden clogs.

Under French rule, students rode free on buses and sampans. That is why the bus and sampan owners disliked them. They didn't pay one cent, but the bus or sampan owners were responsible for their safety. A saying compared students with ghosts and devils:

> First: the devils.
> Second: the ghosts.
> Third: the students.

Many children from other villages attended the school of Laithieu. Bung had a school of which the highest grade was the third one. After receiving their third-grade certificates, students continued their studies in Laithieu or Thudaumot. Children from Binh Nham, Phu Long, Vinh Phu, Thanh Loc, and Nhi Binh studied in Laithieu.

Laithieu was a district, even though its school wasn't as big as the Tuy

An School, which had large front and back yards. Around the school there was much flamboyance with red flowers in the summer. The Laithieu school had a large front yard. Its back yard was narrow. The school was near the market, Road 13, the communal office, the pottery kilns, and Dong Tu hamlet, a rural hamlet with arid and sandy fields comparable to those of Binh Chuan. Some students played hooky and played cards there. The Laithieu school had a beautiful iron fence. Its walls were dark yellow; its doors were brown. These were the two familiar colors in Vietnamese schools under French rule.

The Laithieu school was built in the early twentieth century. Unlike the Tuy An school, it had few local teachers. In the first years of war, there was a serious lack of teachers.

After World War II, teachers, under the influence of French culture, began to wear white clothes. White, standing for purity, was the favorite color of serious people. Few teachers wore colorful shirts. The Vietnamese don't like white because it is the mourning color. Teachers didn't wear white shirts with black pants, which was the style of clothing of waiters. The female teachers were believed not to be serious if they wore colorful clothes, or if they had their hair curled. A few years after World War II, teachers put on pants instead of shorts. Those who wore shorts were deemed not to be serious. Teaching wasn't a lucrative profession, but teachers had to meet many requirements. Teachers had to be exemplary. They had to avoid the four social evils. Otherwise, they would be bitterly mocked by the folks. "Do as I [teacher] say, not as I do," the populace said.

The Vietnamese people coped with corruption, social injustice, severe colonial policies, bloodshed, and differences of culture. They lost their independence and freedom. They tried to conserve their culture, vainly. Traditional culture was paralyzed by French culture. The former was conservative. On the contrary, the latter was progressive and liberal.

The students weren't in uniforms. They wore whatever they had. Rich students had hide bags. Most students used rush bags. Many students were so poor that they couldn't buy copy books and ink. They had to share ink from their friends and be dependent upon them. Sometimes they couldn't finish a dictation because a friend changed his mind and did not allow them to use the ink.

When the drum beat, all the students lined up. They came into class quietly. In class they stood up, saluted their teacher, and recited the times table in French: "Deux fois un font deux. Deux fois deux font quatre..." Thanks to this harmonious recitation I knew the times table. I never learned it at home. I was a bad student. I liked wandering the streets, but I didn't want my teacher to see me on the streets or at the market. When I saw him in the distance, I tried to change my itinerary.

My father got more and more difficult as soon as we joined him in Laithieu. He was more meditative, taciturn, and angry with his children. He missed his native village. He suffered for his country and his lost fortune.

My brothers were good students. My father was very happy about that, but he worried a lot about me. My grandmother was proud of me, but my father wasn't. His colleagues laughed at him, saying, "You are a teacher. But your son will be a bookseller." I wasn't concerned about that. I accepted the "as is" without any anxiety. I never thought of making artificial progress or improvement by copying my friends' homework and giving them something in compensation for their "kindness." I considered that a shameful act, and I tried my best to keep cowardice away from me. I accepted kneeling, to be whipped, scolded, and ridiculed by the teacher. I knew that I was neither stupid nor lazy. I wasn't a rude, impolite, and turbulent boy. On the contrary, I was polite, courageous, and helpful. I was fond of games and spent all of my time for them. I disagreed with some of my teachers about their pedagogy and prejudice. But I was too young and too small to say it. I didn't like their small-mindedness. They were happy to see their colleague's son in a bad rank in class. It wasn't the good behavior of great men.

One day, I let my father's paradise fish fight Mr. Khinh's. The two fish were strong and stubborn. Neither of them gave up fighting although their mouths were swollen and their fins torn. I brought the blind fish home. Its body was fully scratched. My father was very angry because I hadn't asked for his authorization. I just gave him a fait accompli. My father got more angry, thinking of my bad rank in class. He broke the big jar and all of my bottles with colorful paradise fish. That night I was badly beaten. I felt dolorous to hear the hammer hitting the jar. I imagined how unhappy my fighting fish were for lack of water.

Raising paradise fish was over. I turned to cricket fighting. This game couldn't last all year 'round like fish fighting. Besides, it was dangerous to dig holes to catch crickets. Sometimes I didn't see crickets but I did see snakes or grenades.

Feeding paradise fish was more interesting than feeding crickets. It is possible to multiply paradise fish but it is impossible to have small crickets. A cricket's lifespan is much shorter than a paradise fish's. Crickets are noisy. Paradise fish are quiet. Crickets sing loudly, but they aren't tenacious and stubborn. The paradise fish are quite different. They make no noise, but their bite is deadly. Crickets are "the cries of the empty barrel" while paradise fish are brave samurais ready to die on the battlefield, accepting death rather than shame.

My games shrank. I played tip cat (a game involving two pieces of wood — one used as bat and the other as the "ball") very well, but it was a rural children's game. In the city no child knew it. So I had no partner to play it. Playing ping-pong was expensive. I had no money to buy rackets, ping-pong balls, tables, and nets. The French and some Vietnamese played table tennis in Mr. La's house. All the children had to keep away from that place.

I was too young to play soccer. In the 1950s Laithieu had a good soccer team sponsored and financed by a French lieutenant of the Deuxième Bureau and Captain To. Vu Hong Khanh, the minister of youth, came to Laithieu to inaugurate its stadium. I became a soccer fan. I followed the Laithieu soccer team to Thu Duc, Thudaumot, Hoc Mon, and Saigon. I knew all the stadiums in Saigon and Cholon. I knew the good soccer teams there, including the AJS team, the police soccer team, the French military soccer team, the Star of Gia Dinh, and the Star of Ba Chieu. I admired the goalkeepers Quyen, Rang, and Lam Kinh. In 1952, Tran Van Thuc led Vietnamese athletes to the Olympic Games in Helsinki, Finland. I admired the Czech runner, Zatopek, and respected the tenacity of the Vietnamese athlete Tran Van Ly in the marathon race. I became a sports fan with many dreams in mind. I dreamed of being a good goalkeeper, a cyclist like Coppi in the Tour de France, a runner like Zatopek.

I was a soccer player without a ball, a cyclist without a racing bike, and a runner without shoes.

I wasn't quite pleased with watching soccer. There were no regular matches. I didn't know what to do on Thursdays and Sundays. I thought of reading newspapers. It was a good idea, but who would let me read them while I had no money? How could I read many newspapers? I was covetous to read news from the battlefields throughout the Indochinese peninsula, about the war between Israel and the Arab countries in the Middle East, about the Korean War. I also liked to read sports, local news, novels by Phu Duc (a Vietnamese Alexandre Dumas), and Chinese stories. The Laithieu Hall of Information became my library. Mr. Hoanh, who worked there, became my intimate friend in spite of our age difference. We belonged to different generations, but books and newspapers made our friendship closer. The small penniless reader made friends with the librarian like the patients were friendly with the doctors.

I read *Than Chung, Dan Quyen, Phuc Hung, Anh Sang, Tieng Doi, Le Song, Buoi Sang,* and *Tieng Chuong.* Each of them had its own attractive articles. I was so fond of reading newspapers that I would forget the closing hour of the Hall of Information. "It's five o'clock," Mr. Hoanh would say. I arranged the newspapers, said good-bye to him, and left the "library."

My father worried a lot about me. Being a teacher, more or less, he knew that children's psychology predicted their futures. I had many opposite and incompatible characteristics that confused my father's evaluation. I was a bad student without either playing hooky or hating school. Many people praised me. I neither blamed my teachers for their severe punishments nor had submission to the good students. I was fearless when speaking to the French although my vocabulary was poor and my grammar was lamentable. I told all events clearly and accurately. My sincere insistence moved Leo's father and converted my father into paradise-fish breeding. I did somehow reach my purpose without either telling a lie or deceiving anybody. At this point my father consoled himself that I would be a good student and an honest man. His self-consolation was fortified by Mr. Tam Sum's insistence. "I am sure that this boy is an intelligent and courageous one. Don't worry about him. I see something special in him," he said to my father.

Mr. Tam Sum became one of the most experienced jailors in South Vietnam but he was put in jail as soon as the Communists took over Binh Duong in 1975. He spent six years in the reeducation camps in North Vietnam. He was released and came home to Binh Duong (Song Be). That night, he was arrested by the Song Be police and sent to the Nha Do reeducation camp. He died there after learning that his son had been arrested by the Communists. Mr. Tam Sum was a fervent Buddhist, but his last request was to be baptized and buried in a Catholic cemetery.

My father liked to listen to the news I summarized. He didn't encourage us to read Chinese stories, but two of my brothers read almost all the Chinese stories sold in Vietnam.

I found out my father's feelings. I knew what he liked and what he disliked. I used this knowledge to save myself from terrible thrashings. I always had some sensational news to tell him when he got angry.

One day, I went to Saigon barebacked to watch soccer. I came home at dark. My father was very angry with me. I prepared some important news to neutralize his anger.

"Where did you go all day?" my father asked furiously.

I didn't answer his question directly. I told him some important news he needed to know.

"My sister-in-law was delivered of a baby," I said.

"How do you know that?" my father asked with surprise.

"I went to Stade Saigonais. On the way, I stopped by my brother's house and learned that the baby was born this afternoon," I replied.

"How did you go to Saigon? Did you go there bare-backed?" my father asked skeptically.

"I got into a military truck carrying the soccer players to Saigon. I didn't have enough time to come home to get dressed," I replied.

My father called my mother to inform her of the good news. He told her to prepare some gifts for a visit to their daughter-in-law and first newborn granddaughter the next morning.

In 1949, I was chosen to cheer General De La Tour and Governor Tran Van Huu. The pictures of General De La Tour, Governor Tran Van Huu and myself appeared on the front pages of the newspapers and in the news bulletins published by the Directorate of Information of South Vietnam. General De La Tour and Governor Tran Van Huu asked me two basic questions, which I had learned in the second grade. They gave me a first honor and credit. A few months later, I passed my third-grade test with *mention française* and was chosen to recite "Je vais à l'école" at the award ceremony. A year earlier, on the same day, my brother had recited "Le Loup and l'Agneau" by La Fontaine. The guests of honor praised him. "His French is very good," they said. Twenty-four years later, he found his death on the battlefield in the Mekong Delta after witnessing "La raison du plus fort est toujours la meilleure" (the reason of the stronger is always the best), which he had recited.

My recitation was very simple. It consisted of these four lines:

> Maintenant je vais à l'école.
> J'apprends chaque jour ma leçon.
> Le sac qui pend a mon épaule
> Dit que je suis un grand garçon.
> (Now I am going to school. I learn my lesson every day. The bag hanging on my shoulder says that I am a big boy.)

The canton chief came to the stage. He shook hands with me, praising me, and gave me an award. That was my childhood honor.

All of these favorable things allowed me to gain my father's trust.

I was still a child with passions for wandering, playing, watching soccer, and reading newspapers. In the award ceremony of 1949, I received the third award, consisting of a collection of historic children's tales, a world geography book, a book on Chinese philosophers, and some French fairy tales. I read tales at home and newspapers at the Hall of Information. I learned how to locate all the countries on the map. I drew the map and named the important capitals of the world.

One day, at the Laithieu market, I was given a book entitled *Aux Pieds du Maitre* (Duoi Chan Thay; At the Feet of the Master) translated into Vietnamese by the Vietnamese Theosophical Society. I was fond of reading about the life of Buddha. I went to Giac Nguyen Pagoda in Phu Long to pay my respect to Buddha and to enrich my knowledge of Buddha, whose philosophy is scientific, realistic, and practical. I made acquaintance with a Buddhist monk at Giac Nguyen Pagoda, but I don't know his name. People called him "the dwarf" because he was about three feet tall.

The Buddhist monk was very nice. He didn't treat me as a child but as an especially religious child. He gave me two books: one about punishments, judgments, and blessings after death and one about the life of Buddha. I read them many times and thought a lot about karma; determinism; past, present, and future lives; life and suffering; Nirvana; and seed and fruit (causality and finality).

I began to make friends with Mr. Hai Ky, who was living a retired life in Laithieu. Hai Ky was Sau Cu's brother. He originated from Tuy An village. He studied in Hanoi when his father worked for the French general government there. He was an educated man with vocations for music, chess, poetry, and drawing. His secular life came to an end after his wife's death. After that, he quit playing music and chess to focus on studying Buddhism. He didn't eat meat, only vegetables. He spent his time drawing, reading the Buddhist bible, and writing religious poems. He used to draw European landscapes, the four-season flowers, and Buddha under the shady fig tree of India. I liked to watch him draw. My regular visits and my love for his work consolidated our relations. One day, he gave me one of his favorite paintings, the picture of Buddha on a lotus blossom. I hung it on the wall. Every time my friends came to my house, I asked them to cross their hands to pay respect to Buddha. They offered Buddha any flowers and fruit they had.

In class I had an altar in my drawer. I used to say to my friends, "You see, I am not a good student. But I haven't ever stayed in the same class twice. I received my third-grade certificate with *mention française*. Why? God and Buddha blessed me."

My words were simple, but they were truthful. My friends brought fruit and incense sticks to offer them to Buddha on the fifteenth day of the lunar calendar every month. One day, seeing the smoke from my drawer, the teachers were scared. They opened the drawer and found the smoke was from incense sticks. They laughed loudly to ridicule the superstition of their innocent students. My father didn't say a word. He shared my faith silently.

My intelligence developed visibly. But my passion for games seemed to be unchanged. The historic children's tales excited my patriotism. I wasn't upset with my lot, that of a bad student. I shared the shame of a people in a dependent country. I didn't like haughty secretaries who worked for the district government. I disliked Mr. Kiem, the pitiless torturer. I disliked Captain To and his soldiers sowing terror in Dong Ba, Binh Chieu, Binh Hoa, and Tuy An. They cleared the woods in Binh Hoa and Tuy An. They cut down the trees and displayed many thousand of steres of firewood along Road 13 and along the river in Phu Long village. In order to show their faithfulness to the French the soldiers killed the Viet Minh, cut off their heads, and hung them at Phu Long railroad station. All the pedestrians felt horrible and had mercy for the victims. On July 14, 1952, French Marshal Juin came to Laithieu to give Captain To the *Légion d'Honneur* medal.

Captain To was from a rich landowner's family. His education was very limited. Before the Franco-Vietnamese War, he was a member of the *Conseil des Notables* in a small village in Thudaumot province. He was called *Xa To* (Mayor To). In 1948 he became a second lieutenant in Phu Long. The French allowed him to recruit soldiers in Phu Long, Tan Thoi, Binh Chieu, and Binh Hoa. He paid them monthly. The French supplied him with some old guns and tanks. His highest rank was captain of his back-up troops. The Laithieu dwellers called him *Ba* To (Captain To).

His soldiers were farmers, gamblers, hooligans, and defected Viet Minh in Laithieu district. Some defected Viet Minh were warrant officers and second lieutenants in his force. They knew the local Viet Minh cadres in their villages. They arrested and tortured their relatives to get bribes. Captain To hired some youngsters in the Viet Minh–controlled areas as informers. Their duty was to recognize the Viet Minh cadres and their supporters and sympathizers in the city. The latter were those people who paid taxes or made any kind of contribution to the Viet Minh. They could be urban people attending Viet Minh meetings in the war zone at night. They could be functionaries with connections to the Viet Minh. These informers hid their faces for fear of revenge, covering their heads with bags. Each bag had two apertures so that the informers could see and recognize the suspects. The informers at the checkpoint looked at every passenger on the bus. When they indicated somebody with a nod, that passenger was taken off the bus and brought to the Deuxième Bureau or to Captain To's torture chamber. In Laithieu, Phu Long, and Vinh Phu these informers didn't hide their faces. They terrified their own villagers, many of whom were victims of the Viet Minh, the French, and Captain To's back-up force. They sought to leave their villages to live as far from the informers as possible.

Captain To had many rice fields and sugar mills. He sowed terror in the rural areas and in the city as well. He cut down trees for firewood. He could arrest and kill whoever he liked. He sponsored Chu Luc, a Chinese man, to have the monopoly of selling *De* in Laithieu. Mobile casinos mushroomed in Tan Thoi and Phu Long.

De is a Chinese game consisting of forty numbers. Thirty-six numbers correspond to thirty-six animals and the other four correspond to four gods. Number thirty-seven corresponds to God Almighty, thirty-eight to God of the Land, thirty-nine to God of Finance and forty to God of the Kitchen. A number was drawn every day in Saigon.

Like General Le van Vien (Bay Vien) in Saigon, Captain To had many financial resources. He was wealthier than Captain Danh in Bung and Captain Sau in An Son. Captain Danh had his French nationality thanks to his merits and education. Captain To received the *Légion d'Honneur* medal from Marshal Juin thanks to the efficiency of his back-up troops.

Captain To had many wives. When he fell in love with any beautiful ladies in Laithieu district, these ladies should be his wives at any cost. Like Bay Vien, he knew how to use his money to build up power, how to use power to make money, and how to use both power and money to satisfy his desires. In 1953, a lady refused his demand and killed herself. The Laithieu residents protested him passively by attending her funeral and giving her a touching *adieu* speech.

In 1954, Captain To's back-up troops were dissolved. Ten years later, he was assassinated.

The war got worse in North Vietnam after the Communists took control of China (1949). In South Vietnam, the Viet Minh didn't make resounding attacks. However, their war zones remained untouchable. The French built many military posts along provincial and national roads. They were supported by back-up troops and politico-religious forces. Tuy An was circled by Caodaist troops and the back-up forces of Captain To and Captain Danh. The Viet Minh armed force retreated to War Zone D, leaving some militia to prove their presence and to sow terror among the urban people. After 1951, many Viet Minh cadres left the jungle for different reasons. Some couldn't live with the shortages of food and medicine. Some couldn't continue their resistance, not accepting Communist dictatorship and terror. In 1952, a typhoon devastated Bien Hoa and Phan Thiet provinces. The number of Viet Minh cadres leaving the jungle for the cities increased.

The French and Khmer commandos consolidated power in Laithieu. Khmer children went to the rural hamlets and damaged crops. They dug up graves to catch reptiles. The French took advantage of the historic and racial divergence between Khmers and Vietnamese; they shut their eyes and let the Khmers bully the Vietnamese in their own country. Khmer children beat up Vietnamese children, checked their pockets and bags, and took whatever they liked. I was very displeased and reacted by knocking down one of them. I couldn't imagine that this victory would lead me to a series of continual shames. After that, when he saw me, the Khmer boy menaced me with his knife. I had to run like the wind.

Running wasn't a good solution for me. I temporarily accepted this kind of shame because of my father's honor. I wouldn't like him to be dishonored for having a son who was a hooligan. The more I paid attention to honor, the more I lost it. "Get me a pocket knife and sharpen it for me," I said to Khoa, my uncle's son, who lived in my house. Khoa bought a *canife* and sharpened it for me. I put it in my pocket. The naughty Khmer boy had the habit of stopping me midway home and threatening me with his knife. This time, I didn't run. I decided to fight him with my *canife*. When I showed my knife, he didn't dare move forward. I rushed him. He was visibly fearful. He ran without looking back. After that, he stopped all of his aggressive acts. As for me, I was happy that nothing regrettable happened to give my father troubles. I threw the *canife* away.

The Viet Minh didn't attack Laithieu, but they threw grenades regularly in Bung and Tan Thoi. Many civilians were killed or injured. Grenades exploded in the theaters. Women, children, and men died while watching *cai luong* (reformed theater). A train hit mines in Dong Nhi hamlet. Many passengers were killed or injured. All the victims were Vietnamese. The Viet Minh paralyzed all the activities in the cities and forced the Vietnamese to boycott the French and the Nationalist government led by Emperor Bao Dai. They threw grenades at the markets, in the theaters, at the bus stations, at the railroad stations, at the restaurants and coffee shops. During the war, people tried to avoid any crowded places.

In the rural areas, the Viet Minh printed and circulated bank notes called "Ho Chi Minh bills." They bought goods from farmers and paid them with these bank notes. Nobody refused to accept them although it was dangerous for them to keep these bills at home. They would be badly tortured by the French if the latter found Ho Chi Minh bills in their homes. They must hide the bills issued by the Banque de l'Indochine. If found, the Viet Minh would confiscate them and give their owners unpredictable troubles. The Viet Minh devalued the bills issued by the French by cutting them into two pieces. For example, they cut a 100-piastre bill into two pieces. This practice spread from the Viet Minh–controlled zones to the cities. It existed in South Vietnam for a few years after the partition.

The French got more and more furious. After five years of war, they weren't successfully defeating the Viet Minh. At the beginning of the resistance, the Viet Minh had been militarily weak. They lacked officers, trained soldiers, and ammunition. The longer the war lasted, the more and more mature they became. At the beginning of the war, they were equipped with sharpened bamboo sticks. A few years later, they had guns, machine guns, and cannons. Their government was recognized by the People's Republic of China, the Soviet Union, and other Communist countries in Eastern Europe. The Viet Minh began to receive aid from China. They built up their forces and their international relations from negative to positive.

France was ravaged by the war. In 1940, France had been easily defeated by the Germans. In 1945, all the French colonialists were imprisoned by the Japanese within twenty-four hours. In the eyes of Ho Chi Minh, France was no longer an invincible power. The erosive war in Vietnam ruined not only the French economy but also French will. It caused social and political crises in France. In 1950, France received American aid to continue the hopeless war in the Far East.

In 1951, the Viet Minh shelled Thudaumot. The damage was negligible, but the effect of the first thunder of the Viet Minh cannon was immense. The provincial government ordered all the residents to have sandbags and to light a lamp on the veranda at night. The police gave tickets to house owners who neither had sandbags nor lit lamps at night.

Most collaborators were unpopular. They abused their power. The partisans menaced the grassroots. They gave themselves the right to eat free, to watch *cai luong* free, and to plunder people's properties. A village chief stole the wife of the bike repairman by throwing Viet Minh tracts into his house and informing the French, who put him in jail. The victim lost his wife and his freedom at the same time. The French allowed Captain To to associate with the Chinese and poison the Laithieu residents with *De*. Laithieu became a city full of social evils. Many people were addicted to *De* and to opium. Many were syphilitic because there were many brothels in the city. Some were so addicted to *De* that they forgot their daily lives. They bought newspapers not to read the news but to look at the cartoons that were deemed to help them choose a right number. *De* players spent a lot of time reading many conundrums before choosing a number. Sometimes they had to use their knowledge of etymology and the history of China to interpret the conundrums. They knew what animals corresponded to what historic persons. They chose the numbers using their knowledge of history, their dreams, and some coincidences. They used to ask children what they saw in their dreams to help choose a number. Those people who played *De* got poorer and poorer. They had no future but debt and misery. Not a few gamblers killed themselves. Some hanged themselves. Others drowned in the Saigon River.

The Korean War broke out. The demonstration of the Saigonese students was bloody. Many students were imprisoned. Many were wounded. Tran Van On was killed. In North Vietnam the Viet Minh threatened to march to Hanoi. They were defeated by General De Lattre de Tassigny whose only son, Bernard, was killed in Ninh Binh. All of these events weren't important in Laithieu. People seemed to live harmoniously with the French, Captain To's soldiers, and the Viet Minh. The opium smokers cherished their opium pipes. The gamblers paid attention to *De*. The hedonists led their riotous life in the brothels. Captain To and Chu Luc made much money. Those people selling *De* tickets got a 15 percent commission. They got rich quickly. Poor urban people were mistreated and despised by the French, the Chinese, the Hindus, the collaborators of the French, and even by the Khmer soldiers and their children.

I saw a French soldier beating a skinny Vietnamese soldier in the military post. I saw Captain To and the local notables cowering before the French while they showed themselves arrogant toward their people. Even Chief of State Bao Dai had no real power.

Vietnam was independent. It had its own government. Its national day, Hung Quoc Khanh Niem, was the day King Gia Long reunified the country after defeating the Tay Son. But how many Vietnamese knew that day? On the contrary, July 14, Bastille Day, was solemnly celebrated with parades, the sounds of trumpets and drumbeats, and a forest of French flags. The government headed by Chief of State Bao Dai was a puppet one. The real power was in the hands of the French high commissioner like the governor general.

I was unhappy to see a Vietnamese flag the size of two sheets of paper while the tricolor was as long as a mat. I felt that our Vietnamese honor was seriously hurt. On October 5, 1950, I said to my friends, "I am going to go to the jungle to fight the French. Who wants to join me?" My friends looked at me and laughed. I couldn't understand their laughter. What did it mean? They laughed at me. They gave me a speechless message. They wanted to tell me, "You go by yourself." However, two of them responded to my appeal. They were Sam and Pierre.

Sam was an orphan. One of his aunts took care of him and his brother. He was mistreated by her and her children. They considered him and his brother a burden. His aunt's husband was a teacher. He joined the Viet Minh in 1947, leaving his wife in the city to take care of five children and two nephews, who were an extra burden for her family. That was the reason why Sam wanted to join me for he was displeased with his aunt and her children.

Pierre was from a Catholic family in Nhi Binh. His father was dead. His mother had orchards of mangosteen and durian and sugar cane plantations in Nhi Binh. She had a nice house and a lime kiln in Phu Long. Pierre was always well dressed. Students wearing wooden clogs were beaten and scolded by the teachers, but he wasn't, although he wore shoes. That proved his family was rich and powerful.

I didn't know why Pierre decided to join me with enthusiasm. During our stay in Binh Chuan, he let me know that his father had been killed by the French as soon as the war began.

Sam and Pierre joined me for two different reasons. One was displeased with his aunt. The other nurtured revenge.

I told them to meet me at the gate of the school at noon. We left Laithieu, crossing many pottery kilns to get to Binh Nham, avoiding Road 13 for fear of seeing our friends. We walked in the mangosteen orchards. Crossing Binh Nham, Hung Dinh, An Thanh (Bung), and Thuan Giao, we arrived in Binh Chuan as the herdsmen and their water buffaloes were coming home.

I was very happy to see my grandmother and the old house where I had lived in my childhood. Everything was mostly unchanged. My grandmother was a little older. The bamboo hedge remained green. My grandmother's life was almost the same. She looked carefree in spite of many ups and downs in the course of her life, in the village, and in the whole country. Old Bay Anh was happy to see me again. He asked me, "You just came home, didn't you? How are your parents? Who are these two boys?" I answered his questions respectfully and introduced him to my friends, Sam and Pierre.

My grandmother was happy to see me. But she wondered why I came to Binh Chuan to see her on a schoolday and why Sam and Pierre had followed me. She didn't ask me in front of them. As for me, I wasn't in a hurry to let her know our plans. My grandmother prepared a good dinner for us. It was dark when we finished eating. My grandmother lit the lamp and prepared the divan for the three of us. Then she brought me to the ancestral altar and asked me to say hello to my ancestors. I crossed my hands and saluted them with respect. As soon as I finished the rite, my grand mother asked me, "Grand-son, today is a schoolday. Why have you come here? Were you whipped by your parents?"

"No, Grandma," I replied.

"Why did you quit school? I guess your parents will suffer a lot since they don't know where you are now," my grandmother said.

"I won't go to school any more. I am going to the jungle."

My grandmother's face got pale. She tried to remind me of something, saying, "You are too young, grandson! You have to go home and go to school. I'll escort you home so that your parents won't give you any troubles. Rely on me. Don't be scared."

I kept silent. Sam and Pierre looked at me anxiously. Both of them didn't want to go back to Laithieu. They were afraid that they would lose face or be arrested by the local government.

"I would like to see Uncle Muoi Sang," I said.

"It's too dark tonight. What do you want to see him for?" my grandmother asked.

"The three of us decided to leave the city. None of us wants to go back there. I need a torch to get to Uncle Muoi Sang's house."

Knowing that it was difficult to prevent me from going to the jungle, my grandmother reluctantly lit a torch and gave it to me. We walked to Muoi Sang's house. Seeing me, Muoi Sang was surprised.

"When did you get here?" he asked me, smiling.

"This evening," I replied.

"Who are these two boys?"

"They are my friends from Laithieu. This is Sam and this is Pierre."

"What are you coming to see me at night for, dear nephew?" he asked.

"The three of us want you to take us to the jungle in Khanh Van," I said.

I told him the purpose of our visit to his house in the dark night. He listened to me attentively. "Khanh Van is in danger now. It is impossible for the resistance to accept children. Go back to Laithieu and continue your studies. You are young. You must study. It is too late to regret that you are illiterate when you are in your adulthood," he said.

We said good-bye to Muoi Sang. He gave us a new torch to walk to my grandmother's house. The three of us walked heavily on the sandy path. We felt discouraged and uncertain after our homecoming.

My grandmother sat on a chair waiting for us. She looked very sad. She wanted to know what Muoi Sang told us. "What did he say?" she asked me.

"He gave me the same advice as you did," I replied.

My grandmother seemed to hear this as good news. She was visibly happy. She smiled and comforted us, saying, "Go to sleep and get up early tomorrow morning. I'll escort you to Laithieu."

There were different rumors about us in school during our absence. Some students really knew where we went. The others made up stories with some imaginary details, scaring and confusing my parents, Pierre's mother, and Sam's aunt. Some people said that they saw us crossing the pottery kilns. Some said firmly that they saw the Viet Minh arresting us by the Chinese restaurant. Some of our friends said that we had joined the Viet Minh.

My parents were in a panic. Pierre's mother and Sam's aunt contacted my mother. Sam's aunt blamed me. Of course, she never told the reason why her nephew sought to leave her family. Pierre's mother was sweeter.

In Laithieu, my parents were detained by Mr. Kiem once. They stayed in the investigation bureau all day long. Mr. Kiem assumed that my mother had connections with the Viet Minh, that she had gotten their permission to exchange goods in Binh Chuan and Tan Khanh. He didn't torture my parents for my father was his colleague, a functionary like him. Besides, he didn't have any evidence to accuse my mother of connections with the Viet Minh. My brothers and I were so scared that we didn't dare to go home. One of our neighbors sheltered us until my parents were released.

Pierre's family was rich. His religion was helpful to his family. They didn't have any troubles from the local government.

Sam's aunt was very fearful. Her husband was a Viet Minh cadre. Until 1954, he stayed in South Vietnam and taught in a village school in Bien Hoa province. His family moved out of Laithieu.

All three families had their own worries. In such an insoluble crisis, people blamed each other and attributed mistakes to others.

Sam's aunt blamed my parents for not watching me. My mother blamed my father for being too severe. My father didn't say a word. That didn't mean he accepted that my mother was right. He noticed that, lately, I was fond of reading, talking about the news, and studying the map. My passions had their transcendent characteristics. However, he hadn't known that I had decided to go to the jungle. Only Khoa, my uncle's son, did but he said nothing. If I was discontented with my father's severity, I would have run away by myself without letting Sam and Pierre come along.

Looking for us vainly, my mother had suggested to the other two women that they see a medium. The three women agreed to see the medium. They walked to her house. There, they lit incense sticks. Closing their eyes, they prayed in low voices. The medium gaped and gaped. Then she remained motionless. Her eyes were closed. A minute later, with a shrill voice, she said, "Hello, girls. I am the spirit of Uncle Hai. What do you want to ask me, girls?"

The three women crossed their hands and said, "Amitabha! Amitabha!" (prayer to Amitabha or Amida in Japanese).

My mother began, "Uncle Hai's spirit, please show me where my son, Lan, ten years of age, and his two friends are. They left this afternoon."

Pierre's mother raised her voice, "Yes, Uncle Hai, my son is Pierre, twelve years of age."

Sam's aunt added, "My nephew is Sam, thirteen."

The medium laughed loudly. She said, "I see where they are! Two of them have short haircuts. The third one has long hair. Is that right?"

It was true. Pierre and I had short haircuts while Sam's hair was unkempt.

The three women replied together, "Yes, Uncle Hai. It's right! It's right! How are they, Uncle Hai?"

"They are eating dinner. They all are sad," the medium said.

The three women burst into tears. They said, "Oh, my God. They were arrested. They look sad because they are homesick."

"What are you seeing, Uncle Hai?" my mother asked.

"I see many people with guns standing by them. They look mean," the medium said.

"When will they be back?" my mother asked with impatience.

"In the late autumn," the medium said.

"It's a long time," my mother said.

"Good-bye, girls! I am leaving," the medium said, giving a signal that showed that the spirit rode a horse.

The medium then looked normal. She looked at the three women and smiled. "What did Uncle Hai say?" she asked.

My mother summarized the story. The medium laughed happily and said firmly, "If Uncle Hai said so, your children should come home this autumn!"

My mother took some money from her pocket and gave it to the medium. So did Pierre's mother and Sam's aunt. They all were in a hurry to go home.

The streets were deserted. All the stores were closed. They heard some shots in the distance. Laithieu became a ghost town where reigned darkness, silence, and horror.

A bus stopped at the Laithieu post office at 7:30 A. M. My grandmother, Sam, Pierre, and I got off the bus. Seeing us, the students shouted, "They've come back! They've come back!"

Curious students stood by the iron fence to look at us. The three of us waved to them to thank them for their concern. We walked to my house. My father came home from school. A few minutes later, Pierre's mother and Sam's aunt came. Everybody was happy to see us back in Laithieu. Our homecoming demolished all the previous rumors. At break time, some of my friends ran to my house to see me. Pierre and Sam went home with their relatives.

In the afternoon, a military jeep stopped in front of my house. A Vietnamese came in and talked to my mother. Then he took me to the jeep. I saw a Vietnamese driver and a French officer there. I sat in the back seat beside the Vietnamese escorting me from my house in the military Jeep. They brought me to the Deuxième Bureau office in Phu Long, on the other bank of the Laithieu River.

The Deuxième Bureau office was a large brick house belonging to a rich Chinese businessman. Its walls were dark red. The foundation was high. The floor was covered with red tiles. But the house had lost its tender beauty and become a man's slaughterhouse, where blood was spilled everywhere, on the walls and on the floor, and the moaning resounded endlessly during the torture. Some people fainted. Others found their deaths there. The house had a deadly atmosphere.

There were two categories of human beings there: the torturers and the tortured. The torturers glared at the tortured as if they would like to take their lives in the most atrocious ways. The tortured victims were the prey of the torturers. They were tortured with drumsticks, whips, punches, and kicks. They were hung by their hands horizontally, like a plane, or vertically, above the floor. They were filled with water, electrically shocked, or put in a barrel full of water. I shivered with fear in the waiting room every time I heard the screams and moaning from the tortured and the furious shouts of the torturers. Most torturers were Vietnamese. They were under the supervision of three Frenchmen. Their eyes were blazing with fury and hatred. They looked indifferent to the sufferings and fear of a child like me.

"What about this child?" the first torturer asked.

"He planned to join the Viet Minh," the second torturer replied.

"Come here!" the first torturer ordered frigidly.

I came into the torture chamber. The first torturer ordered me to sit on a stool.

"Small louse! You wish to be Viet Minh, do you?" he asked me, raising his chin.

I kept silent.

"What's your name?" he asked.

"My name is Lan."

"What did you go the the Viet Minh zone for?"

"That is my grandmother's native village. That isn't the Viet Minh–controlled zone," I replied.

"You say you didn't join the Viet Minh. Why did the two little bastards go along with you?"

"I went to Binh Chuan to see my grandmother. My friends followed me just to know my maternal village. That's it. Do you think the Viet Minh accept children? All the Binh Chuan villagers are Viet Minh, are they? Do you think that all those who go to Binh Chuan are Viet Minh?" I asked the investigator.

He got very angry. He punched the table and shouted, "What a fine talker!"

He rushed at me to slap me but his co-worker prevented him from doing so. This man looked more elegant, intelligent, and important than the other torturers. "He is a child. He can't be a Viet Minh. Let him go," he said.

He saved me from an earthly hell. I was thankful to him. His words saved me from cruel torture. Nine years later, I saw him at my friend's house on Tu Duc Street in Saigon. My friend told me that he worked for the customs office.

I remembered him but he didn't know me. I tried to forget that fearful moment. I wondered why such a sweet man became a torturer. My friend said that he suffered a lot as a result of working for the Deuxième Bureau, that the torture chamber had enriched his spiritual life. He prayed and practiced fasting for the rest of his life to ransom his professional cruelty in the torture chamber. My friend is now practicing medicine in France. Since he moved, I haven't known anything about the generous man. Is he alive? Is he still in Saigon?

Sam, Pierre, and I were back in school. As usual, Pierre was well dressed. He always won the award of cleanliness. Sam was always upset. Shortly after our homecoming, he left Laithieu again. Over the past forty years I haven't had any news from him. Maybe he is dead. In the late 1960s, Pierre lived in poverty. His mother had died. His younger brother died in the Third Tactical Region. After 1975, I met him by chance in Phu Long. We talked about October 5, 1950, to revive our childhood memories. Our conversation got dull when I learned that he had moved to the new economic area in Song Be province to live a miserable life. It rained in my heart.

I returned to my student's life. Everything seemed to be normal. In the summer of 1953 I went back to Binh Chuan to see my grandmother. Once again, I had the opportunity to attend the War Invalid Ceremony in the woods of Tuy An. For the first time I saw a picture of Truong Chinh, general secretary of the Labor Party (Communist Party). I didn't see any pictures of Ho Chi Minh. I asked myself whether this stranger had replaced Ho Chi Minh.

Two of my brothers continued their studies in Saigon. They were students at Lycée Petrus Ky. In 1948, the other two left Laithieu for Saigon to study at Lycée Petrus Ky, too. I was the oldest son at home; my younger brother was one month old.

From Saigon, two of my brothers secretly left Lycée Petrus Ky for Tuy An, responding to Ung Van Khiem's appeal. My father didn't know anything. But the Laithieu Deuxième Bureau did. A few months later, my oldest brother went back to the city. The other was sent to the western part of Nam Bo. In 1954, he went north. Twenty-one years later, he returned to the South. What a big change! When he left Saigon, he was a handsome student. When he returned to the old city and to his native village he was a skinny, fearful, and dissatisfied man. Some of his relatives had left the world. Our father and grandmother died without seeing him. Our brother had died in the Fourth Tactical Region three years before the fall of South Vietnam. Two of our brothers were in labor camps. Our oldest brother lost his job in a French firm in Saigon. I had lost my job and was under investigation by the police in charge of political security.

My oldest brother read many volumes of Chinese stories. He wanted to behave as heroes or gentlemen do, ready to accept disadvantages without bending their backs. He was rational and stubborn. He liked to argue. Rich in common sense, he felt that our society had many anomalies that needed changing. An idealist, he believed in a certain perfection. Like other people, he was confused about life, politics, and ethics. Reality taught him bitter lessons. In the jungle, my oldest brother was proud of his patriotism. He renounced education and his smooth life in the city to accept hardship and danger for the sake of the country's independence. That wasn't only his state of mind but also that of other students joining the resistance. They were disappointed when the Viet Minh denounced petit bourgeois intellectuals. They witnessed stormy debates and mutual liquidation between the Communists and members of Tan Dan Chu (New Democracy). The non–Communists and the pure patriots were disappointed with the Communist dictatorship and its atrocities. My oldest brother jumped from one surprise to another. Many "whys" appeared in his mind. His logic was seriously hurt. He had left the city for the jungle. Facing brutal reality, he sought to leave the jungle for the city. I don't know if his conscience was hurt by the controversial concept that the French colonialists, his enemies, were more generous than the Viet Minh, his companions.

Due to the severe weather and for lack of food and medicine, he was sick during his stay in the jungle. After he recovered, he got a good job at a French bank in Saigon. Three years later, he got married and had his first baby girl, as I told about earlier. (Her birth saved me from my father's punishment for going to Saigon to watch soccer without wearing a shirt.)

My oldest brother had some prejudice against our father. He thought that our father was conservative, fogyish, apolitical, and nonrevolutionary. He was scolded by our father although the latter loved him, his wife, and his children. Our father had to solve all the problems caused by his oldest son. Both my father and my oldest brother were good fathers and good brothers in our family and good people in society. My oldest brother used to react against our father. He was idealistic and utopian while our father was realistic and practical. Our father kept everything in balance. He avoided any excess. He knew how to measure his possibilities and impossibilities. He was helpful but he didn't let anybody abuse his goodness while my oldest brother made himself a welfare office. My oldest brother was more wordy and universal than my father. He believed in the good cause of the Viet Minh while my father remained cautious and skeptical. My father was a victim of both the French and the Viet Minh. If he had been arrested by the Viet Minh he would have been killed by them. He was arrested by the French. Instead of being shot as shown in his file (à fusiller), he was freed and employed by them after he asked them some questions that woke up their conscience.

My father suffered over having a son in the jungle. He got very angry with my oldest brother and his indiscipline. He wasn't scared of Mr. Kiem or

Captain To, but he missed his son, who should have become headsman. The son left his family forever without knowing that he gave his father persistent sufferings and disappointments. In the jungle, a bad rumor was spread to separate the son from his father and family. The son blamed his father and forgot his family in order to be a Communist.

My father had sorrowful feelings. Even my mother didn't understand his thoughts and hopes. I was too young to know them. The four-page newspaper couldn't soothe his sufferings. He restricted his relations with friends to have a retired life in a populous city.

I made some progress in school. But it wasn't enough to please my father. I began to help him correct his students' homework on weekends. I learned how to use an abacus to do addition, subtraction, multiplication, and division to grade the students. I did this work until my father died.

I usually went to Thudaumot and Saigon. My pockets were full of money. I collected money for my mother, selling tobacco to some outlets in Thudaumot. I was in charge of buying necessities from the cooperative there and bringing money to my brothers in Saigon every month. I wore a cork helmet in order to have enough room for my money, which was wrapped in a piece of newspaper. Neither the Viet Minh nor the French noticed a child like me. So none of them bothered me. The Viet Minh used to stop coaches at Son Cay (Trinh Hoai Duc High School) and at the limit between Binh Nham and Dong Tu hamlet, Tan Thoi.

I had much money in my helmet but I couldn't touch it. I ate breakfast at home and was given one piastre per day. A bowl of *hu tieu* (Chinese noodles) cost 1.5 piastres, a packet of *xoi* (steamed sticky rice, coconut, peanuts, sugar with a little salt) cost 0.5 piastre, a usual bicycle cost 800 piastres. A Mercier, the most expensive bicycle, cost 3,000 piastres. A dollar was worth 48 piastres. A brick house in Saigon was worth 12,000 piastres. The house price went up after 1954, when the North Vietnamese refugees went down south. The piastre was devalued many times during the war.

One day, my father punished me and cut my daily allowance. I sought to make money to surmount this financial crisis. I had needs. I seized this opportunity to make much money to buy whatever I liked. I knew what I was going to do to make money. The big problem was to schedule my time so that I could go to school and make money at the same time. A launderer offered me a part-time job selling *De* tickets. He had two jobs to do to make his living. His education was limited. He wrote slowly and had difficulty with some basic problems of math. His main profession was laundering. Selling *De* tickets was a secondary job that brought him much money. Every day he brought 1,500 piastres to Chu Luc and received 225 piastres in commission. This amount was considerable in comparison with the cost of living. He dealt with Chu Luc. I worked part time for him from 6:00 P.M. until 9:00 P.M. My duty was to sell tickets, to count money, and to let him know how much his commission was.

He paid me fifteen piastres per day. It was a big amount for me. It helped Khoa and me have a prosperous life. We wore wooden clogs at home. We could eat or buy whatever we liked.

After a long financial blockade my father hadn't heard any complaints from me. He began to watch me. His suspicion increased as he saw my happy way of life without his assistance. Was I stealing his money? He wondered for I knew the code of the safe and its key as well. But nothing in the house was stolen. He was completely surprised. He wanted to know how I made money. Finally, he found out that I sold *De* tickets! His blockade had been unsuccessful and had bad consequences.

I knew the forty *De* relations between numbers and dream interpretations by heart (number 1: white fish, number 2: oyster, number 3: goose, number 4: peacock, etc.). *De* players interpreted dreams in their own ways. For example, when they saw in a dream a nude lady, they chose number 2 (oyster). They chose number 31 (shrimp) when they saw the male genital organ, number 17 (heron) when they saw an opium smoker, number 21 (swallow) or number 33 (spider) when they saw a whore, etc.

My father persuaded me to stop selling *De* tickets. I listened to him and sacrificed fifteen piastres a day to receive one piastre given by him. What a noble sacrifice!

In the winter of 1951, some Tuy An villagers living in Saigon were arrested and imprisoned in the Catinat jail (Tu Do and Dong Khoi streets). My oldest brother and his wife were among them.

A young man originally from Tuy An village was arrested by the police for collecting money for "our brothers" (Viet Minh). Tortured by the police, he named all the Tuy An villagers he knew. The policeman in charge of investigation was originally from Tuy An. He took advantage of this occasion to extort his countrymen. He arrested my brother and his pregnant wife and tortured them badly although he was our cousin. He had to be frigid and cruel to be trusted by his superior. All the torture chambers were awful, but that of the Catinat Police Department was the most awful in the South. My sister-in-law was pregnant. She was so badly beaten that their first baby girl has had a leg crippled since her birth. My oldest brother took Western and oriental medicine for many years. His wife and he received whips and drumsticks as Christmas gifts in jail. Many Tuy An villagers in Saigon claimed to be sick to be hospitalized in order to avoid extortion and arrest by the police.

The price of freedom of my oldest brother and his wife was 150,000 piastres, equivalent to sixty taels of gold (1 tael equals 37.5 grams; 1 ounce equals 28.35 grams).

Time flew by. I graduated from elementary school and was going to leave Laithieu for Saigon. My parents lived with my younger brother.

My father looked older and weaker. He had sleeplessness and smoked too much. He woke up very early. He smoked. Tears flooded from his eyes when he remembered a bad dream. He wept. He feared. His presentiments informed him of his sudden "return" while my younger brother and I were still so young. He worried about us without saying it to anybody. He had been seriously sick two years before he passed away.

4

Saigon in Wartime

The summer holidays went by.

I had to go up to Saigon. Everything was well prepared a few days before my departure. Once again, I was going to leave my family. All the childhood games weren't important to me anymore. I left Laithieu without regretting them. I felt that I would miss my parents and my younger brother.

On Saturdays, my father used to stand at the gate, waiting for my brothers. I knew that he had made moral and physical sacrifices for us. Only our successes would please him. He accepted a life of solitude because of our future. Nothing deserved his time and energy more than his children. Sometimes he grumbled with disappointment, "Why do they stay there so long?" I knew my father missed my brothers. The more he showed himself difficult, the more he loved his children and thought about their future.

Saigon is the largest, most populous, and splendid city in South Vietnam. In the mid–nineteenth century, the French occupied Bien Hoa, Gia Dinh, and Dinh Tuong provinces. They embellished Saigon with palaces, churches, villas, new streets, and office buildings reflecting architectural works in Paris. Almost all the streets in Saigon bore French names that were mostly the names of admirals and officers participating in the conquest of Nam Ky (Cochinchina), such as Bonard, De Lagrandiere, and Charner, or of French politicians advocating colonialism, such as Chasseloup Laubat. We had some geographic names, such as La Marne, De La Somme, Belgique, and Verdun, which evoked the bloody battles of World War I.

Chasseloup Laubat (Hong Thap Tu; Xo Viet Nghe Tinh), Gallieni, and MacMahon streets were the longest in the city.

Chasseloup Laubat Street wound from Thi Nghe to Cholon. From the seven-street intersection to Cholon it was named Armand Rousseau Street (Hung Vuong). Nancy Street was named Khai Dinh (Emperor Bao Dai's father), then renamed Cong Hoa. Hui Bon Hoa Street (a Chinese millionaire in the early twentieth century in Nam Ky) was named Ly Thai To. Gallieni Street, linking Saigon and Cholon, became Tran Hung Dao after 1954. Mac-

66

Mahon Street (Cong Ly; Nam Ky Khoi Nghia) linked Tan Son Nhut Airport to Saigon.

Streets in Saigon were well asphalted. They were larger and more comfortable than provincial roads and streets. Saigon had more cars than any other city in the country. Many foreign cargo ships came to the fluvial port, carrying goods in and out. On the quays there were many boats and sampans carrying agricultural produce from the Mekong Delta to the metropolitan city.

Many streets in Saigon had shady trees that gave the city more beauty and charm. Taberd (Nguyen Du), Filipini (Nguyen Trung Truc), De Lagrandiere (Gia Long), and Dr. Angiers (Nguyen Binh Khiem) streets were edged with tamarind trees. Hui Bon Hoa Street was bordered with silk trees. The Saigon Zoological and Botanical Garden and the Vuon Ong Thuong or Vuon Bo Ro (Jardin des Beaux Jeux) attracted many visitors. The museum inside the zoo kept many vestiges of Cham and Khmer cultures. The *cercle hippique* inside Vuon Ong Thuong attracted the French, who loved horse riding.

The largest street in Saigon was Norodom Boulevard (Thong Nhat). It ran perpendicular to Norodom Palace, renamed Dinh Doc Lap under President Ngo Dinh Diem. About 200 feet from Norodom Palace was the palace of the governor of Cochinchina (Gia Long Palace).

Norodom was the Cambodian king who, listening to Monsignor Miche, appealed to France to establish its protectorate in Cambodia in the nineteenth century. In his opinion, France was better than Siam (Thailand) and Vietnam. His wisdom and Francophile policy were appreciated by Paris.

Some streets bore Vietnamese names such as Tong Doc Phuong Street and Do Huu Vi Street. Tong Doc Phuong (*tong doc* means chief of the province) was one of the early collaborators with France in the nineteenth century. He was trusted by the French on account of his faithfulness to France when revolts plunged Nam Ky into blood and fire. His son, Do Huu Vi, was the first Vietnamese pilot. His dream was to have his coffin covered with the French flag after his death. He was satisfied. A street and a school of technology in Saigon bore his name.

Ton Tho Tuong, a discontented scholar, also collaborated with the French. His initiative was to create a new class of administrators, the Doc Phu Su, to help the French maintain peace and order in their colony. He adored French *mission civilisatrice* and showed himself fearful before French weapons. He wrote, "It isn't easy to touch the mouths of the tiger and dragon. The children are advised not to play such a stupid game."

He used his defeatist thoughts to advise revolutionaries Truong Cong Dinh, Nguyen Trung Truc, and Nguyen Huu Huan (Thu Khoa Huan) not to touch the French, whose strength was compared to that of the tiger and of the dragon. A street and an elementary school in Saigon bore his name.

Some Francophile Catholics, such as Petrus Truong Vinh Ky, and Paulus

Huynh Tinh Cua, believed in the French *mission civilisatrice* in Vietnam and had their names on small streets. The biggest high school in Saigon was Lycée Petrus Ky. A statue was erected in a garden on Norodom Boulevard in memory of this scholar. Petrus Truong Vinh Ky was a linguist. He knew twelve languages. Paulus Huynh Tinh Cua and Petrus Truong Vinh Ky made precious contributions to journalism, lexicography, and the *quoc ngu* (romanized Vietnamese) literature in Viet Nam. Petrus Ky gave birth to the first Vietnamese newspaper, the *Gia Dinh Bao*.

King Gia Long was a Francophile. He relied on Pigneau de Behaine, a French priest, to sign the Treaty of Versailles in the presence of his son, Prince Canh. This treaty was detrimental to Vietnam. During the reign of King Gia Long, Chaigneau, a Frenchman helping Nguyen Anh (King Gia Long) fight the Tay Son, adopted a Vietnamese name and had the privilege not to bow down before the king. Later, he was appointed consul to Vietnam by the French government. King Minh Mang was cautious with France. He refused to establish diplomatic relations with any countries except China. He was a xenophobe while his father, King Gia Long, was a xenophobe but a Francophile. The French liked King Gia Long. The biggest high school for girls in Saigon was named Gia Long High School. On the Saigon River there was a huge building with two dragons on the roof. That place was called Ben Nha Rong in memory of King Gia Long's friendship with France (*nha* is equal to *gia* in Sino-Vietnamese, meaning house; *rong* is equal to *long* in Sino-Vietnamese, meaning dragon. Nha Rong, therefore, equals Gia Long).

The busiest street in Saigon bore the name of the battleship that carried the French marines who fired on Saigon, the *Catinat*. At the end of this street was Nha Tho Duc Ba, translated from the French *Notre Dame* to evoke the famous Notre Dame de Paris.

Governor De Lagrandiere accelerated colonization and colonial administration in Nam Ky. During his government many palaces and office buildings were built. The Dinh Doc Lap was one of his works. The most comfortable hospitals in Saigon were the Hôpital Grall and the Hôpital Saint Paul. The former was directed by the French government, the latter by the French Catholic nuns. These hospitals were expensive. Only the French and rich and powerful Vietnamese could be hospitalized there. Hôpital Cho Ray was for the Vietnamese. Beside it, there were many infirmaries providing free medical care.

French, Eurasians, and Vietnamese children from rich and powerful families studied at Chasseloup Laubat, Marie Curie, Taberd, and Sainte Enfance. Ordinary children had to pass hard tests to be admitted to Lycée Petrus Ky or the Collège Gia Long. Students from Saigon, Cholon, Gia Dinh, Tay Ninh, Bien Hoa (Dong Nai), Tan An (Long An), Thudaumot (Binh Duong, Song Be), Cap St. Jacques (Vung Tau) participated in the contests. Few of them were chosen. At that time, in spite of my progress, I was far from passing the test.

The oldest private schools in Saigon after World War II were Lycées Huynh Khuong Ninh, Le Ba Cang, Nguyen Van Khue, Le Tan Thanh, Chi Lang, Tien Long, Le Loi, Leuret, and Hong Bang. Taberd and Sainte Enfance were the most expensive private schools belonging to the Catholic church.

All the expensive and comfortable villas, houses, apartments, and commercial buildings belonged to the French, Chinese, and Hindus. Cho Cu (Old Market) was a Sino-Hindu quarter. Cholon (Big Market) was a Chinese town in South Vietnam, like Singapore in Malaysia during the British rule. Cholon was the most important commercial center in Vietnam.

On the two banks of the Ben Nghe River there were many grocery stores, rice processing factories, sawmills, oriental drugstores, and warehouses, all owned by the Chinese. They hatched eggs, salted fish and eggs, dried fruit, and stocked costly dried seafood. The Chinese ran all kinds of businesses in Saigon and Cholon. They had restaurants with expensive food. They sold construction materials (thatch, tiles, sand, bricks, wood, cement, paints, lime); stocked agricultural produce; distributed "nuoc mam" (fish sauce), food, lumber, beer, root beer, lemonade, tobacco, cigarettes, and cigarette papers; and ran opium dens and casinos.

A large number of Chinese lived in Nam Bo. This was the new land with fertile rice fields and numerous rivers, canals, and arroyos favorable to navigation. In the eighteenth century, the Chinese contributed to the territorial expansion in the South. Some of them were defeated by the Manchus. Some disobeyed the Qing dynasty and fled to the South, where Lord Nguyen allowed them to settle in Nam Bo. From Bien Hoa they progressed toward Ben Nghe (Saigon) and My Tho (Dinh Tuong; Tien Giang). In the Deep South, Ha Tien was exploited and ruled by a Chinese named Mac Cuu.

Chinese born in the South were called *Minh Huong* (people of the Ming dynasty, which was toppled by the Manchus in the seventeenth century). Some of them had good reputations in the history and literature of Vietnam, like Vo Truong Toan, Trinh Hoai Duc, Phan Thanh Gian, and Tran Tien Thanh.

The Chinese had their own schools, temples, and cemeteries. They had their assemblies to deal with the colonial government. Few *Minh Huong* integrated into the Vietnamese way of life. Most *Minh Huong* kept their language, beliefs, customs, costumes, music, and lifestyle, that is, their culture. Only poor *Minh Huong* sent their children to the local schools. They had a private school in each city. The tuition was high. Rich *Minh Huong* sent their children to Chinese schools or to the Ecole Franco-Chinoise in Cho Quan to study French. Some sent their children back to Hong Kong to study English. The Chinese schools had more similarities to American schools than to French schools. The maximum grade was 100 while, in the local schools, it was 10 in elementary schools and 20 in high schools. Chinese students played basketball, which wasn't familiar to the Vietnamese students.

Under French rule many wealthy Chinese had French citizenship. Hui

Bon Hoa, the richest and most powerful businessman in Saigon in the first half of the twentieth century, owned many properties in Saigon and Cholon. His family was of *nationalite française*. Tu Du Maternity Hospital used to be called Chu Hoa Hospital.

The Chinese took control of the economy. They were junkmen, farmers, hawkers, peddlers, businessmen, restaurant owners, bankers, physicians, fortune-tellers, and geomancers. Neither the French nor the Viet Minh suspected them for they were never involved in politics. They made fortunes in wartime. The more the war was persistent, the more they got rich quickly. They sold coffins, cement, concrete, incense sticks, and bank notes to the dead and all other necessities to the living. They had casinos to serve people who loved gambling and thinking of lucky money. Those who were tortured by the police came to their drugstores to get tisanes to regularize the five viscera (heart, liver, spleen, lungs, and kidneys). Disappointed people asked them to interpret their divination sticks, their physiognomy, and their horoscope and to show them good land for the burial of their relatives. The sensualists came to their restaurants to enjoy uncommon foods, such as roast piglet skin, fresh monkey brain, and baby dogs steamed with Chinese herbal medicine. They came to the opium dens to let their minds fly in the smoke and to have their muscles relaxed by massage.

High officials of the colonial government loved their bribes. Wealthy people used to deal with them. They bought or sold diamonds and precious stones. Collectors of antiques loved Chinese pots and vases. Those who loved poetry and literature were attracted by Chinese poetry from the Tang and Sung dynasties and by Chinese stories, such as "The Three Empires" and "Journey to the West." The illustrated history of China appeared everywhere, on mobile carts of noodles, on funeral trucks, on the walls of Vietnamese houses during Tet, and in the Chinese restaurants. Chinese culture spread so quietly and profoundly that most foreigners think that Chinese and Vietnamese culture is the same. The Vietnamese folks knew the Chinese heroes better than theirs. This proved that Chinese culture took deep roots in the Vietnamese grassroots. Many of them worshipped Chinese heroes and considered their countrymen who worshipped their Vietnamese national heroes to be "heretics."

The war got more atrocious. All necessities were rare. The price of food and medicine went up regularly. Those Chinese who speculated in food and medicine got rich in a flash. Although born in Vietnam, they behaved as immigrants. They didn't feel any obligation or responsibility for the country. They weren't interested in politics but in trading and making money. They didn't waste their time, hearts, minds, blood, or money for any struggle. With their money, any winners would be their friends. They didn't join any warring factions. They were ready to give bribes to the French and to the Viet Minh to ensure their safety and to make them both addicted to corruption.

The Hindus were more numerous in Saigon than in Cholon. The Brahmans were richer than the Muslims. Most Islamic Hindus were professional guardians for the European factories and firms. They drank a lot of coffee and abstained from eating pork. When fasting, they neither ate nor drank until the sun went down. They prayed faithfully by kneeling and turning to the West (Mecca). Wealthy Hindus sold fabrics, loaned money, and exchanged foreign currencies. The southerners called their debts the "Hindu debts," or the *cinq, six, dix, douze,* due to their interest rate of 5 percent, 6 percent, 10 percent and 12 percent per month. Those debtors who couldn't pay off their debts let their wives or daughters marry the Hindu creditors. They served the Hindus as servants and concubines. These Vietnamese ladies and their children lived the Hindu lifestyle in their own country, but when their Hindu husbands got old, the men returned to India to be cremated after their deaths. The Hindu men rarely brought their Vietnamese wives and children to their country.

The Hindus had many apartments for rent in Saigon and Cholon. They had splendid temples in Saigon. The Muslims had two mosques in Saigon and Cholon.

There was one big difference between the Chinese and Hindus. They both lived in the city, and they both had properties not only in the cities but also in the rural areas. But the Chinese made their fortunes and stayed in Vietnam, although they didn't integrate into the Vietnamese culture. The Hindus, however, didn't want to stay in Vietnam. They let their children in Vietnam inherit their properties.

The Vietnamese seemed to ignore India. They tended to call Malaysia, India, and Indonesia the "austral regions."

The Hindus in the French possessions spoke French and English fluently.

The Hindu guardians didn't improve their lives. Some lived miserably with their Vietnamese wives in poor quarters. Rich Hindus came to Vietnam with gold and foreign currency. They ran businesses in Vietnam and got wealthier and wealthier. On the contrary, the Chinese who came to Vietnam in the 1920s and 1930s were poor. They left China for Vietnam to have better lives and to keep away from the civil war between the Communists and the Kuomintang. They came to this tropical country empty-handed. They built up their fortunes with patience, diligence, skills, labor, savings, credibility, and mutuality.

There were many poor residential quarters scattered throughout Saigon and its suburban areas. Houses were low and humid there. When it rained, the whole quarter flooded. Cockroaches, rats, flies, and mosquitoes had good environments for lack of electricity, water, and sewers. At times, there were fires in Ban Co, Khanh Hoi, Ben Co, Vuon Lai, Cau Muoi, or Cau Ong Lanh. Not many Saigonese had electricity and running water at home. Needy workers and civil servants lived in uncomfortable quarters. They got light at night by using kerosene lamps, which often caused fires for many roofs in the city were covered with thatch. Most Saigonese got water from the public fountains, or water was supplied by professional water carriers. Those who lived by the rivers took their baths in the river to save water. Few houses had bathrooms. Some bushy areas near Khai Dinh Square, Ban Co, and Camp aux Mares became open-air toilets. Such hygiene problems ended in 1955.

Transportation in Saigon was more available than in the provinces. There were pedicabs, buses, and taxicabs. Rickshaws disappeared after 1945. The tramway on Gallieni Boulevard linked Saigon and Cholon. Many bus lines served the city and its suburbs. They led to the center of the city at Ben Thanh Market. From there, bus passengers could go to Cay Mai, Cay Go, Binh Dong, Binh Tay, Phu Tho, Lo Da, Ba Chieu, Binh Hoa, or Go Vap.

Bicycles still played their important roles. Vélo Solex appeared before Mobylette, which was the first motorcycle in Vietnam. Motobécane, Peugeot, and Terrot were famous brands of French motorbikes. Foreign motorbikes, such as Triumph (Great Britain), Ogar and Java (Czechoslovakia), and BMW (West Germany), were rare and expensive. In the 1950s appeared Italian scooters, the Vespa and Lambretta. By the end of the 1950s, Vespa and Lambretta were welcomed by the South Vietnamese. The number of car owners was very limited. French cars such as Citroen, Renault, Peugeot, were popular. American cars were comfortable and luxurious.

Under French rule, bicycle owners had to buy small plates. At night the police stopped the riders to check plates and lights. The riders could be fined for not having plates or for riding bikes without lights at night. Many students received tickets. If they argued with the police, they were temporarily detained at the police station. The colonial police disliked the students who, in turn, disliked the police for different reasons. The students were believed by the police to break the colonial law and order. The police were considered by the students as an oppressive machinery.

Students struggled against the colonial government to free revolutionary Phan Boi Chau in 1925. The next year, they wore black ribbons to mourn the loss of revolutionary Phan Chu Trinh. In 1950, the police worried about the Saigonese students' demonstrations. A student from Lycée Petrus Ky, Tran Van On, was killed by them. His death incited the Saigonese students to take to the streets to protest police brutality. Saigon witnessed its two biggest funerals in the first half of the twentieth century: the one in honor of Phan Chu Trinh in 1926 and the one in honor of Tran Van On in 1950. The solemn funeral of Tran Van On challenged Tran Van Huu, the French, and the Saigon police.

When giving tickets to the students, policemen used to say, "You study to oppress us later!" It seemed that there was a natural struggle between the truncheons and the pens similar to the class struggle between the rich and the poor, to the educational struggle between the illiterates and the intellectuals, to the residential struggle between the rural and the urban dwellers, to the age struggle between young people and old people, and to the ideological struggle between liberals and conservatives.

Saigon had many secret police agents, ring leaders, gangs, and pickpockets. At the public fountains, there were rascals who gave themselves the right to distribute water to water carriers for money. Troublemakers were everywhere, at the bus stations, casinos, markets, and brothels. Cau Ong Lanh and Cau Muoi entered the popular literature of Nam Bo for having many hooligans and ring leaders. Bay Vien was their highest leader.

Le Van Vien, also known as Bay Vien, left the jungle to collaborate with the French, who appointed him colonel of Binh Xuyen Force. Bay Vien recruited his soldiers in Khanh Hoi, Tan Thuan, Binh Xuyen, Nha Be, Cau Muoi, Cau Chu Y, Xom Cui, Binh Dong, and Binh Tay. He directly ran businesses or sponsored the Chinese to run businesses in Saigon and Cholon. He had casinos, opium dens, brothels, fish stalls, vegetable stands, charcoal depots, and bus lines linking Saigon and Cap St. Jacques (Vung Tau). All the dockhands were his men. His soldiers checked all the trucks, cars, and boats trafficking in his controlled areas. In Long Thanh and Baria, they cut down trees to make charcoal. Pickpockets, robbers, and wrongdoers in Saigon and Cholon were under his patronage. Arrested by the police, they were released immediately to continue their activities. Binh Xuyen Force took control of the Saigon-Cholon police. Before the end of the nine-year war, Bay Vien was promoted to two-star general.

Le Van Vien was described as a liberal spendthrift. His men said that he was good at martial arts and that he wore a big black ring made from the hair of the genital organ of a female hippopotamus so he would not be drowned. In the early twentieth century, all the ringleaders had to learn martial arts and about talismans and get tattooed to show their strength and bravery. Bay Vien's Green Berets, the famous assault police, were under the command of Lai Van Sang and Lai Huu Tai, who worked for the French Deuxieme Bureau. Chief of State Bao Dai trusted General Vien. It was said that Bay Vien brought him one million piastres every month. In 1955, the Binh Xuyen Force was defeated by Prime Minister Ngo Dinh Diem, who was backed by the Americans. The force left Saigon for the mangrove areas in Long Thanh and Baria. Colonel Duong Van Minh commanded a military operation to uproot them from their last hideout. General Le Van Vien fled to France and died there in the 1960s.

Saigon had two opposite aspects: Saigon of the rich and powerful and Saigon of the poor, including the petite bourgeoisie. There were Francophile Saigonese and Francophobe Saigonese. At night the divergence between the rich and poor quarters was clear. Rich residential quarters had electricity. Darkness and humidity reigned in the poor quarters. Besides the murmurs, we heard the familiar arguments of couples who had worked all day long without having dinner.

On the right bank of the Saigon River were sumptuous buildings. The proud Majestic, the most luxurious restaurant in Saigon, looked onto Thu Thiem, which was spotted with low-roofed cottages whose bamboo frames were built over the surface of the river. Lamenting songs resounded in the distance late at night. A heart-broken singer expressed the intimate sentiments of a people losing freedom and independence. The songs were deadened by the bullet whistles on the outskirts of the city.

Saigon wasn't new to me. However, I needed to know it better. Saigon was the capital of Vietnam. It was a real city while Laithieu was only a rural town.

I couldn't maintain my games in Saigon. Living beside my brothers, I had the desire to study. I tried my best to please my father. I needed to do something good to make up for past mistakes. I did know that my father worried a lot about me. I understood his state of mind, which led me to the conclusion that severe parents loved their children and that they were eager to see their good futures. My father seemed to leave a message. He thought of me. I thought of him. I had spent many years living far away from my family. This time, too, I lived separately from my parents.

I went back to Laithieu every week. My brothers couldn't read my thoughts. They deemed that I was deeply attached to the rural games and that I missed the city, which had given me many memories. I never told anybody about my noble purpose of lightening my father's hardship. In the past, when I left Laithieu for the jungle, none of my brothers knew it. None of them knew that I was fond of reading newspapers, history books, and patriotic stories. One day, my oldest brother was informed by Sam's aunt that I had helped Sam leave the second time. My brother took me to the back porch and asked whether I had done that. Sam's aunt knew it through young Bo, the Chinese doughnut boy, who saw Sam leaving my house at dawn. I claimed not to know about it, although I said to myself that young Bo was right. One of my cousins, a female teacher, threatened to send me to the Deuxième Bureau for investigation. She believed that Bo's oral report was right. It was a good opportunity for her to get credit from the French. I was very angry at her menace and dirty job. I challenged her to inform the local Deuxième Bureau. My courageous attitude made her ashamed.

Laithieu had its attractive power. My parents lived there. My father waited for me every Saturday evening there. I had a warm dinner with my father, mother, and younger brother there every weekend. My father paid attention to our nutrition and our behavior at the table. He seized any opportunities to educate us. Being a disciplined child, I loved his education and its efficiency.

After dinner I helped my father grade his students' assignments. He used to ask me about my studies. He was happy to see my intelligence develop. He gave me some money for my good achievements. He wanted to tell me something but he hesitated. He only reminded me to be studious, honest, and trustworthy. It seemed that he knew he wouldn't live much longer to take care of us. His health declined visibly. He lost his appetite and had sleeplessness.

My father suffered over not taking care of our ancestors' graves in Tuy An for many years. His hope of returning to his native village was cloudy due to the war. His last wish was to be buried in Tuy An, but Tuy An remained the target of bombardment. He didn't know whether his wish would come true or not.

Flood damaged Bien Hoa and Phan Thiet in 1952. The outskirts of Saigon were flooded.

In North Vietnam, the French troops were more defensive than offensive. The French bombardments weren't effective because of the bad weather and the careful camouflage of the Viet Minh. In France, people were unfavorable to the erosive war in Vietnam. France faced a social, political, and financial crisis. Many governments were successively overthrown. Since 1950, France had depended on American aid. The *jaunissement* (yellowing) policy of the French government was to use the Vietnamese youngsters and American aid to continue the war to make Vietnam its colony. The French asked the Saigon government to declare general mobilization. Many youngsters who wished to stay in their villages became members of the back-up troops or politico-religious troops (Binh Xuyen, Caodaist, or Buddhist Hoa Hao). Some Saigonese entered the Binh Xuyen Force so they could continue to live in Saigon. Students deferring military service must attend the PMS (*préparation militaire supérieure*) weekly to learn basic military training. They wore white uniforms and dark blue berets with two red and yellow pieces of silk behind. The police stopped some of them and asked them for their IDs on the pretext that they didn't know what service arm they belonged to. Quarrels between students and police became an ongoing saga.

The commandos exchanged bullets with the police. The Binh Xuyen Green Berets shot at the security force commanded by Mai Huu Xuan.

The Viet Minh kept their war zones untouchable. They had activities in the cities. They were homogeneous while the Saigon government was heterogeneous and considered a puppet regime. It wasn't effective even in the regions controlled by the Catholics, Caodaists, Buddhist Hoa Hao, and Binh Xuyen. The heterogeneity of the anti–Viet Minh forces and their feudal spirit showed the weakness and failure of the *jaunissement* policy.

The Vietnam Air Force and Navy were developing. Many Vietnamese students were trained in France and Morocco to be pilots. Around Saigon there were the Thu Duc Military Academy and the Quan Tre Military Training Center.

Saigon security in 1952 and 1953 looked good. At the beginning of the war, the French had been intimidated by the sabotage of the ammunition dump in Saigon by a child, who was called later by the Communists the "live torch." A barber slit the throat of a French officer. Some French officers were assassinated while drinking coffee in a restaurant on Catinat Street. The Viet Minh neither launched attacks on Saigon nor sowed terror as they had previously. That didn't mean the French mastered the military situation by paralyzing the resistance force on the outskirts of Saigon, but they were partly successful thanks to the local back-up troops. The Viet Minh infiltrated their cadres into factories, schools, the government, and the army. They took advantage of social injustice, social evils, and the unpopularity of the Saigon government backed by France to criticize French colonialism and the puppet government and to expose a colorful painting of a classless society in which everybody would be equal, free, and happy.

In 1953, the Viet Minh attacked Laos. Many Khmer commandos in Lai-thieu were dispatched there. Many of them died there.

Chief of State Bao Dai lived his royal life in Da Lat. His favorite hobby was hunting. Sometimes he spent his vacation in Cannes, France. It was the French high commissioner who took care of political affairs in the three "associated nations": Vietnam, Cambodia and Laos. The kings of these countries had no real power. Their presence showed the world a facade of national independence and sovereignty. All the prime ministers had to be Francophiles. Prime Minister Nguyen Phan Long, a journalist, was in power only a short time for he lacked absolute loyalty to France. Prime Ministers Tran Van Huu and Nguyen Van Tam gained their reputations through, respectively, the death of Tran Van On and general mobilization. As soon as he came into power, Prime Minister Nguyen Van Tam was noted for his famous statement in French: "*Je fais la guerre.*"

Before being on the books of Doc Phu Su, Nguyen Van Tam was a teacher. During his service in Cai Lay district, My Tho province, he was as the "Gray Tiger of Cai Lay." As chief of his district, he suppressed the revolts in Cai Lay brutally and bloodily. He was minister of the interior before becoming prime minister. Prime Minister Tam had more power than any previous ones. Paris trusted him and his son, General Nguyen Van Hinh, who headed the Nationalist Army at the age of thirty-four. He was a high-ranking officer of the French Air Force. His wife was French. In 1954, he left Vietnam and served the French Air Force as a general.

In 1952, 1953, and 1954 there were fires in Saigon and Cholon. Poor residential quarters, such as Ban Co, Khanh Hoi, and Cau Kho, burned. Khanh Hoi was on fire on Tet in the year of the Snake (1953). Four thousand cottages were reduced to ash. Thousands of homeless lived in the open air.

After a fire, the municipal authority would allow the fire victims to cover the roofs of their houses with tiles or something nonflammable for fire prevention. Doi Tan Tilery produced square cement tiles. This company name appeared on the roofs of many new houses in Saigon, Cholon, and Gia Dinh. It was rumored that Le Thi Gioi, Prime Minister Nguyen Van Tam's wife, ordered her henchmen to burn down poor cottages in order to sell construction materials. Whether it was true or not, the Saigon government was always the target of bitter criticism.

The Viet Minh didn't miss any opportunities to blacken the government's reputation. They tried to give the Vietnamese people the feeling that the Viet Minh were patriotic and the non–Viet Minh were traitors. They called the intellectuals *attentistes* (partisans of a wait-and-see policy). They compared Bao Dai with Ho Chi Minh. The former was fat and fleshy. The latter was skinny and bony. They concluded that Ho Chi Minh thought about his people and country, but Bao Dai didn't. The Viet Minh propaganda was inexpensive but terribly effective. They exaggerated the mistakes committed by the French, their European and African mercenaries, the Saigon government, the politico-religious troops, and the back-up troops to justify their cause. They encouraged the defection and unsubmissiveness of Vietnamese youngsters by saying that the military training centers dyed their skin. It scared their relatives to see their children's dark brown skin after a few weeks of training.

Saigon witnessed a fast increase of population. The provincials and some people from North and Central Vietnam rushed to Saigon. It was not only a commercial city but also the capital of Vietnam. It had relative safety in wartime. The abrupt demographic augmentation led to many social problems. The rate of unemployment was high. So was the cost of living in comparison with the pre-war time cost. The franc (French currency) devaluation led to the devaluation of the piastre. Life got more and more difficult. Many Saigonese lived in poverty, which was favorable for the Viet Minh propaganda and their activities in the city. Writers, dramatists, and musicians focused on the war, on the bad aspects of life and society, on hopeless love stories due to the differences between social classes and the inequality of wealth. Saigonese spectators burst into tears and got angry about social injustice when watching the play *Doi Co Luu* (Ms. Luu's Life). A lady named Quon killed her husband to satisfy her jealousy, stirring panic in Saigon at war and giving a clear message to the polygamists.

In the 1950s, clothing changed due to the influence of American movies. Young Saigonese put on small shorts with angled pockets and loose short-sleeved shirts. They usually wore cotton shoes made by the Bata Company. These shoes needed cleaning and whitening every week. Some youngsters wore black clothes like Zorro and large sunglasses. They lifted weights to try to be as muscular as Tarzan.

Many Saigonese preferred American and French movies to *cai luong* (reformed theater), but they liked reformed music better than classical songs. Most women loved *cai luong*. They admired actors Ut Tra On, Nam Chau, and Ba Van and actresses Kim Cuc, Phung Ha, Nam Phi, and Kim Cuong. Only the elderly loved the *hat bo* (like the *noh* in Japan or *chanson de geste* in France). Ordinary people couldn't understand it. The *hat bo* was based on Chinese stories. It used a lot of Sino-Vietnamese and refined vocabulary. The *hat bo* actors and actresses had to learn basic martial arts in order to know how to use swords, spears, bows and arrows, and how to fight.

Some cinemas in Saigon, such as the Viet Long and the Thai Binh, had a music show in addition to the feature film. Thai Thanh, Thai Hang, Ngoc Ha, and Hoai Trung, Hoai Bac were famous singers in the 1950s. Songs composed by Pham Duy were popular.

Saigon Moi and *Than Chung* were the two most important dailies with many readers. Mrs. But Tra was editor of *Saigon Moi* and Nam Dinh was editor of *Than Chung*. But Tra was also president of the Vietnamese Women's Association. The sixth day of the second month of the lunar calendar was chosen as Vietnamese Women's Day in memory of the two sisters Trung. Nam Dinh's daughter, Cam Van, was a war reporter in North Vietnam. She supplied the *Than Chung* daily with sensational news from the battlefields. In addition, a French reporter, François Sully, enriched *Than Chung* with local and international news. In 1971, he died in an airplane crash with General Do Cao Tri, commander of the South Vietnamese troops in Cambodia.

Than Chung readers loved its fictions by Nam Dinh and Phu Duc. *Saigon Moi* attracted female readers, who loved romantic and sentimental fictions by Duong Ha and Mrs. Tung Long. Tran Van An, a politician, gave birth to the *Doi Moi* weekly. The *Buoi Sang* daily had satiric columns by Tieu Nguyen Tu, the pen name of a lawyer, Duong Tan Truong. *Tieng Doi* focused on sports. Readers seemed to boycott *Phuc Hung* daily because of its Francophile stand. Its editor was killed in an assassination.

Than Chung and *Saigon Moi* were sold in Hanoi. Nam Dinh got rich quickly. He was the first Saigonese to drive a Cadillac, and he owned a huge building on Charner Boulevard (Nguyen Hue Street). This building was one of the oldest American-style buildings in Saigon. The first was on Audouit Street (Cao Thang) and the second on Charner Boulevard.

Saigon newspapers stirred the anti–depraved culture movement, aiming at the novels by Nam Dinh. This movement had its political and commercial color for *Than Chung* had many readers. Nam Dinh and his daughter were powerful. They were friendly with the French and with General Nguyen Van Hinh, Prime Minister Nguyen Van Tam's son. *Than Chung* overcame its challenges in a short time. Other newspapers couldn't compete with it.

Romantic songs emerged from the thunder of the cannons and were sung at the France-Asie radio station. Romantic and melodious songs included "Du Am" (Echo), "Trang Mo Ben Suoi" (Spring in the Dim Moonlight), "Son Nu Ca" (Song of a Female Highlander), "Ghen" (Jealousy), "Cay Dan Bo Quen" (The Abandoned Guitar), "Thien Thai" (Thien Thai Cave), "Han Truong Chi" (Truong Chi's Resentment), and "Chinh Phu Ngam" (Complaint of the Warrior's Wife). We also had some military songs, such as "Quyet Tien" (Forward, March), "Luc Quan Viet Nam" (Army of Vietnam), "Chien Xa Viet Nam" (Cavalry of Vietnam), and "Khong Quan Viet Nam" (Air Force of Vietnam).

At the bus stations and bus stops, blind singers sang "Chi Ca" (Sublime Will), "Nao Doan Ta" (Dear Companions), "Cuong Quyet Ra Di" (Let's Start Out), "Doan Giai Phong Quan" (Liberation Troops), "Tieng Hat Song Lo" (Song on the Clear River), "Tam Vu" (Tam Vu), and "Tieu Doan 307" (Company 307). They sang songs while playing the mandolin. How daring they were to sing "The Nineteenth Day of May Is Uncle Ho's Birthday."

I lived in Saigon for two years.

The war went from bad to worse, but it came to an end in 1954. My father was seriously ill and hospitalized at Grall Hospital. I went there after school to take care of him. Sometimes I slept there. My father seemed asleep in bed. His complexion was pale and wrinkled. He was skinny and bony. From time to time, he opened his eyes, looked at me, and smiled as if he were satisfied with something. Then he closed his eyes. One day, he asked me, "How is your studying this year?"

"Very good, Father. This year I have many classmates who are many years older than I am," I replied.

"When you study, it's your brain working, not your body. Don't pay attention to their age and weight," my father said.

I put this idea in my mind. It gave me more moral force and self-confidence. I showed him my report card. He couldn't hide his joy and happiness when he saw that I was a good student. He encouraged me to make more progress.

Although sick, my father read newspapers in bed. The French were defeated at Dien Bien Phu. An international conference was held in Geneva.

Feeling it was impossible to resist death, my father decided to leave the hospital. He didn't say a last word the night he died. When alive, he had wished to be buried in his native village, Tuy An. We carried out his last dream to rejoin his ancestors in his native land. My father died after the Geneva Agreement went into effect. The burial of my father was smooth as peace was reestablished.

The day we came back to our paternal land was a sad one. That midautumn marked my family mourning.

Tuy An was wildly abandoned during the war. It was bushy and grassy. The roads were bumpy for nobody had repaired them. Old trenches were covered with wild grass and moss. The sharpened bamboo sticks were rotten.

I didn't recognize any familiar sites. My ancestral land had become a steppe. There were some kapok trees left in my father's plantation of kapok. I didn't see any traces of the foundation of our old house. The woods looked wilder not because of some centennial trees but because of weeds and thorny plants.

We bowed down before our father's coffin for the last time.

Tears flooded from everybody's eyes. Our father left the world forever. In a little while he lay quietly in the ground. Just as the grave was filled, it rained torrentially. Everybody ran to the bus. I walked slowly to the car, trying to find my father through the white veil of rain. *Adieu*, Father! *Adieu*!

We went back to Laithieu every week to pray for our father. His death gave my family a vacuum. Not until the fourth year after my father's death was I used to his absence. All of his books were on the desk. His pen was in its place. His white helmet was still on the wall. All of his souvenirs made me sad. I saw them without seeing their owner again. He left forever and forever. I felt that I needed his severity. I wanted him, an alive father, although he had killed my paradise fish. Such a reaction had been necessary to stop me from being stuck in various kinds of games. Human beings are like wood. All sorts of wood are useful. Precious wood needs good joiners to saw, chisel, and varnish it. Otherwise, it won't differ from firewood in the furnace.

I was young when my father died. I only lived with him a short time but his education remained vivid in my mind.

My brothers and their wives loved me. They knelt before my father's coffin and pledged to support their younger brothers in continuing their studies. Everything was determined by God. In the past, our father had supported our uncles financially, when they studied in Saigon. My brothers now took care of us in his place. Later, I supported and educated my younger brother and a son of my uncle. In the United States, my oldest son took care of his brothers and sisters in the first years of their arrival. This family mutual support became the tradition of the Pham.

I was an excellent student after my father's death. I made many efforts to satisfy my father in the Yellow Spring and to respond to the kindness of my brothers and sisters-in-law. I thought a lot about their sacrifices and tried to somehow lighten their financial burden. I skipped from the eighth grade to the ninth grade. My brothers didn't encourage me to do so. But they shut their eyes, believing that I was a capable student. I passed the BEPC (*Brevet d'Etude du Premier Cycle*) test without difficulty and enjoyed a happy summer in the country. My brothers were very happy with my first success in high school. One day, my oldest brother's wife fixed a big dinner in my honor. One of the most delicious dishes that day was curry cooked with eels, coconut milk, turmeric powder, spices, and peanuts.

"The eel is so big. You are lucky. I am sure that, in the future, your salary will be high," my oldest brother said (eel is *luon*; in Vietnamese, *luong* means salary, so *luon* [eel] and *luong* [salary] are homonyms).

"But we eat it up," another brother said. (He meant that my salary would be high but I would spend it all.)

We ate dinner, talking to one another noisily.

Peace was reestablished, but our country was partitioned. Many North Vietnamese went to the South. They were Catholics on the Red River Delta, military men, civil servants, businessmen, industrialists, and employees working for the French firms. They couldn't live under the Communist regime for political, social, and religious reasons. They were targets of the Viet Minh, who described them as "reactionary," "cruel notables," and devoted Catholics who had used "a tooth for a tooth" with the Viet Minh during the war. Some of them went south because they were told that "St. Mary goes south."

The refugees and the anti–Communist media in Saigon insisted on the Communist danger. The pro–Communists considered the Viet Minh engaged patriots. How could the patriots be dangerous? They said the Communists confiscated the wealth of the rich to distribute it to the poor. It was unnecessary for them to know who Karl Marx was, what he wrote, whom he struggled for, or how the Communist regime worked in the Soviet Union. They knew vaguely that Uncle Ho had said that the Soviets were his comrades and that they liberated mankind. So the Soviet regime was perfect. The Soviet society was an earthly paradise. The Soviets were good while the Americans were oppressors and exploiters, boasting about their technology.

At a feast in the country, I heard the guests arguing stormily about Bao Dai and Ho Chi Minh, that is, about Nationalism and Communism.

"Bao Dai is our king, a legitimate one. He studied in France and deserves to be our leader," the first guest said.

"Bao Dai sold out the country. He has taken care of his body only. I think that Old Ho is better than Bao Dai," the second guest said.

"Ho Chi Minh is a Communist," the first guest said.

"What's wrong with that? How good is capitalism?" the second guest asked.

"Ho Chi Minh is a murderer. He has killed people as if he were killing ants."

"Traitors must be killed."

"Rich people and intellectuals are traitors, are they?" the first guest asked.

"Rich people are exploiters. Intellectuals are unpopular. They wished to serve the foreigners and forget their people and country," the second guest said.

"Can the illiterates solve the national problems? What will happen after the victory? No school? No education?"

"Why not? Communist education is different from capitalist education. Communist intellectuals serve the poor and seek to eradicate the capitalists."

"How unrealistic that is. I assume that everything will be fine if everybody is educated and accomplishes their duties well. We liberate ourselves by improving our lives," the first guest said.

"Who allows you to improve your life without a struggle?" the second guest asked.

"Aren't there rich people in the Soviet Union? Isn't there exploitation of man by man?"

"Absolutely not."

"As you say, such a society is very good. So why don't the Soviets let tourists visit their country freely to learn how to make their country a paradise in which everybody is equal and happy and not worrying about riches and poverty?" the first guest asked.

"It's impossible! The capitalists would steal their national secrets. You will see, North Vietnam will be full of industrial plants. The number of doctors and engineers will increase considerably," the second guest said.

"I'm sorry for the refugees. They don't stay in the North to enjoy the fruit of the socialist revolution. I've been a farmer all of my life without having an inch of land or a pair of oxen. I hope to have these things by naming my two sons Bo [bull] and Ruong [rice field]. Both of them went to the North and were sent to East Germany," the third guest said.

"How do you know that?" the fourth guest asked.

"Our 'brothers' said so. All the militants from the South are studying abroad. Some went to the People's Republic of China, some to the Soviet Union, some to Eastern Europe. You know, the Soviets invented an A-bomb that is more destructive than the Americans'," the third guest said.

"What for? Why don't they invent something good for eating instead of the destructive A-bomb?" the fifth guest asked.

"You don't know the capitalists. They are scared only of weapons. In the Soviet Union they have a panacea capable of rejuvenating the elderly. None of the capitalist countries prepare such medicine," the third guest said.

"How is it good for our country?" the sixth guest asked

"Why not? The Soviets are Old Ho's comrades. They give him what they have," the third man said.

"How good they are!" an old man recognized sublime friendship between Old Ho and the Soviets.

"Uncle! What are young Bo and Ruong studying in East Germany?" a young man asked.

"Our 'brothers' said they are studying medicine or engineering. I don't know exactly," Bo's father (the third guest) said proudly and happily.

"Young Bo and Ruong didn't even know *quoc ngu* (Vietnamese). How can they study medicine in German? I guess they study how to vaccinate cows and pigs. They aren't responsible for their deaths. On the contrary then, they'll have meat," the young man said sarcastically.

"If Bo and Ruong stayed here, they wouldn't have a pair of oxen to keep.

North Vietnam is going to be splendid. South Vietnam waits until the country's reunification to see the 'red sunrise,'" Bo's father said with all of his faith.

"Give me a break, Sir! Don't be happy with something we don't see. Each of us was born with a fate. Look! The water jar and flower pot are made from clay. The former is exposed to the sun and rain. The latter is on the altar. Your wife and you salute it every day. Is it determined? Young Bo has his fateful name, which foretold that he should be a peasant. Happy are those who accept their fate with resignation. Competition and struggle are the roots of hatred, suffering, dissatisfaction, and disunion. The success and the failure stunt our hair. If all of us are kings who will be subjects? If all of us are doctors, who will be patients?" an old man asked.

Bo's father got angry. "You are a quibbler! You use determinism and legitimacy to minimize the class struggle. The poor should remain poor forever? The oppressed should keep on being oppressed forever? Life is an endless struggle for progress, for liberation of the proletariat from poverty, oppression, and chains. Overthrow the corrupt Nationalist government. What will we lose? We'll lose poverty and chains. Winners we are, we gain everything. Losers we are, we lose nothing," he said.

The host trembled with fear. He said, "Please, don't speak politics any more. The police will give me troubles if they hear your arguments. I was imprisoned and tortured many times. I am afraid. Please don't. Please don't," he begged all the guests. "Eat, drink and talk, but not about politics."

Everybody ate slowly and silently. The four problems dividing mankind have been politics, religion, ladies, and money. The Vietnamese peasants were politically mature after the nine-year war.

I explored Saigon, Cholon, Gia Dinh, and their outskirts by bicycle. Nothing was new to me. The bicycle helped me see the city shrinking. Nha Tho Duc Ba (Saigon Cathedral) was no longer high. The Saigon River was no longer large. The massive buildings in the center of the city were no longer huge. The Saigonese weren't as bad as some plays described. They were human beings with human ordinariness. They laughed when they were happy. They wept when they were sad. They cursed when they were angry and poor. They joked when they were rich. They were ironical when they were broke. When winning, they were proud. When losing, they spoke bitter and sardonic words. These things were human beings' characteristics. They weren't the monopoly of the Saigonese.

I had many good friends in Saigon. All of my neighbors were good, helpful, and sociable. I respected their sense of mutuality.

I spent my spare time riding around Saigon. I went to the Old Market, Ba Chieu, to watch people playing chess. A professional chess player displayed his strategic chessmen and challenged people to best him. In Dakao and Tan Dinh, the gamblers had their mobile casinos on the sidewalks. When they saw the police, they rolled their game tools and ran as fast as possible.

After 1954, Kim Chung and Dai The Gioi casinos were closed. The gamblers played games for money in the streets, at home, and in their neighborhoods. Women played *Tu Sac* (small cards with four colors: white, green, red, and yellow; *tu* means four, *sac* means color). Men played spinning tops, various kinds of cards, such as *cat te* (six cards), phoneticized from the French word *carte, bai cao* (three cards), and *di dach*, phoneticized from Cantonese (*di* means two, *dach* means one).

Tu sac was an expensive form of gambling. It required a quiet and comfortable place. The gamblers were mostly women, who spent all night long playing it. The gamblers were served delicious food, coffee, cake, and tea by the home-casino owner, who had the right to receive some money after each round of the game.

The street gamblers were poor. They played cards for food. Sometimes they used dishonest tactics, sweeping the board when winning and snatching when losing.

The race course of Phu Tho was still working. There was horse racing once a week. Many people lost much money at the race course.

All the brothels were closed. The police chased the whores, who left the cities for the suburbs. Clandestine brothels mushroomed in Phu Nhuan, An Nhon, Go Vap, Tan Thuan, and Thu Duc.

Open-air coffee shops appeared in South Vietnamese cities after 1954. The local police watched the coffee servers, who considered ladies of easy virtue. Under Ngo Dinh Diem's premiership, the vice squad worked actively, searching hotels, coffee shops, and hidden brothels and arresting whores and their partners.

Banning social evils was supposed to contribute to building a healthy society. It was theoretically good but practically ineffective. It was also a question of saving face for the newly independent government. Social evils have existed everywhere always. They swell up when society reaches the excesses of wealth and poverty. Rich people enjoyed their debauched lives. Hopeless people enjoyed tragic pleasures by plunging into the four social evils: alcoholism, sexuality, gambling, and smoking opium. It wasn't easy to get rid of social evils in an economically backward country ravaged by World War II, by French and Japanese occupation, and by a nine-year war with terrible destruction and no-man's-land tactics. Willy-nilly, the government couldn't shut their eyes to their development.

Ngo Dinh Diem had replaced Prince Buu Loc as prime minister. A few months later, Prime Minister Ngo Dinh Diem and General Nguyen Van Hinh disagreed with each other. Backed by the Americans, Ngo Dinh Diem overcame Nguyen Van Hinh, who left Vietnam for France. Ngo Dinh Diem took control of the army which opened fire on the Binh Xuyen Force in Saigon in 1955. The pro–Americans and the pro–French came into conflict in South Vietnam. Some pro–French left their offices. Some lived in France. A few Doc Phu Su collaborated with Ngo Dinh Diem and held high positions, like Nguyen Ngoc Tho, Vo Van Ngo, and Nguyen Van Vang. General Nguyen Van Vy fled to France. Chief of State Bao Dai was ousted by Prime Minister Ngo Dinh Diem in the referendum of October 23, 1955. South Vietnam became a republic.

Bao Dai was the last emperor of the Nguyen dynasty. He was forced to abdicate in 1945, when Ho Chi Minh came into power in Hanoi, and he became a reluctant advisor to Ho. Ten years later, he was overthrown by Ngo Dinh Diem, who he had chosen as prime minister in France. As chief of state, Bao Dai didn't pay attention to national affairs but went hunting in Da Lat and Ban Me Thuot and enjoyed royal life in Cannes. The referendum took place while he was in France with his family.

Supported by the Americans, Ngo Dinh Diem weakened and defeated the alliance of Caodaists, pro–French Catholics, Hoa Hao, and Binh Xuyen (Cao Thien Hoa Binh). Le Quang Vinh, also known as Ba Cut, a Hoa Hao general, was guillotined in Can Tho in 1956. Caodaist leader Pham Cong Tac fled to Phnom Penh and died there. Trinh Minh The, the leader of Cao Dai Lien Minh (Alliance of the Caodaists), brought his support to Ngo Dinh Diem. This support broke the balance of power between the Nationalist army and the politico-religious troops. General Trinh Minh The died in a clash with the Binh Xuyen on the bridge of Tan Thuan in 1955. His funeral was solemnly celebrated. He was buried at the foot of Mount Ba Den in Tay Ninh where, during the war, his troops had quartered. The Cao Dai Lien Minh fought against the French and the Viet Minh as well. American Colonel Landsdale and the chairman of the CVT (*Confédération Vietnamienne du Travail*), Tran Quoc Buu, convinced them to support Prime Minister Ngo Dinh Diem. Colonel Landsdale actively helped Ngo Dinh Diem consolidate his power in his stormy first years in office.

Ngo Dinh Diem was the first president of the Republic of Vietnam (South Vietnam). The Nguyen dynasty ended after the referendum of 1955.

Ngo Dinh Diem was born in 1901 in Quang Binh, Central Vietnam, into one of the oldest Catholic families in Vietnam. His father, Ngo Dinh Kha, served the Nguyen dynasty as minister. Ngo Dinh Diem served as governor of Phan Thiet under the French protectorate and was the youngest minister at the court. Disagreeing with the French and displeased with King Bao Dai, he resigned. In 1954, Bao Dai appointed him prime minister. He was backed by the French and the Americans and was considered by them to be a fervent anti–Communist in Southeast Asia, like Magsaysay in the Philippines or Syngman Rhee in South Korea. A year later, Bao Dai was overthrown by his prime minister. Ngo Dinh Diem consolidated his power with the support of the

Catholics, North Vietnamese refugees, young officers in the army, including Colonel Le Van Ty, intellectuals, Cardinal Spellman, and the American government. His brother, Ngo Dinh Thuc, was an archbishop. His two younger brothers, Ngo Dinh Nhu and Ngo Dinh Luyen, graduated from French universities.

The Diemist regime was at its golden height in 1956, 1957, 1958, and 1959. The South Vietnamese enjoyed happy lives in peace. They sang while husking rice in the moonlight. One million North Vietnamese refugees had stable lives on the outskirts of Saigon, Long Thanh, Ba Ria, Vung Tau, Cai San, and Ban Me Thuot. Many agricultural centers mushroomed. Agriculture and fishing production increased. Schools and hospitals flourished. Vietnamese was used in high schools and law schools, but French remained important at the College of Medicine and Pharmacy. French professors taught at the colleges of Education, Arts, Medicine, Pharmacy, and Sciences.

Workers' lives were ensured. Landless farmers applauded the land reform laws of 1957. South Vietnamese youngsters did their military service ardently for "doing military service is loving our compatriots." Civil servants and police changed their behavior. Policemen were polite. They saluted before asking someone to show their ID or before giving him a ticket. It is regrettable that those good things didn't last for long. Corruption, bribery, and power abuse grew quickly. Disunion got clearer and clearer.

North and South Vietnam had two opposite political regimes under the direction of two different leaders. Both of them were patriots and extremists. They were from Central Vietnam. They loved authority. One was an administrator. One was a struggler. One believed strongly in his religion. One was absolutely faithful to Marxism and Leninism.

Ho Chi Minh was born in 1890 in a poor family of intellectuals in the revolutionary province of Nghe An. His father, Nguyen Sinh Sac, was a *Pho Bang* (holder of a master's degree). He was banished to Poulo Condore on account of his anti–French activities. Released by the French, he was prevented from returning to his native province in Central Vietnam. He lived miserably in Saigon and died in Cao Lanh (Kien Phong; Dong Thap). Ho Chi Minh's mother died in poverty. His brother and sister were involved in revolutionary activities. As for him, he quit the Quoc Hoc (school) and went to the South. He was a teacher in Phan Thiet before he went to Saigon. From this city, he went to France, working as a mess boy on a French boat.

Ngo Dinh Diem was from an officialdom family. The Ngos had converted to Catholicism when the Portuguese priests came to Central Vietnam in the sixteenth century. Although he was a fervent Catholic, he couldn't hide his Confucian spirit, which emphasized social order, hierarchy in the family and society, and the people's resignation to their fate. This Confucian spirit had to cope with Ho Chi Minh's proletarian spirit.

Religious, social, and economic situations separated them. To Ho Chi

Minh, resigning himself to fate meant waiting for a slow death. He would rather break the social order than wait for death. Ho was equipped with a non–Confucian spirit. Later, he called it the "international proletarian spirit."

Both leaders led the two partitioned territories to two extremes. Atheist North Vietnam was enlightened by Marxism-Leninism. Spiritualist South Vietnam was enlightened by Catholic personalism.

In North Vietnam, Uncle Ho's pictures were found everywhere. We saw Ho on the bank notes and on the walls. We saw his statue in the park. At the bus station, we saw him with his "grandchildren." The Communist cadres venerated him. Poets, writers, and musicians took inspiration from him.

In South Vietnam, we found the same things. Soldiers, civil servants, and students chanted praises of President Ngo every day after the national anthem: "Long live President Ngo! Long live President Ngo! All the Vietnamese people are thankful to President Ngo."

Hoping to get good grades, students tried to have "as President Ngo said" in their dissertations. All speeches usually ended with "as President Ngo said," "according to President Ngo's instructions," or "carrying out the instructions of President Ngo." We saw pictures of President Ngo everywhere in South Vietnam with different captions, such as "President Ngo" or "Ngo, the Great Patriot." The "Double Seven" (*Song That*, July 7) was celebrated in memory of the day Ngo Dinh Diem came to power as prime minister. It was compared to the "Double Ten" (revolution of 1911, the year of the Pig) in China after the fall of the Qing dynasty. President Ngo's sixtieth birthday was solemnly celebrated on January 3, 1961. The twenty-sixth day of October became the National Day in South Vietnam instead of Bastille Day (July 14), since the constitution of the Republic of Vietnam was promulgated on October 26, 1956. On the National Day, there would be a military parade with military bands. The president, wearing the national costume with a turban, addressed his compatriots on the air. He would end his speech with "May God bless you." At night, people would shoot fireworks.

Diem's opponents said that he wanted to return to the feudal regime when they saw him wearing the *khan dong* (turban) and *ao dai* (mandarin's robe). His partisans said that the *khan dong* and *ao dai* were symbols of the Vietnamese traditional culture. Some of them suggested that we celebrate October 26 instead of the traditional Tet to please the president. October 26 was called the "Tet of the Republic." Some officers and generals got familiar with the president by considering themselves his "children" or "grandchildren." Some ministers showed themselves fearful before the president. A general pleased him by kneeling and polishing his shoes when Diem got angry during his inspection in the plateau of Central Vietnam.

The Secret Service, headed by Tran Kim Tuyen, scared not only the Viet Minh families in the South but also the general population, civil servants, and intellectuals. Its agents arrested those who criticized the regime or the president personally. They imprisoned former Viet Minh cadres staying in the South and even members of the nationalist parties, such as Viet Nam Quoc Dan Dang, Dai Viet, and Duy Dan. Scholars Ho Huu Tuong and Tran Van An, advisors to General Le Van Vien, were sentenced to death. French writer Albert Camus, winner of the Nobel Prize for *La Peste*, worked for their amnesty. They weren't executed but were detained in Poulo Condore until 1963. Members of Viet Nam Quoc Dan Dang, Dai Viet, Duy Dan, Viet Nam Dan Xa Dang (Hoa Hao), Viet Nam Phuc Quoc Hoi (Cao Dai), and Mat Tran Binh Dan (Binh Xuyen) sought refuge in France, Cambodia, Laos, and Thailand. Dai Viet members resisted the Diem administration by founding Ba Long War Zone, Quang Tri. But they were defeated by the government. Ha Thuc Ky was imprisoned until 1963. A few months before the coup d'état led by Big Minh, a writer and former minister of foreign affairs, Nhat Linh Nguyen Tuong Tam killed himself. He refused to appear at court on account of his involvement in 1960's coup.

Many Viet Minh cadres in South Vietnam were detained in Phu Quoc, Poulo Condore, Phu Loi, and Hue. Their families had many troubles from the government.

In 1958, the Communists began to destroy the administrative infrastructure of the Republic of Vietnam by assassinating the village chiefs and members of the local government. Continual assassinations paralyzed some local governments in remote areas for lack of leadership.

Lawyer Tran Van Trai, a doctor of laws and art, helped the reestablishment of Tuy An village (called An Phu). He was the younger brother of my uncle's wife. He invited President Ngo Dinh Diem to visit this reborn village and to put a wreath on my grandfather's tomb.

A military post was built at the intersection of the interprovincial roads. A new office building was constructed. But the local government lacked capable commissioners. On the other hand, few villagers returned to Tuy An. They had left the village during the war and had made fortunes in the cities. The returnees had mostly been farmers in past years in the neighboring villages. The village council members were less educated than those of the former *Conseil des Notables* under French rule. They weren't assassinated by the Communists but they received many letters of menace. In 1962, once again, Tuy An village was abandoned. The Communists demolished the military post and the communal office. The village was in wilderness. The villagers who had repatriated left their land for Bung, Binh Nham, Laithieu, Di An, or Bien Hoa to avoid Communist terror and Nationalist suspicion.

An assassination attempt happened to President Ngo Dinh Diem in Ban Me Thuot. The president became more cautious and skeptical. His brother Ngo Dinh Nhu was his active and efficient advisor. He showed himself more proud and more arrogant. Many of Diem's supporters disliked him and his wife. Ngo Dinh Nhu created the Can Lao Nhan Vi Dang (Personalist Labor party) and pretended to give birth to "personalism," which was from Mounier, a French philosopher. He was a theoretician of Can Lao Nhan Vi Dang or Can Lao. Trusted members of Can Lao held important positions in the government. Officers and civil servants wishing promotion sought support from the Catholic priests. Many people converted to Catholicism for this purpose. Not a few former Viet Minh cadres were baptized to get the religious umbrella. Many different rumors were spread aimed at non–Catholics and southerners. Generally, it was rumored that only Catholics were anti–Communist, that southerners were pro–Communist, pro–French, or didn't know anything about Communism. Religious and regional discriminations found their ground. The Diem administration recruited trusted officials based on their family, religion, birthplace (Central and North Vietnam and finally South Vietnam), education, and ability.

The pro–Diemists assumed that these criteria were normal and that there was no religious and regional discrimination, that the government placed the right men in the right positions based on their education and ability.

The anti–Diemists showed that the president only trusted the members of his family and his Catholic entourage from Central and North Vietnam. In Saigon the most influential man was his younger brother, Ngo Dinh Nhu, a graduate of the famous Ecole des Chartes. The president also listened to his brother Archbishop Ngo Dinh Thuc, who was one of the first Vietnamese bishops in the 1930s. His youngest brother, Ngo Dinh Can, played an active role in Central Vietnam although his education was very limited. Advisor Can was very Vietnamese. He chewed betel, ate only Vietnamese food, and wore Vietnamese costumes. Ngo Dinh Luyen was an ambassador in Europe. Ngo Dinh Nhu's wife, Tran Thi Le Xuan, was a representative and president of Phong Trao Phu Nu Lien Doi (Women's Solidarity Movement). She behaved as first lady since president Ngo Dinh Diem was a bachelor. Her daughter, Ngo Dinh Le Thuy, was deemed to be an excellent lady of the Republican Youth. Ngo Dinh Nhu's father-in-law, Dr. Tran Van Chuong, was ambassador to the United States. Lawyer Nguyen Huu Chau, son-in-law of Tran Van Chuong, was a minister. Tran Trung Dung, son-in-law of Ngo Dinh Diem's sister, was a high-ranking official of the Ministry of Defense.

The anti–Diemists could be Communists, pro–French, royalists, civil servants, officers, or those who disliked Ngo Dinh Nhu and his wife. They criticized the family law, which was given birth by Tran Thi Le Xuan to prevent Nguyen Huu Chau from divorcing her sister. They stirred a general discontent, focusing on Ngo Dinh Nhu and his wife, on Ngo Dinh Thuc, who they accused of having the intention of "Christianizing" South Vietnam, on regionalism, and on the unpopularity of the government. Only Ambassador Ngo Dinh Luyen avoided their violent criticism. In 1960, the National Liberation Front was born. Its leaders included lawyer Nguyen Huu Tho, architect Huynh Tan Phat, and Dr. Phung Van Cung. The armed struggle began.

Hoa Hung, Tan Binh, and Hang Xanh changed their faces after 1954. Vegetable gardens along Eyaud des Vergnes Street (Truong Minh Giang Street) were replaced by new brick houses.

In the past the Saigonese knew the French, Hindus, Algerians, Tunisians, Moroccans, and Senegalese. After 1954 they knew the Polish, Hindus, and Canadians working for the International Control Commission and the Americans serving in Vietnam as advisors.

There were some opinions unfavorable to the Americans but favorable to the French in Saigon. It was said that French food was more delicious than American food, that French scent was the best, that French language was harmonious and musical, and that the French gave more generous *pourboire* (tips) than the Americans. People talked about French generosity and compassion toward their collaborators. A Saigonese barber said, "You see, before leaving North Vietnam the French brought their collaborators, partisans, and sympathizers to the South. As Duong Van Minh attacked the Binh Xuyen in Rung Sat, the French submarine saved Bay Vien [General Le Van Vien] under fire." In the memory of a certain golden past he added, "I was a barber. My brother was a cook. We owned two brick houses in Saigon. Now, alas!"

He shook his head with disgust. A chess player stopped playing to chat with him. He said, "You know, poor At and Giap worked for Cercle Sportif Saigonais of which the director was Mr. Nguyen Van Hia, a native of Tuy An village. One served the tennis players. The other was a bartender. They both had their own houses and motorcycles. Their children attended Lycée Chasseloup Laubat and Marie Curie.

"As I told you, the French are better than the Americans," the barber said, conserving his stand.

Barber shops and coffee shops were popular political clubs. All the international, national, and local news and rumors were spread from there. People talked: "Who is who?" "Where are they now?" "What are they doing?" "What happened?" every day. Every barber shop had a newspaper, an instrument of music, and a checker board. The barber and his clients would play chess, sing nostalgic classical songs, play guitar or the *don gao*, whose sound is sorrowful. Some of them sang French songs, such as "J'ai deux amours: Paris et la France" (I Have Two Loves: Paris and France). Others hissed "La Marseillaise" or "L'Internationale" without fear of the police.

French culture remained influential although we heard many anticolonialist, anti–Communist and antifeudalist slogans in the air. Officials, officers, civil servants, and students liked to use French in their conversations. Advisor Ngo Dinh Nhu wrote speeches in French. His staff translated them into Vietnamese and brought them back to Nhu, who reviewed and corrected the Vietnamese translation. Mission Culturelle Française had its important activities in South Vietnam. Lycée Chasseloup Laubat became Lycée Jean Jacques Rousseau. French schools in Saigon, Dalat, and Da Nang welcomed children from rich and powerful families. Students studied English and French in high schools. Many Vietnamese intellectuals returned to their country from France. They were university professors, physicians, lawyers, engineers, or technical experts well respected and well paid in South Vietnam. Others, with French citizenship, left their country for France.

In 1956 the French troops left South Vietnam. The Norodom Palace was returned to the Saigon government, which renamed it Dinh Doc Lap (Independence Palace). President Ngo Dinh Diem and Ngo Dinh Nhu and his family worked and lived there.

French businessmen still played important roles in the economic activities of South Vietnam. French plantations of rubber trees in Dau Tieng, Xuan Loc, and Long Thanh had their regular activities. French companies such as L'UCIA, Denis Frères, BGI, and CEE continued their businesses normally.

The Republic of Vietnam received American aid and welcomed many economic, administrative, and military advisors. In reality, not many South Vietnamese government officials knew English. Education in the Republic of Vietnam was a copy of French education. Pedagogic concepts were almost the same. The curriculum aimed at literature, poetry, and descriptive sciences more than at experimental sciences. There were few laboratories, and they lacked almost everything for experimentation. Math, physics, and chemistry textbooks were based on French ones. In *classe de première* (eleventh grade), French students studied the literature of the nineteenth century, called "the romantic century." In the same grade (*de nhi*), Vietnamese students studied Vietnamese poetry of the nineteenth century. They also studied poems by Ton Tho Tuong and Phan Van Tri. The former was Francophile while the latter was Francophobe. The teachers praised Ton Tho Tuong's talents and intelligence and shared his "case of *force majeure*" and his generosity toward his Francophobe friend, Phan Van Tri, as he had accepted bitter criticisms from the latter without asking the *ma ta* (police) to arrest him. They highlighted Pham Quynh's style in his works in *quoc ngu*. They praised his eloquence in giving lectures in French.

During French rule Vietnamese students knew the history of France better than that of their country. After 1954 the history of Vietnam was in the curriculum. The eleventh graders studied the conquest of Vietnam by the French. They didn't know a lot about the resistance of the southerners against the invaders although this chapter was in the textbook. Willy-nilly, they studied weakness, shame, and dishonor instead of self-confidence, honor, and glory.

In 1956 the general election didn't take place in accordance with the Geneva agreement. A demonstration of North Vietnamese refugees passed in front of the Majestic Hotel, demanding that the Communist general Van Tien Dung leave Saigon for Hanoi.

ĐẠI-HỌC VĂN-KHOA SAIGON

THẺ SINH-VIÊN

Đăng ký

Họ và tên .... Phạm Đình Lân

Sinh ngày .... 01 tháng 03 năm 1942

Tại .... Bình Nhâm (Thủ Dầu Một)

Sinh-viên năm Cao Học .... Lịch Sử

Sinh-viên ký,

Saigon, ngày 25 tháng 3 1966
Khoa-Trưởng

PHAN-KHẮC-TRỪU

Student ID issued by the Faculty of Letters.

The constitution of the Republic of Vietnam was promulgated in 1956. President Diem's power was politically and economically strengthened. All of the opposition parties were defeated. Washington backed him actively and efficiently. He was warmly welcomed by President Eisenhower during his visit to the United States. He had good relations with South Korea, Taiwan, the Philippines, Australia, and even India. More than fifty nations recognized his government.

Diem's partisans said that the Ngos started the independence era in our history. In the tenth century Ngo Quyen defeated the Chinese on Bach Dang River. This naval victory put an end to the ten-century domination of Vietnam by China. Ten centuries later, according to them, Ngo Dinh Diem gave birth to the Republic of Vietnam, which was characterized by its independence, anticolonialism, antifeudalism and anti–Communism. He was compared to Magsaysay of the Philippines, Sukarno of Indonesia, Syngman Rhee of South Korea.

Historians recognized that Ho Chi Minh gained the abdication of Emperor Bao Dai, read the Proclamation of Independence on September 2, 1945, and founded the first republic in Southeast Asia after World War II.

Western observers wondered whether the elections in South Vietnam were clean or not. In the elections of 1956 and 1960, elected representatives were mostly members of Can Lao (Personalist Labor), Phong Trao Cach Mang Quoc Gia (National Revolutionary Movement), and Phong Trao Phu Nu Lien Doi (Women's Solidarity Movement). Ngo Dinh Nhu and his wife, Tran Thi Le Xuan, were elected. It wasn't necessary for them to get in touch with their electors; they still got more than 100 percent of the votes! This political phenomenon has rarely been seen in any democratic countries, such as Great Britain, the United States, or France. In a province near Saigon, when stuck by a question from an elector, a candidate said proudly: "Whether you vote for me or not, I will be elected."

Many independents were denied the right to be candidates for having "relations with the Communists" or other reasons given by the police. Even Phan Khac Suu, the former minister of agriculture and future chief of state, faced many troubles, when running for Representative in Saigon (Third District). Many representatives didn't know a lot about their districts and electors. The results of the elections came from the fraudulent art of the local government more than the prestige of the candidates or the choice of the electors.

Disgusted at this form of democracy, many people weren't happy to cast their votes. Some of them didn't have any real concept of election. Unwittingly, their indifference created an electoral boycott. "Diamonds cut diamonds." The government response was to stamp the voting card after someone cast a vote. Citizens having no voting cards or nonstamped voting cards would be questioned by the police: "Why don't you have your voting card? You boycotted the election, didn't you? Why didn't you vote? What did you do that day? Where did you go that day?

"Why did you cast your vote early?" one man asked.

"To have my voting card stamped," another man replied.

The concept of building democracy by election was eclipsed by the concept of voting to have the voting cards stamped. The government couldn't deny its responsibility for not building real democracy from the birth of the Republic in South Vietnam. Deceived by the Viet Minh, the French, and the Nationalist government, people became skeptical. How could the Diem administration gain their trust without being different from the previous governments?

It was easy to predict the result of the presidential election of 1961. Incumbent President Diem and his vice-presidential running mate, Nguyen Ngoc Tho, were elected. Shortly after the election, Nguyen Dinh Quat and Caodaist general Nguyen Thanh Phuong, their opponents in the presidential election, were brought to court. Such was the treatment of the rulers toward their opponents.

The regime supporters argued that the Vietnamese people's education remained low, but they could catch up with democracy. Their opponents asked whether a free South Vietnam without real democracy would differ from North

Vietnam. Had the South Vietnamese struggled against dictatorship only to consolidate an authoritarian regime for themselves?

The first leader of independent Vietnam had many moral responsibilities. He would leave the future generations good or bad political traditions. That depended on his good or bad leadership. President George Washington was the first president of the United States. His firm decisions angered those people who compared firmness to dictatorship. After two terms in office he refused to be a presidential candidate for a third term. He gave his country a democratic tradition. None of his successors was anticonstitutional, committed electoral fraud, or eternalized his power.

Credit is required in public relations and in business. It is also required in politics. In 1957 South Vietnamese youngsters did their military service with joy because they knew that they were in the army for just three years. In 1961 the government changed the military service regulations, trying to keep the draftees in the army more than three years. The consequence of this change was that many youngsters sought to dodge the draft by changing their age, name, or residence or by damaging their bodies and worsening their health.

Hanoi thought about the reunification of Vietnam by force. Saigon refused the general election for good. Hanoi faced two possible problems: If they directly attacked South Vietnam, they would be denounced by the I.C.C for violating the Geneva Agreement. If they didn't reunify the country by force, South Vietnam would become politically, socially, and economically mature enough to get national and international support. In that case, it would be difficult for the Communists to take over South Vietnam.

The South Vietnamese grassroots got more and more mature in politics. They were aware of Communism through books, television, magazines, and newspapers. The Communist sympathizers didn't know how to explain the farmers' revolt in Quynh Luu and Nong Cong, the bloody land reform in North Vietnam, or the cruel repression of the Soviet tanks in Hungary and Poland. Not a few impartial people had some questions with an "if" in their minds: If the Communist regime was good, there would be neither refugees nor revolts. If Ho Chi Minh was good, he wouldn't applaud bloody repression in Hungary and Poland. If he truly loved his people, he wouldn't plunge them into bloodshed and tears. In the name of the Comintern, the Soviets had no right to kill the Hungarians and Polish, did they?

In 1954 more than 40,000 Viet Minh cadres and militants went to the North. Some of them, however, stayed in the South. A peace movement was born, assembling many well-known intellectuals. The movement was headed by lawyer Nguyen Huu Tho, who would become chairman of the National Liberation Front six years later. He was detained by the Diem administration in

Central Vietnam before being liberated by the Communists and becoming chairman of the National Liberation Front. Nguyen Huu Tho played an active role in the demonstration of the Saigonese students in 1950. It was the first anti–American demonstration in Vietnam under French rule. Both the French and the Bao Dai administration began to receive American aid. Washington sent thirty-five advisors to Saigon and agreed to provide military and economic aid to the Nationalist government.

The flag of the National Liberation Front had three colors: blue, red, and yellow. A yellow star was in the middle of the flag. If the blue half disappeared on the flag, it would be the flag of the Democratic Republic of Vietnam (Hanoi). In reality, the NLF was given birth and directed by Hanoi. The presence of some well-known southerners, such as lawyer Nguyen Huu Tho, architect Huynh Tan Phat, Dr. Phung Van Cung, and Professor Nguyen Van Hieu, was only a facade to show that this was a domestic movement in South Vietnam. The camouflage purpose was to prove Hanoi's innocence in the subversive war.

In 1960 Le Duan replaced Truong Chinh (Dang Xuan Khu). But his title was first secretary. It was Ho Chi Minh who was president of the Democratic Republic of Vietnam, as well as chairman and general secretary of Dang Lao Dong Viet Nam (Communist party). Until 1976 Le Duan's real title was general secretary of the Communist Party.

Le Duan, a Quang Tri native, was in Nam Bo during the nine-year war. He had many political experiences there. In Nam Bo the political parties were almost absent during French rule. But there were many secret societies and local religions (Cao Dai and Hoa Hao). Like Ho Chi Minh, Le Duan was covered with many legends. Politically he was compared to a 500-watt bulb. It was rumored that he was about to be captured by Tran Kim Tuyen's secret police in a small house near Viet Long Cinema on Cao Thang Street. Rumor had it that he was going to disguise himself to run for president in the presidential election of 1961.

Le Duan's promotion in North Vietnam was tied to the birth of the NLF, which served as a shield protecting Hanoi from being accused of violating the Geneva agreement. This was a revolt of the southerners against the Diem administration and American neocolonialism.

Many southerners in North Vietnam were dispatched to the South, fighting under the flag of the NLF. They were really Communist warriors fighting beside the local guerrillas in the familiar landscape of the former Nam Bo. They used rudimentary weapons or funny tactics, such as using bees to sting their enemies. They were underestimated by the Saigon government. Their leader, Nguyen Huu Tho, didn't have an international reputation. He was one of the three youngest lawyers in Saigon after World War II. He was an intimate friend of lawyer Truong Dinh Dzu, a presidential candidate in 1967, and lawyer Nguyen Lam Sanh, chairman of the Asian Anti–Communist Alliance.

Chung Toi Muon Song (We Want to Live), an anti–Communist film, denounced Communist cruelty and reflected the yearning for freedom of the North Vietnamese who came to the South by boat and raft on the immense sea. The anti–Communist movement was stirred by the Saigon government. Its influence wasn't important in the grassroots. Some of the people thought that denouncing the Communists was "speaking ill of the absent." Others believed that the Communists struggled for independence, that Ho Chi Minh deserved to be the leader of Vietnam, that North Vietnam was independent while South Vietnam was dependent upon the French and Americans. The anti–Communists said that North Vietnam was servile to the Soviet Union and the People's Republic of China.

Embezzlement of refugee funds, stealing donations and rice intended for the victims of flood in Central Vietnam, and the abuse of power by Diem's brothers and sister-in-law separated the government from the folks.

The Viet Minh took control of the rural areas during the war. Most landowners left the countryside. Their lands were distributed to the landless farmers. The latter didn't find anything promising in the 1957 land reform because they had to pay for the land they had occupied in the absence of the owners. The landowners weren't happy with the land reform for they lost their lands while the reimbursement wasn't as high as they expected.

There were many farmers' organizations and agricultural banks throughout South Vietnam. Farmers improved their farming techniques. They got loans from the agricultural banks at low rates of interest. In some regions farmers used tractors and pumped water with motors. Agricultural schools were born to teach new techniques of farming, breeding and forest exploitation. Rice production increased visibly. New techniques of farming, fertilizers, good systems of irrigation, and abundant insecticides were the main factors in increased agricultural prosperity. Peace was another factor. The northern part of Nam Bo and the plateau of South Central Vietnam were covered with industrial plants. Farming was partly mechanized. Many farmers had threshing floors, cement pigsties, tractors, and transportation to get their produce to market. Factories mushroomed around Saigon, Cholon, and other provinces, providing employment for specialized and nonspecialized workers.

In general, the standard of living of the farming and working classes saw big progress. During the Vietnam War (1960–1975) most demonstrators were Buddhists, Catholics, journalists, and students. There were few demonstrations from the working and farming classes. That was a big success of President Diem in South Vietnam.

The war destroyed his efforts. Poverty made North and South Vietnam more dependent upon foreign aid. Vietnamese blood was spilled every day. Vietnamese properties were damaged. The bridges collapsed. The roads were mined or dug. The farmers' association offices were demolished. The boats were mined and sank.

In November 1960 Senator John F. Kennedy was elected president of the United States. In Saigon there was an abortive coup d'état led by Colonel Nguyen Chanh Thi. Officers involved in the coup fled to Cambodia and France. Many anti–Diemists in the Caravelle Group were arrested. Ngo Dinh Diem became more cautious with his entourage. The strategic hamlet policy was theoretically effective against Communist sabotage. It was very unpopular. People had to leave their houses and land for the strategic hamlets full of dikes and barbed wire. The local governments forced the residents to dig trenches and to fence the hamlets with barbed wire. Those people who didn't do such *corvée* had to hire laborers to replace them or give bribes to the local governments. In order to attract the attention of the president and his advisor, Ngo Dinh Nhu, the local governments competed with one another, asking their residents to finish their strategic hamlets in a minimum time. The local civil servants in charge of the construction of the strategic hamlets cursed and beat up their unpaid workers, urging them to reach their goals. Discontent had a good environment for development. Viet Cong (Communists) fertilized it by labeling the strategic hamlets "big jails" for rural people and by comparing them with the Great Wall of China. Professor Nguyen Van Kiet was unhappy when he saw his house demolished during the construction of the strategic hamlets in Hau Nghia province. In 1968 he joined Lien Minh Dan Chu Hoa Binh (National Alliance for Democracy and Peace), led by lawyer Trinh Dinh Thao. He was the minister of education of Cong Hoa Mien Nam Viet Nam (Republic of South Vietnam) of which Nguyen Huu Tho was president and Huynh Tan Phat was prime minister.

The battle of Ap Bac wasn't good news on the sixty-second birthday of President Diem (January 3, 1963). The M-113 tactic (M-113 tank to crush Viet Cong) began to face some real difficulties. Washington sent more advisors to South Vietnam. On the one hand, the Saigon government wished to receive more American aid. On the other hand, it wanted to keep its sovereignty. President Ngo Dinh Diem needed American aid. But he wanted to be independent in the struggle against the Communists. He listened to his brother Nhu more than to the American advisors. The Americans doubted the efficacy of the South Vietnamese army. They believed that the fall of South Vietnam would lead to all of Southeast Asia falling under Communist control. The birth of SEATO (Southeast Asia Treaty Organization) reflected their worries about Communist expansion. Divergence between Washington and Saigon was seen. It got worse in 1963.

From 1954 until 1960 Saigon experienced quick changes. Many Saigonese owned motorcycles. A large number of Saigonese households had radio sets. People enjoyed listening to poem recitations, classical music, and reformed theater. Listeners admired Thai Thanh singing songs by Pham Duy and loved the sound of the accordion played by Thuy Nga. Pham Duy, Lam Phuong, Hoang Thi Tho, and Van Phung were the most well known composers at that time. Duy Lan, author of the play *Lap Song Gianh* (Filling the Gianh River), became crippled in a grenade explosion during the performance of his play in Saigon. Saigonese women liked to listen to Thanh Cong singing classical songs. Actress Thanh Nga began to attract spectators with her beauty, pure voice, and the art of her performance. Actress Kim Cuong had a solid position in the reformed theater. Phung Ha and Bich Thuan had good reputations in spite of their age.

In the 1960s, Thanh Thuy and Minh Hieu were noted for singing "Hoa Trang Thoi Cai Tren Ao Tim" (The White Flower Isn't Pinned on the Purple Robe Anymore) and "Doi Tim Hoa Sim" (The Purple Hill of Blueberry Blossoms). The new soldiers loved not only the charm of the singers but also the lyrics and sorrowful harmony of the songs.

The number of Saigonese women wearing *ao dai* (robes) increased. Women's role in society got more important. In 1945 there were some female *fonctionnaires* providing educational, cultural, social, and medical services. After 1954, there were many women involved in political activities. Ngo Dinh Nhu's wife, Tran Thi Le Xuan, considered herself their leader. Mrs. Nguyen Van Tho, Nguyen Phuoc Dai, Nguyen Van La, and Truong Cong Cuu were important figures during the Diem administration. Mrs. Ngo Ba Thanh disagreed with Diem's policy and was imprisoned.

Mrs. Nguyen Van Tho and Ngo Ba Thanh studied in the United States. The latter opposed the government. Her father, Dr. Pham Van Huyen, was expelled from South Vietnam because of his pro–Communist stand.

Mrs. But Tra was noted for her *Saigon Moi* daily and her social activities. Mrs. Huynh Thi Nga ran a private high school in Tan Dinh. Mrs. Duong Huynh Hoa graduated from the French medical school. In 1968 she went to the jungle and was Viet Cong minister of health.

Confucian thoughts lost their color in Saigon and other South Vietnamese cities. Many South Vietnamese women had their hair curled and wore white clothes and high-heeled shoes. Some of them had university degrees. In the 1940s, Vietnamese women rarely wore white clothes or had their hair curled.

After the atrocious war Vietnamese women made giant progress. They could do whatever men could do. We saw women riding motorcycles, driving cars, studying in college. Some studied abroad. The number of female civil servants, social assistants in the army, and employees working for banks and foreign firms was soaring. As the urban population increased, housing got more difficult. The cost of living rose. Women had to work to keep the family budget in balance. Many rural people moved to the cities to look for jobs, to enjoy democracy and freedom, although relative, and to have opportunities to get in touch with urban comforts and new thoughts.

In order to be different from the previous governments, the Diem administration advised the South Vietnamese to get dressed well when shopping or traveling. The police warned bare-backed and barefooted people wandering on the streets.

By the end of the 1950s Japanese slippers were in vogue. Wooden clogs were replaced by slippers, sandals, or leather shoes.

Let's have a look at Binh Chuan and Tuy An (An Phu) between the two Vietnam wars.

The first bicycle appeared in my maternal village. Some farmers had shirts, pants, and sandals they only used during Tet. *Ao dai* were still absent there, even in wedding ceremonies. I didn't see any farmer putting on shoes. When there was a wedding ceremony, men used to borrow or rent *khan dong* (black turbans) and *ao dai* to make the ceremony more solemn and traditional.

Binh Chuan village had an elementary school. Many children went to school. The illiteracy rate decreased.

Alas, peacetime was too short. Naïve childhood dreams disappeared, bowing down before political schemes and carnage.

Parents paid attention to the names of their children. In the past people tended to give ugly names to their children. Some thought that children with ugly names didn't die young. On the other hand, people tried not to give their children the names of their ancestors, their neighbors, or the local notables. The new concepts of how to name children after 1954 reflected a love of democracy and the optimism of a people in a newly independent country. Children born after 1954 rarely had Van or Thi as middle names (Van for males and Thi for females). Ugly names, such as Trau (water buffalo) and Chuot (rat) were replaced by the names of famous actors or actresses or by the names of flowers.

Tuy An was in resurrection after the war. Some farmers living in Bung, Thuan Giao, and Binh Nham repatriated. Those who made their fortune in the cities came back to visit their native land on weekends only. They built cottages and planted fruit trees. My oldest brother had a large orchard in which he planted grafted mango trees and grapefruit trees, which bore fruit just one year later. He went to Ha Tien to study how to plant black pepper (*tieu*). The elderly villagers advised him not to plant *tieu*. In Vietnamese, *tieu* means "waste," "spend," "dissolve," or "burn." Its meaning isn't good. Superstitious Vietnamese never plant *chuoi* (banana trees) in front of their house. In Vietnamese, *chuoi* means "upside down." Of course, my oldest brother didn't pay attention to their advice full of superstitions and negativities. He loved the proverb "Aide-toi, le Ciel t'aidera" (God helps those who help themselves). He used to act contrarily to the experiences of the populace. He worked for Denis Freres, a French firm in Saigon. His salary was high enough, but he spent some of it, trying his luck. He walked from one failure to another because of his stubbornness. He got tired swimming against the stream.

Water was a big problem in Tuy An. It was expensive to carry water from the spring in Tan Phuoc to sprinkle his orchard. His fruit wasn't selling, but he paid Muoi Thua generously every month. Muoi Thua had served our family in the 1930s. He loved us and respected my father, who considered him a member of our family. During the war my father told us about his promise to give Muoi Thua some land in Tuy An and asked us to work out his promise in case he never saw him again. My father died. My oldest brother, Jules, tried to look out for him and carried out my father's promise.

My oldest brother's miscalculation became a funny story for the villagers every time they talked about his business. They said, "Jules' orchard revenue isn't enough to feed Mr. Muoi Thua," "He is in debt to Mr. Muoi Thua," "He never listens to anybody," "He believes in himself only," "He wasn't a farmer. How can he have experiences in agriculture?" and "Nobody can carry water from Tan Phuoc to sprinkle fruit trees except for the government."

In fact, my oldest brother liked to do something impossible. My sister-in-law was so sweet that she couldn't prevent him from doing what he liked. He wasted his money without any remorse. His compassion was ridiculed by the villagers, but it was recognized by God, who gave him a happy life with pious children after intermittent challenges.

My oldest brother liked to drink beer in the country in the moonlight. He came back to Tuy An every Sunday to have a party in his shady orchard. People drank beer and ate roast goose. It was easy for him to have such a weekly party. One day, an old man advised him not to eat geese. "The geese don't eat shrimp, only grass. The male and female run in couples. They are faithful to each other. So they have something religiously different from other animals," the old man said. My oldest brother wasn't interested in this nonscientific advice.

One Sunday, he roasted some geese and invited many of his friends to enjoy eating roast goose and drinking beer. Before lunch was over, all the guests were arguing noisily and were fighting. In 1962 his orchard didn't exist anymore. People cut down the fruit trees to clear the land for the strategic hamlet construction. Shortly after the birth of the Tuy An strategic hamlet, the villagers knew their diaspora again. Tuy An became a free fire zone during the Vietnam War.

My maternal village was happier than my paternal one. The villagers continued their daily activities in spite of the war. In 1962 they had to move to the strategic hamlet that stretched along the interprovincial road linking Binh Duong (Thudaumot; Song Be) and Bien Hoa (Dong Nai). Dismantling houses was big trouble for them. Fortunately, there were no brick houses in Binh Chuan. So the damage wasn't so big. The villagers felt that they had a big loss. They felt attached to the place where they were born, grew up, and lived. Compared to their old residential hamlet the strategic hamlet was more comfortable and organized. They could go everywhere by bike, motorcycle, or bus. Every household had a well and a cement pigsty. Some villagers bought motorcycles, tractors, and sewing machines. Some carried agricultural produce and directly sold it to urban consumers. In the 1960s the lives of the villagers got more comfortable. Their geographic knowledge developed considerably. Many of them rode to Binh Duong, Saigon, Bien Hoa, Thu Duc, and Cu Chi to visit relatives and friends and to sell or buy tobacco, peanuts, and beans. Some children in the village attended Trinh Hoai Duc High School and other private schools in Binh Duong. Before the Franco-Vietnamese War, only Chin Rua, a provincial policeman, could count *un, deux, trois* in French. All the villagers had considered him the most learned man in Binh Chuan although he didn't have a third-grade certificate.

In the strategic hamlets of Binh Chuan and Phu Loi, the villagers killed dogs as they had in 1945. I didn't know who ordered them to do so. Communists or Nationalists? The Saigon government didn't have any reason to release such an order. At that time the South Vietnamese farmers weren't so poor that they couldn't raise dogs to keep at their houses. Only the Communist guerrillas were scared of dogs, which were dangerous to their nocturnal sabotages. Poor dogs! They died in a mass because of their barking during the two wars.

It was torrid in Binh Chuan and Phu Loi in the daytime. The flaming sunlight glittered like a starry noon. Since moving to the strategic hamlets, people planted trees and ornamental plants to make the landscape good looking and less arid. After 1975 the villagers decided to stay in the strategic hamlets instead of returning to their old residences about a mile from the inter-provincial road.

Time flew by. I received the French *baccalaureat* when the Republic of Vietnam was two years old. I was fond of reading. I wanted to enrich my knowledge and to refine my French. My oldest brother was happy with that. He gave me money to buy books and to order some special ones from France and Belgium, if necessary. Influenced by the aridity of my maternal and paternal villages I wasn't romantic, blaming the clouds and weeping for the winds. I loved French romantic literature and poetry, but I disliked hopeless situations with endless sorrow. I was a little dreamy, but I didn't like anything unrealistic in novels or in *cai luong*. I felt uncomfortable when I saw a man being chased by the bad guys stop to finish a long classical song and then be arrested and tortured. It was unrealistic that the clowns argued with the king or their superior. All the kings in the Far East had absolute power. They were not only the political leaders but also religious ones. How did the clowns dare to argue with the kings? It was true that King Le Long Dinh, a tyrant, allowed the clowns to burlesque what the courtiers reported to the king for fun.

When a young man, I loved the movies very much. I loved their local color. I was curious to know the customs, religions, and lifestyles of all the peoples in the world.

Author's *baccalaureat* diploma.

President Ngo Dinh Diem was a fervent Catholic. He believed in miracles but he was against superstition and interdicted ghost tales. Chinese stories by Kim Dung were absent from the newspapers. Did he prefer Western culture to Eastern culture? Was he scared there would be a mass movement against him if people read Chinese stories? In the Chinese stories there were many revolts. In the olden times writers seemed to use the images of ghosts and devils to hint at the cruel government. Our people underwent misery, injustice, and degeneration during two centuries under the Lords Trinh. Many ghost tales and authorless masterpieces appeared in the seventeenth and eighteenth centuries. People used the fairies, ghosts, and animals to express their secret aspirations.

In 1955, 1956, 1957, 1958, 1959, and 1960, Hindu films were spread in South Vietnam. The Saigonese liked French or American films while the provincials were fond of Hindu films. The former were romantic while the latter were mystic.

I had a happy summer after receiving the *baccalaureat*. I went back to Laithieu to see my mother. I walked around the city. Sometimes I walked with my friends. Sometimes I walked by myself with a pocket book I could read whenever I liked.

It is very hot in the summer in South Vietnam. I walked in the shade of the trees to get fresh air.

One day, a sudden shower forced me to run quickly to the nearest house to shelter from the rain. I was welcomed into a large house that had French-style furniture made of precious wood. In front of the house there were many ornamental plants whose legs were mossy. Nice rock work was built on a lake in miniature. Some immortals played chess on top of the mountain. Wood-cutters carried wood on the mountain's flanks. Some fishermen cast nets on the lake.

The house owner was an old man in his sixties. He looked comfortable and benevolent. He welcomed me warmly and poured tea to serve me. It was a special jasmine tea prepared by himself. While we were talking, a beautiful lady appeared. She greeted me and went to the back porch. "That's my daughter," the old man said. I didn't say a word. It seemed that my mind was wandering somewhere. I felt that I was in love at first sight and that she should be my wife. I saw her for the first time for only a few seconds. But I had the feeling that I had known her for a long time. I recognized her long hair, her oval face, her black eyes, and her charming smile. I couldn't sleep that night. I tried to remember where and when I had met her. My memory didn't give any precise answers.

We loved each other. Our wedding ceremony took place seven years later. The house owner became my father-in-law. He knew 3,000 verses of *Kim Van Kieu* by Nguyen Du by heart. He loved the Buddhist philosophy in this masterpiece about karma, determinism, fatalism, and compensation law. He kept on reciting the following verses taken from *Kim Van Kieu*:

> *Don't count on your talents.*
> *The word* tai *[talent] rhymes with the word* tai *[disaster].*
> ....
>
> *The word* tam *[heart, sincerity] is worth threefold the word* tai *[talent].*

My father-in-law was the oldest son in his family. He was a pious son and a disciplined person. He took care of his parents without thinking of his business while his brothers and sisters lived their selfish lives. At times they came back home to sell the lands and antiques of their parents. He didn't say any words to offend them. He accepted all the disadvantages caused by his siblings. My mother-in-law supported his filial piety actively and happily. She pleased her mother-in-law, all the members of her husband's family, and her neighbors as well. She was one of the women I paid respect to. I realized how important women's role in family and society was. I was thankful to my sisters-in-law who helped my brothers fulfill their brotherly love toward me. They didn't consider me their burden. They never discouraged me. On the contrary, they encouraged me to continue my advanced studies. How noble they were.

My future father-in-law had a cozy life during the two Vietnam wars. He lived in harmony with his flowers, poems, and ornamental plants. Like my wife's grandmother he was healthy, happy, and smiling until his last day at the age of eighty-two. On the contrary, his brothers and sisters had many family troubles. They were needy and died in misery.

While I studied at the College of Education and the College of Arts, President Ngo Dinh Diem faced many oppositions not only from the National Liberation Front but also from the grassroots, including the military and the civil servants of the Republic of Vietnam. Religious and regional discrimination and political divergence disunited the South Vietnamese. The coup d'état of 1960 showed the discontent of some officers toward the regime. A large number of generals trained by the French became powerless. Some of them wanted to reshuffle the cabinet with their participation. They were dissatisfied. Almost all of them participated in the coup of 1963 led by General Duong Van Minh.

The Diem administration was accused of oppressing the Buddhists in Hue. Venerable Thich Quang Duc burned himself in Saigon after the death of some Buddhist believers in Hue. Following his example some monks burned themselves as Buddhist martyrs. Their deaths excited the Buddhist believers to struggle against the Saigon government to save their religion.

The Buddhists accused the government of religious discrimination when the government forbade them to hoist Buddhist flags. They attributed responsibility to the Diem administration for the deaths of the Buddhist believers in Hue. The Saigon government said that they were killed by Viet Cong grenades.

The Buddhists said that President Diem, a fervent Catholic, oppressed them and that Venerable Thich Quang Duc burned himself for the cause of Buddhism. The Saigon government denied this denouncement. According to Saigon, Venerable Thich Quang Duc "was burned." He didn't burn himself.

Vu Van Mau, the minister of foreign affairs, shaved his head to go on a pilgrimage to India. Dr. Tran Van Chuong, ambassador of the Republic of Vietnam to Washington and Ngo Dinh Nhu's father-in-law, resigned.

In August 1963 the army and police searched the Buddhist temples in Saigon and Gia Dinh under the command of General Ton That Dinh, who had been appointed governor of Saigon by President Ngo Dinh Diem. Many Buddhist monks were arrested, but Venerable Thich Tri Quang sought refuge at the USOM office on Ngo Thoi Nhiem Street. General Ton That Dinh's roar scared the Buddhist believers. Many of them hid the pictures of Buddha and the Buddhist bibles to avoid any possible trouble when the police searched their houses.

Madame Nhu went to Europe and America to assuage world opinion, but she enraged public opinion in Europe and America. Her mission was completely unsuccessful in the United States where her father, Tran Van Chuong, denounced the Diemist regime. He attracted more of an audience than she did. The coup d'état broke out on November 1, 1963, while she was in the United States.

The leader of the coup d'état was Big Minh, who had defeated the Binh Xuyen in Rung Sat and the Hoa Hao in the Mekong Delta in the mid–1950s. President Ngo Dinh Diem and his brother Nhu fled to Cholon. On November 2, 1963, the Saigonese learned that they had both died on a tank.

South Vietnam witnessed many significant events in the last three years of President Diem. In 1960 there were the Ben Tre uprising and the abortive coup d'état led by Colonel Nguyen Chanh Thi and Lieutenant Colonel Vuong Van Dong. The battle of Ap Bac in 1963 marked the fast growth of the National Liberation Front. In 1962 two officers of the Vietnam Air Force, Nguyen Van Cu and Pham Phu Quoc, dropped bombs on Dinh Doc Lap (Independence Palace). In 1963 the Buddhist monks burned themselves and President Diem was overthrown.

The Buddhists were happy about the fall of Ngo Dinh Diem. So were the antigovernment factions. The newspapers cursed the fallen regime and unveiled the private life of Madame Nhu and her husband's political intrigues. President Diem and his brother were killed. Archbishop Ngo Dinh Thuc stayed in Rome. Ngo Dinh Luyen was in France. Madame Nhu was in the United States. Ngo Dinh Can was brought to Saigon and sentenced to death in 1964.

Most Catholics felt that they had lost their lucid leader. They denounced the generals involved in the coup and American ambassador Henry Cabot Lodge.

Impartial people didn't believe in the leadership of the generals. South Vietnam faced multiple political, military, economic, social, and religious difficulties. People wondered whether South Vietnam would have a military dictatorship regime. Some said that the army should be apolitical, "l'armée, la grande muette." People were disappointed when General Duong Van Minh allowed the demolition of the strategic hamlets and tried to consolidate his power by wrestling support from the Buddhist Church.

The Communists were the true profiteers of the coup d'état of 1963. They gained without fighting. The South Vietnamese generals overthrew Ngo Dinh Diem, the most important anti–Communist leader, who was detained by the Communists in 1945 and whose brother and nephew were cruelly killed by the Communists in the same year. Due to his religion, social class and hatred for the Communists, Ngo Dinh Diem became a fanatic anti–Communist in Asia. In 1954 he was backed by Paris, Washington, and the Vatican. Left by them he was overthrown and killed by his generals. The Communists now had a favorable time to disunite the South Vietnamese. After 1963 disunion got more serious, disunion between Buddhists and Catholics, between pro–Diemists and anti–Diemists, between northerners and southerners, between generals in power and retired generals, between military personnel and civilians.

The anti–Diemists had used any means to predict the fall of the Ngo. They said that Dr. Nguyen Binh Khiem (sixteenth century) had prophesied:

The Nguyen left, then returned.
Touching the fig tree of India [Buddhists],
The pirates should be defeated.

It was rumored that the tomb of former Minister Ngo Dinh Kha, Ngo Dinh Diem's father, was struck by lightning.

People said that the government collapsed when the successive three months (lunar calendar) had thirty days. They also said that Vietnam would have big political changes every nine years. Precisely, when the sum of the last two digits of the year was nine, there would be big changes. Vietnam became independent in 1945. The Nguyen dynasty came to an end in 1945 (4+5 = 9). In 1954 (5+4 = 9) the Viet Minh defeated the French at Dien Bien Phu; the Geneva Accord was signed; Vietnam was partitioned. In 1963 (6+3 = 9) President Diem and his brother were killed.

The anti–Diemists attributed almost all the mistakes to Madame Nhu, who was believed to abuse power and to upset morals. They condemned the president for favoring the Catholics and his family.

The pro–Diemists said that Ngo Dinh Diem deserved to be chief of state. He was handsome, imposing, virtuous, and uncorrupted. He had resigned from officialdom to struggle for the country's independence. His success was to make the national economy stable, to put an end to the feudal forces, and to bring security and happiness to the South Vietnamese. A fervent Catholic, he fought against the Communists to maintain not only faith but also the Confucian social order and hierarchy. The pro–Diemists disagreed with their opponents' violent criticism of Madame Nhu. Their simple argument was that "it wasn't chivalrous to speak ill of a lady." President Diem chose Ngo Dinh Nhu as his advisor. The choice wasn't wrong, for his younger brother was among the elite in Vietnam under French rule. The Republic of Vietnam had 14 million people. Was it wrong that the president appointed his brother as a political advisor to him? Wasn't Robert Kennedy attorney general during his brother's presidency? Nothing wrong happened, because Robert Kennedy deserved his position.

"Ngo Dinh Diem discriminated against the Buddhists," a Buddhist believer said.

"Most ministers in the Diem administration were Buddhists," a pro–Diemist retorted.

"Venerable Thich Quang Duc burned himself to protest the religious discrimination of the Saigon government," a Buddhist said.

"He didn't burn himself. A man poured gasoline on him and he burned," a pro–Diemist replied.

"Venerable Thich Quang Duc became a Boddhisattva. His heart remained fresh at 600 Centigrade," a Buddhist said.

"I have no idea about that," a pro–Diemist said.

Relations between Washington and Saigon became sour and strained after the appointment of the new American ambassador to the Republic of Vietnam, Henry Cabot Lodge, a Republican. The BBC and the VOA transmitted much news unfavorable to President Diem after August 1963. The death of Quach Thi Trang, a student killed by the police at Ben Thanh market, moved the South Vietnamese and made the Saigon government unpopular. Ms. Quach Thi Trang was compared to Tran Van On, who was killed by the police in 1950. The pro–Diemists said that Ambassador Lodge was a Freemason, that he liked Zen and that he was antipathetic to the Catholics. Suzanne Labin, a French anti–Communist veteran, expressed such ideas when she talked about Ambassador Lodge and Venerable Thich Tri Quang.

Ngo Dinh Diem's opponents compared his actions with Nero's toward the Buddhists and with Shih Huang Ti's toward his people and the students.

Many disappointed people were sick of political disorder and chaos after the coup. They felt thirsty for the order before the coup. South Vietnamese had many different viewpoints on the coup d'état of 1963 and the choice of November 1 as National Day.

I began teaching history and geography while President Diem was facing thorny problems. I was in a difficult situation. As a civil servant I couldn't be against government policy, but as a teacher of history I could neither bend the truth nor despise public opinion. On the one hand, my superior and colleagues kept their eyes and ears on me when I taught. On the other hand, some students, I don't know why, suspected me of keeping my eyes on "revolutionary students." In such a dilemma I was conscious of how terrible politics is. Politics and ethics are always incompatible. Politics divides everybody. It seems to be the mortal enemy of love and friendship and to freeze human virtues. Its dear motto has been always "the end justifies the means." Politics cut off the students' respect for their teachers. That disappointed the true and pure teachers in South Vietnam after 1963.

The generals didn't have any political experience. They succeeded in toppling the authoritarian regime led by a former mandarin but they failed to replace it with a democratic one. To them, "democracy" meant "liberalism," which led to political chaos. The previous government was overthrown because of its unpopularity. The new government tried to gain popularity by doing some things contrary to the previous government policy. The Diem administration had banned dancing. The military government didn't. The previous government had forbade Chinese stories by Kim Dung. The military government did the contrary. President Diem was deemed to be overthrown because he oppressed the Buddhists. The new government sought to flatter the Buddhist church leaders. Both generals Duong Van Minh and Nguyen Khanh visited venerables Thich Tinh Khiet, Thich Tri Quang and Thich Tam Chau and favored the construction of Viet Nam Quoc Tu (National Buddhist Temple).

Their pro–Buddhist line displeased the Catholics. In 1964 General Nguyen

Khanh's clumsiness led to bloodshed between the Buddhists and Catholics in Saigon. The police just watched them killing one another. Nguyen Khanh's demagogic policy didn't help him. The students took to the streets to force him to abolish the Charter of Vung Tau. The fearful general shaved his goatee and declared the abolition of the Charter of Vung Tau. He resigned and left Vietnam after having stirred continual political tumults in Saigon in 1964.

5

The Bloody War

Almost all the strategic hamlets were demolished. The Viet Cong took control of many rural areas in South Vietnam. The war escalated. The Communist pressure on Binh Gia got intense. The Americans bombarded North Vietnam. Saigon was afraid of a possible retaliation from the Communist air force.

In 1965 American troops arrived in South Vietnam to help the Republic of Vietnam fight the Communist expansion. Chief of State Phan Khac Suu and Prime Minister Phan Huy Quat transferred power to General Nguyen Van Thieu and Air Vice Marshal Nguyen Cao Ky. They both were young generals compared to generals Duong Van Minh, Tran Van Don, Nguyen Khanh, and Ton That Dinh. General Nguyen Van Thieu became chief of state at the age of forty-two and Air Vice Marshal Nguyen Cao Ky became prime minister at the age of thirty-six.

Three four-star generals — Duong Van Minh, Nguyen Khanh, and Tran Thien Khiem — were in exile. General Tran Thien Khiem was appointed ambassador of the Republic of Vietnam to Washington, then ambassador to Taipei before becoming prime minister (1969–1975). General Duong Van Minh lived in Thailand. In April 1975 he was the last president of the Republic of Vietnam two days before its collapse. General Nguyen Khanh left the country forever.

Generals Thieu and Ky were totally supported by the Americans. Like Nguyen Van Tam, Nguyen Cao Ky called his cabinet "the war cabinet." June 19 became Armed Forces Day. This choice was a historic coincidence for June 19 marked the defeat of Napoleon I at Waterloo in 1815. Our young generals in Saigon wanted to follow the path of Bonaparte. They responded to the needs of the situation. The media spoke highly of the armed forces and military leaders. French general De Gaulle, Chinese generalissimo Chiang Kai-shek, and South Korean General Pak Chun Hy were considered to be good leaders. Many American presidents had been generals. That meant generals Thieu and Ky should be good leaders.

Nguyen Cao Ky, a young air vice marshal, reached the top of power. He was believed to be a "hawk," commanding the South Vietnamese troops to march to the North to wipe out the Communist regime. His supporters said that he spoke fluent English, that he was upright, and that he was a brave pilot when bombarding Vinh Linh. It was rumored that President Johnson preferred him to General Nguyen Van Thieu. Ky's supporters said that Thieu stumbled while Ky had smooth words and presence of mind.

Two years after the coup of 1963 Nguyen Van Thieu was promoted from colonel to three-star general. He was backed by the army. His partisans said that he was courageous and calm and that he loved actions better than words and efficacy better than oral presentation.

Thieu and Ky had nothing in common except for their *Bonapartiste* spirit. Ky was dynamic while Thieu was static. Ky was proud of his premature success. He didn't hesitate to say that "the man in his forties" (Thieu?) wasn't useful anymore. His words prophesied his fate when he was in his forties in 1971. Ky liked to fly. He looked very proud and happy after the bombardment of Vinh Linh. He compared himself with Truong Vo Ky and his beautiful wife with Trieu Minh, a Mongolian princess who fell in love with Vo Ky, a talented Kung Fu fighter in Chinese stories, who struggled against Mongolian rulers in his country.

The air force of the Republic of Vietnam was proud of its two commanders. The first was Nguyen Xuan Vinh, a pilot, a mathematician, a writer, and a famous university professor in the United States. He was compared with the French pilot and writer Saint-Exupéry. The second commander was Nguyen Cao Ky, a young and powerful prime minister in wartime. Colonel Qadhafi of Libya took power when he was twenty-seven years old. Fidel Castro overthrew Bastista and became prime minister of Cuba at the age of thirty-two. Nguyen Cao Ky was among the youngest leaders in the world. And his power was fragile.

Ky became a rising star after many abortive coups d'état in 1964 and 1965. All of them failed for lack of participation of the air force. Prime Minister Nguyen Cao Ky dismissed General Nguyen Chanh Thi in the First Tactical Region and General Dang Van Quang in the Fourth Tactical Region. General Nguyen Huu Co, the minister of defense, was dismissed. Ky firmly repressed dissident troops and Buddhist demonstrators in the First Tactical Region. Buddhists took pictures of Buddha and incense burners to the streets, complying with the order of Venerable Thich Tri Quang. The Buddhist monk who, according to the American media, trembled America, was brought to Saigon. The Unified Buddhist church was divided into two sects directed, respectively, by Venerable Thich Tam Chau (Viet Nam Quoc Tu) and Venerable Thich Tri Quang (An Quang). Prime Minister Nguyen Cao Ky and his friend, Colonel Nguyen Ngoc Loan, built their reputation by repressing the dissidents and Buddhist demonstrators in Hue and Da Nang in 1966. Afterward, the Saigon government stepped down. The Constitutional Assembly was born after the election of September 11, 1966. It was a small spark of democracy after three years of chaos and tumult.

In 1965 housing was expensive due to the increase of population in the cities and to the presence of the American and allied advisors and troops throughout South Vietnam.

The shortage of transportation got serious. Taxicab drivers liked to serve Americans more than Vietnamese. They put a small sign "Not for hire" on the windshields so as not to be disturbed by Vietnamese passengers.

The Vietnamese piastre was eclipsed by the U.S. dollar. There were three kinds of currency in South Vietnam: the piastre, the "red dollar," and the "green dollar." The red dollar was used by American GIs in their PX. The green dollar was the most valuable. Saigonese businessmen went to Bien Hoa, Phu Loi, Phu Giao, and Lai Khe every day to buy American goods and to exchange money.

Snack bars mushroomed wherever American GIs were quartered. Many young ladies left the rural areas for the cities to work for the snack bars and for American companies. American TV sets, radio sets, tape recorders, canned food, apples, and oranges were sold at the open-air markets. Prostitution swelled considerably.

The American culture and lifestyle were found in all of the big cities of South Vietnam. People smoked Salems, chewed gum and said, "Hi" or "Hello." Some Saigonese read *Newsweek* and *Time* instead of *Paris Match*. In Saigon all the English schools were full of students. French was eclipsed by English in the schools. The Vietnamese American Association became the American Cultural Center in Saigon beside the Centre Culturel Français. The American-educated intellectuals played important roles in the South Vietnamese government. In the first Republic of Vietnam (1956–1963), Nguyen Van Tho was cabinet director of the Ministry of Health. In the second republic (1967–1975), he was minister of education. His wife was a representative and senator. In 1964, as soon as Nguyen Xuan Oanh returned to Vietnam, he was chosen by Prime Minister Tran Van Huong as vice prime minister in charge of the economy. After him Nguyen Van Hao and Hoang Duc Nha held leading positions in the South Vietnamese government. Nguyen Ngoc Linh was successful with his school of English and his bank. Truong Hoang Lem, Cao Thi Le, Pham Thi Tu, Nguyen Manh Hung, and Nguyen Quoc Tri were university professors. Nguyen Quoc Tri was president of the National Institute of Administration after the death of Nguyen Van Bong.

In 1965 the first Honda appeared in Saigon. They became the most popular means of transportation in South Vietnam. They weren't as heavy as the

Italian scooters and European motorcycles. Their price was less expensive than the Vespa and the Lambretta.

Saigon got more populous. Many provincials and rural people moved there to have safety and job opportunities. The Communists tried to infiltrate Saigon to sow terror. The American and allied headquarters and offices were carefully protected. Some streets were closed.

All the streets in Saigon were old and narrow. The U.S. military trucks were too big for the South Vietnamese roads and streets. Traffic jams occurred every day. The first highway linking Saigon and Bien Hoa was built with a thousand-meter bridge, the longest bridge in the Saigon-Cholon area. This bridge was more convenient than the old ones built by the French in the early twentieth century. It was the first evidence of American civil engineering in Vietnam. The big problem was that the South Vietnamese didn't know how to drive on a highway. Many deadly accidents occurred because of the high speed and ignorance of highway traffic law.

Japanese television sets, radio sets, refrigerators, and electric appliances inundated Saigon. The South Vietnamese enjoyed more comforts than they had previously. Almost all the cinemas were equipped with air conditioners. Wealthy Saigonese and provincials had them at home. The first escalator appeared at the Rex, one of the largest cinemas in Saigon, in the 1960s.

The three-wheel motored Lambretta replaced the coaches to carry goods and pick up passengers. French cars were very popular before the importation of Japanese cars and were used heavily as taxicabs. The interprovincial buses were bigger, speedier, and more comfortable. Most of them consumed diesel. Tricycles and motored tricycles played an active role in transportation. On the rivers and canals many sampans were motored. Big boats were pushed or pulled by motored sampans.

The ironic thing was that, during the catastrophic war, the lives of most urban and rural South Vietnamese improved. They had comfortable houses with electricity, running water, radio sets, television sets, and refrigerators. They celebrated Christmas and Tet solemnly and optimistically.

The conservatives complained about social value reversal. Learned men now earned less money than laborers. The radicals said these were the characteristics of democracy and social justice. "How disgusting this is!" The pedicab driver's income is higher than that of an educated man," the conservative said.

"What are you disgusted at? That is social improvement. Why are you disgusted at it instead of welcoming it happily?" the radical asked.

"I wonder if education is necessary or not. I can't agree that a noneducated man should earn more money than an educated one," the conservative said.

"Education is always necessary. But you see, laborers work hard. Sometimes their work is dangerous. The more they work the more they earn. But their promotion is very slow while the educated man has many opportunities to reach the top of his profession," the radical said.

The conservative didn't argue further with the radical but he didn't accept his arguments. He felt that he had lost something he couldn't find again.

I heard different opinions on the presence of American troops in South Vietnam.

"South Vietnam becomes prosperous thanks to the Americans," the first man said.

"It is an artificial prosperity. In the past, did Vietnamese die for lack of American aid?" the second man asked.

"Without American aid, in the past, we were backward. Nobody had a radio set. The Americans differ from the French," the first man said.

"They are white and physically alike. I don't see any difference," the second man said.

"The French came here as invaders. The Americans came here as helpers. They're helping South Vietnam stop the Communist expansion. We have to thank them. The United States is a superpower. It helped Western European countries in World War I and World War II. Germany, Italy, and Japan surrendered. They saved South Korea from the red tidal wave. Ho Chi Minh isn't lucky this time," the first man said.

"The Americans are foreigners. Our country was under foreign domination for a long time. Our people are cautious with foreigners. Ho Chi Minh labels the Americans 'new colonialists,' and 'imperialist invaders' to clarify his cause. He will attract many supporters inside and outside Vietnam. Well-trained troops with modern weapons won't win the war if they don't have a good cause. The American and allied troops in South Vietnam will cause social, economic, and political disorder. Misunderstandings between them and the Vietnamese are inevitable due to the difference of culture. Hanoi will take advantage of this inevitable friction and contradiction between the American and allied troops, the donors and helpers, and the Saigon government and its people in the South, the takers, to divide them and to excite the Vietnamese people to stand up against the Americans and the puppet government.

"People say the American advisors bully Vietnamese officers," the second man went on. "They say that a Vietnamese officer beat up an American advisor; Mrs. X and Mrs. Y left their families to live with the Americans; and that the American bombardments destroyed houses and killed innocent people in South and North Vietnam. They say that the Americans backed Ngo Dinh Diem and watched his death with indifference. Now they are backing the military regime, sending South Vietnamese youth to the battlefields to kill Viet Cong and to be killed by them. Both the killers and the killed are Vietnamese. Some day Thieu and Ky will have the same fate as Diem.

"Such problems help the Communists in their struggle for popularity and help them gain their cause," the second man said.

"The Americans went to Europe to fight the Germans in two world wars. Nobody said they were invaders. On the contrary, they were welcomed by the Europeans," the third man said.

"England, France, and other European countries are different from Vietnam. They were independent while Vietnam was ruled by the Chinese and the French for eleven centuries. In Europe the Germans were aggressors. In South Vietnam Hanoi launched the war behind the shield of the National Liberation Front. North Vietnam didn't send troops to cross the Demilitarized Zone at the 17th Parallel to attack the Republic of Vietnam like North Korea did in 1950. Hanoi secretly sent the South Vietnamese who had gone north in 1954 back to the South along the famous Ho Chi Minh Trail. Not a few people deemed that it was an internal affair in the South between the Saigon government and the National Liberation Front," the second man said.

This conversation reflected different opinions on the Vietnam War and the presence of the American and allied troops (fromThailand, South Korea, Australia, and New Zealand).

The rightists called the leftists "doves" and "defeatists." They believed in American invincibility.

The leftists predicted the difficulties the Americans were going to face, like the French in 1954. Their arguments were that, in 1945, the Viet Minh fought the French with sharpened bamboo sticks. After nine years of bloodshed they won the war. In the 1960s the Communists consolidated their power in North Vietnam and acquired political and military expertise. They were economically, technically, and diplomatically supported by the Soviet Union, the People's Republic of China, the other Communist countries, and the newly independent countries in Africa and Asia. In the Franco-Vietnamese War they faced multiple difficulties until the Communists took over China in 1949. This time their situation was better although they coped with a superpower.

The Saigon government brought undeniable comforts to the South Vietnamese. But these things couldn't help it achieve popularity. Between the government and the populace, there was a deep abyss. The grassroots were mostly needy peasants, workers, soldiers, and civil servants. They doubted their leaders who, in turn, despised them. Most people thought that their government had nothing "Vietnamese" but was very "French" or "American." The government assumed that the grassroots were conservative, narrow-minded, fogyish, and noncooperative with the government's attempts to modernize the country and to fight the Communists. The grassroots expected their leaders to be more popular. Their leaders expected them to be more obedient.

Ordinary people blamed the intellectuals imbued with Western culture for ignoring their own country's realities. Worse, many of them knew their country only through foreign books and magazines. Although at the top of their power, they felt isolated. Physically, they were Vietnamese. But morally, they were foreigners. They were really Vietnamese mandarins trying to make much money to live happily in Europe or America after leaving their offices.

Saigon was noisy with the roar of vehicles, airplanes, and tanks and the explosion of bombs and mortar shells from the warring factions. American B-52s bombarded Dong Xoai, Dau Tieng, and the Ho Chi Minh Trail. The bombardments cost many Communist lives and damaged their food and ammunition storage. In retaliation, the Communist commandos, the *dac cong*, damaged American aircraft with bombs. Communist guerrillas destroyed bridges, roads, and railroads every day in revenge for the terrible raids in North and South Vietnam.

As long as the war lasted, the Vietnamese on both sides faced more sacrifices. The war ruined the economy of both sides. South Vietnam counted on the United States to survive. North Vietnam turned to the Soviet Union, the People's Republic of China, and other Communist countries for food and ammunition. Both North and South Vietnam lost their independence. Saigon didn't play an active role in the war. North Vietnam suffered from the presence of Chinese "voluntary" troops, which came to North Vietnam to "help" Hanoi reconstruct roads and bridges destroyed by American bombs.

Hanoi was ready to prolong the war to demoralize the American people, their leaders, and soldiers. The latter were young Americans, who enjoyed the most comfortable lives in the world. Sent to South Vietnam, their lives were threatened. They had to fight in a tropical country far away from their country. They weren't used to the severe weather there. It was hot, humid, swampy, and muddy in the Mekong Delta. It was sultry and dry along the coast. Malaria reigned in the mountainous regions. In the West the forests were almost virgin with all kinds of wild animals, venomous snakes, poisonous plants, and various kinds of mosquitoes and insects. The enemies were like ghosts. They appeared and disappeared quickly after sowing terror. They had no boots, no uniforms, no helmets, no rucksacks. They knew their enemies. But their enemies didn't know them. They hated the Americans. But the Americans didn't hate them. They moved quickly while their enemies moved slowly and heavily. They knew the landscape and were used to the regional weather while their enemies were physically weary and morally homesick. They missed their happy memories of families and schools during Christmas and Thanksgiving. The war was bloody and persistent without any prospect of victory. It was an obstacle to their futures.

The United States is a democratic country. The Americans elect their president every four years. The more the Communists fought ardently, the more the American people lost their patience and became antiwar protesters. The Communists launched attacks every four years in the hope of putting pressure on the presidential election. In 1960 the National Liberation Front was born to direct the "uprising of the South Vietnamese countrymen." We had the battle of Binh Gia in 1964, the Tet Offensive in 1968, and the bloody, flaming summer in Binh Long, Loc Ninh, Quang Tri, and Dong Ha in 1972. The South Vietnamese government was on alert on historic days, such as September 2 (National Day of the Democratic Republic of Vietnam), May 19 (Ho's birthday), December 19 (National Resistance), December 20 (birthday of the NLF), and July 20 (Geneva Accord).

In early 1965, five months before the arrival of American troops in South Vietnam, I saw Jesus in a dream. He informed me of a "big war." These two words seemed to electrify and chill me. I felt gooseflesh on my body. I knelt and made informal prayers: "My Lord, please keep my country away from the big war. My country has been in continual wars. All of my people will be destroyed if the big war occurs in my country." Jesus turned and walked away without saying a word.

My heart beat fast. I couldn't continue my sleep. I knocked at the door to wake up my brother. He asked me: "It's late night. Aren't you sleeping yet?"

I told him about the dream. It seemed that he wasn't interested in it. He lay on the bed and rejoined his sleep. I was stupefied and sat on a chair until dawn.

This short dream has remained vivid in my mind. I didn't tell it to anybody except my brother for fear that people would laugh at me for believing in nonsense or for making up mysterious stories.

Since my childhood I have believed in God, in Buddha. I have paid attention to national and international news. As a teacher of history I have had more interest in historic events. I have dreamed of peace and prosperity for my country, which has undergone intermittent sufferings for many centuries in darkness and shame. I have dreamed of social justice and happiness for all the Vietnamese people under the direction of lucid and righteous leaders who have true love for their country and people. I have dreamed of honor and glory for Vietnam. My dear country should be equal to other countries in the world community. I have dreamed of the effective contributions of future generations to building a democratic, free, and prosperous Vietnam in the world in love, in peace, and in abundance. I had many dreams during the catastrophic war. My dreams were always dreams of a war-ravaged country in which disunion, selfishness, and hatred reigned. Some people considered the then-situation as a "golden time." Others considered it a "dark time," preventing them from having bright futures.

The bloody war stole the hopes and ideals from many Vietnamese. They thought that they couldn't take care of themselves. What could they do for their country and their people? A large number of Vietnamese thought that, as long as their country was the ground of opportunists and corrupt people, it should remain in its persistent backwardness and immobility. Ultra-nationalism and national pride lead to racism, xenophobia, and war in the world community.

The Communists believed strongly in the perfection of Marxism and

Leninism and in the incomparable strength of the Soviet Union, the bastion of the socialist world. The war became a Communist Crusade against Capitalism.

The Saigon government counted on the technical and financial strength of the United States and its support. The government lacked self-sufficiency and failed to gain the trust of the grassroots or even the good and zealous people in the government and in the army. Soldiers of different service arms fought one another. The people were scared of them. The military despised the civilians. The marines, parachutists, and rangers despised the police and the militia. The American- and French-educated people watched one another. The urban residents despised the rural folks. Domestic disunion was irreparable.

In the rural areas the peasants called the Communists "brothers" or "gentlemen." These words showed their friendship and fear as well. They showed us how the Communists acquired their popularity. They conquered sympathizers and supporters with attractive promises, phraseology, and demagogy. They used force to repress those people who disobeyed or resisted them. Terror, assassination, and corporal suppression intimidated the so-called reactionaries and the undecided people.

Urban people attributed to the Communists all the good characteristics, such as "good at politics," "good orators," "courageous and bold," "virtuous," "uncorrupted," "patriotic," "engaged," and "altruistic."

In South Vietnam good military personnel and civil servants, who served the grassroots with zeal and were admired by them, were suspected of being Communists. Unwittingly, in such cases, the South Vietnamese government admitted that the Nationalists had the opposite characteristics of those attributed to the Communists.

In mid–1963 I wrote "The Nuclear War" for *Thoi Bao* daily. When we talked about the territorial disputes between the Soviet Union and the People's Republic of China and about the doctrinal divergence between these two Communist countries, some of my friends disagreed with me totally. They said that the Communist world was united, that there was no dispute between the Communist countries. "Communism is universalism. All the peoples in the world are brothers in the same house. All the countries are borderless. Why is there territorial dispute? The Russians occupied Port Arthur and North Manchuria in tsarist feudal times. Now the Soviet Union and the People's Republic of China are in their warm friendship," they said.

I smiled without arguing with my friends. Such a discussion was dangerous to them if the police heard us talking politics. In case they were arrested by the police, my argument would be the reason for the iron chain. In 1969 Soviet and Chinese troops exchanged bullets in Damansky. None of my friends reminded me of the Communist brotherhood.

In schools every time the teachers told about what was going on in the

Communist countries, especially in North Vietnam, some students didn't feel comfortable. They assumed that their teachers spoke ill of the absent. They neither wanted nor dared to hear it although they knew that it was true. Their own safety and that of their family were more important than such a political truth. Many of them were reluctantly anti–Nationalist or antirepublican (South Vietnamese government). They would rather choose prison (anti–Nationalist) than bloody terror (anti–Communist).

In 1964 a student of mine came to see me at home. He informed me that he had quit school. I asked him why he did so.

"I'm going to go to the jungle," he said sadly.

"What's the cause of your decision?" I asked.

He looked at the ceiling sadly to avoid my question.

This student was from a North Vietnamese family that, looking for freedom, had come to South Vietnam in 1954. He was a good and polite student who pleased all of his teachers. He looked poor. He was in rags. His complexion was sunburnt. He loved history. So he liked me. He liked to smoke water pipes. Addiction to this strong tobacco soon made him mature and experienced in his twenties.

My reaction to his bold decision was to advise him to weigh the advantages and the disadvantages, the "must" and the "must not" carefully. Since then, I haven't seen him. I don't know why he went to the jungle. I haven't heard any news from him. Maybe he died.

Four years later, another student came to my house and let me know that he had returned to the city from the jungle. He told me that one of my ideas appeared in his mind when he played games with death.

"What's that idea?" I asked.

"You said, 'This is a challenge between the will and weapons.' The Communists try to make American weapons ineffective with their strong will and endurance. As for the Americans, they use their technology to wear down stubbornness and to try the patience of their enemies," he replied.

Then he added, "I was demoralized in the rain of bombs and rockets. I sought to leave the jungle for the city. I don't know why I am still alive after undergoing many hours in the ocean of fire."

A few months later, he entered the Thu Duc Military Academy. In 1970 he came to my house in the uniform of a second lieutenant. Shortly after that, I heard of his demobilization after a car accident in Phan Thiet. After the fall of Saigon I learned that he headed a district board of education in Ho Chi Minh City (Saigon). In 1984, when visiting one of his friends, he asked about my family and my own safety after the fall of the Saigon regime. He told his friend to advise me to leave Vietnam for my freedom and survival.

❖ ❖ ❖

In the 1960s Japan restored its postbellum economy. Taiwan and South Korea were on the way to economic and industrial development. In 1964 Japan was the first Asian country to successfully organize the Olympic Games. That year the People's Republic of China tested its first A-bomb, which made the world tremble. Japan and the Soviet Union watched this nuclear test with fear. Khrushchev was deposed. But his policy of "peaceful coexistence" with the free world was respected by his successor. The Japanese stormily criticized their government for spending a lot of time, energy, and money on the Olympic Games. Willy-nilly, Japan felt uncomfortable with the Chinese A-bomb.

The Japanese economy soared. Japan had good commercial relations in the world, including with the Communist countries. It exchanged goods with both North and South Vietnam. The construction of the hydroelectric Da Nhim Dam by Japan in the program of war indemnification ended in early 1964.

The Saigonese and the suburban people had enough light at night. Almost all the streets of Saigon were electrified. People bought Japanese electric appliances to make their lives more comfortable.

West Germany, Japan, and Italy restored their economy. They realized the danger of war and the necessity of peace for economic recovery. Ultranationalism and racism led Germany to war, to defeat, and to partition. West Germany became an economic power while East Germany, rigidly controlled by the Soviet Union, paid more attention to faithfulness to Marxism and Leninism and to total submission of the folks to the Communist Party than to economic restoration.

The revolutionary heroism of the Vietnamese Communists made Vietnam an anticapitalist bastion in Southeast Asia. It led our country to intermittent wars, carnage, and partition. It disunited our people and made them skeptical of their future. The wars ruined the country and impoverished its people. Ninety percent of them were farmers. Under French rule rice and rubber brought Vietnam foreign currency. During the Vietnam War both North and South Vietnam got poorer and poorer. They couldn't survive without foreign aid. Instead of exporting rice they had to import it. In a certain measure, the Vietnam War helped some countries recover their postbellum economy. Some neighboring countries of Vietnam in Southeast Asia became independent and on the path of reconstruction and development. Saigon was called "the Pearl of the Far East," but compared with Bangkok, Kuala Lumpur, Singapore, and Manila, Saigon showed itself inferior to these cities.

The Vietnamese people have been laborious, patient, studious, and progressive. They made up heroic pages of history. They struggled for their survival and for their country's independence. Their inventions weren't abundant. However, they have had enough intelligence to keep up with technical and scientific progress and the new streams of thought in the world. Vietnam faced bitter realities. It was backward. Its economy was controlled by the Chinese

Vietnamese. In the 1960s and 1970s many Chinese Vietnamese were elected village chiefs, municipal council members, representatives, and senators in South Vietnam.

The Vietnamese must be impartial when thinking about the roots of their country's backwardness. Vietnam has been endowed with natural resources and valuable manpower. Lacking union and capable, lucid, zealous, and open-minded leadership, they lacked the factors necessary to the development of their country.

Ho Chi Minh was a good organizer capable of exciting Vietnamese patriotism in wartime. But he was unable to give his people inspiration to contribute to national construction and prosperity. In North Vietnam Ho Chi Minh and his disciples heightened the working class and tried to get rid of intellectuals, landowners, and businessmen. They preferred muscle to *eminence grise*.

In South Vietnam the military regime praised the new samurais without being interested in the productive forces. All the young Vietnamese of both sides were soldiers. They killed one another cruelly to polish the greatness of their leaders. Ho Chi Minh considered himself a Communist soldier, making his country an anticapitalist bastion. Ngo Dinh Diem and Nguyen Van Thieu considered themselves anti–Communist champions in Asia, making South Vietnam an anti–Communist bastion.

The Vietnamese people were sick of continual wars. They wasted time, energy, lives, and money for vain glory. Some didn't know why they killed one another. Some wondered what they struggled for. For independence or dependence? They had a lot of pain without any gain. As soon as their country became independent in 1945, they witnessed horrible vendettas. After defeating the French they saw their country in partition and their compatriots in separation. They took off one yoke to carry two! They made history by denying their national heroes and lauding Marx, Lenin, Stalin, and Mao. During his stay in Pac Bo cave (Cao Bang), Ho Chi Minh named the spring and the mountain there after Marx and Lenin.

In the 1960s many British and French colonies in Asia and Africa became independent. After Vietnam, Tunisia, Morocco, and Algeria weren't French colonies anymore. The newly independent African and Asian countries staggered between capitalism and Communism. Their favorite choice was to be neutral between the two antagonists. India, Indonesia, and Yugoslavia played important roles in the Third World. Prince Sihanouk of Cambodia, a fervent Gaullist, advocated neutralism but leaned toward the Communists.

India, although neutral, was very friendly with the Soviet Union and the Democratic Republic of Vietnam. Yugoslavia, although Communist, was independent from Moscow. Indonesia was a former colony of Holland. President Sukarno had struggled against the Dutch colonialists. More or less, he appreciated Ho Chi Minh as a revolutionary.

Prince Sihanouk of Cambodia was unfriendly with the Saigon government backed by the Americans. He had good relations with the People's Republic of China, the Democratic Republic of Vietnam, and the Democratic People's Republic of Korea. In 1970 he was ousted by Lon Nol and became a victim of his controversial stand for more than two decades (1970–1991).

In Vietnam, scholar Ho Huu Tuong had advocated the neutrality of Vietnam and Southeast Asia since 1954. In 1962 French president De Gaulle proposed the neutralization of South Vietnam. Hanoi accepted the idea. Saigon rejected the suggestion, arguing that neutralization meant suicide. To the Saigon government, it was unfair to neutralize only South Vietnam while North Vietnam remained Communist. Neutralizing South Vietnam at that time would have been the first step toward Communist victory.

Impartial outsiders thought that neutralization of South Vietnam was the best way to put an end to the war. Saigon got angry at this suggestion and was deemed to be warlike. The aggressors were believed to love peace and their victims were believed to be the hawks. The South Vietnamese government suffered for its failure to make its reasoning understood. Its situation was compared to a story: There was a deafening scream at midnight while everybody was sleeping. Everybody woke up. Their reaction was to curse the one who yelled without knowing that the man they cursed was the victim of an assault and battery. In order to rejoin their sleep, they advised the victim to accept all the demands of the aggressor.

It was the case of the Republic of Vietnam. Nobody saw the aggressors slapping their victims. But everybody heard the scream interrupting their sleep.

Since 1965, supported by the American and allied troops, Saigon could say "an eye for an eye and a tooth for a tooth" to Hanoi and the National Liberation Front.

In 1962 President Kennedy successfully confronted the Soviet Union over West Berlin and Cuba. The Soviet Union stepped down before his firmness and obstinacy even though Mao Zedong labeled the United States "the paper tiger." In November 1963 President Kennedy was assassinated. Vice President Johnson assumed his presidential responsibilities. In 1964 he defeated Goldwater, a conservative Republican presidential candidate, who won only six states in the election.

President Kennedy was one of the youngest presidents of the United States in the twentieth century. His charisma attracted American voters. He was born into one of the richest families in America. His wife, a beautiful and charming lady, was a journalist. His brothers were senators. President Kennedy got tough with Khrushchev, the leader of the Soviet Union. He accepted the space race with the Soviet Union with self-confidence and promised the landing of the first American on the moon although the Soviet Union was the first country to launch an artificial satellite in space (1957).

President Johnson faced more difficulties than any president of the United States. American public opinion on the Vietnam War differed deeply. Many Democrats disagreed with President Johnson on the war. The antiwar protesters, the doves, got more and more numerous. They protested American involvement in the Vietnam War while the hawks wanted President Johnson to end the war triumphally. Secretary of Defense MacNamara resigned. President Johnson was torn between war and peace. President Ho Chi Minh was firm in his stand. He dissipated all the hopes of peace in a thundering speech predicting the war could last "five, ten, twenty more years or longer."

Failing to respond to the true aspiration of the American people, President Johnson decided not to run for reelection in 1968. The Democratic presidential candidate, Vice President Humphrey, was defeated by Richard Nixon. The Republican president promised to "Vietnamize" the war and to "end the war and to win the peace." In Nixon's war Vietnamization was similar to the *jaunissement* (yellowing) policy of France in the 1950s.

In 1968 the Chicago police confronted the antiwar demonstrators outside the Democratic National Convention. There were many other events in the United States in 1968. Senator Robert Kennedy and Dr. Martin Luther King, Jr., were assassinated. In South Vietnam the Communists launched attacks on many cities, including Hue and Saigon.

I went back to Laithieu after my marriage. Sometimes I lived in my mother's house. Sometimes I lived in my father-in-law's house.

Laithieu was plunged into darkness at night. All the electric lines had been destroyed by Communist guerrillas. This populous city, eleven miles from Saigon, had no lights for five years. Communist guerrillas appeared at dark in Binh Chieu and Dong Ba to destroy what the Saigon government built and rebuilt in the daytime.

The urban and the rural people were confused by a series of strange rumors. In An Son a sow farrowed an elephant. A banana tree flowered a dragon. In Phu Nhuan a lady gave birth to a bag of eggs. Some people believed these strange rumors were signs of the end of mankind. Others assumed that Buddha would come to our planet to save mankind on doomsday. Catholics believed that Jesus would come to Earth and that the Soviet Union would return to the world community and denounce atheism. The anti–Communists were optimistic, believing that the following prophecy would come true:

> *When the stone emerges,*
> *The hair immerges,*
> *The lakes and rice fields dry up,*
> *Our people will be happy.*

The Vietnamese called Chiang Kai-shek "Tuong Gioi Thach." *Thach* means "stone." In Sino-Vietnamese *mao* means "hair," hinting at Mao Zedong. *Ho* means "lake" and *dong* means "field," hinting at Ho Chi Minh and Pham Van Dong.

Chiang Kai-shek died without shaking the Communist regime from the mainland. He didn't defeat the Chinese Communists militarily but he won them economically.

Mao Zedong wasn't ever deposed. The Cultural Revolution launched by him and his third wife, Jiang Qing, in 1966, cost the lives of his former comrades in the Long March (1934–1935), of many Communist cadres, and of innocent people.

In North Vietnam President Ho Chi Minh died in 1969. Prime Minister Pham Van Dong stayed in his premiership for thirty-two years. He retired in 1987, suffering from stomach ache and diabetes.

There were big changes in China and Vietnam after the death of Mao Zedong and the withdrawal of Pham Van Dong from the government.

Flares gave light to Laithieu and its neighboring villages every night. The center of the city was relatively safe. Communist guerrillas used to assemble the rural folks and force them to get involved in their sabotage activities. They ordered them to beat gongs to expose their presence in order to provoke the Laithieu subsector to shell. The deaths of innocent people and the damage to their property deepened the hatred of their relatives for the Saigon government.

In 1967 the constitution of the second republic was promulgated. There were eleven tickets in the presidential election of 1967. Both generals Thieu and Ky wanted to be presidential candidates. Prime Minister Nguyen Cao Ky deemed that he was capable of defeating the civilian candidate thanks to the support of Washington and of the South Vietnamese armed forces. We found the motto "Nguyen Cao Ky's cabinet is that of the poor" everywhere. In 1966 he attracted the attention of President Johnson with his "Great Society" at the Honolulu Conference.

The situation needed a military leader. Prime Minister Nguyen Cao Ky was a young and flamboyant air vice marshal. He was a fluent speaker ready to command the South Vietnamese troops to invade the North. However, in the eyes of American ambassador Bunker, the man of situation was General Nguyen Van Thieu, chief of state. Under pressure from the generals, Nguyen Cao Ky agreed to join Nguyen Van Thieu on the military ticket as the vice presidential candidate. If there were two separate military tickets, South Vietnam would have a civilian president. Civilian candidates, such as Truong Dinh Dzu, Phan Khac Suu, and Tran Van Huong, were likely to be elected.

The Thieu-Ky ticket won the election. Lawyer Truong Dinh Dzu was ranked second. He accused the government of electoral fraud. After that, he was arrested and imprisoned.

During the campaign Truong Dinh Dzu promised, if elected, to have a coalition government with the National Liberation Front and to free all the prisoners. Most rural people voted for him. Were they tired of the war? Did the Communists tell them to do so? Some observers said that Truong Dinh Dzu had friendly relations with Nguyen Huu Tho, chairman of the NLF. The presidential election of 1967 was a political test for both South and North Vietnam. The South Vietnamese had the opportunity to choose war or peace, military or civilian leaders. The Communists fighting in South Vietnam must have been afraid of the war, since they told people in the rural areas to vote for the "white dove," the emblem of Truong Dinh Dzu. The election of 1967 legalized the military regime in Saigon.

Apparently South Vietnam was politically stable after the promulgation of the constitution of April 1, 1967, and the presidential election. South Vietnam kept on receiving American aid regularly. American troops launched a series of "search-and-destroy" operations. In 1967 they tried to sweep the Communist stronghold in Binh Duong province. Thousands of inhabitants were forced to leave this "iron triangle." They were resettled in Binh Hoa village, Binh Duong. Many of them got wealthy by farming and raising chickens and quails. After 1975 most of them returned to their native land.

Corruption and smuggling got serious in the last ten years of the South Vietnamese government. The assassination of Representative Tran Van Van raised the suspicion of the southerners. Some of them attributed responsibility to Nguyen Cao Ky's partisans without thinking that the Communists killed Van to enlarge disunion between the southerners and northerners.

Tran Van Van, a graduate of the French Haute Etude Commerciale, was involved in political activities after the return of Emperor Bao Dai from Hong Kong. In 1966 he was elected a representative to the Constitutional Assembly. He was killed the next year. His son, Tran Van Ba, was sentenced to death by the Communists in Saigon in 1984 after returning clandestinely to Vietnam from France to organize the resistance against the Communists.

In 1967 and 1969 South Vietnam witnessed a vice presidential regime. The real power was in the hands of Vice President Ky. Colonel Nguyen Ngoc Loan of the air force, one of Ky's friends, was in charge of the national police. Lawyer Nguyen Van Loc, who had been chosen by Ky as the vice presidential candidate, became prime minister.

On the second day of Tet Mau Than (the year of the Monkey, 1968) the Communists launched attacks throughout South Vietnam. Hanoi changed the lunar calendar in 1967. Its lunar calendar became a little different from that of China. It showed the divergence between Hanoi and Beijing. It was also a sign of Ho Chi Minh's insubordination to Mao Zedong and his Cultural Revolution. The Tet Offensive broke out on the second day of Tet in Saigon. But it was the first day of Tet in Hanoi. The skeptics didn't believe that the Communists broke the truce regardless of the traditional Tet. They thought that Vice President Ky had led the coup to oust President Thieu, who was spending the Tet holidays with his wife's family in My Tho. People didn't know anything about the president. They only heard the voice of Vice President Ky on the air. Some worried about the president's safety.

The South Vietnamese troops and the Communists clashed on the outskirts of Saigon. Binh Loi, Hang Xanh, Cau Kinh, Binh Hoa, Xom Thom, Nga Tu Bay Hien, and Xom Cui witnessed bloody skirmishes. The inhabitants tried to move to the safety zones. The newspapers in Saigon said the South Vietnamese voted for the Communists with their feet. The Communists called the Tet Offensive an upheaval of the South Vietnamese people to overthrow the military regime led by Thieu and Ky and backed by the Americans. Seeing the folks leaving the combat areas, the South Vietnamese government thought that they hated the Communists.

Attacking Saigon, the Communists gained a resounding reputation. Some Communist militants smashed in the U.S. Embassy compound in Saigon. They all were killed after killing five Americans. Most Communist militants were sixteen or seventeen years of age. They got lost in the big city after losing contact with their guides. What surprised the South Vietnamese officers after checking some dead bodies was that the Communist militants had many South Vietnamese bank notes and that they were armed with AK-47 automatic rifles while the South Vietnamese soldiers kept on using the old carbines. After the Tet Offensive they were armed with M-16 automatic rifles. '

Americans were shocked by the picture of Nguyen Ngoc Loan shooting a captured Communist militant in the head. This famous picture was taken by Eddie Adams, who won the Pulitzer Prize. Later, he was a friend of General Loan.

In Hue the Communists killed more than 3,000 persons. They were civil servants, officers, soldiers, collaborators with the Americans, Catholic priests, and even some German university professors.

In May 1968 the Communists launched another attack. This time General Loan, general director of the national police, was seriously wounded. Many colonels were killed in a war accident at a Chinese school in Cholon. General Luu Kim Cuong of the air force died in combat. They all were active partisans of Vice President Ky. Prime Minister Nguyen Van Loc was replaced by Tran Van Huong, who had been prime minister in 1964. The vice presidential regime ended.

The Communists suffered heavy casualties in the Tet Offensive. The Hue massacre remained horrible in the minds of the South Vietnamese. The Communists started shelling Saigon and the South Vietnamese cities. The Saigonese lived in horror betweem sunset and sunrise.

Many clandestine establishments of the National Liberation Front (Viet Cong) were destroyed. The rural construction cadres worked actively in the remote areas to bring popularity to the Saigon government.

Many Viet Cong surrendered to the South Vietnamese government. They became *hoi chanh* (returnees) for different reasons. Some were sick and hungry. Some were demoralized by bombs and rockets. Some didn't believe in victory. Some felt that they had been sacrificed and betrayed by the North Vietnamese Communists.

The Phoenix Operation eliminated some 6,000 Viet Cong and wiped out many of their bases. It took time for them to restore the situation. Their military activities decreased visibly.

Hanoi agreed to talk with Washington in Paris. The peace talks lasted more than four years before the four warring factions signed the Paris Agreement in early 1973.

After the Tet Offensive the optimists believed that the war would be on the wane. President Ho Chi Minh died in 1969 after knowing a lot of bitterness during the Tet Offensive, which had made General Vo Nguyen Giap a star. His role got less important after the death of Ho Chi Minh. His star grew dim after the fall of the Republic of Vietnam in 1975.

Both Saigon and Hanoi praised their victories. The Communists tested the capacity of the armed forces of the Republic of Vietnam and American will and firmness. They clandestinely brought weapons to Saigon and prepared the Tet Offensive smoothly. South Vietnamese security didn't know anything about that. The residents didn't inform the local government of their clandestine activities in the capital. When the Communists opened fire, many people thought about a coup d'état. They weren't successful at occupying a city of the Republic of Vietnam. They failed to excite the South Vietnamese to revolt against the Saigon government. They had a big loss of lives. They didn't win. But they didn't lose. They showed their military capacity and their presence everywhere in South Vietnam to demoralize their enemies and to confuse the South Vietnamese.

According to the Saigon government, the Communists attacked Saigon and other South Vietnamese cities on the day everybody was busy celebrating the Lunar New Year, when the defense was loose, but they were expelled from the cities and left many bodies. In the eyes of the Saigon government, the Communists were losers for not reaching their goals. They had expected an uprising. But the Saigonese ran when they saw them.

After the Tet Offensive Hanoi agreed to send its delegation to the peace talks with Washington in Paris. The Vietnam War remained an insoluble problem until President Johnson decided not to run for reelection.

President Nixon was tough toward the Communists. Many Americans considered him an "anti–Communist fanatic." On the one side, he resumed the bombings of North Vietnam and the Ho Chi Minh Trail. On the other side, he tried to please the antiwar protesters with his Vietnamization program. He welcomed President Nguyen Van Thieu at the Midway Conference. He praised the South Vietnamese leader as an excellent leader. In the past few years American Secretary of Defense MacNamara had praised Nguyen Khanh, who was president and prime minister in 1964. The next year Nguyen Khanh left South Vietnam.

President Thieu's position was consolidated under the presidency of Nixon. The delay of President Thieu in sending the South Vietnamese delegation to the Paris peace talks showed that he favored the Republican candidate, Richard Nixon, at the expense of the Democrats. Dr. Henry Kissinger became the most influential advisor to President Nixon. His diplomatic activities were more important than those of Secretary of State William Rogers. Kissinger met with Le Duc Tho, a member of Dang Lao Dong Politburo (Workers' Party–Communist Party), in Paris to find a settlement for the Vietnam War.

Kissinger was a Jewish German. He immigrated to America in 1938 after Adolf Hitler had launched his brutal anti–Semitic movement. In the nineteenth century there were many eminent statesmen in Central Europe, such as Austrian chancellor Metternich and German chancellor Bismarck. The former cherished the *equilibre de force*. It was he who separated France from Russia and who contributed to the collapse of the Napoleonic regime. The latter contributed to the unity and prosperity of Germany by defeating the Austrians and French and industrializing his country. He was called the "iron chancellor." These two statesmen influenced Kissinger.

The United States became the promised land for the Jews in diaspora. They have been economically, financially, intellectually, and socially successful there. They haven't faced as much intolerant treatment as they did in Europe. The United States was the first country to recognize the birth of the State of Israel in the Middle East in 1948.

Since the creation of their state, the Israelis have struggled against their neighboring Arab countries. The United States supported them. The American involvement in Vietnam was a disadvantage for them.

The Vietnam War eroded not only the American economy but also American will. The Americans weren't used to such a dirty war. People killed one another not only on the battlefields but also in the churches, schools, snack bars, restaurants, and entertainment centers. It was difficult for Americans to distinguish friends from enemies. But it wasn't for the Communists. The Communists were mobile while their enemies gave them fixed objectives. They weren't attached to any laws or rules of war. On the contrary, all the activities of the American and South Vietnamese troops were minutely watched by the media, the U.S. Congress, the South Vietnamese Assembly, the American people, antiwar activists, and international bservers. It was easy for the photographers to take touching pictures of the My Lai massacre and the killing of a Viet Cong by General Nguyen Ngoc Loan. But they didn't have any pictures of the Hue massacre during the Tet Offensive. No picture. No proof. No massacre? No guilt? British philosopher Russel denounced the Vietnam War. So did French philosopher Jean-Paul Sartre. French journalist Jean Lacouture admired Ho Chi Minh in his book. Jane Fonda protested the war. So did American students and politicians. Black Americans struggled for civil rights. The American people were touched by the pictures taken at Khe Sanh and at the U.S. Embassy in Saigon and by some articles about American bombings of North Vietnam, which included some terms like "stone age barbarism" or "savage and senseless."

In Saigon, representatives Ngo Cong Duc, Ly Qui Chung, Nguyen Huu Chung, Kieu Mong Thu, and Nguyen Cong Hoan were antiwar protesters. The funny thing was that the aggressors were always innocent and considered peace lovers while their victims were considered ugly hawks. *Tin Sang* daily had long editorials favorable to the National Liberation Front and Hanoi. It gave Representative Tran Ngoc Chau more of a reputation and discredited President Thieu for giving the order to arrest a representative, that is, to trample down his immunity. All of these representatives protested the dispatch of South Vietnamese troops to Southern Laos. One newspaper noticed that the role of tearful actress Kim Cuong in *La Sau Rieng* (The Durian Leaf) excited the class struggle *à la communiste*. Immediately, the author of that article was violently attacked and blackened by these people. Songs by Trinh Cong Son describing the sufferings of the Vietnamese people due to the destruction of the war were widely spread. After the fall of Saigon, Trinh Cong Son was in charge of information and culture in Ho Chi Minh City. *Tin Sang* daily survived for only a short time after the Communists took over South Vietnam. Nguyen Cong Hoan became a Communist representative in 1976. Soon after, he left smoothly and arrived in the United States. Kieu Mong Thu was a member of the Ho Chi Minh City People's Council. Kim Cuong played an important role in the Communist theatrical field.

Communist infiltration into the Saigon government had occurred since the country's partition in different forms. Some claimed to be defected Viet Minh; some used religious umbrellas; some had national or international connections to play important roles in the South Vietnamese government. They made themselves trusted by giving their superiors the feeling that they were really anti–Communist and that they were loyal, zealous, dynamic, and good organizers.

Colonel Pham Ngoc Thao, a former Viet Minh officer and a friend of the influential Archbishop Ngo Dinh Thuc, was from a rich Catholic family in Saigon. He was well known in the Saigon government from the birth of the Republic of Vietnam until his death in 1965. He participated in all the coups d'état in South Vietnam. In the coup of February 19, 1965, he didn't hesitate to call it the "bourgeois revolution," a favorite political term used by the Communist party. Lieutenant Colonel Tran Ngoc Chau was Thao's successor as chief of Kien Hoa province. He was elected a representative in 1967. He was arrested and charged with having contacts with his brother, Tran Ngoc Hien, a Communist spy.

Huynh Van Trong, advisor to President Nguyen Van Thieu, and Vu Ngoc Nha, a favorite of Hoang Quynh, an anti–Communist priest, were brought to court on account of their Communist activities. It was rumored that Nha made Trong advisor to President Thieu and that he planned to make Nguyen Van Huong prime minister. An American-educated correspondent, Pham Xuan An, who had given American reporters sensational news, was a Communist officer of intelligence.

The South Vietnamese armed forces and allied troops were numerous, well-trained, well-equipped and well-fed. But how could they win when they were fighting with bound hands and without any moral support?

In 1970 Prince Sihanouk was deposed by Marshal Lon Nol. The Cambodian monarchy ended. Lon Nol founded the Republic of Cambodia, which was friendly with the Republic of Vietnam. In the past Sihanouk had shut his eyes and let Communist militants seek safe refuge in his country every time they were defeated by the South Vietnamese and allied troops or when B-52s destroyed their bases in South Vietnam. The war would be "internationalized" if American and South Vietnamese troops chased the Communists into Cambodia. President Lon Nol was a rightist. Friendly with Saigon and Washington, he allowed the South Vietnamese and allied troops to pursue their enemies into Cambodia.

On the one hand, President Lon Nol was friendly with Saigon. On the other hand, he brutally mistreated the Vietnamese immigrants in Cambodia. Did he use *cap duon* (killing the Vietnamese) to please the Cambodian people? To get some credits from the Cambodian people, who preferred Sihanouk to him? The Vietnamese were barbarously killed and thrown into the Mekong. Many women were raped before having their throats cut. Others were robbed and badly beaten before being stabbed or hammered to death. The Vietnamese refugees in Cambodia returned to their country empty-handed. Saigonese students protested the Phnom Penh *cap duon* policy in front of the Cambodian Embassy on Le Van Duyet and Phan Dinh Phung streets. They asked the Saigon government to agree with their attitude toward the savage *cap duon*.

Most Vietnamese immigrants in Cambodia got wealthy by trading, fishing on Lake Tonle Sap, and working for the government offices. Most of them lived in Phnom Penh (called Nam Vang by the Vietnamese), in the eastern provinces, where there were French rubber plantations, and along the Gulf of Thailand. Their influence was considerable in the capital of Cambodia, where many Cambodians spoke Vietnamese when dealing with the Vietnamese. The Cambodians didn't like them. Historic hatred? Jealousy of their success? Or both? When a certain Cambodian leader excited their anger and hatred, the Cambodians stood up to kill the Vietnamese and threw them into the Mekong to feed the fish and shrimp.

The South Vietnamese were displeased with their government, which, due to the Vietnamese-Cambodian friendship, was indifferent to the bloody *cap duon*. The Cambodians blamed Lon Nol for bringing them war. Sihanouk called for an uprising to topple President Lon Nol, who was backed by the Americans. Sihanouk's stand moved from Paris to Beijing, Pyongyang, and Hanoi.

The South Vietnamese troops had military operations in Cambodia. There was no war without bloodshed, destruction, piracy, and senselessness. This rule had no exception when the South Vietnamese troops were in Cambodia.

It is said that Cambodia has much gold. It is the land of opportunity. It is easy to make much money but it is impossible to keep it. This observation isn't a postulate but it is a long-time accumulation of experiences from those Vietnamese immigrants who lived in Cambodia for many generations.

The military operations in Cambodia cost the lives of generals Nguyen Viet Thanh and Do Cao Tri. They both died in a plane crash. General Nguyen Van Hieu was in critical condition after the battle of Snoul.

After the Tet Offensive many political parties appeared in South Vietnam to prepare a political struggle against the Communists. *Agrégé* Nguyen Van Bong and Dr. Nguyen Ngoc Huy founded Phong Trao Quoc Gia Cap Tien (National Progressive Movement). General Tran Van Don and Dr. Nguyen Xuan Oanh founded Mat Tran Cuu Nguy Dan Toc (National Salvation Front). Tran Quoc Buu, chairman of the CVT (*Confédération Vietnamienne du Travail*), planned to give birth to Dang Cong Nong. Professor Truong Cong Cuu, former minister under President Diem, founded Viet Nam Nhan Xa Dang, of which the members were from Can Lao Nhan Vi Dang. President Nguyen Van Thieu prepared a ruling party, Dang Dan Chu.

There were more than sixty newspapers in Saigon. They represented different political, religious, and professional tendencies. The Catholics had *Xay Dung* and *Thang Tien*. Radical Catholic priests, like Phan Khac Tu, Chan Tin, and Nguyen Ngoc Lan, had *Doi Dien*. *Chanh Dao* belonged to the Buddhist church, *Cap Tien* to Phong Trao Quoc Gia Cap Tien of Nguyen Van Bong and Nguyen Ngoc Huy. Representative Ngo Cong Duc ran *Tin Sang*. Representative Ly Qui Chung had *Dai Dan Toc*. *Chinh Luan* belonged to the Dai Viet party. The army had *Tien Tuyen*, *Dieu Hau*. *Than Chung* attracted many readers. Its editor, Nam Dinh Nguyen The Phuong, had many experiences in journalism. *Than Chung* released many documents on the Franco-Vietnamese War and the Geneva Conference.

Tu Chung, a well-known columnist, was killed in an assassination. Chu Tu, editor of *Song*, was seriously injured in an assassination attempt. Some university professors were assassinated. Dr. Le Minh Tri, minister of education, and *Agrégé* Tran Vy were killed. In 1971 *Agrégé* Nguyen Van Bong, president of the National Institute of Administration and Chairman of Phong Trao Quoc Gia Cap Tien, also died in an assassination.

The National Progressive Movement was opposed legally and constitutionally to the Saigon government. Its members were intellectuals, military personnel, civil servants, and businessmen who were anti–Communist without sharing the Saigon government lines. Some people thought that Professor Nguyen Van Bong was killed by the military, who wished to get rid of a brilliant chessman from a future civilian government. The suspicion lasted for a long time after his death although the murderer, a Communist student, confessed that he had killed Bong in compliance with the order of his superior. After the fall of Saigon, the Communists confirmed that they had killed *Agrégé* Nguyen Van Bong.

Corruption became a big problem, a daily topic of the South Vietnamese newspapers. In South Vietnam the president, vice president and prime minister were generals. The local governments were in the hands of high-ranking officers. Usually, the chief of the province was a colonel and the chief of the district was a major. All the key positions were held by military officers. Corruption became so cynical and awful that MacCoyle wrote a book on it. He detailed the history of corruption in Vietnam under Chief of State Bao Dai, President Ngo Dinh Diem, Prime Minister Nguyen Cao Ky, Tran Thien Khiem, and President Nguyen Van Thieu. General Le Van Vien, a Binh Xuyen ringleader, was a successful example of corruption that was followed by all the governments of South Vietnam. He made money by founding a network of economic and financial establishments in Saigon, Cholon, and other provinces in South Vietnam. Connecting with Chinese *compradors,* he focused on casinos, brothels, restaurants, opium dens, and bus stations, like the ringleaders in Shanghai. In the 1960s and 1970s corruption spread from the cities to the rural areas, from the Saigon government to the local authorities. MacCoyle mentioned corruption in the army, the air force, and the navy.

Tran Thanh and Ly Long Than were the powerful Chinese businessmen in South Vietnam. They influenced all the South Vietnamese leaders at that time. In 1963, at a critical time, President Ngo Dinh Diem and his brother Nhu were sheltered by Ma Tuyen, a Chinese businessman in Cholon. Ma Tuyen was faithful and courageous as he shared the danger with the president at that moment.

Both prime ministers Nguyen Van Loc and Tran Van Huong were unable to stop corruption. Prime Minister Tran Van Huong said frankly that "if we kill all the corrupt, we won't have any collaborators." What a sad observation. Corruption became an incurable disease. Corrupt people were numerous and powerful. *Dieu Hau* released a list of "clean generals" and "dirty generals." The clean were powerless or erased from the political stage while the dirty got more and more important.

Soaring corruption in South Vietnam was similar to that of China after World War II and during the civil war there between the Communists and Nationalists. Corruption was the root of the fall of Chiang Kai-shek's regime. Would President Nguyen Van Thieu follow his path? Or would he be an exception thanks to the presence of American troops?

In 1970 South Vietnamese disabled veterans took to the streets. Their aspiration was to have an "inch of land." The Saigon government was led by three generals, but apparently only President Thieu carried all the burdens. The problem was how to satisfy those who bore arms and sacrificed parts of their bodies for the national cause without touching the private property of folks. The disabled veterans occupied the lands of the Catholic church and faced violent reaction from the Catholics in northwest Saigon. In order to avoid the occupation of the disabled veterans, landowners fenced their lands with barbed wire. The "inch of land" movement regressed and fell into oblivion.

In 1971 South Vietnamese troops were dispatched to South Laos. The foreign strategists paid attention to this strategic zone. Some assumed that those who took control of South Laos would conquer Southeast Asia.

Laos is a sea-less and mountainous country with virgin forests. During the Franco-Vietnamese War Viet Minh militants were sent there in 1953. Hanoi supported Pathet Laos led by a Communist prince, Souphanouvong, a stepbrother of Prime Minister Phouma. Prince Souphanouvong was pro–Vietnamese. He studied in Hanoi and married a Vietnamese lady. During the Vietnam War the Communists used the Laotian corridor to infiltrate South Vietnam. As for the Americans, they trained and backed the Hmong headed by General Vang Pao. Laotian neutrality was uncertain due to violent disputes between the rightists and leftists.

Military operations in Laos were unsuccessful. Colonel Nguyen Van Tho, a young hero during the Tet Offensive in Hue, was captured by the Communists. Both Hanoi and Saigon claimed to be victors. It was rumored that the Communists had been made aware of the operations. Some attributed the responsibility to General Nguyen Huu Co, former vice prime minister and minister of defense, who was dismissed on account of his corruption.

In 1971, once again, Vice President Nguyen Cao Ky planned to run for president. Retired General Duong Van Minh didn't conceal his intention of being a presidential candidate.

President Nguyen Van Thieu's prestige had declined after four years in power. However, those four years gave him a good opportunity to consolidate his power and to multiply his supporters at home and abroad. Most generals were on his side. The Americans appreciated his efficiency.

Thieu, Ky, and Minh were military. Although retired, General Minh would share the military votes with Generals Thieu and Ky. He would be backed by the Buddhists in Central and South Vietnam, by the moderates, and by the silent majority.

If there were three tickets, headed by Thieu, Ky, and Minh, General Minh would win for General Ky would divide the military votes with General Thieu.

If there were two tickets (Thieu-Ky or Thieu-Minh), General Thieu would win the election without any difficulty. The incumbent president had more means than the other candidates. Many representatives, senators, and municipal council members were his partisans. These lawmakers helped him prevent any dangerous candidates from running for president. The electoral laws disappointed Nguyen Cao Ky and Duong Van Minh. Both of them quit the race for the Dinh Doc Lap. There was only the Thieu-Huong ticket left. Prime Minister Tran Thien Khiem was chosen as the reserve vice presidential candidate. This only-one-ticket presidential election didn't embellish the infant democracy of the second Republic of Vietnam. President Thieu had no choice in spite of some violent demonstrations. The demonstrators protested the only-one-ticket election and American support of the military regime. The students set fire to American military trucks on Truong Minh Giang street. The presidential election took place as it was scheduled. General Thieu was re-elected president. Former Prime Minister and Senator Tran Van Huong was vice president. General Tran Thien Khiem remained prime minister. He had held this position since his return from Taiwan in 1969. Air Vice Marshal Nguyen Cao Ky left officialdom for a villa at Tan Son Nhut Airport. He had no power. Air Marshal Tran Van Minh was appointed commander of the air force of the Republic of Vietnam.

There was nothing in common between Hanoi and Washington at the Paris Conference. It seemed to be a conversation between two deaf men.

The firm stand of Hanoi was to ask the Americans to stop bombing. Hanoi talked with Washington about the American bombings of North Vietnam. The National Liberation Front talked with the Saigon government about South Vietnamese affairs.

The Americans considered the National Liberation Front a political instrument of Hanoi but they accepted it as a political entity. It hurt President Nguyen Van Thieu a lot. According to the Americans, North Vietnamese Communists had invaded South Vietnam. Hanoi rejected this denouncement, saying that they had the right to support their people in South Vietnam to expel "American imperialists" from their country. They denounced the American bombings.

Saigon said that the NLF was just a name given birth by Hanoi. In 1969 the government of the Republic of South Vietnam (Cong Hoa Mien Nam Viet Nam) was born. Architect Huynh Tan Phat was prime minister, Madame Nguyen Thi Binh was minister of foreign affairs. Saigon called it the phantom government without people, land, or capital. The NLF said they represented two-thirds of the South Vietnamese population and therefore took control of two-thirds of the territory of South Vietnam.

All the demands of North Vietnam were satisfied after a long boring talk. Representatives of the Republic of Vietnam and of the Republic of South Vietnam came to Paris. The chief of the Republic of Vietnam delegation was Pham

Dang Lam, a pure and simple *fonctionnaire* working for the Ministry of Foreign Affairs. His advisor was Vice President Nguyen Cao Ky. Madame Nguyen Thi Binh led the delegation of the Republic of South Vietnam (Viet Cong). It was a good choice not because she was a good diplomat but because she was a lady at the Paris Conference. It heightened women's role on the political stage of a country influenced by Confucianism, with its unfair assumption of the inferiority of women to men. It attracted the attention and curiosity of the Western media. At home Madame Nguyen Thi Binh was deputy commander in chief of the NLF.

The South Vietnamese deemed that Binh was the daughter of revolutionary Nguyen An Ninh, a French-educated intellectual who, as a young man, had struggled for the independence of Vietnam in the 1920s. He created *La Cloche Fêlée*, a newspaper in French, to expose his political stand and the true aspirations of the Vietnamese people. He spent money, time, and energy to write, print, and sell *La Cloche Fêlée* by himself. Like Theodore Hertz, he was lonely. The colonialist police watched him and the readers of *La Cloche Fêlée*. Everybody was scared. *La Cloche Fêlée* died. Nguyen An Ninh spent many years in prison. When World War II broke out, he was imprisoned and banished to Poulo Condore Island where he died in 1943. Nam Dinh, editor of *Than Chung*, confirmed that Nguyen Thi Binh was Nguyen An Ninh's daughter. Nam Dinh knew Nguyen An Ninh, Ta Thu Thau, and Phan Van Hum (Trotskyites), and Duong Bach Mai and Nguyen Van Tao (Stalinists).

Nguyen An Ninh was originally from Hoc Mon, Gia Dinh. Nguyen Thi Binh was born in Quang Nam (Central Vietnam) to a revolutionary family. Nguyen An Ninh had a daughter named Nguyen Thi Binh and a son named Nguyen An Tinh. The latter attended Lycée Petrus Ky and vanished after the demonstration of the Saigonese students in 1950. Nobody knows for sure if he is alive or dead.

The Viet Cong woman diplomat launched diplomatic attacks in Europe and Third World countries. Asked by the foreign correspondents about the two-thirds of South Vietnam claimed to be controlled by the Viet Cong, she said that wherever there were breaches or the vestiges of bombing there was the presence of the NLF. Western correspondents were excited about her positive and smart answer, as well as its sophistication. They were impressed by the roles of the two women in the NLF, Nguyen Thi Dinh and Nguyen Thi Binh. It was possible for a woman to be a diplomat. But it was rare to have a woman commander like Madame Dinh. Everything worked smoothly, but she was only a facade. The true commander was the Communist four-star general, Nguyen Chi Thanh.

The Communists attacked the Americans and the South Vietnamese government politically, militarily, economically, culturally, socially, and diplomatically. They called the Americans "new colonialists," "imperialists," "invaders," and "international *gendarmes*" and the Saigon leaders "puppets," "tyrants," and "American lackeys." The South Vietnamese government focused mostly on military activities in which it played a defensive and secondary role.

The aggressors respected the collective decision. The defenders used to respect individual decisions from their leader. The former heightened the leadership of the Communist Party. The latter disdained the role of political parties. The Soviet Union and the People's Republic of China helped North Vietnam actively. Both countries wanted North Vietnam to be in their orbit. South Vietnam received American aid, but that could change after every election, depending on American Congress, on American public opinion, and on the political, social, and economic situation of the United States. South Vietnam didn't decide war and peace but the White House did. That was South Vietnam's diplomatic weakness before Hanoi and the National Liberation Front.

Many South Vietnamese students had left their homeland to study abroad. Some of them were pro–Communist. Or worse, they worked for the Communists. The Saigon government chose and sent students abroad but it failed to bring them back and to make them friends. Did the embassy of the Republic of Vietnam have an interest in them? Did it let the Communists or overseas Communist sympathizers take care of them in their first days in a foreign land? Nguyen Thai Binh, studying in the United States, soon became an antiwar protester. So did Doan Van Toai. Binh was killed on an American airplane when it was in the air over Nha Trang. A high school in Ho Chi Minh City bears his name.

The Vietnamese immigrants in Thailand, New Caledonia, Cambodia, Laos, and France turned to Hanoi more than to Saigon. After the signing of the Paris Agreement the Vietnamese immigrants in Thailand had a big feast to welcome "victory." Expelled by the Thai government they returned to North Vietnam. Many Vietnamese immigrants in New Caledonia, descendants of those people who had been recruited by the French in the 1930s to work in Cochinchina (Nam Ky) and New Caledonia, traveled to North Vietnam to visit their native villages and relatives (many were in the South) without knowing the existence of the Republic of Vietnam.

The Saigon government tried to put in the minds of the South Vietnamese civil servants and military personnel an anti–Communist ideology. But the result seemed nebulous.

Hanoi and the National Liberation Front taught their people hatred for the American invaders, for "the puppet government selling out the country," for the "regime of police," and for "the conspiracy of the country's partition." They also taught them national pride and liberation of their "blood compatriots" in the South from "American new colonialism."

A partisan of the Saigon government said: "We are against the Communists because the Viet Cong are enslaved by the Soviet Union and Communist

China. They impoverished our people and forced them to deny their family, religion, and homeland. The Viet Cong sold out our country and plunged our compatriots in North Vietnam into misery. Now they want to put the rest of the country into Soviet and Chinese claws."

A pro–Communist retorted: "What's wrong with the Communists? Ho Chi Minh fought the French for our country's independence. Now he is fighting the Americans for national unity. He is wrong, is he? North Vietnam is industrialized and economically mature while South Vietnam was and is totally dependent upon France and the United States. It isn't an honor to be a beggar. Who are the 'Nationalists'? Are they those people whose masters were and are French, Japanese, and Americans? Is this their political cause?"

In the eyes of foreign observers, Ho Chi Minh was a man of action, a Nationalist, and a Communist. Some compared him to Tito. In the eyes of many Vietnamese, he was a patriot who struggled against the French, the Japanese, and the Americans; they didn't believe that he did everything for the sake of the Comintern.

In feudal times the civil war between the Trinh and the Nguyen lasted less than half a century (1627–1672), but it sent the northerners and southerners to misery, hardship, suffering, separation, oppression, and social injustice.

In the North the Trinh had a well-organized administration, a stable economy, and a well-trained and disciplined army. The Red River Delta and the Ma Delta were more populous and fertile than the littoral plains in Central Vietnam.

The Nguyen took control of the sandy and rocky land with many lagoons and dunes of sand. The weather was severe. The land was almost sterile and was permanently threatened by drought, floods, and typhoons. Administration in the South was in its infancy but less feudal than that of the Trinh. It lacked laws and scholars in the new land, most of whose residents were adventurous, banished, and discontented people. Defense was ensured by the farmers in the latifundia. They enlarged croplands, practiced farming, and fought, when necessary, to keep their lands and crops. The Trinh couldn't defeat the Nguyen. They both were seconded by Europeans. The Dutch brought assistance to the Trinh, as did the Portuguese to the Nguyen. At that time the influence of Holland on the Trinh and of Portugal on the Nguyen wasn't as profound as that of the Soviet Union and China on Hanoi and of the United States on Saigon three centuries later. The Nguyen resisted the attacks of the Trinh heroically. One time their soldiers crossed the Gianh River (Quang Binh) to go up to Nghe An to frighten the Trinh. The Nguyen succeeded because the southerners supported them totally.

Nationalist leaders (Bao Dai, Ngo Dinh Diem, Duong Van Minh, Nguyen Khanh, Phan Khac Suu, Nguyen Van Thieu) couldn't build up their popularity although they received huge aid from America before and after 1954. South Vietnam didn't have a strong political party able to give the country a capable, zealous and patriotic leader. Corruption, bureaucracy, and disunion were bad aspects of the Saigon government. They showed the lack of credibility of the officials in the country's future. They cut off relations between the government and the masses. The government didn't need the masses. They needed international support only. The masses didn't believe in the government. The government machinery was deeply divided into small groups. They sought to harm one another to hold lucrative positions.

Some showed their anti–Communist ardor by labeling as "Viet Cong" those people who disagreed with them. Some showed their hatred for the Communists by displaying Viet Cong bodies in the sun along the roads or by disemboweling them after cutting out their livers and gall bladders. Some said they hated the Communists because the latter killed their relatives and confiscated their properties. Some said they fought the Communists to protect their religions.

Some thought that they would use the Communist way to dominate the Communists. They attributed Communist efficiency to dictatorship. As a result, they praised dictatorship *à la Hitler* and the *despotisme éclairé* of the eighteenth century in Europe.

Some thought about achieving popularity by living with the masses, being polite to them, helping them clean their houses, fetching water, planting rice paddies, wearing black clothes and conic hats, smoking tobacco, and drinking rice alcohol.

Some showed their enthusiasm by working twenty-four hours a day.

Some showed their integrity by going to work by bicycle. Popularity was associated with demagogy. These above ways were unsuccessful for their owners didn't perceive the depth of Vietnam's problems. Such political phenomena disappeared silently.

In 1972 the Communists attacked Loc Ninh, Binh Long, Dong Ha, and Quang Tri and occupied them temporarily. South Vietnamese warriors were sent to the battlefields to expel the Communist troops from the occupied territories. American B-52s bombarded Binh Long and Quang Tri. Road 1 and Road 13 became bloody and horrible. South Vietnamese troops recaptured Quang Tri and Binh Long, but the inhabitants of Binh Long evacuated to Phu Van, Binh Duong province. They didn't return to Binh Long, which had been ravaged by the war. They resettled in Rung La and stayed there until the fall of South Vietnam.

This time the Communists controlled day and night some districts in South Vietnam. Loc Ninh, about seventy miles from Saigon, was the most important city they occupied.

In the United States, President Nixon prepared for his reelection. He sought to keep his promise of 1968: ending the war and winning the peace. Kissinger and Le Duc Tho met secretly in Paris to give birth to a draft agreement at the expense of the Republic of Vietnam. Kissinger flew to Saigon to discuss with President Thieu the draft agreement. He was frigidly welcomed by Thieu. The proposed agreement was favorable to Hanoi and, of course, harmful to Saigon. Kissinger was in a hurry to see its premature birth, which was necessary to the reelection of President Nixon. Vietnamization must be successful. The American president had to bring all the GIs home. The future of South Vietnam would be determined by the Vietnamese. In other words, the Communists would take over South Vietnam after the withdrawal of American troops.

The Paris Agreement was signed on January 27, 1973, after B-52s dropped some 40,000 tons of bombs around Hanoi and Hai Phong (December 18–30, 1972). On January 28, in a televised address, President Thieu expressed his disagreement with the Paris Agreement. He couldn't hide his anger and used many *soldatesque* terms, such as "if the enemy uses short guns, we will use the long ones. If they use the long guns, we will use cannons and tanks."

South Vietnamese civil servants studied the contents of the Paris Agreement and tried to interpret it as a diplomatic success of the Republic of Vietnam.

Not long after the signing of the agreement, the warring factions exchanged war prisoners. American pilots captured and imprisoned in North Vietnam prepared for their homecoming. American and foreign troops withdrew from South Vietnam. Viet Cong General Tran Van Tra was present in Saigon.

The Saigon government ordered their cadres to paint yellow flags on the house roofs and front doors of their residences with the motto "My family doesn't hide any Communists." They took pictures of all the members of each household holding a yellow flag with three red stripes with the motto. Each household paid for its own paint and pictures. Without such pictures, the residents could be considered "Communist," "pro–Communist" or "antigovernment."

The Saigon government seemed to lose its lucidity. It remained unpopular for giving the South Vietnamese many troubles.

In the rural areas Viet Cong hoisted their flags and assembled peasants to keep them informed of the Paris Agreement. South Vietnamese troops took Viet Cong flags down and tried to stop the Communist guerrillas from occupying more land with more dwellers.

On October 26, 1972, during the visit of Kissinger to Saigon, the Viet Cong attacked South Vietnamese troops in Bung, a small town fifteen miles from Saigon.

On January 28, 1973, while President Nguyen Van Thieu was talking to the South Vietnamese people about the Paris Agreement, the Viet Cong opened fire on South Vietnamese troops on Road 13 in Binh Nham, one mile from Laithieu. They appeared in many villages of Quang Ngai province, hoisting their flags (red and blue with a yellow star). The Viet Cong exchanged war prisoners with Saigon in Loc Ninh, a district of Binh Long province, which they had occupied in 1972.

In the United States, a few days before the signing of the Paris Agreement, former President Johnson died. His successor, Nixon, had succeeded in ending the war for which the Democratic presidents were responsible. In November 1972 President Nixon was reelected. His opponent, McGovern, lost the election bitterly although he had made himself a white dove. Many Democrats, such as Edward Kennedy, Fulbright, Mansfield, and McGovern, disagreed with President Johnson on the Vietnam War. In reality, it wasn't President Johnson's initiative. He had continued President Kennedy's line, but President Johnson became the target of criticism from different sides for sending more than 500,000 GIs to South Vietnam and bombing North Vietnam without either ending or winning the war. McGovern tried to please the antiwar protesters with his pacifism in the presidential election of 1972. However, the dove didn't bring the olive branch. What were the true aspirations of the American people? Ending the war by force? Ending the war at any cost? Disengagement? Helping South Vietnam without dispatching American troops there? Ending the war and letting the Vietnamese solve their affairs themselves?

In two decades (1952–1972) no Democratic president had won reelection. Vice President Harry Truman became president after the death of President Franklin D. Roosevelt. He defeated Republican Thomas Dewey in a famous upset victory to win election to a new term. But he didn't run for reelection in 1952. Republican Eisenhower defeated Democrat Stevenson twice, in 1952 and 1956. Democrat Kennedy was elected president in 1960. He died in 1963. Vice President Johnson became president (1963–1964). He won the presidential election of 1964. He supported his vice president, Humphrey, in the election of 1968, but the latter was defeated by Republican Nixon because Humphrey carried all the political burden left by President Johnson.

President Eisenhower put an end to the Korean War, which had broken out in 1950. In 1949 Chinese Communists took over the mainland; the Soviet Union had its first A-bomb. These events were factors in the defeat of Adlai Stevenson in 1952. In 1959 Cuba became the first Communist country in the Americas. The first artificial satellite of the Soviet Union was launched in 1957. An American U-2 reconnaissance plane was shot down by the Soviet Union. This incident led to the cancellation of the Paris summit conference (1960). These were bad signs for Republican Nixon in the presidential election of 1960. Richard Nixon, a two-term vice president, an experienced statesman, was defeated by a young, rich, handsome, charismatic, and eloquent Democratic candidate, John F. Kennedy. Eight years later, Nixon became president of the United States and sped toward Vietnamization and the end of the Vietnam War without hurting American honor and position in the world. The Domino Theory was adjusted after the visit of President Nixon to Beijing and Moscow in

1972. The Sino-Soviet repugnance was undeniable after the exchange of fire on an inhabited island in the frozen Ussuri River. Chairman Mao needed a reconciliation with the United States to offset the Soviet threat. President Nixon was warmly welcomed by Chairman Mao and Premier Chou. He turned on the green light and welcomed the People's Republic of China to the world community in 1971. He made Mao more open-minded and mysterious China metamorphosed to become politically Communist and economically capitalist.

The Nixon administration faced multiple difficulties at home. The Kent State University killings sparked protests across the country in his first term. Many universities and colleges shut down. Students and professors staged strikes (1970). Vice President Agnew resigned in 1973 and pleaded no contest to a charge that he failed to report income from payoffs by Maryland businesses. The scandal of the Watergate affair led to the resignation of President Nixon on August 9, 1974.

Support for President Thieu was diminished during the second term of President Nixon. Le Duc Tho asked the United States to stop supporting President Thieu, who considered the Paris Agreement a "surrender agreement." He knew that both South Vietnam and he were sacrificed. Le Duc Tho was the first Vietnamese to win the Nobel Peace Prize, sharing it with Henry Kissinger in 1973.

General Thieu was a leader in wartime. His role declined visibly after the signing of the Paris Agreement. He tried to console himself when he said that he would be a good leader in peacetime. President Nixon invited him to the United States but limited him to a family dinner in San Clemente, California. Although the peace agreement was signed, the president of the United States still feared the antiwar protesters. In Europe President Thieu wasn't welcomed as a chief of state. He was believed to be a hawk, a warlord, and an obstacle to peace. The South Vietnamese didn't appreciate his regime, blackened by corruption, the monopoly of presidential elections, and the militarization of the South Vietnam.

People didn't sympathize with Hoang Duc Nha of Bo Thong Tin Dan Van (Ministry of Information and Propaganda). People joked and changed *Dan Van* (people's propaganda and agitation) to *Dan Gian* (people's anger). This young minister was proud of his position, age, and American education. He was President Thieu's cousin. He had studied in the United States and was deemed to be backed by the Americans. He was a powerful minister in the Saigon government in his thirties. His arrogant speeches and manner hurt the generals and even the prime minister. Nobody knew how he was helpful to the regime that was getting more and more unpopular.

Nguyen Van Hao, another young official, played an important role in the national economy as soon as he returned to Saigon. He was vice premier in charge of the economy until the fall of South Vietnam and then stayed in

Saigon in the hope of serving the Communist regime. In April 1975 he called on the South Vietnamese not to leave the country and threatened to confiscate the property of those who left Saigon before April 30. His chances at power in the new regime were nebulous. He was disdained and suspected by Mai Chi Tho. Disappointed, he left Vietnam, ostensibly to join his wife (the ex-wife of Hoa Hao general Ba Cut) in the United States. For fear of violent reactions from Vietnamese refugees in America, he stayed temporarily in France, then worked in Haiti before having a quiet and secret life in Florida.

Corruption and horrible living conditions in Poulo Condore prisons became headlines in the newspapers in Saigon. Some American senators and congressmen called the Poulo Condore prisons "the tiger's cage" and asked the Saigon government to improve the living conditions of the prisoners (mostly Communists and political prisoners).

President Thieu challenged public opinion by giving corrupt generals, such as Dang Van Quang and Nguyen Van Toan, important roles. The second Republic of Vietnam was marked by the so-called ghost soldiers and ornamental soldiers. Many Chinese Vietnamese were elected communal council members in the last five years of the regime. Many officers became village chiefs. Usually a lieutenant colonel headed the provincial department of police; a captain headed the district department of police and a second lieutenant headed the communal department of police. The graduates of the National Institute of Administration were subordinate to the military men in charge of the local government. They were mostly deputy chiefs of the provinces or deputy chiefs of the districts. Their number grew but there weren't enough positions for them. The Saigon government planned to insert the new graduates of the National Institute of Administration into the administrative infrastructure by making them village chiefs. Colonel Quach Huynh Ha was assigned to study administrative reforms, which had been in limbo until the fall of the Republic of Vietnam.

The star of President Thieu grew dim. American vice president Agnew resigned. So did President Nixon the next year. Former House minority leader, Gerald Ford, became president of the United States.

Hanoi and the NLF endlessly criticized President Thieu. They accused him of violating the peace agreement, of being an obstacle to peace and to the execution of the Paris Agreement. Tran Huu Thanh, a Catholic priest, released documents proving President Thieu's corruption in Saigon. A Buddhist nun, Huynh Lien, led the demonstrators to the streets. Journalists marched in Saigon, struggling for the right to a decent life.

The Communists prepared a new attack. Some predicted that they would launch attacks in 1976 to pressure the American presidential election as usual. This prediction wasn't true. They attacked South Vietnam in 1975 without fearing American bombings and the return of the American troops. This time South Vietnamese troops fought by themselves. They had to contain Viet Cong and North Vietnamese troops while American aid became uncertain. The Paris Agreement had given them two years to prepare the attack. In a short poem Ho Chi Minh wrote: "Fight the Americans until they go home!/ Fight the puppet government until it falls down!"

In 1973 the American troops left South Vietnam. The Communists had successfully carried out 50 percent of their goal. With the Ho Chi Minh Campaign, they reunified the country by force. The Saigon government collapsed.

Lugubrious South Vietnam after the signing of the Paris Agreement was beautified by the magnificent wedding ceremonies of Prime Minister Tran Thien Khiem's daughter and of President Nguyen Van Thieu's daughter. Saigon was busy and noisy, celebrating the Lunar New Year, Mid–Autumn, Christmas, and the New Year. Restaurants mushroomed in Saigon, Cholon, Gia Dinh, Phu Nhuan, Binh Loi, Binh Dien, Binh Chanh, and Thu Duc. It was the same in other South Vietnamese cities from the 17th Parallel to the headland of Camau. The urban residents consumed much foreign beer and brandy. They smoked American cigarettes, drank Coca-Cola and Pepsi-Cola, and ate American fruit and cheese. Skating was in vogue in the early 1970s. Tea rooms and coffee shops attracted teenagers. They rode their Hondas at full speed and crossed in front of loaded trucks running on the highway to win bets. Fortunately none of them were crushed by the trucks.

The Saigonese enjoyed watching Hong Kong Kung Fu films. Ly Tieu Long (Bruce Lee) revived the Chinese martial arts. South Vietnamese teenagers admired him and studied Chinese martial arts. They were muscular. Their punches were strong enough. But most of them loved the violence and fighting more than the ethics of the boxers.

In Saigon we had Korean, Japanese, Chinese, and Vietnamese martial arts classes. The Vietnamese martial arts, the Vo Vi Nam and Vo Binh Dinh attracted a large number of teenagers trying to discover the essence of their ancestral art of fighting. Martial arts books in Vietnamese, French, and English were for sale at Khai Tri bookstore, the biggest bookstore in Saigon.

Studies of history and politics became more important than they had been under French rule. Many books on World War II, Germany, Italy, and Japan, translated into Vietnamese from French or English, were published. Some books talked about the Nationalist parties, such as Viet Nam Quoc Dan Dang, Dai Viet, and Duy Dan, and their clandestine activities during French rule. Some books focused on Marxism and the Indochinese Communist Party.

In a confrontation with international Communism, Truong Tu Anh had given birth to the Dan Toc Sinh Ton (National Survival Doctrine) by the end of 1938. This doctrine was developed and systematized by Dr. Nguyen Ngoc Huy.

DEPARTMENT OF STATE

𝕬𝖌𝖊𝖓𝖈𝖞 𝖋𝖔𝖗 𝕴𝖓𝖙𝖊𝖗𝖓𝖆𝖙𝖎𝖔𝖓𝖆𝖑 𝕯𝖊𝖛𝖊𝖑𝖔𝖕𝖒𝖊𝖓𝖙

CERTIFICATE OF ACHIEVEMENT

This certifies that, under the Program of the Agency for International Development of the Government of the United States of America in cooperation with other Governments,

PHAN ĐINH LÂN

has successfully completed participation in a technical cooperation program

in the field of: L I B R A R Y   S C I E N C E

for the period: July 31, 1973   -   August 11, 1973

ISSUED AT _____ SAIGON - VIETNAM

THIS 15th DAY OF December 19 73

ADMINISTRATOR

Author's Certificate of Achievement in Library Science.

Nguyen Ngoc Huy, also known as Dang Phuong (poet) or Hung Nguyen, was a member of the Dai Viet Quoc Dan Dang. Returning from France after the fall of President Diem, he was general secretary of the Tan Dai Viet (New Dai Viet) and founder of the National Progressive Movement, of which he was general secretary and *Agrégé* Nguyen Van Bong was chairman. Nguyen Ngoc Huy was a professor, a poet, a playwright, a columnist, a lecturer, and a political theoretician. He wasn't an orator with resonant words, but he was a fluent lecturer, who attracted listeners with his abundant knowledge, scientific and synthetic arguments, and modesty and simplicity. He was very Vietnamese although he had been a graduate of the Sorbonne. He sacrificed his heart, body, and mind for his country's independence, democracy, and prosperity. He avoided irresponsible criticism. His firm stand was to look for the right direction for a free, democratic, and prosperous Vietnam.

Spending almost all of his life thinking of this right direction for our country, a former colony, in which the level of education of the grassroots was very limited and the standard of living was terribly low, he didn't accept Communism as being either humanistic or realistic. He felt that it couldn't help our country be democratic or our people be free and happy. He conquered the hearts of almost students, officers, and intellectuals who came into contact with him. They shared his thoughts and accepted his stand and his enthusiasm. In him we found the strong persistence of revolutionary Phan Boi Chau, the vigor of Nguyen An Ninh, the yearning for freedom and democracy of Phan Chu Trinh, and a national doctrine, which had been absent from Vietnam in the past. In 1975, once again, he had to leave Vietnam, but he continued his struggle for democracy and a free Vietnam by founding Lien Minh Dan Chu (Alliance for Democracy) and by giving lectures in Europe, North America, and Australia, advocating the birth of the International Committee for a Free Vietnam. He wrote many political articles and books in Vietnamese, French, and English. He worked without knowing that he was worn out, that his health had declined awfully, and that his speech was broken. He died in Paris in 1990.

Curious South Vietnamese sought to read history books published by the Hanoi Institute of History. They secretly listened to the BBC, VOA, Radio Hanoi, and Radio Giai Phong. Both readers and listeners were disappointed. Communist historians weren't impartial as they were expected to be. Radio Hanoi and Giai Phong were bellicose and falsified the truth. They disgusted impartial listeners from the silent majority.

The South Vietnamese who were displeased with the Saigon government thought simply that the Hanoi government would be better. According to their judgment, what was bad in Saigon would be good in Hanoi. It was said that the South Vietnamese police and soldiers used to say rude words. On the contrary, the Communist police and *bo doi* (Communist soldiers) neither said rude words nor beat up the captives. They deemed that North Vietnam had no corruption, no oppression, no exploitation, and no social injustice. They suggested some good leadership factors based on Ho Chi Minh's background: celibacy, involvement in revolutionary activities, imprisonment, efficacy, and virtue. President Ho Chi Minh was successful in giving himself this aura. In 1945 he was fifty-five years old but his cadres taught the Vietnamese to call him *Cu Ho* (Old Ho) with respect. Like other Communist leaders he let his cadres and the people sanctify him. His picture appeared on bank notes, in books, at bus stations, in front of government offices, in factories, and in many households. He was the source of inspiration for poets, writers, painters, musicians, sculptors. In North Vietnam, after his death (1969), the Communist government celebrated his birthday and made him an incomparable hero in history. Upon learning that he had died, some representatives in Saigon suggested a minute of silence in his memory.

The war became more bloody. Facing the death menace, human beings turned to voodoo and horoscopes. They looked for Taoist priests or wizards and asked for safety, a peaceful life, and success in business. Officers, generals, civil servants, businessmen, and taxi girls had their "masters" as sponsors and divine advisors. Great masters usually lived far from the capital. They could be in Dalat, Long Xuyen (An Giang), Thot Not, Chau Doc, Hoc Mon, or Tay Ninh. Their disciples had to see the masters every month to change talismans. Usually women chose masters for their husbands. Once in a while, the masters traveled to Saigon, where all of their disciples welcomed and served them, by turn, at home. It was an honor, a pleasure, and good luck for them to serve their masters.

In war time people faced sudden death. Wild boar's tusk was believed to protect people from fire. As a result, it was expensive. Some craftsmen engraved a picture of Buddha on a beef bone and sold it as a wild boar's tusk. People verified the real wild boar's tusk by rolling it in hair and burning it. If the hair wasn't burned, the tusk was real.

Chinese astrology, chiromancy, and physiognomy were in vogue. *Maitre* Khanh Son, Minh Nguyet, Huynh Lien, and Le Ba Hoa were well-known fortune-tellers and astrologers in Saigon. In Cholon there were many Chinese astrologers and geomancers. Their disciples were of the upper class of South Vietnamese society. They needed to know about their fates, fortunes, love lives, families, and officialdom. Women needed to know about their husbands' private lives and their futures as well. Some quarreled with their husbands because the fortune-tellers said that their husbands had more than one wife and that they had children with other wives. They compensated the astrologers for speaking well of them. Intellectuals, officials, and generals used physiognomy and astrology to choose loyal subordinates. If the birth year (Mouse, Water Buffalo, Tiger, Cat, Dragon, Snake, Horse, Goat, Monkey, Rooster, Dog, Pig) and its elements (metal, wood, water, fire, earth) of the subordinates were incompatible with those of their superior, they would be transferred to another place. The Chinese horoscope book by Van Dang Thai Thu Lang was the best seller. Others authors, such as Nguyen Manh Bong, Nguyen Phat Loc, Thien Luong, and Thanh Long, were also well known for their Chinese horoscope books. Minh Duc University, headed by a Catholic priest, mentioned oriental medicine in its curriculum. The book of mutations was translated into Vietnamese. Oriental philosophy was taught at Saigon University and Van Hanh University (Buddhist University). Acupuncture books appeared, reviving oriental medicine. Venerable Thich Tam An and acupuncturist Thuong Truc played an active role in this movement.

Eclipsed by Western culture for a century, oriental culture sought its reemergence. It is undeniable that every culture has its specific beauty. Westerners brought Vietnam technology, comforts, concepts of freedom and democracy, and scientific organizations. They came to Vietnam as conquerors. They despised and tried to erase the existent culture in their colony. Consequently, there was violent friction between East and West. At the dawn of their history the Vietnamese had realized that their existence was tied to that of their culture. They therefore modified what they learned from the Chinese colonialists. They learned Chinese characters without speaking Chinese. They knew that culture is like delicious food, which can make eaters healthy and sick at the same time.

Political schemes and tricks have been the same always. Two thousand years ago, Trieu Da succeeded in stealing the secret of the magic crossbow by letting his son marry An Duong Vuong's daughter. In the eighteenth century General Nguyen Hue, future Emperor Quang Trung, hired an astrologer to harass Pham Ngo Cau, a general of the Trinh in the South, before launching attacks and defeating him. Were the South Vietnamese generals affected by ordinary schemes in the second half of the twentieth century? It was rumored that General Tran Van Don hired a fortune-teller to predict the brilliant future of General Ton That Dinh before convincing him to participate in the coup d'état of 1963. The fortune-teller said that General Dinh was born to be a minister. It was said that this ambitious general wished to be the minister of the interior or of security. His dream came true after the coup of 1963.

There was a rumor going about that a fortune-teller had said that Nguyen Cao Ky, when still an officer of the air force, would be a chancellor. In 1965 he reached the top of his fate.

It was said that President Nguyen Van Thieu believed in Chinese astrology and geomancy, that Colonel Nguyen Van Y, former director of the CIO and the national police, was good at Chinese horoscopes and that the purpose of the construction of Duy Tan Square, according the advice of a Taiwanese geomancer, was to exorcise ghosts and devils and prevent them from bothering the president in Dinh Doc Lap. Thong Nhat Boulevard was perpendicular to Dinh Doc Lap. For that reason, the French governors and Vietnamese presidents in the palace faced endless troubles. Traffic was prohibited on the portion of the boulevard leading to the palace.

President Thieu's partisans said that he was born in the year of the Mouse, in the month of the Mouse, on the day of the Mouse, and at the time of the Mouse. His lot was the best one, that of the richest and the most powerful man. In other words, he was born to be king. They said this even though the president was born in 1923 (the year of the Pig).

In early 1975 astrologers predicted something unfavorable to President Thieu. They decided that the location of the Dinh Doc Lap was geographically bad. No leader could stay there for a long time. They said that President Thieu's daughter was pregnant. The baby would come out in the year of the Cat, which wasn't good for the president, who was born in the year of the Mouse! His position would be shaken in the year of the Cat (1975). President Ngo Dinh Diem was overthrown and killed in the year of the Cat (1963). President Nguyen Van Thieu resigned and the Republic of Vietnam collapsed in the year of the Cat (1975).

Some South Vietnamese were in a hurry to buy a cactus and put it at their front doors to prevent ghosts and devils from entering their houses. The children wore paper ties so as not to be disturbed by ghosts, devils, and kidnappers.

Ong Dao Vuot, a charlatan with a religious appearance, claimed to heal any diseases by touching the patients. He made love with many superstitious ladies, killed them, and buried them in his small temple. His barbarity scared the religious South Vietnamese, who thought that the time of Satan had come.

The last five years of the Republic of Vietnam were marked by people in power with bad reputations. The grassroots didn't know whom to trust. Senators, representatives, and government officials wasted the national budget when traveling abroad. High-ranking officers had many houses for rent. They chose some soldiers to serve them at home or to take care of their farms and orchards. Their families lived luxuriously in a country at war. The disabled veterans lived from hand to mouth by selling lottery tickets or cigarettes. Many warriors' widows were so poor that they pawned everything they had. When a soldier died, his family couldn't receive his death pension smoothly without paying a bribe.

Bribery spared nobody. A deputy chief of a province moved to a littoral province eighty miles from Saigon, driving in a truck full of conveniences of every sort. A policeman stopped the truck and asked the deputy chief to give him 200 piastres as a bribe so that he wouldn't check the truck.

"What do you have on the truck?" the policeman asked.

"Furniture," the truck driver replied.

The deputy chief of the province didn't say a word.

The policeman checked the truck in the twinkling of an eye. He kept a long silence without giving any decision.

"May I leave, Chief?" the truck driver asked.

"No," the policeman replied.

"What's wrong, Chief?" the truck driver asked.

The policeman didn't answer the question. In a few seconds he said: "Give me 200 piastres to drink coffee."

The deputy chief had no reaction. He took 200 piastres from his pocket and gave it to the policeman. The truck driver continued on his way while the deputy chief of the province wrote down the policeman's name and the date, time, and place of the incident.

After taking office, the deputy chief invited the policeman to present himself at his office. He asked his subordinate to get hot coffee for the policeman. Time passed. The policeman drank much coffee without receiving any instructions from the deputy chief of the province. He got a little embarrassed and asked himself why he was at the office of the deputy chief. When the latter wasn't busy, he politely asked him, "Sir, I'm at your disposal. I'm ready to follow your instructions."

The deputy chief of the province shook hands with him and said kindly, "I invited you to come here to have some coffee."

"Sir, I drank a lot of coffee this morning," the policeman replied.

"I asked my subordinate to get 200 piastres of coffee for you," the deputy chief of the province said.

"Thank you, Sir. It's enough for today. I only have a cup of coffee a day."

"Oh, no. You have to drink 200 piastres of coffee. Everything is ready."

"Sir, it's impossible for my stomach to drink 200 piastres of coffee."

"I think so too. But when you stopped my truck and asked me to give you 200 piastres for coffee, I thought that you must drink too much coffee," the deputy chief of the province replied.

At this, the policeman found out that the bribe giver had been the deputy chief of the province. Both of them smiled.

Not everybody hated corruption. The arrivistes and opportunists argued that business would be difficult without corruption. They compared business and corruption to fish and water. Fish can't live without water. They can't live in clear water, either!

Corrupt people ridiculed the uncorrupted by qualifying the latter as "less intelligent" or "unrealistic." They told this funny story as a warning to uncorrupted officials after their retirement:

> Long ago, there was an upright courtier. He did his duty without thinking of bribes. His wife and he had a hard life after his retirement. Their life got more and more difficult. At their ages, they couldn't do anything to earn money.
>
> One day, the courtier's wife gave him delicious food with expensive rice alcohol. He was very surprised.
>
> "We are poor. How do you have enough money to get good food and rice alcohol?" he asked his wife.
>
> "Honey, don't get angry with me. I'll explain to you the reason why." She chewed betel and continued, "When you were a courtier, you helped many people. One of them came here and gave me a bag of money. I refused to receive it."
>
> "Please, Madame, this money shows that I am grateful to my generous Great Man. This is a gift, not a bribe," the man said.
>
> "No, bring it back home. My husband will get angry when he knows this story.
>
> "He asked me about your birth year. I let him know that you were born in the year of the Rat. Three days later, he came to our residence and gave me this golden Rat. Thanks to it, we have survived until now," the wife said.
>
> "Why didn't you say I was born in the year of the Water Buffalo?" the former courtier asked sadly.

In the 1960s there were many banks in South Vietnam. Nguyen Tan Doi had Tin Nghia Ngan Hang, which was as important as the military bank. Many generals, lawyers, and politicians were on its board of directors. Its interest rate was high. Tin Nghia Ngan Hang had many branches throughout South Vietnam. Its customers were civil servants, retired people, and military men who were excited by its high rate of interest. Nguyen Tan Doi was well known in South Vietnam. He was not only a businessman and a banker but also a representative. He had a newspaper in Saigon. In 1971 he ran for representative in Rach Gia and was elected. Some praised him as the only Vietnamese businessman running a business *à l'americaine*. They said that, in the eyes of the Americans, he would be a president capable of restoring the economy in peacetime. His advisors were mostly lawyers and retired generals. It was rumored that President Thieu was afraid that Colonel Nguyen Be or millionaire Nguyen Tan Doi would steal his presidential seat. Nguyen Tan Doi's level of education was limited but he was very successful in business. He knew how to take advantage of a situation to make money. He got rich by producing tiles during French rule. He had a big brick factory that made expensive bricks and floor tiles in Binh Loi. His economic success led him to political ambitions that didn't stop at the House of Representatives. Shortly before the fall of South Vietnam, Tin Nghia Ngan Hang was in bankruptcy. Nguyen Tan Doi was imprisoned and many people lost their money due to the bankruptcy of his Tin Nghia Ngan Hang. He was released when General Duong Van Minh became president, and he left Saigon after the Communists took over South Vietnam.

It was difficult for the South Vietnamese government to gain popularity and credibility. After the Tet Offensive some South Vietnamese raised quails. The price of quails and of their eggs increased every day. Sometimes a pair of quails was more expensive than a tael of gold. So were their eggs. Everybody was excited to buy quails and to build cages to raise this precious kind of bird in the hope of getting rich quickly, although they didn't know who they would sell them to. They talked a lot about the characteristics of these tailless birds, which can't fly much but run and hop. Their meat and eggs are good for sex. Before 1968 only the Chinese knew how to raise and multiply quails. The secret of quail keeping was revealed by South Vietnamese soldiers when they fought in Cholon during the Tet Offensive. Quails became rare and very expensive. Almost all of the South Vietnamese urban residents raised them. Baby quails and quail's eggs became priceless, but few quail keepers got rich quickly. Suddenly, one day, the quail keepers were cleaned out. Only some generals, government officials, and Chinese businessmen in charge of importing quails from Taiwan and Hong Kong made huge money.

In olden times Vietnam was deeply influenced by Confucian thoughts. Politics were separate from business. Merchants were ranked fourth in the four cardinal occupations. In the monarchic regime only scholars held high positions in the administration. It was the same under French rule.

In the late 1960s South Vietnam tried to get used to the new concept that a successful businessman could be a successful politician. This concept had been familiar to the Americans but was new to the Vietnamese. Eyeglasses, fashionable suits, neck ties, and Samsonite briefcases constituted the specific appearance of a businessman and a new politician in South Vietnam in the early 1970s. The image of a pale and skinny revolutionary with an unshaved chin in the revolutionary and romantic eras was replaced by a fat, tall, handsome, and open-minded politician with a large face and big ears, who loved sports and movies.

6

The New Owners
of South Vietnam

The Saigon government was unhappy with the Paris Agreement. But it consoled itself by believing that the Americans wouldn't abandon South Vietnam. South Vietnam claimed to be the anti–Communist bastion in Southeast Asia. The Americans wouldn't abandon it for they had spent a lot of money in the Vietnam War. They had huge installations in Cam Ranh Bay, Chu Lai, and Da Nang. They wouldn't shut their eyes and let the Communists take over South Vietnam. Some South Vietnamese hoped that the visit of President Nixon to Beijing and Moscow in 1972 would ensure the existence of the Republic of Vietnam.

President Thieu worried about his presidential seat in the new political circumstances. Was it good for him to execute the Paris Agreement? What would happen if he violated it? What would happen if Hanoi resumed its attacks?

The Paris Agreement had nothing good for President Thieu and was detrimental to the Saigon government. The American and allied troops left South Vietnam while the North Vietnamese troops stayed there. In the past the South Vietnamese troops fought beside the American and allied troops and received American aid regularly. After 1973 they fought alone. American aid decreased and got more and more uncertain. Would the South Vietnamese troops contain the North Vietnamese and Viet Cong militants efficiently without any help from Washington?

The Communists had many advantages. The Paris Agreement gave them enough time to strengthen their forces in the occupied areas of South Vietnamese territory. The Communists didn't worry about the return of American troops and their aerial interventions. The United States faced a series of domestic problems. The Paris Agreement helped the Americans end their involvement in the Vietnam war. President Gerald Ford continued the policy of disengagement in Vietnam.

In 1975 North Vietnamese troops used Soviet T-54 tanks to attack the South Vietnamese army. The Communists had occupied Phuoc Long in early January 1975 and Ban Me Thuot in March 1975. A French correspondent was killed at the national police headquarters for spreading the news of the fall of Ban Me Thuot. President Thieu ordered the retreat of South Vietnamese troops from the plateau to the littoral plains. During the retreat they suffered many casualties due to Communist raids. Da Nang and Hue became the target of the Communist attacks. Da Nang was an important military base. People thought that there would be a bloody battle there. In reality, the resistance of the South Vietnamese troops was negligible. The evacuation was tragic and chaotic at the airport and at the harbor. People pushed one another to get into the airplanes and battleships. They mugged, shot, and killed one another. The soldiers were demoralized after the so-called strategic evacuation. The Communists conquered Da Nang, the largest and the most important city of the First Tactical Region, without any difficulty.

Nha Trang, another important base and a city in the Second Tactical Region, was empty nine days before the Communists took it over. Road 1, winding along the coast of Central Vietnam, was full of military trucks, buses, cars, motorcycles, and evacuees.

The death of the French correspondent at the national police headquarters angered the Paris government. President Thieu was domestically and internationally lonely. He was pressured to resign. Some believed strongly that his resignation would lead to peace. General Duong Van Minh (Big Minh) was deemed to be the leader of the silent majority, the third faction. Some thought that national reconciliation would be easier if he replaced President Thieu.

In early April 1975 Prime Minister Tran Thien Khiem resigned. The Speaker of the House, Nguyen Ba Can, was appointed prime minister by President Nguyen Van Thieu. Nguyen Ba Can, a graduate of the Dalat Ecole d'Administration, had been deputy chief of Dinh Tuong province before being elected representative. His premiership was so short that few Vietnamese knew him or his ministers. Nguyen Van Hao was still deputy prime minister in charge of the economy.

In mid–April 1975 Dinh Doc Lap was bombarded by a pro–Communist pilot, Nguyen Thanh Trung. After the bombing he flew to Phuoc Long. A few days later, President Thieu resigned. Vice President Tran Van Huong became president, but Thieu's opponents weren't satisfied. They said that Thieu resigned but his hard line still existed. In their opinion, with Tran Van Huong as president, South Vietnam kept on having Thieu's regime without Thieu.

Everybody was eager to know the "que sera sera" of South Vietnam.

"What will happen next in this political situation?" the first man asked.

"Everything will be OK if General Thieu resigns. 'These gentlemen' [the Viet Cong] fought for the execution of the Paris Agreement," the second man replied.

"General Thieu resigned. But we have no peace. According to the Communists, peace comes only when they take over South Vietnam," the third man retorted angrily.

"General Thieu resigned. But his successor is his vice president. Nothing is new," the second man said.

"It is said that the American and North Vietnamese leaders concluded a secret agreement dividing Vietnam into three zones. North Vietnam is the Democratic Republic of Vietnam [Communist]. The Republic of South Vietnam [Viet Cong] stretches from the 17th Parallel to the 13th Parallel. The rest belongs to the Republic of Vietnam. Hanoi is the capital of the Democratic Republic of Vietnam, Hue the capital of the Republic of South Vietnam, and Saigon the capital of the Republic of Vietnam," the first man said, trying to be optimistic.

"The Republic of Vietnam will be the loser, won't it?" the fourth man asked.

"It has the portion of land stretching from the 13th Parallel to the Mekong Delta," the first man said.

"I have a headache because of all these rumors. It is said that South Vietnam will be neutral, that France mediates between the warring factions, that the Vietnamese solve their own problems, and that there will be a coalition government. You see, all of the South Vietnamese officials fled by air or by sea without fearing that their property would be confiscated by Nguyen Van Hao. If you want to leave, try to find a way. Don't waste time arguing. The Communists will stop fighting only when they take over South Vietnam," the third man said.

President Thieu, Prime Minister Khiem, and their families left Vietnam secretly. The Communists attacked Long Khanh to pave the path for their march to Saigon. The air force of the Republic of Vietnam had to drop CBU bombs to stop their advance. Many Communist soldiers were killed. It was expensive for them to put pressure upon the Saigon government by attacking Long Khanh and Bien Hoa. They used Long Thanh as a shortcut to reach the capital of the Republic of Vietnam without facing any fierce resistance from South Vietnamese troops. Other Communist troops used Roads 1 and 13 to put Saigon in their pincers.

President Tran Van Huong resigned. A few days before, he had refused to resign in favor of General Duong Van Minh. He was applauded by the representatives when he said, "Power is not a handkerchief in the pocket I can give you [General Minh]."

That night, the Communists shelled Saigon. Many generals, senators, representatives, officers, and civil servants sought to leave Saigon. The next day, the congress accepted the resignation of President Tran Van Huong. General Duong Van Minh took office on April 28, 1975. Senator Nguyen Van Huyen became his vice president. Senator Vu Van Mau was prime minister without a transfer of power for Prime Minister Nguyen Ba Can had left Saigon.

During the inaugural ceremony of President Duong Van Minh the Communists bombed Tan Son Nhut Airport. South Vietnam was at the point of death. The voice of President Minh wasn't firm. It was interrupted by bomb explosions at the airport. The Saigonese were anxious and fearful about what would happen in the days to come.

Agrégé Vu Van Mau was a university professor and former minister of foreign affairs under President Ngo Dinh Diem. At the sunset of the regime, he turned against President Diem, shaved his head, and planned to go to India as a pilgrim. As a result, he was supported by the An Quang Buddhist Church when he ran for senator under the symbol of the lotus. His cabinet was composed of many young ministers who were noted for their antigovernment stands. Representative Ly Qui Chung became the minister of information.

On April 28 Communist troops encircled Saigon. The chief of Binh Duong province planned to build a series of earthworks to prevent the Communist tanks from entering the capital. Former vice president Nguyen Cao Ky said that he had stayed in South Vietnam to fight the Communists and that he had 50,000 gunmen in Saigon ready to execute his orders. President Thieu had called on his soldiers to fight to the death. In his resignation address he denounced the United States for abandoning its ally and vowed to fight the Communists as a soldier. Not long afterward, President Thieu, Prime Minister Tran Thien Khiem, Prime Minister Nguyen Ba Can, and General Cao Van Vien left Saigon. Former vice president Nguyen Cao Ky had the same promise but he couldn't keep it. He was in a hurry to leave Saigon, which was being besieged by the Red Army. Some soldiers kept on fighting to their deaths for fear of being brought to the martial court.

The U.S. Embassy in Saigon, Tan Son Nhut Airport, and the Saigon wharf were crowded, noisy, and chaotic on April 28, 29, and 30. On the morning of April 30, Communist troops and tanks arrived in Saigon. A Communist tank with a big National Liberation Front flag hit the gate of Dinh Doc Lap (Independence Palace). President Duong Van Minh surrendered to the Communists. As a high-ranking officer in the presidential palace at that time, Colonel Bui Tin, deputy editor of *Quan Doi Nhan Dan* (The People's Army), the North Vietnamese army newspaper, accepted his capitulation.

American ambassador Martin left Saigon safely a couple of hours before the fall of the Republic of Vietnam. In the United States President Ford and Secretary of State Kissinger, coauthor of the Paris Agreement, were indifferent when learning of the fall of South Vietnam. The American involvement in South Vietnam had ended. No American was killed by the Communists in

April 1975. No American airplane was shot down. No angry South Vietnamese soldier shot any Americans.

In Paris the fall of the Republic of Vietnam didn't surprise anybody. Those who turned to Paris believed in a "pink regime." Their belief was consolidated when President Giscard d'Estaing appealed to the French immigrants to stay in South Vietnam. General Vanuxem, who had served in Vietnam during the Franco-Vietnamese War, came to Saigon to advise President Duong Van Minh on how to save the dying Republic of Vietnam. It was too late.

Like Washington and Paris, Beijing wasn't excited about the fall of South Vietnam. Didn't Beijing force Ho Chi Minh to accept the partition at the Geneva Conference in 1954? China wouldn't have any advantage with the unity of Vietnam.

Radio Hanoi and Radio Giai Phong talked endlessly about the Communist victory under the direction of the Communist party and the leadership of "Great Uncle Ho." The Vietnamese Communists' haughtiness irritated the People's Republic of China, the Soviet Union, and other Communist countries in Eastern Europe. The Vietnamese Communists were proud of beating the "American imperialists," the "international *gendarmes.*" Wild with victory, they insisted that they would "defeat any enemies regardless of their greatness or origin."

These haughty words displeased China and the Soviet Union as well. The Vietnamese Communists were showing disrespect to their former "masters" and givers. Advocating "peaceful coexistence" with the United States, Khrushchev hadn't favored the liberation of South Vietnam for fear of a confrontation with the "paper tiger with nuclear teeth." In 1957 Moscow had suggested that the United Nations accept both Vietnams as members.

Mao Zedong had launched the Cultural Revolution to eradicate all of his adversaries who had been his comrades in the 1930s. He had called the United States a "paper tiger." But in 1972 he became very friendly with the "paper tiger," which was less dangerous than the northern white bear.

Enlightened by Marxism-Leninism Ho Chi Minh accepted neither revisionism nor Maoism. He disliked Mao's Cultural Revolution. He led his disciples to reunify the country by force to show his independence and to present a *fait accompli* to the Soviet Union and the People's Republic of China.

Most foreign observers thought wrongly that Mao had given birth to the "people's war" without knowing that, since the birth of Vietnam, the Vietnamese had used it to resist and defeat Chinese invaders. In the fifteen century Le Loi, with the active assistance of Dr. Nguyen Trai, defeated the Chinese after ten years of resistance. Ho Chi Minh followed his path, using the same tactics and strategy to defeat the French and to confront the Americans in South Vietnam.

China, Korea, and Germany were partitioned. Chinese Communists couldn't take over Taiwan by force due to the presence of the American Seventh

Fleet in the Pacific Ocean. In 1950 North Korea had failed to reunify Korea by force. East and West Germany managed to avoid ideological war and civil war. They realized that war would lead to national destruction and disunion. In 1989 Germany was peacefully reunified.

After April 1975 Vietnam became a Communist country and a military power in the Communist bloc. The Vietnamese Communists were extremely faithful to Stalinism and supported the Soviet repression in Poland, Hungary, and Czechoslovakia in 1956 and 1968. They didn't praise Khrushchev's "destalinization."

In 1975 former French Indochina became Communist. The Communist victory in the Indochinese peninsula encouraged Angola, Ethiopia, and Nicaragua to join the Communist world. Cuba sent its troops to Africa while the Vietnamese *bo doi* invaded Cambodia. From the 1960s until the collapse of the Soviet Union in 1991, Cuba and Vietnam showed themselves faithful to the world's "socialist bastion" (the Soviet Union) by doing their "international duties" and contributing to the growth of orthodox Communism in the world.

I was thirty-five years old in 1975. When I was five years of age, my father had faced a big challenge. Thirty years later, I had the same problem as he did. April 30 marked a big change in my life. Unpredictably, it separated me from my country forever.

As a South Vietnamese I shared the loss with the Saigon government.

On May 1, I sought to contact my relatives and friends in Saigon. I made a tour around Saigon, Gia Dinh, Quan Tre, Hoc Mon, and Thu Duc. I saw the red flags and those of the National Liberation Front everywhere. The Communist *bo doi* watched the passersby coldly. But they were well disciplined. I heard deafening songs and voices on the air. The traffic was in disorder for lack of police and regulatory lights. Everybody looked fearful, but they claimed to be excited and waved to the *bo doi* on the military trucks or tanks. Some Saigonese civilians wore red ribbons. They seemed to be very busy. They were in a hurry to shuttle from one street to another. They were Communist sympathizers living in the city. Maybe they paid taxex to the Viet Cong. They were possibly draft dodgers or local opportunists. Some hung pictures of Ho Chi Minh on the walls. Some Chinese Vietnamese hoisted the red flag of the People's Republic of China in Cholon. Some elderly people told about the Communist revolt in Nam Ky in 1940. They said they knew many revolutionaries during World War II. They called Nguyen Thi Minh Khai, who was from a revolutionary and Communist family, Co Hai Bac Ky. In the 1930s she was sent to the Soviet Union. Her husband was Le Hong Phong, a commissar of the Comintern. Her sister was the first wife of General Vo Nguyen Giap. She died heroically in a colonial prison. Minh Khai's teacher was Tran Phu, the first general secretary of the Indochinese Communist party. Le Hong Phong and Nguyen Thi Minh Khai were killed by the French. We had two heroines, Nguyen Thi Bac and Nguyen Thi Giang, in the Viet Nam Quoc Dan Dang. In the Indochinese Communist party we had Nguyen Thi Minh Khai and her sister, Nguyen Thi Minh Giang. Many Communist party members were killed after the revolt plunged the country into blood and fire. Some talked about Huynh Tan Phat, Mai Van Bo, and Huynh Van Tieng in the Autumn Revolution (1945). Some Saigonese were proud of their relatives who had adhered to the Communist party in the 1930s and 1940s. They guessed they would hold important positions in North Vietnam. A famous professor of sciences in Saigon showed his passport, saying that he had decided to stay in Saigon to serve the country. He kept his word.

In northwest Saigon, on Road 1, some South Vietnamese tanks and military trucks were burned. The quadrilateral surrounding Quang Trung Military Training Center was full of military clothes, boots, steel helmets, and T-shirts. A bloody dismembered man was thrown on a communal route near Hoc Mon district. How in pain the victim was. He puffed and blew before leaving the world. This was the beginning of Communist vengeance aimed at policemen, informers, spies, and intelligence service agents.

All the professors in Thu Duc University village were expelled. Their villas were requisitioned by the revolutionary government. A year later, the Communist cadres returned them to their former owners after having dismantled all the conveniences.

Laithieu, a quiet city during thirty years of war, witnessed a short exchange of fire between *bo doi* and a fleet of military trucks of the 25th Division on Road 13. In fifteen minutes many military trucks and some tanks were destroyed in Binh Nham, Tan Thoi, and Phu Long. Many South Vietnamese soldiers died. The Communists didn't help the wounded, who were exposed to the sun. They were thirsty and in pain. They groaned and asked for water. But nobody dared to take care of them. They died slowly under the torrid sunlight on Road 13. No soldier from the fleet of military trucks survived. When their bodies got rotten, the local people's committee ordered the residents to collect and bury them. Some *bo doi* were killed or wounded in the clash. Their companions roared awfully.

A grenade exploded as a Communist soldier tried to open the door of the Tan Thoi Communal Office. *Bo doi* then burned down this building, a vestige of the oldest French architecture in the city.

The Communist *bo doi* captured a drug addict who had cursed Ho Chi Minh and lowered the liberation flag. They planned to shoot him at the flag pole to show their iron discipline, but the mother of the drug addict asked them to spare her son's life. The drug addict was imprisoned before being sent to a reeducation camp.

One Viet Cong tied a military security service agent to a coach. The victim ran behind the coach until he was worn out and then he was dragged on the road. He died but his family didn't know where he was buried. Another Viet Cong sowed panic by shooting in the air. Then he began searching some wealthy houses along Road 13 to loot jewelry and money. Nobody said a word. The losers were looted and humiliated by the winners.

Some differences between the *bo doi* and the Viet Cong were visible. The *bo doi* were the true winners. The Viet Cong only shared their victory but they behaved as true victors. The Viet Cong couldn't have defeated the armed forces of the Republic of Vietnam without the *bo doi*. The latter looked well disciplined while the former were arrogant and greedy.

On afternoon of May 1, I saw my brother in Saigon. We talked about our futures.

"What do you think about this situation?" my brother asked me.

"We are in a desperate situation. Let's think about what to say and what to do in the very near future. Thieu's regime was corrupt but it gave us opportunities to live. On the contrary, the Communist regime is going to get rid of us any way they can. Last January I received your letter from France. I was in a hurry to write to you, asking you to stay there to 'wait and see' at least until July. You were eager to return to Saigon. Now we all are in the trap," I said.

"I know. I was eager to return to Saigon after learning of the fall of Phuoc Long. I was afraid that my wife couldn't take care of our eight children. On the 28th I planned to leave. Unfortunately one of my children had scarlet fever, and I had to bring him to the hospital. That day most doctors left Saigon, while others stayed home or sought to leave before the Communists came," my brother said.

"In the days to come the Communists will send military and civil servants to concentration camps for brainwashing. Physical and moral punishment will make the detainees bloody, sweaty, and tearful. Can you move to another place to avoid the mass punishment?" I asked my brother.

My brother looked anxious. Instead of answering my question he asked me, "How about you?"

"It's easy for me," I replied.

"What do you mean by that?"

"I'm sincere but not naïve and stupid."

After this short conversation with my brother, I left his house to see my former teacher and some friends of mine in Saigon.

My teacher had studied in France in the 1920s and then lived there for thirty years. His life was miserable in Paris during the economic depression and World War II. When the Germans occupied the capital of France, he was sent to Berlin as a laborer. He returned to France after the Germans lost the war. The French suspected him of collaborating with the Germans. Fortunately, they didn't have any evidence to bring him to court.

My teacher was a virtuous man. Born to a rich family and having experienced a long difficult time in France he was very altruistic. His happiness and joy was teaching and helping others, working out the spirit of "Il y a une espèce de honte d'être heureux à la vue d'une certaine misère" (There is a sort of shame to be happy in the sight of certain misery). During his three decades in France he knew many Vietnamese students who became important persons in South Vietnam in the 1950s, 1960s and 1970s, like Ngo Dinh Nhu, Tran Van Trai, Trinh Dinh Thao, Nguyen Van Kiet, Chau Long, and Pham Hoang Ho.

Ngo Dinh Nhu graduated from the famous Ecole des Chartes.

Tran Van Trai received doctoral degrees in both law and arts.

Nguyen Van Kiet was the minister of education of the Republic of South Vietnam.

Pham Hoang Ho, a doctor in physics and an *agrégé* of biology, served as president of the University of Can Tho and as minister of education.

Chau Long, a doctor of history, was director of the cabinet of the Ministry of Agriculture.

My teacher refused any involvement in political activities. He preferred education to politics. He used to help needy people without thinking that they would abuse his kindness. He ignored tricksters who triedf to deceive him, taking advantage of his compassion. He never thought about the advantages and disadvantages of his services. Some deemed that he was pro–Communist. His wife and he were of opposite characters. However, they lived together happily. One day during Tet, his wife and he were arguing with each other about his excessive way of spending money when I arrived.

"You just had 100,000 piastres in your pocket. For what did you spend 100,000 piastres in an hour?" his wife asked.

"I gave it to the taxicab and pedicab drivers in front of our house to wish them good luck and happy new year. They are poor. They have to work hard to earn their living even on Tet. On this occasion, I helped their families with a little lucky money. We are happy. We had better think of needy people," he said.

One day, my teacher and I were walking along Nguyen Trung Truc Street. I was surprised to see the taxi and pedicab drivers saluting him politely.

"Good morning, Ong Nam," they greeted him.

They called him "Old Nam" because they knew neither his name nor his profession. They had heard my teacher's neighbors call him Ong Nam.

My teacher used to wear sandals and a three-pocket shirt. He rarely left the house, but every time he did, he had at least 50,000 piastres in his pocket. While we were walking and talking, a man ran to us.

"Good morning, Old Nam. How are you?" the man greeted us.

"Good morning. I am fine," my teacher replied.

"My family is in need of money. I have this to sell. I would like Old Nam to have it. Old Nam has a car. You need these tools to repair it, when necessary. I am unhappy to sell them."

My teacher didn't know how to fix a car. But he couldn't let the touching words of the man go in one ear and out the other.

"How much is this tool set?" he asked the taxi driver.

"Ong Nam can give me as much as you like. My family is in need of money," the man said.

"I will give your family 50,000 piastres, but I don't need this tool set. I am not a car repairman," my teacher said.

"Old Nam, I can't lie to you. If you don't take this set home, I don't dare to take your money," the man said.

My teacher gave him 50,000 piastres and took the small box of rusted screwdrivers, pliers, hammers, and cutting wheels. I carried it for him. He looked at me, saying, "I bought it so that his family has some money. I don't know how to use the tools." As soon as he came home, he said to his wife with joy, "Honey, I just bought these tools from a taxi driver."

"How much?" his wife asked.

"Fifty thousand piastres," he replied.

"Oh, my God! Why did you buy these rusted pieces of iron at that price?"

"His family is in need of money. I suggested giving him 50,000 piastres without taking these things but he looked unhappy about my suggestion."

"Fifty thousand piastres isn't a big amount. The danger is that you trust everybody blindly and automatically. What did you get these things for? Can you fix your car? If they are stolen things, you will have problems. Anybody can cry famine," his wife said angrily.

"It isn't so serious, honey," my teacher consoled himself.

I will never forget my sweet, generous, sinless teacher. He lived harmoniously with people of different levels of education and character, ideology and social class. He didn't have the appearance of a fervent Buddhist, Catholic, or Confucian, but he carried out Buddhist benevolence, Christian charity, and Confucian brotherhood. He neither accused his wife of selfishness nor disliked those people who didn't share his opinions and actions. He didn't pay attention to superficial criticisms or congratulations, for his goodness was innate. It wasn't led by concern for honor or self-interest. It illuminated him. It made him immortal in my mind and heart.

He liked me. Our relationship changed from master-disciple to friendship, as he predicted. He was very sincere, pure, and simple. He kept away from the political arena at any cost. Once, in France, his friends introduced him to a rich and beautiful lady, who was in widowhood after the sudden death of her husband, a famous medical doctor in Nam Bo. He thanked them without thinking about marrying her. He told me that there was no common ground between him and her. He was in his forties while she was young, beautiful, charming, and accustomed to luxury.

Asked about Ho Chi Minh, he just said, "His eyes are bright." That was his feeling when seeing Ho Chi Minh for the first time in Paris in 1946.

In 1965 I stopped by his house and learned that he had been arrested by the police for signing a peace petition. I had arrived just as he was released. I asked him why he had signed. He answered my question with innocence: "A friend of mine invited me for lunch in memory of his parents. Many of the guests were my friends. When the lunch was almost over, they passed a peace petition with all the signatures of the guests. I was the last person they invited to sign. I was a little embarrassed. I would have been a coward if I refused to sign. So I signed."

Then he added, "One of the guests said, 'What's wrong with the peace petition? We have nothing to be scared of. Do we prefer war to peace?'"

Whether I agreed or not, I understood that he was on the horns of a dilemma.

General Nguyen Van Thieu was chief of state then. He smiled when seeing my teacher's name on the peace petition. He said to my teacher's wife, · "Don't worry. I see his name on the peace petition. Leave him there [in prison] a couple of days. He will be released."

My teacher was in jail for a week. Having kept far away from political activities, he was imprisoned on account of political affairs. I shared his suffering. As for him, he remained indifferent. He didn't get angry with those people who arrested him. He didn't curse his friends for pushing him into jail either. He thanked Chief of State Nguyen Van Thieu for saving his freedom. But he wasn't involved in the political dispute between the Communists and the Nationalists.

In 1975 one of his brothers looked for him after fifty years of separation. Both brothers burst into tears. They hadn't seen each other for fifty years. One brother had adhered to the Indochinese Communist party while his younger brother was studying in France. The younger brother spent thirty years in a foreign land. When he returned to Vietnam, his brother had gone to the North. Then, the brother appeared suddenly. He came to see his younger brother in his seventies. His younger brother tried to give him some money, but he refused to receive it without any explanation. He didn't say what he was doing or where he was living. After this visit, he never came back to see his younger brother, who died in 1979.

My teacher was very happy to see me on May 1, 1975, in Saigon. He knew a lot about me. He loved me and my family. He knew that the new regime would give me many troubles, and he worried about my freedom and safety. He didn't say it frankly but he insisted that I had better see him regularly.

After the fall of Saigon all of his money in the bank was blocked. He had to "offer" his properties to the revolutionary government, but he kept his cool temper. That didn't mean he accepted the Communist policy. He had his own view about the precariousness of our earthly life.

That evening one of my childhood friends came to see me after twenty years of separation. We hadn't seen each other for twenty years. I made my living by teaching. He practiced medicine. Sometimes I lived in Saigon. Sometimes I lived in Laithieu. My friend lived far away from Saigon.

I faced many challenges in the course of my life. However, my life didn't have more vicissitudes than my friend's. His father died when he was seven years of age. His mother sold kerosene and vegetable oil at the market so she could support him and his sister. In such a humble and lonely life, my friend turned to religion in search of consolation. When a student, he would fast. He accepted any difficulties and social injustices with patience and courage. I was his only friend in Laithieu. Unlike the other children, I neither despised his poverty nor bullied him although he was a weak and fearful child.

At one time, he was head of the health department in a remote district of Binh Duong province. A few years later, he left this post for Thu Duc Military Academy. After the training all of his colleagues were assigned as officers to their former medical posts except for him. He never complained about his exceptional treatment. In 1975, in the reeducation camps, the Communists, in their turn, accused him of being an anti–Communist fanatic for preferring fighting to healing patients.

My friend saw me on the day Berlin was besieged, as VOA repeated many times before the fall of Saigon. We drank strong tea before walking to the bridge across the Saigon River that linked Binh Duong and Gia Dinh provinces. We walked and talked as if we didn't have any worries. The Communist *bo doi* in their loose uniforms wore Binh Tri Thien sandals made from car tires. They looked serious with their AK-47s, watching people walking. Between them and the folks, there was a certain distance although they weren't as arrogant as the Viet Cong. We neither hated nor feared them. They did their duty while we were walking to the Saigon River to enjoy the fresh air of peace. Arriving at the bank of the river, we began to talk about our futures.

"Do you think that the situation is reversible?" my friend asked.

"It's too soon to think about it. I'm a little pessimistic about the reversibility of the situation by force. Nobody can do it. Nobody needs another war," I said.

"I agree with you. So far, no Communist country has been defeated and become capitalist."

"The Communist government controls its people rigidly. No revolt is possible in a Communist country, but that doesn't mean the Communists are invincible. In reality, they are economically unsuccessful. As a result, their people are poor and worry about the food, clothes, and daily lives. In this matter the Communist regimes can't hide their undeniable weakness."

"South Vietnam was in tatters, and it still took time for the Communists to take it over. That proves they aren't eagles," my friend said.

We jumped from one topic to another. Sometimes we felt pessimistic. Sometimes we felt optimistic.

It was dark. We walked home slowly with confusing thoughts in our minds.

My friend considered me his advisor. In reality, I admired his tenacity, endurance, acceptance, and adaptation to circumstances. In the reeducation camp he lived on the meager food provided by the Communists and on the snakes or rats he caught. His mother was old and had her chronic asthma. She stopped selling kerosene and vegetable oil at the market before 1975. Her son took care of her. Detained in the reeducation camp, he couldn't look after her. His mother had a miserable life at home. Her daughter-in-law carried all the family burden by selling fried bananas. Seriously underfed, all the members of the family were at risk of tuberculosis. They had no money to go to the reeducation camp to see my friend and to supply him with decent food. He had no visitors in the camp while the other detainees had food supplied by their families. They also had a list of Communist relatives in their backgrounds while my friend had nothing to write. His curriculum vitae was very simple. His relatives were his mother, sister, wife, and three children. However, he didn't feel lonely. He wasn't displeased with his lot. He tried to accomplish his duties in the camp and to improve his skill at killing snakes and catching rats to have some meat. People are usually scared of snakes, which are dangerous and a sign of bad news and bad luck. But these poisonous reptiles were scared of the reeducation detainees like my friend. Every time they saw a snake, they chased and sought to kill it any way they could. Snakes and rats supplied the Communists' victims with their meat.

In 1980 my friend was released. He came to see me. We talked about our adaptation to the new regime and about keeping ourselves healthy under difficult conditions.

In the past my friend had been unfairly treated by the old regime. He stayed in the army while all of his colleagues left their uniforms for their medical practices. When the Communists came, they retained most teachers and physicians in their posts, but after being released, my friend faced the same situation he had before 1975. The two opposite regimes had made the same decision. In other words, the same person had the same fate in two different circumstances.

At that time the Communist government encouraged the South Vietnamese to copycat the North Vietnamese farmers and use human waste as fertilizer. The local government made toilet bowls in Phu Van to sell them to farmers to save human waste. My friend worked there as a laborer and got paid two new piastres per day (1 new piastre = 500 old piastres). The local government had to deal with the reaction from the South Vietnamese farmers, who refused to fertilize their fields with human waste. It was a big loss for the local government. The production of toilet bowls ended. My friend was unemployed. He had to make his living by carrying charcoal he bought from the new economic areas and sold in Ho Chi Minh City.

Carrying charcoal is a hard work. A small quantity of charcoal couldn't ensure his daily needs. If the weight of the charcoal was over 400 pounds, he couldn't ride. The bike would be broken. He didn't ride on the highway but in the forest, along the springs, and on the sandy paths in the remote areas. Like other charcoal carriers he chose the longest and the most dangerous itinerary in the hope of avoiding the local militia. The latter could confiscate his bike and charcoal and detain him. In that case his family would sleep hungry.

Most charcoal carriers were military or civil servants who had spent some years in the reeducation camps. After their release they made their living with their muscles and sweat for the rest of their lives in a country that was bloody in wartime, sweaty and tearful in Communist peacetime. The Communists humiliated them in the reeducation camps, separated them from their families, and plunged them into tragic and desperate situations. It wasn't enough. They didn't kill them, but they impoverished them and their families, refused education for their children, and sent them to despair and slow death. Humiliations stunned them. Hopelessness dazed them and made them nervous. My friend was among these miserable victims of the new regime. His family relied on his illegal labor. His asthmatic mother had neither medicine nor nutritional food. His daily income couldn't ensure meaty meals for his family. They used to have boiled, salted, or fried bindweed every day. Rice was expensive. Most people cooked rice mixed with sweet potatoes, cassava, beans, or sorghum. Age, anxieties, and a shortage of food and medicine brought his old mother closer to death. I suggested that he think about traditional Vietnamese medicine. He had no choice. Fortunately, it helped. His worries about his mother's asthma decreased. He began to help me fertilize my garden of medicinal plants.

Threatened by poverty and starvation, my friend let his oldest son quit school to help him carry charcoal. The other son wandered on the streets, along the rivers, and around the dumps to collect plastic bags. The father was physically and morally punished. His children didn't get an education. They lived their futureless lives with other children, struggling for survival.

7

Communist Peace

The Communists took over South Vietnam. Since that time rural people haven't heard the blasts of bombs, rockets or the whistle of bullets. They don't see the flares at night anymore. Urban residents are no longer scared of Communist shelling.

A returnee, who had been a Viet Cong physician, said to me, "There won't be burglars and gangs. You can sleep safely without closing the doors."

In 1974 I had heard something similar from the general director of a state-run factory in Thu Duc. After the fall of Saigon I heard the Communist cadres repeating this idea several times at meetings as if they would like to show their authority and efficacy.

I verified if the Communist propaganda was accurate by drying clothes at night. Nothing happened the two first nights. On the third night all the clothes were gone. The burglars didn't fear the revolutionaries.

Prostitution stepped down temporarily on April 30. Not long afterward, it sped up unbelievably.

All the residents were awakened every morning by deafening songs broadcast from the Hall of Information. The local cadres woke them up by knocking at their doors and asking them to do physical exercises. I heard "The Party Gives Us the Spring," "From This City He Left," and "March on Saigon." Then a Communist singer sang "Ho Chi Minh, the Most Beautiful Name." To Lan Phuong, a female singer of the party, was sorrowful in "Visit to Uncle Ho's Native Land." The loudspeaker was busy all day long with a series of announcements. The word "registration" became most familiar to the South Vietnamese after the collapse of South Vietnam. Soldiers, officers, civil servants, businessmen, landowners, and farmers must present themselves at the People's Committee for registration. A son of a neighborhood chief was bitten by a dog. The People's Committee then asked all the residents to register the dogs they raised.

All the public offices were open. The civil servants presented themselves at their old offices to receive new instructions from the new government. They got paid based on their old salaries and shared rationed food with the Communist cadres and the employees who took over the government offices before they were sent to the reeducation camps.

Saigon was renamed Ho Chi Minh City. Binh Duong became Binh Thu, then Song Be. Gia Dinh province was annexed to Ho Chi Minh City. The local government was changed to the People's Committee; *quan* (district) was changed to *huyen* like in feudal times; chiefs of the provinces and of the districts were called chairmen of the People's Committee. Most of the cadres taking over South Vietnam were Viet Cong (NLF) or North Vietnamese Communists who had fought in the South. The Viet Cong became Cadres B while the Communists from North Vietnam were Cadres A.

The flag of the Democratic Republic of Vietnam was displayed beside the NLF flag. The picture of Ho Chi Minh was displayed in every household. Some people put it at the front door. Some put it on the altar with a flowerpot and an incense burner. When talking about Uncle Ho, all the Communist cadres choked up. Tears flooded from their eyes like the poet To Huu, a Vietnamese Gorki, wept in his poem when learning of Stalin's death in 1953. When talking about Uncle Ho, they bowed their heads to show respect and sorrow toward their eminent leader. They never forgot their adjectives, such as "very lovely," "great Uncle Ho," and "great President Ho," and some of his favorite slogans were found everywhere in Vietnam, from the Presidential Palace in Hanoi to the open markets in the mountainous regions:

> Nothing is more precious than independence and freedom.
> Vietnam is an indivisible country
> The Vietnamese people are inseparable.
> The rivers would dry up.
> The mountains would be eroded.
> But that truth should be unchanged.
> South Vietnam is in my heart.

The Viet Cong and the *bo doi* looked proud of their uniforms, their *dep rau* (rubber Binh Tri Thien sandals), and their cotton hats. Female cadres were in black *ao ba ba* with long, striped scarves. They looked more dogmatic, enthusiastic, and fanatical than the males. All of them were pale. Their eyes were roguish. It seemed that they were surrounded by enemies not by friends. They were cautious when eating something in the presence of strangers for fear of poison. When someone invited them to a wedding ceremony or to the anniversary of the death of his relatives, they severely chastised the host about his luxurious life. The new regime fined those families that had big wedding ceremonies or funerals. The fine was called "stupid money." Most South Vietnamese were ready to be fined instead of simplifying the wedding ceremonies and funerals of their relatives. To the Vietnamese they are the most important events in their lives.

The Communist cadres used aggressive words. They spoke of their enemies roughly. They called the members of the Communist party "comrades." They used rude words for the South Vietnamese leaders, such as "poor Diem," "poor Thieu," "poor Minh," and "poor Americans."

The North Vietnamese Communist cadres talked about the prosperity and industrialization of North Vietnam. They spoke so fluently that everybody thought that they were educated men. Their reading and handwriting unveiled their limited education. Cadres A (from North Vietnam) were scientific liars and talkative. They hurt the South Vietnamese and Cadres B (Viet Cong, NLF) as well. Their lives reflected their poor knowledge and the material shortages in the North. A *bo doi* said that the streets in North Vietnam were flooded with "Honda milk." He said this after seeing the sign "Sua Honda" (Honda Repair) in a South Vietnamese city. In Vietnamese, *sua* means "to fix, to repair" (verb), but *sua* also means "milk" (noun). Our dear *bo doi* misunderstood the meaning of the sign, thinking that *sua* meant "milk" and that "Honda" was the milk brand.

Bo doi and cadres A and B liked to watch television and to listen to the radio. In the first months of liberation *bo doi* went to market to buy purses, watches, and radio sets. They preferred watches with "windows" (date) and "three pilots" (three hands). Many Saigonese and provincial hawkers got rich by selling used watches and radio sets to the *bo doi* and the *can bo* (cadres). The photographers made much money as every *bo doi* wanted to have some color pictures taken in South Vietnam. How did they have money? Their money came from different sources. Some sold gas they stole from tanks or military trucks. Others sold what they took from the South Vietnamese and American bases and military posts (barbed wire, tools, wood, steel, iron, aluminum sheets, chemical products, cement, bricks, clothes, cigarettes, cigarette papers, metal chairs, tables, etc.). Former noncommissioned officers of the air force and navy and civil servants retained by the new regime in their posts became useful to the Communist bosses. They helped the latter sell all the stuff they stole. People of the old regime were usually in charge of receiving and distributing necessities to cadres and employees in the government offices. They knew what was rare and expensive at the market, where to sell stuff, and how to report to their superior and colleagues. Some pleased their new bosses and became members of the Communist party. A noncommissioned officer of the South Vietnamese air force in Bien Hoa, reemployed by the new regime, enjoyed all the rights of a Communist cadre. His boss gave him 120 liters of gas per month (usually an employee owning a motorcycle had four liters of gas per month). His duty was to provide transportation to his boss from Bien Hoa to Cholon, where he sold some expensive stuff he had stolen from Bien Hoa Airport.

A sawmill owner in Binh Duong got richer after transferring his ownership to the local government. The Communist head of the sawmill didn't know how to manage it. The circular saw broke. He didn't know where to get a new one or how to weld it. But the old owner did. Only the Chinese Vietnamese in Cholon sold or welded circular saws. They didn't work with strangers, only with people they had known. The saw broke almost every three days. The Communist head asked the old owner of the sawmill to buy a new saw or to weld the old saw. The latter seized the opportunity to get some benefit from welding the saws. He pleased the Communist head by giving him some money. The sawmill didn't need a new saw. It needed only the welded ones so that both the Communist head and the old owner shared money every three days. The losses of the state-run sawmill were made up by the government.

One of my friends sold his house to live in the countryside. For lack of money and experience in farming, he spilled rice seeds instead of hiring workers to plant the paddies. His rice seedlings looked pretty. They attracted the attention of the local government, which was hungry for local economic merit. My inexperienced friend was invited to talk about the technique of sowing rice seeds without bedding out plants. He became a reluctant "agricultural hero" in the village he lived in. His family was still short of rice. They had to cook rice with sweet potatoes or sliced cassava.

Like other farmers following the instructions of the Communist government, my friend planted sorghum and cassava. After the harvest of sorghum, his wife and he didn't know how to husk it, so they used it to feed chickens. In 1977, 1978, 1979, and 1980, food shortages were serious in South Vietnam. Rice production regressed. Chickens died for lack of food and immunization. The South Vietnamese ate rice mixed with sweet potatoes, cassava, or barley donated by the European Economic Community and sold by the Communist cadres at the market. Hungry people stole cassava every night. Farmers spent a lot of time watching over their cassava fields. One night, as my friend patrolled his cassava, he heard noises being made by the wrongdoers. Discovering the presence of my friend in the dark, the burglars raised their voices, asking, "Who's that? What are you doing here at night?"

Keeping his cold temper, my friend said, "It's me. I'm very hungry. I came here to steal some cassava to fill my empty stomach."

Understanding his pitiful situation, the wrongdoers ordered, "Uproot some plants and take some roots!"

My friend uprooted some plants and got out of the cassava field as fast as possible.

Burglary techniques improved. The wrongdoers could uproot many hectares of peanuts in one night. That proved they were numerous and had enough means of transportation. Sometimes they uprooted cassava or cut sugar cane deep inside the fields, leaving some plants on the edges. The wrongdoers stole oxen, water buffaloes, pigs, dogs, cats, chickens, and ripened rice. They even excavated some new graves to steal coffins and materials.

Due to malnutrition people began to eat snails. At low tide they rushed to the rivers to catch fish, shrimp, and helixes. The Communist government encouraged them to raise dotted catfish. The Communist cadres said that they are good for eating and that they grow fast. These dotted catfish are omnivores. They like to eat stinking snails. The pisciculturists spent much money buying small catfish and their stinking food. In the course of their growth, the fish ate not only smelly food but also the other fish in the pond. After some months there were few fish left, but the heaviest one could weigh ten pounds. They are black with some red and yellow dots. The Vietnamese eat more fish than meat. But they are scared of big fish with strange colors. For that reason they wouldn't buy such an ugly kind of fish. The pisciculturists went bankrupt. Some of them became interested in planting medicinal plants. But the result was always negative.

Some areas in Saigon, Cholon, Gia Dinh, and Go Vap were ruined as the residents sold tiles, iron sheets, doors, windows, and the door frames of their houses before leaving the cities for the new economic areas. The families of the reeducation detainees were forced to move there. Most of them tried to live in the cities by selling cigarettes, tobacco, medicine, and rice at the flea markets. When the Communist police came, they ran and hid what they sold. They gave bribes to the neighborhood chiefs so they wouldn't have to go to the new economic areas and to the police to continue their activities at the flea markets.

The Communists controlled the circulation of goods rigorously. The Chinese Vietnamese tried to take advantage of the tough policies of the Communist government. Apparently they lost all of their businesses and were condemned by the new regime. Clandestinely they sold foreign cigarettes or chemicals. Many of them, who had paid taxes to the Viet Cong during the war, became "patriotic capitalists." Politically, they had no problems from the new government, but the revolutionary government gave capitalists and wealthy people many troubles when it issued the new bank notes. A new piastre was worth 500 old piastres. Each household had the right to change a maximum of 100,000 old piastres, which was only 200 new piastres. Those people connected with the local People's Committee could change an unlimited amount of old currency on the condition that the Communist cadres received 80 percent or 90 percent. Chinese Vietnamese businessmen had a big amount of money to stock cigarette paper, chemicals, gold, and diamonds, which weren't bulky but were expensive. The Chinese were born to be businessmen, skillful craftsmen, and hard-working laborers. They are wise, pragmatic, flexible, and quickly adapt to any circumstance. They didn't plant paddies but they sold rice and were rice granary owners. They didn't use fish sauce but they produced and distributed it. They didn't live in the rural areas but in the cities, along the river banks, along the coast, and on large streets. When the Manchus took control of China, the Chinese immigrants in Vietnam were called *Minh Huong* (countrymen of the Ming dynasty). China was among the Big Five in World War II. The Chinese immigrants were well treated by the French. China brought support to the Viet Minh during the Franco-Vietnamese War. In 1954 North Vietnam became Communist, and Chinese influence was politically and culturally important there too. Chinese immigrants were more numerous in the South than in the North. Their economic role was very important. When the South Vietnamese government collapsed, some of them became patriotic capitalists in the new regime, but the Communist policy wasn't favorable to their private enterprises. Many of them left Vietnam by boat. Some poor Chinese Vietnamese applied for repatriation. Relations between the People's Republic of China and the Socialist Republic of Vietnam turned sour in the late 1970s. Temporarily Vietnam wasn't the land of opportunity for the Chinese immigrants. Since 1988 their economic role has been soaring.

The Communists denounced trading. The South Vietnamese didn't protest their policy but they didn't believe it. Smuggling developed quickly in South Vietnam. Many women went to Nha Trang and Phan Thiet to buy seafood, which they sold in Bien Hoa, Di An, Thu Duc, Binh Loi, and Saigon. The former Chemin de Fer Trans-Indochinois was the seafood road. Road 4, leading to the Mekong Delta, was the rice road. It was also the ceramic road. People carried jars, pots, and plates from the pottery kilns in Laithieu to the Mekong Delta by bicycle. Foreign cigarettes and cigarette paper also reached Ho Chi Minh City along Road 4. It was lucrative to sell foreign cigarettes and cigarette paper. A ream of American cigarette paper was worth four to six taels of gold. The cigarette paper cutter charged 200 new piastres (⅕ tael of gold) per ream. The cigarette rollers needed chemicals to counterfeit foreign cigarettes. Sugar mills needed chemicals to whiten brown sugar. Soap producers needed chemicals to make expensive soap. It was time for the Communist heads to steal chemicals and cigarette paper and to sell them in Cholon. The whole country lacked everything while Cholon had everything.

In the rural areas the Communist cadres in charge of the collective and state farms stole fertilizer, plants, seeds, gas, and oil. Some tractor parts were stolen and sold at the junkyards in Cholon.

Latex rubber in Tay Ninh, Go Dau Ha, and Dau Tieng was stolen. It was used to make bicycle tires.

Expensive necessities in the state-run stores, such as fabrics, oil, sugar, kerosene, condensed milk, and monosodium glutamate, were always stolen. Fabric was expensive. Each household had the right to buy some feet of material per year. Some men who wore two-color shorts were warned by the Communist police against "dishonoring" the regime. Urban youngsters put on neither shoes nor socks. They seemed to lose the habit of getting dressed properly. In the rural and economic areas people were in rags. Many women used empty sand sacks to make their shorts.

During the Japanese occupation the Vietnamese were short of food and many kinds of necessities due to the war and the harsh policies of both France and Japan. There were neither war nor foreigners in Vietnam after 1975. The

Vietnamese people were punished and impoverished by the revolutionary government to become more obedient and submissive to the Communist regime. What an irony! After thirty years of struggle the Vietnamese people lost more freedom and happiness than they had during the wars and under foreign rule.

Poverty was the main root of burglary. Everything could be sold. Consequently, everything could be stolen. People sold old newspapers, copy books, plastic bags, iron or aluminum sheets, and fuel tanks, which were used to bake bread and to make bike frames. After the Communist government struck one-piastre coins in aluminum, many electric wires were cut and stolen. They were used to make counterfeit money. The wrongdoers stole iron sewer grills from the streets. Some cyclists and motorcyclists were injured when they fell in the sewer. Professional thieves could steal bikes, motorcycles, or their parts, such as pedals, chains, tires, and wheels, for ransom. Careful people padlocked their bikes or motorcycles at the parking places although the parking attendants were paid. The latter were mostly retired Communist cadres or members of the revolutionary families. They stole expensive bikes and promised to pay for the lost bikes or motorcycles based on the invoices. Expensive bikes were the old ones made before 1975. Many owners had lost the invoices, so they lost their bikes or motorcycles. Before 1975 a bike cost 10,000 piastres. The unlucky owners would be repaid twenty new piastres while the stealers would sell them at the price of 1,000 new piastres each. Many people were injured while riding new bikes made from aluminum sheets or fuel tanks. They broke when the riders went up hills or down hills.

The Vietnamese Communist clothing was very simple. The Communist leaders wore neither neckties nor suits. They put on short-sleeved shirts and dark blue pants.

The Communist *bo doi* put on neither boots nor steel helmets but they wore *dep rau* (Binh Tri Thien sandals) and *casques coloniales* (cork helmets). The Viet Cong had cotton hats on. All of them looked pale and sick while their leaders were rosy with large faces and big ears. The grassroots looked anxious and skinny for they were underfed.

President Ton Duc Thang, eighty-seven in 1975, was two years older than Ho Chi Minh. But he remained rosy and chubby.

First Secretary Le Duan was tall and heavy. His voice was still clear and strong. He moved his hand in the air and called on the Vietnamese people to move forward to socialism.

Prime Minister Pham Van Dong looked stunted because of his chronic diseases. Like Le Duan he was tall with a victorious smile. His face was bony and his teeth were prominent.

Nguyen Huu Tho, chairman of the NLF, looked stunted. His voice was hoarse. Imitating other Communist leaders, he praised the Communist party and the leadership of "great President Ho."

Pham Hung was always smiling while General Vo Nguyen Giap was taciturn. Generals Van Tien Dung, Tran Van Tra, and Le Duc Anh seemed to be rising stars.

On May 15 the Communists celebrated their victory in a solemn parade in Saigon. All the Communist leaders of the Democratic Republic and those of the NLF were on the grandstand. Liberation heroines were proud of their black peasant uniforms, striped scarves, cotton caps, and medals.

It was sunny that day. The Communist cadres protected their leaders from the heat of the sun with umbrellas. From time to time they gave them some fresh air with paper fans. Everybody seemed thrilled to listen to the eighty-seven-year-old president, Ton Duc Thang, read a long speech prepared by the Communist party. People didn't expect to hear something interesting or new. They were afraid that he might not read smoothly or that he wouldn't reflect the content of the speech faithfully. President Ton Duc Thang read and reread the same page. One of his attachés turned the page of the speech and prompted him to go on reading the new page.

The Communist *bo doi* and the Viet Cong paraded on the streets. Soviet tanks, military trucks equipped with rockets and rocket launchers moved slowly on the streets. Radio Giai Phong kept on repeating "Our country is clear of enemies. South Vietnam is in my heart."

Deafening pieces of music such as "It Seems That Uncle Ho Is Present on the Merry Day of Liberation," "The Party Gives Us the Spring," and "The Liberation of South Vietnam," were on the air.

The price of bicycles was raised in early May 1975. Another era began.

The South Vietnamese tried to pedal. They couldn't use their motorcycles, scooters and cars for lack of gas. They didn't have any problems in the first days, but little by little, they were worn out. So were their clothes and bicycles. Their health declined due to food shortages. They realized that it was hard to ride a mile in thunderstorms or in the torrid sunlight. At Binh Loi people had to carry their bicycles on the bridge, which had had some planks removed.

The Communist cadres and employees went to work with a sack for food and a vase for fish sauce or kerosene. So did the university professors. Worse, they were ordered to write articles praising the Communist party and government. A professor of sciences wrote an article about cassava and its contributions to nutrition. He exaggerated some characteristics of cassava leaves.

In June 1975, officers, civil servants, senators, representatives, and members of the political parties registered for reeducation. In late June brainwashing classes began. South Vietnamese soldiers spent three days at the reeducation centers in Ho Chi Minh City. Former civil servants retained by the new regime studied the cruelty of American global strategy, the victory of the Communist bloc, and the duties of the cadres after liberation. High-ranking officers and officials were concentrated in Long Thanh, Tay Ninh, Long Khanh, and a few other places throughout South Vietnam. Most detainees in Long Thanh were sent to North Vietnam by the end of 1975.

What scared the detainees most was to write about their backgrounds. They told about their grandparents, parents, and siblings, their social class, profession, and activities from 1945 until 1975. They read their crimes to their group and listened to their criticism. They had to remember all the details of their crimes and rewrite them in the next days. If someone criticized their backgrounds for any reason, they lost not only credits but also time to adjust their backgrounds. The more crimes they wrote, the more sincere they were. The detainees were very anxious, nervous, and depressed when writing and rewriting their curriculum vitae. The Communist cadres examined their cases based on their own criteria. In their eyes, journalists, intellectuals, those who worked for the Americans, and those who knew foreign languages were CIA agents. They disliked detainees who wore eyeglasses.

The detainees reflected on what they learned and recognized their crimes in the past. According to the Communist cadres, everybody was guilty. Physicians were guilty. Teachers were guilty. Soldiers were guilty. Civil servants were guilty. Priests were guilty. Their actions could be guilty. If they weren't guilty in their actions, they would be guilty in their thoughts. A Viet Cong killer was less dangerous than a teacher, a writer, or a priest with their anti–Communist thoughts. Therefore, the members of the political parties, priests, writers, poets, and journalists were subject to severe punishments in the Communist regime.

The new regime retained a number of teachers, nurses, and technicians of the old regime for a few years. Many of them were gradually replaced by Communist-trained employees. Some resigned or were forced to resign.

The Communists soon established a thick network of security to prevent counter-revolutionary activities. The Communist police rarely asked people to show their IDs. They gave everybody the feeling that they had the freedom to travel anywhere they liked. Watching the daily activities of the dwellers was the responsibility of the neighborhood cells and the local People's Committees. The heads of the neighborhood cells noticed any lesser attitudes, gestures, speeches, or social relations of the residents and reported them to the neighborhood sector chiefs. A resident wishing to move from one place to another had to get permission from the local police department, based on the approval of the cell head. The applicant explained the reason for his travel and told where he would arrive and how long he would stay there. When he got there, he must present himself at the police department to get local police certification.

Trash collectors watched the lifestyle of the residents through their waste.

The heads of the neighborhood cells and sectors watched over strangers in the neighborhood. They had many suspicions in their minds. Smuggling? Escaping? Anti–Communist activities? They also tailed those people who did nothing but who had regular parties. They were taught to suspect anybody by asking questions, such as "how do people have so much money?" "How can they not live in poverty if they aren't financed by foreigners?" "Why don't people have any complaints?"

The Communist police watched the coffee shops and the barber shops. They kept their eyes on people talking in the coffee shops and the barber shops. The Communist policemen separated them from each other and gave each of them a sheet of paper to write what they had talked about. From this experience, before the conversation, people prepared in advance what they would write. If the contents of their reports of their conversation were different, they would be investigated by the police.

Communist society had many social classes. The members of the Communist party had many privileges. The high-ranking members of the party had more special privileges to compensate them for their faithfulness to the party, to Marxism and Leninism, and to Uncle Ho. Many old members of the party didn't hold any important positions because of their bourgeois families or their rightist or leftist deviation. Those members who reached leading positions were very flexible. They knew how to take advantage of a situation and avoid any new initiatives, hiding their true thoughts. Pure patriots and idealists were soon expelled from the party for their ideological deviation and political inflexibility. Most South Vietnamese Viet Minh going north in 1954 faced such bitter reality.

Revolutionary families were divided into many categories based on their social classes, involvement in the Communist revolution, contributions during the wars, and noncooperation with the Saigon government.

"Clean" families were poor families having no children in the army or in the government of the Republic of Vietnam. They could be pro–Communist or not.

The non–Communist and anti–Communist families were classified based on the backgrounds of their parents and of their grandparents back to 1945, their position in the Nationalist government, and their danger to the new regime.

Social class discrimination was clear. High-ranking cadres had more comfort than low-ranking ones in the hospital. Sick members of the grassroots didn't have enough food, medicine, or comforts like the Communist cadres. In school the Communist cadres' children held important positions in the Communist youth organizations, such as the Komsomol and the Red Neckerchiefs. They were prepared to be college students, future members of the party, and future leaders. Some studied in other Communist countries. Some studied in Vietnam. Politically, they were chosen although their education was insignificant.

On the streets, through the means of locomotion and the weight of their owners, we could tell who was who. Skinny people in rags, wearing worn-out slippers, walking or riding old bicycles were the South Vietnamese grassroots. Chubby and cocky people, waring leather slippers, bearing bags on their shoulders, and riding Hondas or Vespas or having their own drivers were middle-ranking cadres. They had inherited the wealth left by the collaborators of the old regime and their wives and daughters as well.

Words also reflected the social classes. When speaking of President Ho, the Communist cadres used mandatory groups of words such as "the most respectable," "great President Ho," "great Uncle Ho," and "the father of our people." They called his grave *lang* (mausoleum), a feudal term used to indicate the kings' graves. When talking about Lenin, they had to use the terms "gifted leader" or "talented leader." The Communists began their speeches with "Dear Comrade Le Duan." In Communist Vietnamese there was no hyphen except for Truong-Chinh, the pseudonym of Dang Xuan Khu, former general secretary of the Communist party. Without a hyphen between the two words *Truong* and *Chinh*, all the books or newspapers couldn't be distributed. (*truong chinh* means long march).

Communist vocabulary was a little different from that of South Vietnam. Some times we had vulgar terms like *linh thuy danh bo* (marines) instead of *thuy quan luc chien; may bay len thang"* (helicopter) instead of *truc thang; ho xi* (toilet) instead of *cau tieu; xuong de* (maternity) instead of *nha bao sanh,"* etc. Sometimes we saw some strange, uncommon, complicated and incomprehensible terms borrowed from foreign languages like *xa hoang* (tsar), *so vanh* (chauvinistic), *lo-gic* (logic), *Xo viet* (Soviet), and *ABC* (anti-bolché-viste). Many Communist terms were more American than French. On the contrary, the South Vietnamese terms were more Chinese and French than American. In the Communist vocabulary there were many words that were absent in Saigon but were current in America, such as *quan che* translated from "probation," *tem phieu luong thuc* from "food stamps," *cung thieu nhi* from "children's palace," *dan phong* from "neighborhood watch," *quan ly* from "management," and *xu ly* from "handle."

Communist reports and speeches consisted of long sentences with many commas and without the conjunction *and*. Little by little, the detainees and South Vietnamese became used to some phoneticized words like *Pa-ri* (Paris), *Gio-Neo-Vo* (Geneva), *Mot-co-va* (Moscow), *Me-hi-co* (Mexico), *At-hen-ti-na* (Argentina), or *To-rot-ky* (Trotsky). They became used to some specifically revolutionary terms, such as *gian don* (*don gian* in Saigon, "simple"), *han che* (*gioi han* in Saigon, "limitation"), *tron ven* (*hoan toan*, "whole, entire"), *khan truong* (*khan* in Saigon, "urgent"), *can* (*can thang*, "tense, strained"), *le me* (cumbersome), or *lech lac* (deviation). The word *Quoc Gia* (national) was almost absent in Communist books and newspapers, but at the top of the bank notes there were the words Ngan Hang Quoc Gia (National Bank).

The reeducation detainees absorbed revolutionary terms faster than the grassroots. It was a must for them to understand the policy of the new regime enlightened by Marxism and Leninism.

The Communist cadres called one another comrades. The words "Mr." and "gentlemen" disappeared from conversation. They evoked "bourgeois politeness." People called one another *anh* (brother) but not *ong* (Sir), which evoked something ceremonious and unequal. Young people called the elderly *chu* (uncle, father's younger brother) and avoided the word *bac* (uncle) except forBac Ho (Uncle Ho).

We saw how serious and important Communist terminology was. Nevertheless, there were many popular songs and funny stories that appeared in South Vietnam after 1975. The song "Co Gai Dat Do" (The Young Lady of Dat Do) by Tran Long An had its lyrics changed and it spread in the South Vietnamese schools. The revolutionary song became funny and counter-revolutionary.

> *Let's break the bent hoes*
> *So that we don't go to the fields.*
> *As the "liberators" come here,*
> *We have to go to the new economic areas,*
> *We have to work hard all day long.*
> *But we eat only roots.*
> *Oh, dear Homeland! Why so forever?*
> *Since the "liberation" we have eaten*
> *Rice mixed with roots for good.*

It was a favorite song of the children, but it embarrassed the People's Committees. School principals assembled students' parents and asked them to take responsibility for their children if the latter continued to sing this song. I persuaded my children not to sing it. Otherwise, my security would be threatened.

A large number of streets in Saigon had their names changed. Phan Dinh Phung Street was changed to Nguyen Dinh Chieu Street. Truong Minh Giang Street became Nguyen Van Troi Street. Tran Quoc Toan became 3 Thang 2 (birthday of the Vietnam Communist party).

Phan Dinh Phung had been a *lettre*, a courtier, and a resistance leader. Nobody knows why the Communists denied his heroism and patriotism. Because of his education? Because of his high position at court?

Nguyen Dinh Chieu was a patriotic poet. There was a street bearing his name in Tan Dinh. Was it fair to praise Nguyen Dinh Chieu's patriotism and to deny that of Phan Dinh Phung only because the former was a poor scholar while the latter was a laureate of the doctoral contest and a courtier

Truong Minh Giang was governor of Tran Tay Thanh (Cambodia) under the reign of Minh Mang. According to the Communist viewpoint, he was inferior to Nguyen Van Troi, an electrician who had planned to assassinate American secretary of defense MacNamara with a bomb. All the Vietnamese students had to read "Song Nhu Anh" (Live Like You) and imitate Troi who, according to Communist propaganda, shouted, "Long live Ho Chi Minh! Long live Ho Chi Minh!" before his execution.

Tu Do Street (*tu do* means freedom) became Dong Khoi Street (*dong khoi* means uprising); Cong Ly Street (*cong ly* means justice) became Nam Ky Khoi Nghia Street (The Revolt of Nam Ky), etc. The change of street names gave birth to this following verse: "The Revolt of Nam Ky toppled down Justice./ After the Uprising we lost Freedom."

The Saigonese children were bothered by Uncle Ho a lot. They invented a strange game in which they walked, danced, put their hands together, and chanted:

> *Con duong* Bac di *la con duong* bi dat
> *Con duong* siet vo *la cong duong* Xo Viet.
> *(The path Uncle Ho walked on has been a tragic one.*
> *The despotic way has been the Soviet one.)*

Bac di euphonized with *bi dat*. *Siet vo* euphonized with *Xo viet*. *Bac di* means Uncle Ho walked; *Bi dat* means tragic; *Siet vo* means to tighten, to grab, to grip. In Ho Chi Minh City there is *Xo Viet Nghe Tinh Street*, which replaced Hong Thap Tu Street.

The South Vietnamese also paid disrespect to Uncle Ho when they sang: "Last night I saw Uncle Ho in a dream. His beard was as long as ..." The picture of Uncle Ho waving his hand in the air was interpreted as a promise of five kilograms of rice per capita per month.

In 1980 President Ton Duc Thang died. So did Vice President Nguyen Luong Bang. The following funny story appeared in Ho Chi Minh City:

> Uncle Ton and Vice President Nguyen Luong Bang had a meeting with Uncle Ho in the Yellow Spring. Uncle Ho looked tired and anxious. He worried a lot about his unfinished mission on the Earth as a Communist soldier.
>
> "What did you do up there after my death?" Uncle Ho asked Uncle Ton and Nguyen.
>
> "When you were alive, your favorite motto was: 'Khong co gi/ qui hon doc/ lap tu do.' (Nothing is more precious than independence and freedom). Our comrades and I carried out one-third of your favorite motto," Uncle Ton replied, politely and sincerely.
>
> "What do you mean by that?" Uncle Ho asked.
>
> "Your motto has nine words. One-third of it consists of the three first words, *Khong co gi* (nothing)," Uncle Ton explained.

XHCN, the abbreviation of *xa hoi chu nghia* (socialism) was read as *xuong ho ca nuoc*" (the whole country falls into the pit) or *xep hang ca ngay* (line up all day long). Many plays on words, such as *long kieng* (fitting glass) turned into *lieng cong* (throwing in the sewer) and *bang do sao vang* (red board with the yellow star) turned into *bo dang sang giau* (quitting the Communist party to become wealthy), were considered reactionary thoughts.

Disappointed with the durability of the despotic regime, people thought about *qui ma*, which euphonically turned into *qua My* (going to America), or about *ma qui*, a play on the words of *My qua* (the Americans come).

The more people thought of the past, the more they felt sorrowful. They had lost their relatively happy time, even wartime under the military regime had been better. They compared the Communist regime to the military regime in Saigon in this verse: "Down with Thieu, Ky! We could get whatever we liked./ Long live Ho Chi Minh! We must register to get a nail."

An actor was arrested for saying, "Don't listen to what he says. Watch what he is doing carefully." It reminded the South Vietnamese of a statement made by President Thieu in Vinh Binh a year before the fall of the Republic of Vietnam.

The Communists multiplied more prisons and reeducation camps to detain counterrevolutionaries and those people who slurred the regime. The more prisons they had, the more wealthy the police were. At the height of the exodus the police made much money. The Chinese Vietnamese sought to leave the country semi-officially or secretly by boat. Those people who didn't escape consoled themselves with prophecy and metaphysical phenomena. We heard the following story:

> In the Mekong Delta catfish killed one another. Many of their bodies were afloat on the surface of the rivers. The grassroots believed that it was a sign of carnage between the North Vietnamese Communists and the Viet Cong. The North Vietnamese Communists really eliminated the Viet Cong and those Communists dispatched by Hanoi to the battlefields in the South during the war. The Vietnamese Communists exchanged fire with the Khmer Rouge and invaded Cambodia. The Chinese Communists attacked some northern provinces of the Socialist Republic of Vietnam. Cadres A purged Cadres B, and the pro–Soviet eliminated the pro–Chinese.

In the 1970s and 1980s some people confirmed without any caution that Trang Trinh Nguyen Binh Khiem, a famous scholar and prophet in the sixteenth century, wrote:

> *Ngay nao* Sen *moc bien Dong,*
> *Dong Phuong* troi moc, sao *roi day duong.*
> *(When the lotus grows in the East Sea,*
> *And the sun rises in the East,*
> *The stars fall like rain on the streets.)*

In Sino-Vietnamese, *sen* is *lien*, hinting at *Lien Xo* (the Soviet Union). "The lotus grows in the East Sea" implies the presence of the Soviet navy at

Cam Ranh Bay. "The sun rises" is the symbol of the Japanese flag. "The stars fall" represents the collapse of Communism. The interpretation sounded good, optimistic, and politically scientific although, based on reality, it wasn't quite right.

At the end of 1975 the ammunition dumps at Long Binh and Bien Hoa exploded. Some people wished the return of the Americans to Vietnam. The Americans never came back. Some people expected Japanese military intervention or interference from the United Nations. All of their hopes became nebulous. They turned to the celestial machine, waiting for the birth of a clairvoyant king. Time flew by, leaving in their mind intermittent despair and sorrows.

Children adhered to the youth organizations in the first days of liberation. In school they were divided into various groups. They had meetings everyday. They sang Communist songs praising the Communist party and teaching faithfulness to Uncle Ho for his endless concerns about the Vietnamese children. They were taught to be proud of being born in Ho Chi Minh's era. They knew a lot about Kim Dong, Le Van Tam, "the live torch," and hero Ho Van Men, but heroic children in history, like Phu Dong Thien Vuong, Dinh Bo Linh, and Tran Quoc Toan, were ignored.

Children of *nguy* (officials, officers, reeducation detainees) had no right to belong to the Communist youth organizations, such as the Red Neckerchief group or Komsomol. Each school had a Communist party cell whose secretary directed the principal, the teachers, and all the youth organizations politically.

The students learned to hate Americans and their lackeys. All the school subjects focused on the Communist party, its lucid leadership, the greatness of Uncle Ho and his contributions to the independence era. The students were taught to be "red and assiduous." They weren't forced to be obedient to their teachers for "You [teachers] don't follow the party. I don't follow you."

In addition to hatred for the American imperialists and their lackeys, the students learned hatred for social classes. Many of them blamed their parents for their involvement in the puppet government. As a result, their future was dim. They didn't blame the Communist government but attributed all the mistakes to their parents. Children whose parents had belonged to the South Vietnamese government couldn't enter college. They were forced to quit school after finishing the ninth or twelfth grade. Each province had its own committee in charge of choosing college students. Children of reeducation detainees couldn't be selected regardless of their high grades. The recruitment committee explained that they had passed the written test but they had failed due to the political backgrounds of their parents. The political curriculum vitae determined their future. The recruitment committee was very powerful. The students' futures depended on its decision.

Recruiting college students based on their family's backgrounds was harmful to national development. Good students were eliminated while incapable students were selected. Even those students studying in the Soviet Union, China, and Eastern Europe were far from being experts. Famous physicians and engineers, such as Dr. Pham Ngoc Thach, Ton That Tung, and Tran Dai Nghia, were French-educated. It was said that the North Vietnamese were very scared of surgery. They didn't trust Communist physicians, who were technically and educationally bad. The fear moved from Hanoi to Saigon after 1975. I saw some South Vietnamese ladies burst into tears at Hung Vuong Hospital when they learned that they would be operated on by Communist surgeons.

Education focused on forming a new generation faithful to Marxism-Leninism, to the Communist party and to the government. Vietnamese literature, poetry, history, politics, and language insisted on the roles of the Vietnam Communist party and Ho Chi Minh in the revolutionary wars to liberate the country from the foreign yokes and the proletariats from oppression, chains, and poverty.

The sciences were more descriptive than experimental. Students were intent on learning poems by To Huu by heart to show themselves "red and assiduous" in the hope of having brighter futures.

Foreign languages didn't have any role in the curriculum. In North Vietnam, as a rule, students learned Russian and Chinese. In reality, they didn't learn foreign languages for lack of teachers of languages. In South Vietnamese schools English and French were retained. But, after 1975, teachers of English and French were few. Many of them had quit their jobs or left the country. Elementary school teachers were promoted to teaching in middle schools and high schools. Unqualified teachers couldn't give birth to capable students. Worse, bad students were selected to enter college. Their true capacities were incompatible with their titles and social positions. In 1980 Russian was taught in South Vietnam. What a strange thing! Children of the reeducation detainees were forced to study Russian while the Communist cadres' children studied English. Russian became a punishment for the detainees' children. Many of them burst into tears at being forced to study Russian. They seemed to say good-bye to the Soviet Union while their leaders worshipped Lenin and praised Stalin, the October Revolution and the patriotic war against the Germans during World War II.

At night there were continuing education classes for the cadres. In these night classes teachers respected their students, who were middle-ranking cadres whose seniority in the Communist party was high enough. Teachers had to ensure their graduation as soon as possible in spite of their irregular attendance. Some Communist physicians were in the seventh grade of these night classes.

Teaching wasn't lucrative in the Communist regime. But teachers had many duties and responsibilities. The Communists claimed to praise them with beautiful words. They watched them carefully and made them into policemen, who had to investigate suspected students, and propagandists, who had to advocate Communist policies. They had to be modest with minimum benefits. They were subject to criticism from the party cell, fromKomsomol, from their colleagues and students. A teacher from North Vietnam working in Ho Chi Minh City used to eat sweet potatoes for lunch every day. Asked by a South Vietnamese teacher about what she ate, she answered bitterly: "I eat earth ginseng."

Most Vietnamese ate rice mixed with roots. Animals ate rice bran mixed with sliced banana stems and aquatic plants. Engines ran on gas mixed with diesel or petroleum. Motorcyclists had to have small bottles of pure gas to start their motorcycles.

The consequences of the food shortage were visible. Children didn't grow up normally due to malnutrition. They looked passive and lazy. Adults got sick. Many of them lost memories. Their sight and hearing got worse. Many ladies had goiters or uterine tumors. Many people living in the new economic areas had tuberculosis, hepatitis, or malaria.

Meat got more and more expensive. Breeding was paralyzed. At one time, the South Vietnamese didn't eat pork because it was rumored that the Communists fed pigs with aborted fetuses.

With the shortage of food and a tight network of police, the new regime succeeded in maximizing the people's submission and minimizing their hostility to the Communist government. It was said in a joke that President Ho Chi Minh asked Ta Duy Hien how he could dominate fierce animals, such as tigers and panthers, in his circus. "Let them be hungry," Ta Duy Hien said. It was a real joke. Didn't Ho Chi Minh learn anything from Lenin, Stalin, and Mao Zedong? He knew that human beings were dependent on food.

Living with the burdens of poverty, hunger, illiteracy, and imprisonment, the South Vietnamese were soon stunted. Their hair got white; their teeth decayed. They smoked too much to dissipate their worries and relax their minds. They smoked any kind of domestic cigarettes made from tobacco mixed with the sliced leaves of cassava or papaya. Before 1975 the South Vietnamese were fond of smoking Rugby, Capstan, Bastos, Cotab, and Mélia. After 1975 Communist Cadres A and B smoked Phu Dong, Hoa Mai, Da Lat, and Vam Co, made by state-run factories. These cigarettes were sold at the market. People didn't have enough money to get a whole pack but some sold individual cigarettes. Candy, cake, and even foreign medicines were sold at the cigarette stands. In the 1980s Thai, British, and American filtered cigarettes appeared in South Vietnam. They played an important role in public relations between the folks and the Communist cadres.

Mobile coffee shops mushroomed everywhere. People roasted corn, ground it, and mixed it with real coffee. Sometimes they roasted wild berries and ground them to replace coffee. The Vietnamese people have had the pleasure of drinking coffee in the morning and in the evening. Some people drank coffee to save their daily meals. Coffee relaxed the drinkers and gave them the feeling that it was a tonic and made the drinkers feel full. Before 1975 needy people ate *xoi* (steamed sticky rice with mung beans, peanuts, salt, sugar, coconut, fried onion, and lard) and drank coffee for breakfast. After 1975 *xoi* was expensive because all of its components were costly.

Many people made friends with rice alcohol to forget their disgust. Some of them suffered from poverty. Some suffered from bankruptcy, separation, and an uncertain future. Others suffered from mistreatment and trouble with the local government.

The government controlled rice production and circulation rigidly. Farmers distilled rice alcohol clandestinely. Rice alcohol was abundant at the market. Not a few drinkers died after drinking rice alcohol distilled with cassava that had been dusted with insecticide powder. In the 1980s the South Vietnamese were frightened by insecticide powder. Its danger was widespread. People thought that it made fish, shrimp, ducks, and chickens full of pus. In Song Be (Binh Duong) a lady died when she used it to kill lice. The lice died. So did the lady.

Many families of the reeducation detainees were in catastrophic circumstances. Some left the cities for the new economic areas. Some returned to their native villages to practice farming. Some tried to escape from Vietnam. Some decided to stay in the cities. They lived from hand to mouth by doing anything they could. They were threatened by poverty and separation.

Dwellers in the new economic areas lived miserably. Their children were illiterate. They were surrounded by starvation, malaria, tuberculosis, hepatitis, and the local government. They couldn't return to the cities where their houses had been sold or demolished. Their household certificates were revoked after they left the cities. They cut down trees and cleared the forests for housing and farming. They fired wood to make charcoal. The local government sought to confiscate the charcoal or to interdict the dwellers from selling it. After the harvest, they were forced to leave their farm land and continue cutting down trees and clearing the forests. The new regime made them agricultural slaves doing forced labor, like war losers in feudal times. The Communist government planned to concentrate the reeducation detainees and their families in the forests and the mountainous regions to keep the enemies away from the cities, to force them to work these deserted regions with their severe weather, and to let them struggle against malaria, food shortages, poisonous snakes, wild animals, and all kinds of harmful insects. Fortunately, Hanoi didn't carry out this plan because the Socialist Republic of Vietnam faced many domestic and international problems.

The reeducation detainees were prisoners without a trial. None of them knew how long they would stay in the camps. In the North Vietnamese camps they were threatened by severe weather and food and medicine shortages. They expected their families to supply them with sugar, salt, dried food, and other basic necessities. Not all of their families had enough money to travel to North Vietnam to supply them with food, medicine, and clothes. In order to visit the detainees their relatives had to get a permit from the local government and to have enough money to prepare some dried food, to pay for train fare, and to hire a North Vietnamese to pick them up from the railroad station and take them to the reeducation camps. The train stations in North Vietnam were crowded and busy. Robbers and pickpockets assembled there to make their living. Many detainees' relatives were mugged and spent miserable days in North Vietnam until they met their friends from the South and borrowed some money to get train tickets. In the camps the detainees looked forward to visits from their relatives with impatience and disappointment. Many couples separated from one another because the wives were so poor that they couldn't visit and feed their husbands in the camps. Not a few detainees were abandoned by their families when their wives left the country or lived with the Communist cadres or with Chinese businessmen for economic reasons.

I presented myself at the office on the first day of liberation. I felt a little perplexed. Everything had changed quickly. Everything seemed new to me. My colleagues looked at one another with prudence. Everybody kept their golden silence. When speaking, they seemed to choose words that wouldn't be harmful to their security and safety. The students changed their attitude toward their teachers.

A friend and colleague saw me. This time he wasn't as friendly as he had been before. He looked mysterious and dangerous. He seemed to show that he was involved in revolutionary activities in the South Vietnamese government and that he was aware of his colleagues' political viewpoints. He put many black-and-white photos on the table and said, "Look at these pictures and you'll know what I have done!"

I was surprised at his arrogance. In the past I had been friendly with him. I loved his sweetness and politeness. But just one day after the fall of Saigon, he had lost all of his lovely characteristics. He used "thou" and "thy" in his speech to show his superiority to me. Pretending not to pay attention to that I looked the photos on the table. I saw pictures of Uncle Ho, of his wooden house behind the old palace of the French governor general, and of his activities. I wondered why my friend had these pictures. Was he a Viet Cong? Was his family Communist or pro–Communist?

His birthplace and name, "a forest of red flags," reminded me of his father's political stand. In the South Vietnamese government he had enjoyed all the benefits of a Category A civil servant. Then the regime collapsed. He tried his best to have a new position in the new regime. He showed himself enthusiastic and excited about harming and endangering his colleagues. I was not only his friend but also his classmate in the Saigon College of Education. He knew a lot about me. But I didn't know anything about him. I knew that his father had been a barber. He was dead. His mother was a sweet widow who was dependent upon her son and daughter-in-law, who was an elementary school teacher. His family was humble. All of its members were polite.

There were many variations and changes in the course of our lives. Some people changed their characters due to their age. Some changed their characters before their death. Some changed their characters because of a change in their social situation. Some changed their characters to adapt to the new situation. My friend changed his character because of his innate perfidy, which he had hidden cleverly in the past. He had deceived all of his colleagues. I was seriously mistaken for having had friendly relations with him.

As soon as the Communists took over Saigon, he behaved as a stranger to his colleagues and gave them serious troubles. I didn't know what he reported to the Communists about me, but they called me several times and stuck me with many thorny questions. They said that I was counterrevolutionary, that I spoke ill of Karl Marx, and that I had relations with reactionary intellectuals. I realized that my friend had betrayed me to build up his credits with the new regime. He danced on my suffering. I was forced to quit my job. My fate depended on the police of my residential province. Four years later, I learned that he left Vietnam to be a refugee.

I was unemployed. But my family didn't know it. Neither did my neighbors. I got up early every morning and claimed to ride to work as usual. My children went to school regularly as if nothing had happened to me.

The Communist *bo doi* watched my house. They asked my neighbors about me. All of them spoke well of me. I had good relations with them and helped them when they had serious problems. The *bo doi* didn't give up their investigation. They went to my wife's native village to ask the villagers about me and my past activities. Most villagers confirmed that I was a good man and a good teacher. They said that I was an ordinary man unharmful to anybody and to society. Some said sincerely that they didn't know me.

My safety was protected by my neighbors and my father-in-law's. But it was troubled by one of my cousins, who gave the local police some information about me. His mean intention was to ask the Communists to confiscate my property and to put me in jail for avoiding reeducation. My younger brother was arrested when he came back to Laithieu to see my mother. The local police searched my house. They confiscated my car and my scooter, giving as a pretext that they belonged to my brother. I showed them the titles. They kept them, saying that they were false one. I lost my car and my scooter. But the Communists said that they had only requisitioned them temporarily.

In a short time after liberation I underwent many catastrophic vicissitudes. I lost my job. I was under investigation. I lost some of my property. The local police sought to confiscate my house and to put me in jail when somebody gave them some evidence of my "reactionary" past. I was endangered by my friend and by my cousin. I calmed myself in order to comfort my wife and children. But I knew that I couldn't hide the brokenhearted situation for long. My family's circumstances got worse. I sold my wife's jewels gradually to keep my family's survival. I tried not to touch anything in my living room, especially my ancestral altars and furniture, to safeguard my family's morale.

Having eaten rice mixed with cassava for more than a year, my wife was hospitalized for surgery. My children got pale and skinny for lack of meat, milk, and eggs. Their growth was very slow. As for me, I weighed eighty-five pounds. My sight and hearing weren't good. I lost my memory not only because of malnutrition but also because of my daily worries. Sometimes I forgot my friends' names. It would take me a few minutes to find them again in my subconscious. I suffered for I was unable to bring happiness to my family. I had to destroy what I loved and what I owned. What I lacked became precious and more valuable. I burned many books in Vietnamese, French, and English. My wife and children tore some and made small paper bags, which my daughter sold to the peddlers. One evening, I put my typewriter in a bag and threw it in a deserted field five miles from my house.

Some of my cousins and friends advised me to sell all the furniture in my living room. I thanked them without noticing their advice. I loved history. I loved my country. I paid respect to my ancestors. I cherished bygones and moral values and thought a lot about the future. I had a large altar dedicated to Emperor Quang Trung. There was a large map of Vietnam and a long sword on it. I kept everything intact there although the Communists called on the residents to give the People's Committee all weapons, swords, spears, and bayonets. My pure faith and patriotism didn't allow me to be so fearful that I would give the sword of a national hero to anybody although my freedom was seriously threatened.

I was so curious that I forgot that I was watched by the local police. I rode to Saigon, Cholon, or Gia Dinh everyday. I watched the activities of the populace and their adaptation to the new regime. I had many things to learn from the Saigonese and from the North Vietnamese, who had lived more than two decades under the Communist regime. I learned how people adapted to the social, economic, and political changes after the fall of South Vietnam. Some patients were accustomed to their chronic diseases. Some people spent a long time in misery or in jail and survived only when they were optimistic and capable of adapting to the existing life conditions. The North Vietnamese and the South Vietnamese Viet Minh who went north in 1954 gave their relatives in the South some suggestions about how to live with the Communist regime. In their opinion, life in the city was much better than life in the rural areas. The future of the reeducation detainees' families would be uncertain. In the Communist regime smuggling, corruption, murder, robbery, and rape were minor offenses. But the regime wouldn't tolerate those people who were against it.

After 1954 one million North Vietnamese left the North for the South. There weren't any high-ranking officials or officers of the nationalist government left in North Vietnam. The Communist government sent the soldiers of the Nationalist army to the reeducation camps for brainwashing and forced labor for at least seven years. Their families were forcibly expelled from the cities. They moved to the mountainous regions up north. Under the agrarian reforms the instructions of the Communist party were that each village would have 2 percent of landowners be denounced and sentenced by landless farmers. Mechanically, the Communist cadres had the list of the 2 percent in their villages. These landowners were humiliated, tortured, and accused by the villagers, including their relatives. They were forced to admit their "crimes" before being killed. Many victims who were accused of being "tyrannical landowners" in the agrarian reforms almost died of hunger in the famine of 1945. This proved that the Communists were intolerant and frigid, blindly and mechanically obedient to the regulations of the Communist party.

The South Vietnamese were politically mature. They didn't show any violent reaction against the new regime. Their attitude was uniquely passive. They had neither opinions nor signs of hostility. Apparently they were docile. In reality, they neither listened to the Communist cadres nor complied with Communist policies. The Communist cadres called businessmen "parasites" or "scroungers." The grassroots tried to exchange goods at any cost to make money and to earn their daily living without making any actions or speeches hostile to the Communist regime.

The Communist party praised proletarians and denounced intellectuals severely. The ironic reality was that all the vanguards of the Communist movements in the world were intellectuals. Karl Marx received his doctorate in philosophy when he was twenty-three years old. Lenin, a law school graduate, was from a petit bourgeois family. Mao Zedong, an educated man, was born into a rich family in Shao-shan, Hunan province. Chou En-Lai and Deng Xiaoping studied in France. Ho Chi Minh was a sixth grader. But his father, Nguyen Sinh Huy held a *pho bang* (master's degree) and worked for the Nguyen dynasty before being banished to Poulo Condore Island on account of his anti–French activities. In the Vietnam Communist party, Truong Chinh, Pham Van Dong, Vo Nguyen Giap, and Le Duc Tho weren't from the working or farming classes. Huynh Tan Phat, Nguyen Huu Tho, Trinh Dinh Thao, and Duong Quynh Hoa in the National Liberation Front and the National Alliance for Democracy and Peace were famous intellectuals in society during French rule.

Another strange thing was that all the members of the Communist party had neither the time nor the ability to read and understand *Das Kapital* by Karl

Marx. However, all of them were fanatic and fervent Communists faithful to the doctrine they knew only vaguely.

Communist propaganda was scientific, efficient, and systematically deceptive. The Viet Cong believed that they beat the Americans and their lackeys with the help of North Vietnam. They thought that they would inherit the bonanza left by the Saigon government. They couldn't predict that they would be victims of Hanoi. Nguyen Huu Tho and Huynh Tan Phat became their puppets. Trinh Dinh Thao, Duong Quynh Hoa, Phung Van Cung, Truong Nhu Tang, and Nguyen Van Kiet fell into oblivion after the birth of the Socialist Republic of Vietnam.

Nguyen Van Kiet, minister of education in Huynh Tan Phat's cabinet, returned to Saigon as a victor. He couldn't hide his pride and arrogance. Before going to the jungle in 1968 he had taught French at the College of Arts and Education in Saigon. He was well known in the Saigon intelligentsia. After April 30, 1975, returning triumphally to Saigon, he considered himself a wise man who chose the right side while his colleagues belonged to the puppet government.

One day, I went to Saigon to see my former teacher. He was happy to see me safe and sound. After asking me about my family, he said to me. "Mr. Trinh Dinh Thao called me and invited me to visit his new villa on Tu Xuong Street near Mr. Kieu's."

"Teacher, if you have an appointment with him, go to see him. I will see you another day," I said.

"By the way, I want you to come along with me," my teacher said.

"I think that would be very inconvenient, teacher." I said.

"Don't worry. Mr. Thao is a good friend of mine. He is different from Mr. Kiet. The latter was proud and haughty. If Mr. Thao hadn't called me I wouldn't go to see him. I know that Mr. Thao is more open-minded than Mr. Kiet. The former is jovial and open-minded. On the contrary, the latter is fractious, narrow-minded, and taciturn. They both were my friends in France. Let's go! Come along with me and make acquaintance with him," my teacher said.

My teacher drove his Peugeot to Tu Xuong Street. It took some time for him to find a parking lot. We both walked to a pretty villa on Tu Xuong. A *bo doi* in khaki holding an AK-47 stood at the gate to ensure security for the VIP in the villa and to check people contacting him. My teacher went and talked to him. I saw him writing without knowing what he wrote. A few minutes later the *bo doi* allowed us to enter the villa.

Lawyer Trinh Dinh Thao, in pajamas, shook hands with us, smiled, and showed us our seats. I was attracted by many large pictures on the walls. Trinh Dinh Thao stood up and went over to these black-and-white photos. So did we. He told us about the history of each picture. These photos were taken in China, the Soviet Union, and Eastern Europe.

It seemed that Thao wanted to tell us about his diplomatic activities in the Communist bloc and Third World countries. Taking advantage of that favorable moment I began my conversation with him. I called him *bac* (uncle, father's brother) with respect.

Trinh Dinh Thao was one of the first Vietnamese to receive French doctorate in law after Dr. Tran Van Chuong, Ngo Dinh Nhu's father-in-law. He was a North Vietnamese who practiced law in South Vietnam almost all of his life. He was fond of *cai luong* (reformed theater in Cochinchina).

"Dear Uncle, please tell me the reason why you decided to go to the jungle," I said.

"I practiced law in Cochinchina during the French rule. At that time no solicitor defended the Communist party members except for me. In 1945 I was minister of justice in Tran Trong Kim's cabinet. As soon as I took office, I released all the political prisoners in Poulo Condore. Comrade Le Duan, first secretary of Dang Lao Dong Viet Nam, was among them. President Ho considered me a patriotic lawyer. In 1968 he wrote me a letter calling me to go to the jungle," Trinh Dinh Thao said.

"How did you go to the jungle?"

"A motorcyclist picked me up."

"What province of South Vietnam did you go to?"

"I went up north, not to the war zone in the South. We crossed the forests and mountains in Cambodia and Laos to arrive in Quang Binh province. The American bombings were awful when I got there. Uncle Ho ordered the local government to bring me to Hanoi at any cost so that I could avoid any danger caused by the American raiders," he replied.

"You stayed in Hanoi, didn't you?" I asked.

"Yes, I did. I lived on Gambetta Street. Hanoi was familiar to me. I am a North Vietnamese, born in Tu Liem, Ha Dong province," he said.

I asked him about his relations with Nguyen Huu Tho, chairman of the National Liberation Front.

"Brother Nguyen Huu Tho misunderstood me. He is president and I am vice president of South Vietnam. It's clear."

I wondered why, after the liberation of South Vietnam, the chairman of the National Alliance for Democracy and Peace had free time to welcome my teacher and me. What did Lawyer Nguyen Huu Tho, chairman of the National Liberation Front, misunderstand Lawyer Trinh Dinh Thao about? Was there a power struggle between the two famous lawyers in Saigon? It was certain that they both thought about their positions in the new administration in South Vietnam: they had replaced President Nguyen Van Thieu and Vice President Tran Van Huong or the two-day president, Duong Van Minh, and Vice President Nguyen Van Huyen.

"Are you a member of the Communist party?" I asked.

"I told Pham Hung about that the day I came to Tan Son Nhut Airport to welcome him. He said to me, 'You are over sixty years old. What do you adhere to the party for? Let the young members work for us.'"

"How often do you see President Ho?" I asked.

At this, lawyer Thao looked meditative but happy and smiling.

"I remember the day I arrived in Hanoi. I was informed that I would see Uncle Ho at the Presidential Palace the next week. That Saturday evening Uncle Ho came to see me at home. It moved me and made me burst into tears. I thanked him for his special visit. He said, 'You came here from the South. I have the duty to visit you first.' Then Uncle Ho asked me, 'You are tired from the long journey and the American bombings, aren't you?'" Lawyer Thao said all of this with deep respect and gratitude toward President Ho Chi Minh.

He was very happy to tell us about this short conversation with President Ho. I never saw this leader, but I read many books, magazines, and newspaper articles on him. I heard a lot about his intimacy with any persons in conversation with him. He deeply impressed my teacher in Paris in 1946, then Thao in Hanoi in 1968. His charisma and intimacy illuminated his popularity.

Being a mess boy on *La Touche Treville*, a laborer in France and England, a journalist, a writer struggling for the independence of Vietnam, and a Communist soldier in France, the Soviet Union, and China, he wasn't as haughty and finical as feudal mandarins in Asia. He knew Western democracy and the artful leadership of European despots, who gained popularity by looking for support from children, women and youngsters. Nguyen Manh Tuong, Nguyen Manh Ha, Tran Dai Nghia, and Tran Duc Thao were conquered by him. So was Trinh Dinh Thao.

Taking advantage of this conversation with lawyer Trinh Dinh Thao, I wanted to verify some international news regarding Sino-Soviet relations.

"Uncle, did you visit the People's Republic of China, the Soviet Union, and other socialist countries?" I asked.

"Yes, I did. I went to the People's Republic of China, the Soviet Union, Hungary, Romania, etc.," lawyer Thao said.

"For many years the domestic and foreign media have told us about a Sino-Soviet dispute. I think that it is a distortion," I said.

Lawyer Trinh Dinh Thao didn't confirm whether I was right or wrong. He said, "I arrived in Beijing before visiting the Soviet Union and other socialist countries in Eastern Europe. Prime Minister Chou En-Lai welcomed me warmly. We were happy to see each other. It was a good opportunity for both of us to speak French. We told about our memories in Paris, about the Sorbonne, Quartier Latin, the metro, and even about some familiar peddlers in the capital of France. Our conversation lasted five hours. All the foreign correspondents could think about were diplomatic abnormalities or about some thorny problems from both sides. That evening a communiqué was released showing the common ground of both sides. Moscow wasn't happy with this communiqué. When I arrived there, the Soviets welcomed me frigidly. I got angry and left Moscow for Budapest, where I was warmly welcomed. The Soviet ambassador in Budapest suggested that the Soviet government invite me to visit Moscow again. This time the Russians welcomed me solemnly. They saw me off at the railroad station when I left for Beijing on the way back to Hanoi."

The conversation with Trinh Dinh Thao was interesting. He was jovial, sincere, and open-minded. He was friendly with my teacher. He resisted the ban of *cai luong* performances after April 30, 1975. All the *cai luong* actors and actresses suffered from this ban. He praised Ms. Thai Thi Ngoc Thanh, a lawyer and talented linguist in Indochina. She hid her intelligence and talent and chose a quiet life. Few Vietnamese knew this especially intelligent and talented lady. As a *cai luong* fan, Trinh Dinh Thao advocated for the *cai luong* performances successfully. The *cai luong* actors and actresses returned to the stage.

Reverend Huynh Van Cua was detained by the Communists in Song Be (Binh Duong) before becoming bishop of the diocese of Phu Cuong. Phan Huy Duc came to see my teacher and asked him if he knew how to get Father Cua out of jail. My teacher was very helpful although he didn't know Father Cua. He got dressed and drove to Tu Xuong Street to see lawyer Trinh Dinh Thao who, without any hesitation, called Pham Hung, a member of the politburo and a political commissar in South Vietnam. The latter ordered the provincial government to release Father Cua so that he could attend his Episcopal investiture at the diocese of Phu Cuong. The investiture had to be simple. That day militia in Tan Thoi and Phu Long wouldn't allow Catholics from other regions to go to Phu Cuong, Song Be province (Binh Duong).

A Catholic priest asked a nun to drive a Volkswagen to Saigon to pick up my teacher, his wife, and Mr. and Mrs. Phan Huy Duc to take them to Giong Ong To, Thu Duc district, for lunch in honor of Bishop Huynh Van Cua. On this occasion, on behalf of Bishop Cua, he thanked my teacher for playing an active role in the release of the new bishop. My teacher died. So did Trinh Dinh Thao. But Bishop Cua is alive in the United States. Probably he didn't know anything about the silent work of these two unknown benefactors. But Mr. Duc, Phan Quang Dan's brother, and his wife did.

In 1976 Vietnam was reunified and became Cong Hoa Xa Hoi Chu Nghia Viet Nam (Socialist Republic of Vietnam). The flag of the National Liberation Front didn't exist anymore. The leaders of the NLF and the National Alliance for Democracy and Peace, such as Nguyen Huu Tho, Huynh Tan Phat, Nguyen Thi Dinh, Nguyen Thi Binh, Nguyen Van Hieu, Trinh Dinh Thao, Duong Quynh Hoa, and Truong Nhu Tang, were less important. So were Cadres B

(Viet Cong). The latter were hated by the South Vietnamese for harassing them, confiscating their property, and performing vengeful acts. They were gradually replaced by Cadres A from North Vietnam. Some of them were sent to Nguyen Ai Quoc School to study Marxism. Many of them were dismissed because of "corruption," "bureaucratic spirit," "bossy manner," or "ignorance of the party line." The leaders of the NLF and the National Alliance were of *petit bourgeois* or *bourgeois* intellectual families. Their relatives and friends in South Vietnam held high positions in the Saigon government. During the war they had been in the jungle. These relatives and friends brought their families financial assistance. When they rejoined their families, their relatives and friends became victims of the new regime. Didn't Nguyen Huu Tho, Huynh Tan Phat, Trinh Dinh Thao, and Duong Quynh Hoa suffer when they saw their relatives and friends in the reeducation camps and in foreign lands after the whole country was "clear of foreign enemies"?

Lawyer Nguyen Lam Sanh, chairman of the Asian Anti–Communist Alliance, helped Nguyen Huu Tho's family although they were on opposite sides. Personally they were friends. Professionally they were colleagues. Politically they were adversaries. After 1975 Nguyen Huu Tho was the winner. Nguyen Lam Sanh was the loser. The winner was in power. The loser was a the reeducation camp. The loser was the benefactor of the winner's family. More or less, Nguyen Huu Tho was strained by the call of conscience. On the one hand, he had power, honor, interest, and Communist ethics. On the other hand, he had conscience, gratitude, righteousness, and human virtues. Which side did he choose? He couldn't choose both sides at one time but one of them only.

In 1980 Nguyen Lam Sanh was released. Shortly after that, he rejoined his family in France. Nguyen Huu Tho had a political title without real power in the Communist regime, which he had believed in and spent thirty years struggling for its birth.

Trinh Dinh Thao, Huynh Tan Phat, and Duong Quynh Hoa made no exceptions when the regime associated patriotism with Communism. Love for the country had to be tied to love for socialism. Love for socialism had to be tied to the class struggle. The cadres couldn't be shaken by family attachment, friendship, or common sense, if it would make them deviate from their political stand.

Architect Huynh Tan Phat, prime minister of Cong Hoa Nam Vietnam (Republic of South Vietnam), returned to Saigon the day his mother passed away. Her funeral was solemn not because of the reputation of Huynh Tan Phat, her son, but because of the piety of her granddaughter, whose husband had just been sent to a reeducation camp. Huynh Tan Phat was bitterly criticized by the party because of his mother's solemn funeral. He was deputy prime minister after the birth of the Socialist Republic of Vietnam. Nobody knew how important he was in Hanoi. At times, he was seen in Ho Chi Minh

City. He used to wear a three-pocket shirt and a pair of leather slippers when he visited his friend in the Thu Duc University village.

Dr. Duong Quynh Hoa was used to liberalism, which she had learned in France. Rationalism and liberalism lost their ground in Communist society. Duong Quynh Hoa was one of the richest physicians in Saigon. She had a splendid villa with many worthy antiques. She sacrificed her luxurious life for the revolution. Her brother, a lawyer, was assassinated by the Saigon government. One of her children died in the jungle. After 1975 she was no longer minister of health of the Republic of South Vietnam. She worked for a children's hospital in Ho Chi Minh City.

Truong Nhu Tang, Viet Cong minister of justice, studied in France. In South Vietnam he held an important position, but he quit his job to go to the jungle in 1968. After the fall of the Republic of Vietnam he returned to Saigon where he fell in love with a young and beautiful air hostess. The Communists criticized him for loving a lady of the opposite side. He was politically and socially discredited. Finally, he decided to leave the regime he had dreamed of. His assistant, Dr. Tang Kim Dong, sought to leave Saigon for France.

Engineer Huynh Van Dai, a member of the French Communist party, a high-ranking expert on the Republic of Vietnam, had believed in the perfection of a Communist society without social evils. He was soon disappointed with the new regime. He found his sudden death, although nobody knew the cause. He was disappointed and sick of life. Some of his friends thought that his illness wasn't serious. They assumed later that the Communist physicians had accelerated his death under orders from the party to get rid of a discontented member.

The Vietnam Communist party evaluated its members based on their social class; unconditional faithfulness to the party, Marxism, Leninism, and Uncle Ho; obedience, discipline, and efficiency; and physical and moral sacrifices for the party. The members of the Vietnam Communist party were proud of their merit over the past fifty years. They scorned the Vietnamese who adhered to the French Communist party. Most of those members were bourgeois intellectuals and idealists. They weren't completely godless, familyless, and stateless. They weren't fond of armed struggles. Their discipline wasn't rigid. In brief, they weren't fanatic Communists. Therefore, according to the Communist view, they were rightist or leftist deviationists. In the two Vietnam wars they lived in the cities or in foreign countries without facing any danger or hardship, without spending a day in jail, or playing and dancing with death like their comrades in the Vietnam Communist party.

Nguyen Khanh Toan taught Russian in Moscow before the arrival of Nguyen Ai Quoc, the future Ho Chi Minh, in the Soviet Union. Few Vietnamese knew his name. His highest position in Hanoi was deputy minister of education.

In 1945 and 1946 Dr. Nguyen Manh Ha had a good reputation while Do

Muoi, Le Duc Anh, and Vo Van Kiet were unknown. His name fell into oblivion until 1975. Do Muoi, Le Duc Anh, and Vo Van Kiet became rising stars after undergoing many dangers during the two wars.

Many Vietnamese students in France became Marxists. Marx and Lenin had lived in Paris. In the nineteenth century this city witnessed stormy political, revolutionary and ideological debates. The communes of Paris was the first Communist government in the world during the First International. The famous "L'Internationale" was born. As far back as the revolution of 1789, Babeuf was considered a precursor of Communism. Weren't Nguyen An Ninh, Phan Van Hum, Ta Thu Thau, and Ho Huu Tuong influenced by Marxism? Nguyen Tat Thanh (Ho Chi Minh) left Saigon for France in 1911 and became a member of the French Communist party in 1920 before going to Moscow. Phan Chu Trinh and Phan Van Truong were repulsed by Marxism. There was an ideological divergence between Phan Chu Trinh and Nguyen Ai Quoc (Ho Chi Minh). The former was a colleague of the father of the latter. He came to France in the early twentieth century to study Western democracy. He advocated reforms and nonviolence while Nguyen Ai Quoc loved violence. Ho was a Communist of action but not a Marxist. Some Vietnamese studying in France were fond of Marxism. But they weren't Communists of action.

Tran Van Giau was an excellent Marxist theoretician. His star got dim after he left Saigon for the jungle. Some well-educated men, like Nguyen Manh Tuong and Tran Duc Thao, were well known in France but they were mistreated in their country and underwent multiple calamities due to their ideological "deviation." After 1975 many Marxists in Saigon were deeply disappointed. Some of them sought to escape or to leave the country officially. The new regime wasted natural and human resources. All activities seemed paralyzed for the government used the wrong people or incapable people in the wrong places. In the 1980s a bridge broke in Bien Hoa. Many passengers on a bus were drowned. Hundreds of people died in a train accident near Bien Hoa. The Communist government didn't take any responsibility for that. The Communist cadres were proud of their ignorance, saying that the Bolshevik governor of the National Bank of Russia didn't know how to sign his name. He pressed his fingerprints the day he took office in 1917. They said that he ran the national bank smoothly, though.

After April 30, 1975, the law school was closed, but all the professors of the College of Arts presented themselves there every day. They got paid without teaching. A famous professor of chemistry in Saigon was criticized by his students for not using "socialist" scientific terminology. An engineer was criticized by the secretary of the party cell for wasting oil and grease because he suggested lubricating engines periodically. Such boring sagas suffocated the Saigonese intellectuals. Some of them had been Communist sympathizers. They now were conscious that nothing was more important than politics in the Communist regime. Politics illuminated science, technology, economies, etc. Under the leadership of the party an illiterate like the governor of the National Bank of Russia could run a business smoothly.

The big losers in the war were the South Vietnamese Viet Minh who had gone to the North in 1954. During twenty-one years in North Vietnam they were politically, socially, and regionally discriminated against by the Communist government and by the populace. They lived in misery. Many of them sought their slow death by drinking much rice alcohol. Some went up north to get married to highlanders. They earned their living by farming, hunting, and raising poultry. Many of them fought in South Vietnam. Some were killed by American and South Vietnamese bombings during the war. Some died of starvation and of malaria. The survivors took part in the victory. Shortly after liberation, they were dismissed and returned to their native villages to practice farming. Many South Vietnamese Viet Minh in North Vietnam returned to the South without the permission of the Communist party. Some didn't attend party meetings.

Their homecoming was mostly dolorous. Those who had honor and position in society weren't warmly welcomed by their villagers. Neither were the poor and retired cadres. They suffered and returned to their native villages in rags.

These Viet Minh had their relatives, children, and sons-in-law working for the Saigon government. They couldn't imagine how comfortable their families' lives were. Their relatives were surprised to see their miserable appearance. There was a big difference between them and their relatives. Their accents, vocabulary, thoughts, and life concepts separated them from their families. Some were married in the South before going north. There they got married again and had children while their wives in the South were working hard to take care of their children and looking forward to their homecoming. They wasted their beauty and buried their youth. Twenty-one years had passed and the young ladies in wartime had succumbed to the age burden in peacetime. Their husbands' homecomings weren't their families' reunification but their separation.

Huynh Van Nghe, Dong Van Cong, To Ky, and Dao Son Tay were well known in Nam Bo during the Franco-Vietnamese War. To Ky, Dong Van Cong, and Dao Son Tay were only two-star generals. They didn't have any important role after 1975. Huynh Van Nghe wasn't a general but a *thuong ta*, a middle-ranking officer. He was in charge of forestry in South Vietnam before he died. Dao Son Tay commanded the Seventh Military Zone, but he was replaced after a scandal when he built a big house in Di An. To Ky and Dong Van Cong retired in silence. Ung Van Khiem, former minister of foreign affairs and a member of the politburo, spent the rest of his life in bitterness and shame.

After thirty years of continual wars the Vietnam Communist party jumped from one victory to another. Prime Minister Tran Trong Kim dissolved his cabinet; Emperor Bao Dai abdicated; the French were defeated; the

Americans withdrew from South Vietnam; the Republic of Vietnam collapsed. The most disadvantaged were not only the war losers but also contributors to the victory. The Vietnamese people carried all the political, economic, social, and cultural burdens left by these two wars.

8

Persistent Sorrows

Number one is studying.
Number two is farming.
When rice runs out,
Number one is farming,
And number two is studying.

I and many other people gave up our pens and desks to work in the countryside and forests. I decided to practice farming to get some agricultural produce for my family and to avoid the periodic investigations of the Song Be political security police. They came to my house once or twice a month. They wanted to know whom I contacted, how I lived, what I did before and after 1975, etc. They asked me almost the same questions every time they came.

One day, they came to my house but I was not there. They asked my wife where I had gone. My wife told them that I was farming in Tuy An (An Phu). They asked her how to get there. They rode to Tuy An to investigate me.

"Why are you here?" one of them asked me with arrogance.

"This is my paternal village. We have some land here," I replied.

"Why don't you stay home?" he asked.

"You didn't tell me when you were coming so that I could stay home to welcome you. Now, you are here. You can see what I am doing to make my living. You can ask me any questions you want. As you know, I need to work to feed my family instead of staying at home and looking forward to your coming," I replied angrily.

The two young policemen looked a little embarrassed when I talked about working. They were afraid of violating the policy of the party and of the government. Henceforth, they came to my house regularly but their attitudes were less arrogant and less brutal than they were previously. If they didn't see me at home they wouldn't go to Tuy An to verify whether I was there or not.

In 1977 they asked me, "Do you plan to escape by boat?"

"No, I don't. You see, my family is miserably poor. How could I have gold to escape by boat?" I replied.

195

They looked at me and seemed to believe that my words were true and sincere. They had pity on my family situation. Seeing many books on the shelves one of them asked me, "Why don't you give these debauched books to the Department of Information and Culture?"

Realizing that he didn't know anything about my books in French and English, I replied to him as if I were a real Communist: "This is *Le Capital* by Karl Marx, translated into French from German. It is composed of twenty-eight volumes. It is rare in Vietnam. Those books focus on the geography and economy of the Soviet Union, Hungary, Poland, and East Germany."

Both of them kept silent. They felt ashamed for misplacing their questions. Their shame increased for being Communists without knowing Karl Marx.

I worked the land owned by my father in Tuy An village, but I had no household certificate there. I was considered by the local government to be a "stranger" invading the farmlands of the village. I had no right to buy fertilizer or seeds. I couldn't bring anything out of the village. I had to "steal" my own agricultural produce or sell it in Tuy An after the harvest.

I didn't know anything about farming. Strictly speaking, I was a reluctant farmer. I bought seeds and fertilizer from the black marketeers. I hired villagers to plow my lands. Intentionally, they plowed the land superficially. When I sowed seeds, grass prevented them from growing. The plowmen received my money and then damaged my crops to discourage me so that I would give them more farmland. Wrongdoers stole my cassava and corn before the harvest. They knew my weakness as a "stranger" in the village. I wasn't protected by anybody. They used any ways to repulse me from the meager land left by my father in my paternal village. It had been abandoned during the war, but it became important after 1975. The mean-minded were always active. They updated their tactics of sabotage to force me to leave my paternal land as soon as possible. They let their chickens destroy all of my seed sprouts. They encouraged their children to play on my land during growing season.

One year, my wife was very excited about our black beans and mung beans. On harvest day her joy became a nightmare. Someone had picked our beans, leaving a big pile of leaves on the field. My wife and I were very disappointed. We rode back to Laithieu empty-handed.

Returning to my maternal village I faced the same difficulties from the local government and from a few villagers. I understood their state of mind. Our country was unstable. Our people had undergone many sufferings, witnessed horrible changes, and experienced many ups and downs. They were used to their own sufferings and to those of others. Continual hardship, poverty, and suffering seemed to kill their generosity and compassion and fertilize the development of selfishness, jealousy, and hatred.

It was difficult for me to adapt to the new environment and society overnight. My profession was teaching not farming. I was out of place. I had to do what I had ignored and what I disliked. Coming back to my paternal and maternal villages I was watched by the local government and by the villagers as well. The local People's Committee considered me a residue of the puppet government, an illegal farmer. Some villagers thought that I was obstinate, taciturn, and overly cautious. I kept away from the crowd. I didn't drink rice alcohol. But they had no reason to hate me. They used to tell me about their agricultural experiences. They asked me to spend some nights in the village to drink rice alcohol in the moonlight. I refused politely. I was afraid that I would get used to drinking rice alcohol. The drunkards spoke of their discontent and cursed the Communist regime. Both speakers and listeners were arrested by the police for speaking ill of the regime. Ba Trong and Nam Loc were the two drinkers regularly detained by militia. They both were noncommission officers of the army of the Republic of Vietnam.

Ba Trong was an airborne warrant officer who had fought in Laos and North and South Vietnam during the two wars. He was a brave Red Beret and a lucky soldier in love. He was present at all the bloody battles during the two wars. In 1967 his right arm was wounded and paralyzed. He was demobilized. In 1973 Tuy An village was restored. He left Saigon for his wife's native village, where he had happy days and a quiet life thanks to his veteran's pension. One of his arms couldn't move. He couldn't use a hoe. He counted on his monthly pension, which permitted him to get food and rice alcohol to share with his new friends in the village. After 1975 his life became miserable for he lost his pension. He was mistreated by his wife and children. Many of his new friends kept away from him. They didn't let him join them when they had parties. The Communists considered him a bad element. Every time he got drunk, he talked about his military life and spoke sarcastically of the Viet Cong. As a result, he was detained at the People's Committee office to be bitten by mosquitoes. When he was sober again, he had to do *corvée* before being released.

Nam Loc was a scout sergeant. He was stronger and healthier than Ba Trong. He had the habit of leaving the village for another place without having the permission of the local government. He had to make money to get food and rice alcohol. The local People's Committee asked him to present himself at the committee office but he turned his deaf ears to its order.

Nam Loc was a strong drinker. He walked steadily after drinking many bottles of rice alcohol. In order to have meat, he hunted hares in the woods and caught fish in Tan Phuoc. He had a wandering life and didn't worry about his wife and children who, in turn, didn't care about his presence or absence. They didn't take care of one another. Sometimes he trapped dogs, killed them, and sold their meat to get rice alcohol.

Like Ba Trong he liked to talk about his military merits as a Viet Cong killer. Detained by the militia at the committee office, he always claimed his innocence. He asked the local People's Committee why they took away his freedom while he was working to execute the teachings of Uncle Ho. The duty of the militia was to arrest the charcoal carriers and those people who tried to carry their agricultural produce out of the village. Were Ba Trong and Nam Loc harmful to society? Did the Communists have a prejudice against them because they had been South Vietnamese soldiers? That was a long saga in Vietnamese society after the war.

The People's Committee had a prejudice against the Pham in Tuy An village. In 1973 my brother called the villagers to reconstruct the *dinh* (village temple) and restore Tuy An village. The Viet Cong didn't appreciate his work, which they thought was harmful to their activities in this "free fire zone." They ordered a lady, one of our cousins, to approach and assassinate my brother. She didn't have any opportunity to accomplish her mission because of the presence of the bodyguards. After 1975 she confiscated my brother's house in Tuy An and took a lot of china. The local committee categorized my grandfather and my father as "landowners." They called the *dinh* the "temple of the Pham." They sought to destroy it at any cost. A stepbrother of my father denied his father, my grandfather, and called on the villagers not to come to the village temple to pray for peace and prosperity but to celebrate War Invalid Day annually on July 27. The villagers were displeased with his godlessness. He denied his father, his local deity, and his native village. The villagers considered him ungrateful to his parents and unfaithful to his countrymen and to his native land. Shortly after that, he was demoted. His wife killed herself. His children quarreled with one another because of their ideological divergence. One of his daughters got married to an officer of the South Vietnamese army. She was a civil servant. She brought financial assistance to the big family during his absence. After 1975 her husband was sent to a reeducation camp. She was unemployed and isolated from her father and siblings. She revolted against her Communist father and brother and left the house without saying good-bye to them.

There was a kind of cold war between the local People's Committee and the villagers. The former ridiculed the faith of the latter.

Some villagers had left their native land over the past thirty years. They had happy lives wherever they lived. Their children were educated. Some of them were economically, socially, and politically successful in Saigon and other South Vietnamese provinces. The village temple was destroyed during the war. Vice Prime Minister Phan Quang Dan assisted my brother in restoring Tuy An village and reconstructing its *dinh* in 1973. Tuy An village was reborn. It appeared on the administrative map of Binh Duong province. The villagers came back to their native land to offer food, fruit, and flowers to the local deity at the new *dinh*. So did many people from the neighboring areas.

Tuy An was a "free fire zone" during the Vietnam War. There were many unexploded bombs and mines underground. However, after 1975, no villager was killed by them. Some cows died when trampling on them.

The villagers weren't underfed during the food shortage period. Many of them received gifts from their relatives in Europe, America, or Australia. Farming has always been difficult in Tuy An for lack of water. In 1973 Tuy An had two artesian wells (from Artois, France), 400 feet deep, punched by the experts of the Ministry of Public Works, and two big motors to pump water from the wells. These artesian wells supplied the villagers with abundant water. Unfortunately the Communists dismantled and sold them on the pretext that they were a vestige of the puppet government. The wells are still there. But the villagers are short of water.

The Communists wanted to make the *dinh* a warehouse. They decided to demolish the statue of the tiger in front of the *dinh* and its gate. A Communist policeman named Ba volunteered to execute the plan of the local People's Committee. He walked to the statue of the tiger with a big hammer. Suddenly he fell down and groaned on the ground. Nobody knew what had happened to him or why he fell down. He became crippled. His legs were completely paralyzed. Consequently, he couldn't serve as a communal policeman. He stayed motionless in bed day after day, hearing his wife and children cursing him. His misfortune saved the traditional belief of the villagers.

As soon as the Communists took over Saigon, my oldest brother lost his job at a French firm. Leaving his desk he became a farmer in Tuy An, where he faced all the difficulties I did. He was disappointed with the regime he had liked in the past. He had taken part in its construction but was detained and tortured in Saigon. He criticized the Communist regime violently. One night, he was detained at the committee office for farming illegally and living in the village without a household certificate. It was the first warning for him. It made him tired and fearful. He drank a lot of rice alcohol and got drunk every day to forget all the bitter realities. Cigarettes and rice alcohol spoiled his lungs and ruined his optimism. I advised him to go to France. He told me that he didn't want to leave our ancestral land and that he had to take care of our ancestors' graves. "I was born and grew up in this country. I live and will die in this country," he said.

Some Vietnamese called the Vietnam War an ideological war. Some called it a civil war. It disunited the Vietnamese people and divided the Vietnamese families into different political tendencies: Communism, capitalism, and neutralism. In North Vietnam we had the pro–Chinese and pro–Soviet Communists. In South Vietnam the rightist wing was composed of the pro–American and pro–French rightists. The neutralists or centrists were mostly pacifists. They were scared of the war. Some believed that Sihanouk was smart.

The decline of our bodies led to the development of our minds. When people were short of food and clothes, they became more spiritual. They went to church and to the pagoda regularly regardless of the Communist police. Fatima Center in Binh Loi was crowded with Catholics and non–Catholics. I taught my wife and children to practice meditation to forget our present suffering. I healed sick people using acupuncture. Most of them were so poor that they didn't have money to get medicine. Many South Vietnamese physicians had escaped. Others didn't practice medicine officially; at the same time, the South Vietnamese didn't trust the Communist physicians. Meditation, acupuncture, and traditional medicine were useful to our health in this critical period. They helped us to be more optimistic, healthy, and adaptable in this stormy situation. Acceptance gave me more energy to cope with the incessant troubles circling me and my family. All of my plans were unsuccessful. I worked hard but the result was always negative. I cooperated with some of my friends to make noodles so I would have the right to live in the city. But my family didn't have any opportunity to enjoy the noodles made by our company. I didn't make much money and I wasted a lot. I wasn't allowed to do what I could and was forced to do what I couldn't. If I stayed unemployed, I would be suspected by the local government. I lost money in every business I tried. In addition to this stormy life, I had to present myself at the Ho Chi Minh City Police Department every Wednesday.

One evening in early 1978, I stopped by my friend's house in Thi Nghe, Ho Chi Minh City. He was general secretary of a religious university in Saigon. He was also a talented musician and originally from Hue. We knew each other and had become friendly because both of us loved history.

I went to his house but didn't see him, only some strangers. Three strange youngsters asked me many questions such as "What do you come here for?" "Who is your friend?" "How long have you known him?" and "Under what circumstances?"

I knew that I had a big trouble, but I couldn't withdraw. The three youngsters asked me to come into the house and continued to ask me thorny questions. There was no doubt that they were Communist policemen. They gave me a sheet of paper and told me to write my curriculum vitae. They kept on asking me, "How long have you known poor Luong?" "What is your religion?" "Are you Catholic?" "What is your profession?"

I respectfully answered their questions. Suddenly they shouted with joy, "Poor Luong was arrested!"

I answered their questions smoothly. I pretended not to pay attention to the bad news. One of them reported to the police department by phone.

I finished writing and gave them my background. They read it carefully then reported to their superior. I became a big fish for these hungry policemen. I was under their surveillance in my friend's house. That night I slept on the sofa in the living room with shackles on my legs. The three policemen loaded their pistols and told me that I couldn't move off the sofa without their permission. Otherwise, they would shoot me.

At 7:00 P.M. a teenager came in. "How much do you charge to teach music?" he asked.

"Whom do you ask?" one of the policemen asked.

The teenager didn't hear his question. He continued asking about the music class. A policeman held his hand up and asked him, "When did you meet poor Luong?" He repeated the question twice.

"Who is poor Luong?" the teenager demanded.

"What did you come here for?" another policeman asked angrily.

"I want to study music."

"Who teaches music?" the policeman asked.

"I don't know. I saw an advertisement on this street and came here to get some information about the music class."

The three policemen looked very happy, as if they had just caught an enemy. They told the teenager to sit on a chair and gave him a sheet of paper.

"Write!" one of the policemen ordered.

"What do I write?" the teenager asked, surprised.

"Your curriculum vitae and self-criticism," the second policeman said.

"I don't know what to write," the teenager complained.

"Did you go to school?" the third policeman asked.

"Yes, I did."

"Until what grade?" the third policeman asked.

"Ninth grade."

"So, write!"

"I don't know what curriculum vitae and self-criticism mean. How can I write?" the teenager asked.

"Write your name, address, and profession. Tell us why you came here, how you know poor Luong, etc."

"I don't know who poor Luong is. How can I write about him?" Looking at me, he suggested, "Uncle! Please write for me."

"No. That's impossible. You are a real counterrevolutionary. Don't play games with us," the second policeman said angrily.

The teenager looked fearful and angry. "Be careful with your words. What did I do to be a counterrevolutionary?" he screamed.

The three policemen didn't say a word. Their hands gently touched their guns to show that they had the right to kill anybody they liked.

The teenager wrote some lines. Then he gave the sheet of paper to one of the policemen. He looked exhausted on his chair as if he had left on a bad day and at an ill-fated time.

"Are you hungry?" one of the policemen asked me at about 8:30 P.M.

"Yes, I am," I replied.

"Give me your money. I'll get food for you," the policeman said.

The teenager felt hungry. He said to me, "Uncle! Please tell him to get two loaves of bread, one for you and one for me."

I took a ten-piastre bill from my pocket, gave it to the policeman, and asked him to get food for both of us.

After eating the loaves of bread with some thin slices of meat, we asked the policeman to give us some water. An hour later, someone called the police-men and ordered them to free the teenager.

I was alone on the sofa. I felt worn out. I lay on the sofa and slept soundly. That night I saw Jesus in white. He put his hand on mine and both of us flew over the clouds. I was very scared of falling and saw three layers of black clouds coming toward me. Startled, I opened my eyes. Lights were on in the living room. The three Communist policemen were snoring. I shut my eyes to rejoin my sleep. I felt very happy. I thought firmly that I would be released. But my life would be surrounded by three layers of black clouds. The next morning I was released but the Communist policemen kept all of my papers. I had to pre-sent myself at the Ho Chi Minh City Police Department once a week.

My family coped with the darkest situation in 1978, 1979, and 1980. I didn't make a penny. My health was languishing. My safety seemingly hung by a thread. I was visited by the provincial police in charge of political secu-rity every month. It was my turn to visit the Ho Chi Minh City Police Depart-ment every week. The local police terrorized me by searching my house many times. They wrote a petition and went to every house to collect signatures so they could arrest me. Fortunately all of my neighbors refused to sign it.

I restricted my relations with friends and cousins. Some of them had pity on me. Some were afraid to be implicated in my political business. They sought not to approach me. Some blamed me for not adapting to the circumstances. They advised me to sell everything I had and ridiculed me for sending my chil-dren to school. Some consoled me and advised me to give up farming. These people understood Communist policy and knew the art of living in a Com-munist society in which "The more people work hard, the more they are hun-gry. The more people speak, the more they are full. The flatterers have happy lives. The stubborn have to die."

A friend of mine built a boat. He suggested he would help me escape. I refused. "You are miserable. Why do you refuse my suggestion?" he asked me with surprise.

"I have a big family to take care of."

"I'll let your family escape with me. You don't have to pay a penny. Tell me your opinion," he said.

I smiled and kept silent to say "thanks" to him. It was rumored that I liked to live with the Viet Cong. Consequently, nobody talked about escape with me.

My state of mind was very complicated. Bad luck and unfavorable things came to me incessantly. They made me pessimistic and skeptical. I wondered whom I could trust after being harmed by one of my close friends. Would this friend be truly good? Was he sent by the Song Be Police Department to check if I planned to escape or not? In this unlucky situation I had to choose exist-ing misery instead of possible chains and prison.

I was indifferent before the massive exodus of the Vietnamese people. Strictly speaking, I was in contradiction with myself, oscillating between "stay" and "leave." Staying meant accepting the status quo. Leaving meant missing and renouncing everything for good. I shuddered to think of it. I would leave my country and spend the rest of my life in a foreign country. Everything would be new and strange to me there: sights, activities, ways of thinking, language, habits and customs, and daily food. I was neither a lettuce with small roots that would easily grow accustomed to a new land nor a centennial tree capable of withstanding violent storms. I shuddered when I thought of strangers looking at me with curiosity and disdain. Would I leave my country? Would I live far away from my mother, my ancestors' graves, my relatives and friends? Would I leave the familiar sights of my wartorn country? Would I leave it because of its poverty? Would I stay and see my family languishing, my children having no future, and my freedom and security being seriously threatened by the regime?

I had a headache because of these questions. I felt that stupidity reigned in my mind. I spent many white nights smoking cigarettes and turning to the altar of Emperor Quang Trung to ask for advice.

In school the teachers asked my children about my activities. My children couldn't be members of the Communist youth organizations. In reality, they weren't interested in that. They were tired and too lazy to study. Of course, they were underfed. Politically, they couldn't be good students. They had to be inferior to students from revolutionary families. In the new society I had become a thirteenth-category citizen. My children belonged to this category. They were sick of Communist literature and poetry. It was difficult for them to distinguish history from literature and politics. Like other students they coined stories to please their teachers who, in their turn, pleased the party with their literary flatteries.

One of my former professors at the College of Arts used to come to Laithieu to see me after the fall of Saigon. I felt broken-hearted to see him riding an old bicycle from Thu Duc to Laithieu just to supply my family with rice and say hello to us. Our mutual comprehension and respect grew. One day, he came to Laithieu and learned that I was farming in Tuy An. He rode there to see me. Tears flooded from his eyes when he saw me sweating blood on the arid and sterile land, exposed to the rain and sun. Putting his bicycle against a jack tree he rushed to me and hugged me, crying.

My professor had studied in France after World War II. He graduated from La Sorbonne with a doctorate in history. He returned to Saigon in 1954, when Vietnam was partitioned. He was the director of the cabinet of the Ministry of Agriculture under President Ngo Dinh Diem and taught at the College of Arts. His wife and he were sweet and virtuous persons. They were simple, compassionate, and devoted to Buddhism. They practiced fasting twice a month. After 1963, in addition to teaching at Saigon University, he taught at Hue University, Da Lat University, Can Tho University, Van Hanh and Hoa Hao Universities. He knew almost all the politicians in South Vietnam and the leaders of the National Liberation Front and the Alliance for Democracy and Peace. He was friendly with former Prime Minister Le Van Hoach, architect Huynh Tan Phat, Huynh Van Dai, and Ta Ba Tong. Venerables Thich Tam Chau, Thich Tri Quang, Thich Minh Chau, Thich Quang Lien, and Thich Thien An sympathized with him. He was thought to be a leftist or at least to believe in a "pink regime."

Before 1975 our relations were loose. He knew that I didn't believe that the Communist regime would bring democracy, freedom, and happiness to the Vietnamese people given that the Communists held all the trumps in the war. It was hard to win the war. But winning the war was easier than bringing freedom and happiness to all the Vietnamese. At that time he disagreed with me. However, he liked to hear my opinions. He was attracted by my opinions about revolution, reform, and proletarian dictatorship.

All revolutions are bloody and lead to horrible consequences. The revolution of 1789 led France and its people to terror, dictatorship, revolts, wars, glory, and shame and then to the resurrection of the monarchy.

The proletarian revolution of 1917 led the Russian people to bloodshed, imprisonment, banishment, poverty, famine, and the most systematic dictatorship.

The revolution of 1945 in Vietnam followed the same path. Its leaders praised freedom and democracy while consolidating dictatorship. They praised equality while nurturing oppression and injustice. They praised union while sowing hatred, carnage, and disunion. For the sake of independence they asked their people to sacrifice their lives, property, freedom, and happiness.

Great Britain is a monarchy. The British prefer reform to revolution. Their country is the oldest democratic and industrial country in the world.

The renovation of Japan in the nineteenth century was very successful. Japan was economically, militarily, politically, and socially Westernized and played an undeniable role in the world after thirty years of reforms.

Compared to feudal despotism, bourgeois dictatorship *à la Robespierre*, and fascist dictatorship *à la Hitler*, Communist dictatorship has been the most awful one. In feudal times, although the kings considered themselves to be God's sons and had absolute power, there were intermittent *jacqueries* (rising of peasants) in Europe and Asia. But they were absent in the Communist regime. People didn't like it. They feared it. They were scared of being arrested, tortured, brainwashed and brutally repressed by the Communist government. It was impossible for them to revolt. They sought to leave their country to look for freedom and better lives.

These observations kept my professor close to me although, after 1975, he was a member of the Ho Chi Minh City Fatherland Front in which his rank was inferior to that of Le Van Nuoi, a high school student. He knew that I had problems with the Song Be and Ho Chi Minh City police. However, he wished to see me regularly.

One day, he told me that his family was sponsored by a former general consul of the Republic of Vietnam in Paris. He didn't know what to do for he was in the Fatherland Front. I suggested that he see Vo Van Kiet, the chairman of the Ho Chi Minh City People's Committee, and tell him about his case. He was hesitant. He asked me to write a letter to Vo Van Kiet and to use the best arguments to tell him why his family would like to leave Vietnam without hurting the government. Two weeks later, my professor informed me that Vo Van Kiet allowed his wife and two daughters to leave but that he must stay in Vietnam. According to Kiet, his departure would dishonor the regime after *Agrege* Tran Ngoc Ninh escaped by boat. This decision disappointed his family for it prevented them from going to France officially. My professor was worn out. He died and was cremated in 1984.

My two respectable professors passed away. I felt that I had many big losses after liberation. I lost my job, wealth, friends, cousins and respected teachers.

Time flew by. The losses continued incessantly in the rest of my life in Vietnam. I had the feeling that God pushed me into a dead end to force me to make some firm decisions. Those people I loved went bankrupt. Some were in jail. Some had gone away or left the world forever. The death of my father-in-law and my two professors sent me to loneliness. I had nothing to cling to and no confidant to talk to, except for God. I was patient and waited for His determination. Would a righteous man be punished? If it wasn't a punishment, it would be a challenge. I comforted myself. I avoided reeducation and imprisonment. Hardship and poverty would be the price of my freedom. At least, I had shelter. I had the opportunity to take care of my family and to educate my children.

I used to get the flu before 1975. I had to have a flu shot every month and try to keep my throat warm. After 1975 my flu disappeared. I used traditional Vietnamese medicine and acupuncture to heal myself. I did the same when other members of my family got sick. We had no choice in this hopeless situation.

I got more and more spiritual. Rationalism was replaced by spirituality. My body shrank while my mind got more lucid. The development of my intuition and impartiality was considerable. In 1962 I had begun to read the Bible, which helped me surmount all obstacles miraculously in this period of challenge. Sometimes I was tired of a life full of absurdities. When I was at the height of my disappointment, some good signs made me more optimistic.

One night, I felt very happy. It seemed that all the points and meridians in my body were in harmony and in balance. When I got up the next morning, I didn't know why I felt happy. All the fruit trees around my house were verdant and bore a great deal of fruit. The sparrows flocked on the trees and made a lovely chatter at dawn and at sunset. I healed many patients from their chronic diseases.

An old man was almost dying after a stroke. He was mute and unconscious in his bed. His family invited a Buddhist monk to pray for his smooth death. His son-in-law came to ask me to heal him. "While there is life, there is hope," he said.

I was hesitant. I didn't want the local government to watch me. Besides, his father-in-law was at the doorstep of death. The son-in-law invited the neighborhood chief to come to my house and promised before the chief that his family wouldn't attribute any responsibility to me in case his father-in-law died. Fortunately, the patient recovered after three days of treatment. He spoke normally. On the fourth day he went to the coffee shop with his friends, forgetting that he was on acupuncture therapy.

One morning, a former correspondent of the *Journal d'Extrême Orient*, a French daily in Saigon before liberation, came to see me.

"I have constipation. To say the truth, I would like to see you and speak French with you. It's my pleasure and addiction," he said.

"Please don't speak French," I said.

Being deaf he didn't hear anything.

"What did you say?" he asked.

I didn't answer his question. I wrote some lines on a piece of paper. He read it without knowing why I was so prudent.

His constipation was gone. He asked me whether I could heal his deafness.

"I don't know the cause of your deafness. For that reason, I couldn't say if I can or can't. Maybe it is due to your age. Maybe it is due to your eardrum. If your eardrum is broken, I will be at the end of my resources," I said.

"I am eighty-two years old. But my eardrum is normal."

"Let me try. Within a month, if everything is unchanged, we'llknof if I failed to heal your deafness."

On the fourth day of treatment, according to him, he heard an "explosion" inside his ears as if somebody beat a drum. I continued the treatment and his hearing became normal on the thirty-fifth day.

The newspaper had an article about acupuncture and mentioned one of the most sensational success stories of mine. Many of my friends wondered whether the acupuncturist's name was mine. They came to my house and asked whether the newspaper talked about me in the article entitled "The Needles Made the Mute Speak." They looked happy when they heard my confirmation. They hugged me and said, "You make a difference."

A friend of mine, who taught at the University of Can Tho, had a stiff neck. His head couldn't move. He rode to Laithieu for treatment. After two days of treatment his head moved normally.

One early morning, a young man came to my house. He looked old in his twenties. He was skinny, pale and slow. His speech was weak. His lips were dark brown.

"Master, please help me. I have a serious heart disease. I sold everything I had just to pay the physicians and to get medicine. Now, my house is empty. My health gets worse. Death is waiting for me," he said, crying.

"What can I do for you?" I asked.

"Some friends of mine advised me to see you. So did a physician in Phu Long."

"I am not so great! I am sorry to say so."

"Master, please," he solicited.

"How can I heal you when famous heart specialists have failed?" I asked.

Frankly, I had lost my self-confidence. On the other hand, I knew who I was. I wasn't a physician. I was unemployed and watched by the police. They would take advantage of any mistake to arrest me, to put me in jail, and to confiscate my house.

The young man didn't lose his patience. Maybe I was his last source of hope. "I am sure that you can save me," he said.

I oscillated between responsibility and conscience. The patient could die any time. I would be his last physician and would take responsibility for his death. What would happen to me? I couldn't imagine.

I felt ashamed for not saving a man on the brink of his death only because he was poor. It wasn't my true nature although I didn't have the willpower of a superman.

The young man went on soliciting me.

"Master, I can't sleep without taking medicine. I can't ride from my house to the market, about three hundred yards. If I could, I would say that my heart disease was gone," he said.

I prayed before healing him. The next day he came, smiling.

"Master, I slept deeply last night. As I said yesterday, I am sure that you can heal me," he said with optimism.

On the seventh day he said to me, "Master, I would like to go to Dong Ba with you."

"I don't think that you can ride that far. Dong Ba is two miles from here," I said.

"I have the feeling that I am healthy now," he said.

He rode to Dong Ba with me on the sandy paths. We were back home in the evening. Nothing wrong happened to him.

Three weeks later, he told me that he wanted to see his doctor in Saigon for a cardiogram.

"How will you get there?" I asked.

"By bicycle."

"Are you able to ride that far?"

"I think that I am. I feel good now."

"I have two pieces of advice to give you. First, you must be escorted by a friend of yours. He will help you, when necessary. Second, when you see Dr.

Canh, don't tell him anything about your acupuncture treatment so that his conclusion will be more impartial. Otherwise, your disease could be dramatized. Tell him that you followed his instructions, that you took his medicine, and that you need him to follow up your case," I said.

"Yes, Master. I will listen to you," he said.

He told me about his trip to Saigon by bicycle after he returned to Laithieu. He looked happy for he had no trouble during the trip. Three days later, he rode to Saigon to see his doctor again.

"What kind of medicine did you take?" the doctor asked him with surprise.

"All the medicine you gave me," he replied.

"Are your relatives physicians?" the doctor asked.

The patient was afraid that the doctor would prescribe some more medicine and he didn't have the money. After 1975 many physicians in South Vietnam got rich by selling French medicine.

"I have many relatives who are doctors in France, Canada, Australia, and the United States. They sent me a lot of medicine for heart disease," he lied to the doctor.

"Really? That is why your heart disease is almost recovered. How are you feeling now?" the doctor asked.

"I am feeling good, Doctor."

"Next time, bring me all medicine you took. Good luck to you," the doctor said.

"Thank you, Doctor," the patient said, leaving the doctor's office.

The patient was recovered. He was very happy. As for me, I was morally satisfied.

One day, two old men came into my house. One was the former correspondent of the *Journal d'Extreme Orient*. The other was an old man in his seventies. He was a former civil servant who had worked for the Ministry of Education. He looked pessimistic since he had learned that he had cancer.

The first old man sold coffee on the sidewalk near the bus station. He knew the second old man from the Binh Nham Catholic Church. Seeing his friend, the first old man asked, "Where are you going?"

"To Saigon," the second old man replied.

"Why do you look pale and weak?" the first old man asked.

"The doctor said I have cancer. Today I'm going to Cho Ray Hospital to see the doctor. I am old and broke after liberation. How can I live with such an incurable disease?" the second old man asked sadly.

"Don't worry. Don't go to Saigon. Sit here. I will introduce you to a 'good doctor.' Don't be afraid," the first old man said.

The second old man listened to his friend without asking a question.

The first old man was very optimistic after his recovery from deafness. He talked a lot while the second man was taciturn. He spoke only when I asked him something directly.

I found out that he had hematuria. I tried to restore his morale by assuring him that his disease was curable. I treated him with acupuncture and asked him to take some fresh leaves of the *kalanchoe pinnata*.

He didn't come back after the fourth day. I thought that the treatment was inefficacious.

Two months later, he came to my house, smiling.

"I am sorry I did not inform you that my hematuria was gone after four days of treatment. Now, I can ride to Thu Thua, fifty miles from here, to carry some rice. You are an excellent doctor," he said.

"I am happy to see you in good health."

"Many people in Thu Thua thought that I would die of cancer. They were surprised to see me riding an old bicycle from Laithieu to Thu Thua. I told them about you. They would like to come here. Please tell me your opinion," he said.

"It is a long way. It is inconvenient for them and for me. The local police would give me trouble due to their presence."

"I understand what you mean," he said.

He invited me to have breakfast with him. After that, he came to see me regularly.

On the sixth day of Tet of the year of the Pig (1983), an old man walked slowly and heavily to my house with the help of a bamboo stick. He looked very sick. His back was bent. He seemed to look at the sky the whole time he walked.

"Are you a doctor?" he asked me.

"No, I am not."

"Are you Master Lan?"

"Yes, I am."

"Master, I am a farmer. I have been sick for a year after lifting heavy bags of fertilizer. My back is bent, as you see. I spent 30 million piastres without making my illness regress. I am desperate and am waiting for my slow death. My son-in-law told me about you during Tet. I didn't believe him because he was drunk. That day two other men talked to me about you. I was eager to see you and ask you to heal me. I pray to have my head shaved after recovery," he said.

"Where are you living?" I asked.

"In Dong Ba."

"How did you get here?"

"By coach."

I began to treat him.

On the fourth day he walked without a bamboo stick and had his head shaved. "I am certain that you have saved me from my persistent pain," he said.

After forty-five days of treatment he rode to my house with two chickens and some vegetables to thank me and inform me of his good news.

Sick people who came to my house were residents of Laithieu. Some were from Binh Nham, Bung, Phu Van, Nhi Binh, Thanh Loc, Hoc Mon, Tan Khanh, Tan Uyen, and Saigon. Among them there were some former military men who now earned their living by carrying charcoal, jars, and bowls. Sometimes they came while I was teaching at home. I treated them in the classroom without paying attention to my students' curiosity. Teaching and healing became my pleasures in the darkest days of my life.

9

Fatherland or New Land?

At the end of 1978 Vietnamese *bo doi* invaded Cambodia, overthrew the Khmer Rouge government led by Pol Pot, and backed a pro–Vietnamese government. After this event the Southeast Asian refugee camps welcomed not only "boat people" but also "walking people."

Most boat people were fishermen or people living in the littoral plains in the first years after liberation. Many Chinese Vietnamese left Vietnam semiofficially by contacting some provincial government officials and giving them nine to ten taels (37.5 grams) of gold per head. The Hanoi government kept four taels. Communist cadres and intermediaries shared the rest.

The Communist government created a lucrative service, "exporting" refugees for gold. Many Chinese Vietnamese registered, paid gold, and left Vietnam secretly. Some Vietnamese bribed the Communist cadres to change their backgrounds to Chinese ethnicity to be eligible for this semiofficial registration. The applicants registered, paid gold in advance, and waited for their departure that, once scheduled, couldn't be delayed for any reason. Therefore, many people were drowned because of typhoons and because of the boat's fragility.

Boat building was very lucrative during the diaspora of the Vietnamese people. Boat builders had neither good wood nor good nails or bolts. Nails were made from rusted barbed wire. They were soft and breakable. At sea, when faced with strong waves, the boats broke in pieces. The Communists weren't responsible for the safety of these boat people. Their purpose was to accumulate gold only. Boat people could be robbed, raped, or killed by Thai corsairs on the Gulf of Thailand. They could die from starvation.

If they arrived in the Southeast Asian countries, UNHCR (United Nations High Commission for Refugees) would take care of them. If they were drowned near the Vietnamese coast, the local governments would have one last opportunity to get some more gold from their bodies.

Rich Chinese Vietnamese didn't want to leave the country semiofficially because of these dangers. Besides, they couldn't bring much gold. They went on organizing their escapes by boat.

Escaping became the main topic of daily conversations in South Vietnam in the 1970s and 1980s. The escape organizers got wealthy quickly. They didn't accept Vietnamese bank notes, only gold. They could be Communist policemen, members of revolutionary families, or their intermediaries.

Many people were victims of fraud. Many were robbed and killed. Many lost their gold, freedom, and even their lives. Rich people used their money to buy comforts in jail. Otherwise, they had many troubles. They had to pay the Communist cadres to have good food and to smoke filtered cigarettes. After receiving money from the prisoners, the cadres ordered them to present themselves at their office for "investigation." They felt at ease to eat, drink, and smoke there. Jailed escapees had a collective shower. A Communist cadre "watered" them with a hose. They soaped. The cadre moved the hose to give them some water to wash off the soap. Their shower was over. In order to get some more water the prisoners had to negotiate with the cadre in advance.

The prisoners had to do labor every day. They grew vegetables for the camps. The cadres sold the vegetables or used them to feed pigs and chickens.

I was used to the news of the diaspora such as "Mr. X already left," "Mr. Y arrived at the refugee camp in Indonesia," "Poor Tung was arrested in Camau," "Poor Chay lost his gold and was imprisoned," or "Mrs. Ba, the jeweler's wife, wants her son to escape."

People talked about escape everywhere, at the open markets, in the restaurants, at the barber shops. From time to time I heard some sensational news: "The son of the Song Be commissar escaped on a military truck. Arriving in Cambodia, he was robbed and shot by *bo doi*. His father, a provincial commissar, got angry and decided to investigate who killed his son."

Businessmen escaped. Officers and civil servants of the Saigon government escaped. The South Vietnamese escaped. The North Vietnamese escaped. The Communists escaped, too. Telling a joke, Tran Van Trach, an exceptionally talented singer and musician, said, "If the electric poles could walk, they would escape."

Some escaped in search of freedom and *raison de vivre*. Some escaped in the hope of having a better life. Some escaped because they couldn't live under the Communist regime for political and religious reasons. Some thanked the new regime for giving them a good opportunity to send their children abroad. In the Hong Kong refugee camp, the North and South Vietnamese refugees fought and killed one another because of their different viewpoints on "April 30." American president Jimmy Carter opened his arms and welcomed all the Vietnamese who left their Communist country for any reason. The first North Vietnamese refugees were settled in the United States during his presidency (1977–1981).

In 1978 many officers of the navy were released. The escape organizers hired them as navigators. They needed mariner's compasses, motors, and maps. Some escapees bought release certificates so they would be qualified to settle in America as collaborators of the South Vietnamese government.

People were excited by the pictures taken in the refugee camps and in the new countries and by lovely letters describing the paradisaic life in America, Western Europe, and Australia. People said, "Ms. At is very beautiful!" "All the sites are attractive," "Poor Giap received his doctoral degree," or "Everybody drives. Nobody walks or rides like us."

Everybody said the same things. It seemed that people had the same dream. Some hoped to go abroad to eat chocolate, candy, cheese, fruit, and other delicious food. Some hoped to have better lives. Some hoped to do advanced studies. Some hoped to have cars to travel from one place to another.

Most people were needy except for the Communist police, tax collectors, customs officers, foresters, and the families of the "escapees." Rich citizens had food, medicine, and cigarettes. They rode Japanese motorcycles and used TVs, radio sets, tape recorders, clothes, and sandals. They received gifts every month from their relatives in America, Europe, or Australia. The quantity and quality of these gifts showed not only the prosperity of their relatives but also the prosperity of the countries they lived in. Gifts from the United States were always more abundant than gifts from other countries.

Gifts helped the receivers to have good relations with the local government. These people became the new arrivistes in the Communist society. They contacted one another to exchange pictures, news, and activities of the boat people in the asylum camps and in their new countries. They also exchanged expertise in dealing with the Communist cadres about sponsorship, registration, and application for exit permits.

I was unsuccessful at farming in my paternal and maternal villages. I was unsuccessful at running the noodle company for lack of flour. I had to teach English and French at home to make my living in spite of many difficulties from the local government. I taught languages and healed needy people at home. The Communists never encouraged these things. Under the Communist regime only the Communist police and diplomats studied foreign languages. They were trained in Hanoi or in the Soviet Union and recognized by the Ministry of Foreign Affairs. Non–Communists who knew foreign languages were suspected of having connections with the CIA or the Deuxième Bureau. Teaching foreign languages was politically unlawful. It encouraged people to escape. The Hanoi government and its cadres received tons of gold from the Chinese Vietnamese and escapees. However, in order to save face, the Communists condemned the refugees.

When healing needy people, I tried not to think about the danger I faced. I could be arrested and prosecuted for practicing acupuncture illegally. In a certain way, honest and innocent people were more dangerous to the regime than the dishonest ones. When I thought about it, I felt a little scared. *What is to be done?* I wondered.

Everything was determined by God.

The chairman of the Red Cross came to see me after seeing my name in the newspaper. He asked me to heal him of his migraines. We had the opportunity to talk to each other. I told him about my worries. He dissipated them and encouraged me to continue helping people. He promised to give me needles, cotton balls, and alcohol. A Chinese Vietnamese gave me alcohol and told me I could get more any time I needed it. He was happy that I had healed his son of insomnia and stomachache.

One morning, a female physician brought a Communist captain of police to my house and asked me to relieve his persistent headache. The patient was a South Vietnamese Communist who had gone to the North in 1954. He had returned to South Vietnam and was appointed police chief of Tan Thoi. He was rude and brutal. Every time he had a headache, his eyes got red and blind. He screamed all day long when the pain surged. When the pain was gone, he confided to me, "You know, I am rough because of my headaches. When the pain surges, I could be homicidal. At one time I hated everybody and everything around me. In 1972 an American B-52 dropped bombs over Kham Thien, Hanoi. A piece of shrapnel hit my head and stayed there. Doctors said they could take it out of my head with surgery. But, according to them, such an operation could damage my speech or sight. Consequently, they remained indecisive."

Acupuncture regularized his temper.

One of the two policemen in charge of political security, who came to my house every month, asked me to heal him of backaches. After he recovered he brought me to the coffee shop. My neighbors and friends thought that I was being arrested by the police. Some thought that I was being friendly with the police. Nobody knew the ironic reality that the patient (policeman) was healed by the man he had harassed and investigated.

I was invited by the Tan Thoi People's Committee to give a *causerie* about acupuncture and traditional Vietnamese medicine to 200 people. The *causerie* was broadcast so that a large number of residents could hear. Its success was unexpected. Right after I spoke of some of the characteristics of the *kalanchoe pinnata*, all the medicinal plants in my garden were stolen.

The *causerie* ended. The chairman of the People's Committee shook hands with me and thanked me for giving this interesting *causerie*.

"In my opinion, this is the best *causerie*. Everybody listened to you presenting a dry, difficult but interesting topic. At meetings, people used to talk to one another about their personal business or look at the lizards biting their tails on the ceiling more than they listened to our cadres speaking. We need to have some more *causeries* like this," he said.

He got to know me through this occasion. He then began to stop by my house to invite me to have coffee with him. Sometimes he brought some food to my house and had breakfast with me. He liked to converse with me. He knew my past and present. He understood and shared it with me instead of pushing me in the mud like his comrades did. Our friendship flourished after many breakfasts and conversations. In his eyes, I wasn't a dangerous and despicable man. As for me, I didn't find anything awful in him. I didn't have such feelings when I saw his comrades.

He went north in 1954 on board a Polish boat. His arm was wounded in an exchange of bullets with the French. A Polish surgeon operated on his arm on the boat. He got married to a North Vietnamese peasant. Their life was miserable. His infirmity prevented him from being a strong farmer. Living miserably in his wife's village and being crippled, he was despised and bullied by the villagers and by his comrades. One day, he argued with a member of the collective farm and was badly beaten by him. He fell down and lay unconscious on the ground until his wife found him.

Due to poverty and shortages of food and medicine for a family of six persons, his wife fell ill and died. His family got darker. He was unable to feed his four daughters, to educate them, and to take care of them. They were too young to be motherless. A young lady helped him manage the family. She became his second wife. She wasn't beautiful, but she was joyful, modest, sweet, sincere, and sociable. Behind her bad-looking appearance hid many invisible beauties.

She wasn't hesitant to speak about her state of mind. She said, "I was moved by his situation. I was a young lady. He was a widower with four daughters. Many bad rumors were spread in the village while I was morally anguished about his motherless daughters. In North Vietnam people observed customs rigorously. I had to ignore criticism from different sides. I looked forward to the liberation of the South in order to go there with my husband. We worked hard in the collective farms but we were always in the pinch of poverty. We were in need of food, heavy clothes, medicine, and a safe shelter."

Her dream was simple and realistic. South Vietnam was a new horizon for her. The important thing was to have two meals a day. It was enough. Her dream came true after 1975. She followed her husband when he returned to Laithieu. She was a citizen of the Democratic Republic of Vietnam. Her husband was a Cadre A. He was elected chairman of the People's Committee of Tan Thoi, the most populous and prosperous village in Laithieu district. She became a council member. Our lovely lady wasn't interested in these titles, but many people cowered before them while she tried to accomplish her duty as a worker at a pottery kiln. From work she brought home some bark and firewood. I sympathized with this couple. They both were simple and sincere. I loved sincerity and simplicity because, in the course of my life, I had faced lies, deceptions, and complications, especially after the fall of South Vietnam.

One evening, while the husband was conversing with me, one of their sons ran home crying.

"What is the matter?" the mother asked.

"Poor Tung beat me up," the son cried.

"OK! OK! Stop crying! Poor Tung was clumsy with his hands. He didn't beat you up intentionally," the mother said, comforting her son.

The son was displeased with his mother's reasoning. He ran to his father yelling, "Poor Tung beat me up. I am in pain!"

The father looked at his son and said, "Stop crying, son. You deserved it."

Disappointed, the son stamped his feet on the floor, screamed, and went out.

I was satisfied with the behavior of this couple. It differed from that of a neighborhood chief the time a dog bit his son. He had used the loudspeaker to order all the neighborhood residents to register their dogs one sultry afternoon.

Are kindness, sincerity, and simplicity innate? Do they depend on time, space, education, or social position?

I knew two men. Both of them were the same age. They were born in the same village. Their education was almost the same. But their behaviors were different. The first man joined the resistance in 1945. The second worked for the French Red Berets during the Franco-Vietnamese War. The former wasn't proud of his participation in the resistance or of his present position in the village. But the latter behaved as if he should be a viceroy in his neighborhood due to his imaginary anti–American activities. This comparison didn't lead us to the conclusion that all the former Viet Minh were as modest as the man in question.

The Communists denied religions. They considered them to be like opium, which enchanted human beings. They tried to paralyze them. Nevertheless, all the religions still existed not only in the minds and hearts of the population but also in the minds and hearts of some members of the Communist party.

There was an altar in the house of the chairman of the People's Committee of Tan Thoi. The altar had neither statue nor picture. It had a small incense burner only. The husband was more cautious than his wife. I saw her lighting incense sticks and praying.

One year, the village chief and his wife went back to Ha Nam Ninh with their two sons. I thought that she was homesick after many years of separation from her family in North Vietnam. Returning to the South she told me about their trip to the North and its true purpose. She said, "This trip to North Vietnam was horrible. The train was noisy, dirty, and unsafe. The muggers on the train were cruel. They would have killed us if we had resisted. When the train entered a tunnel, it was very dark. The muggers could do what they liked. We lost all of our luggage. In addition to that, we were detained and checked by the police. What shame."

"You went back to North Vietnam to visit your family, didn't you?" I asked.

"My husband and his first wife had no son, only four daughters. When he married me, he prayed to have sons to carry on his lineage. We have two sons. Now our oldest son is twelve years old. We went back to the North to make some offerings to thank God for giving us two sons and for protecting their health," she said.

"Why didn't you give offerings to God here instead of traveling to the far North?" I asked curiously.

"My husband is chairman of the committee here. It is inconvenient for him to do it here. Very inconvenient," she said without any hesitation.

The provincial political security police watched my English and French classes. One time they sent two new young policemen to my house. These guys looked rough and rude.

"Did you register to teach English and French?" one of them asked me with arrogance.

"No, I didn't. The number of students varies constantly. How can I have money to pay my taxes if I register?"

"You teach English and French to the escapees, don't you?"

"I compare my classes to a store. When a customer gets something at the store, the store owner doesn't ask him what he buys it for. Neither do I. I teach languages. The students come here to study them. I never ask them what they learn them for. Such curiosity would prevent them from coming," I replied.

"Did you get a teaching permit from the Department of Education to teach foreign languages?" one policeman asked.

"No, I didn't. But everybody in this area knows my classes. They aren't harmful to either the local government or the residents of this city."

"Who knows your classes?"

"The local committee."

After five years under investigation I stopped presenting myself at the Ho Chi Minh City Police Department. Throughout the five years they kept on asking me the same questions about my relations with "poor Luong" and with Father Nguyen Van Vang, about my family, my daily activities, about *Agrege* Nguyen Van Bong, and Dr. Nguyen Ngoc Huy, etc.

The investigator had clandestine activities in Saigon during the war. He said that he knew me and that he had taught Vietnamese in some private schools in Saigon. I didn't know if that was right or not. He had the appearance of a teacher and a professional officer of intelligence. He wasn't as rude as the policemen in Song Be. But he was more dangerous than those rude rural Communists. He knew a lot about the Saigon government and the social, educational, religious, and political problems in South Vietnam. All of his questions seemed to be traps for me.

"What is your religion?" he asked.

"Ancestral worship. I worship Buddha and Emperor Quang Trung."

"Were you baptized to be a Buddhist follower?"

"No, I wasn't. I believe in Buddhist philosophy."

"So you aren't a Buddhist. Worshipping ancestors isn't a religion."

"In the past I said so when somebody asked me about my religion," I said.

"Under what circumstance did you know 'poor Luong'?" he asked.

"We both taught history."

"Poor Luong followed a reactionary Catholic priest, Nguyen Van Vang, who worked to overthrow the revolutionary government. Did you know that?" he asked.

"No, I didn't."

"What did you go to Luong's house for?"

"To talk with him about tutoring a student," I said.

"Who will teach?" he asked.

"I will."

"Why not poor Luong?"

"Luong is busy teaching music."

"Luong and you had an antirevolutionary conspiracy," he accused me.

"You overestimate me. In the past the South Vietnamese army and the American and allied troops were numerous and well equipped, but they couldn't defeat the revolution. How would Luong and I overthrow the revolutionary government? We have a certain level of education. We aren't stupid to try what we can't do," I said.

The investigator diverted me by saying, "Poor Luong told me about you. He said you know many Catholic priests."

"It's true. I taught in many Catholic schools in Saigon and Gia Dinh."

"Why did you teach in the Catholic schools?"

"I liked to make money. They needed good teachers. We needed each other. Besides, I taught in the Buddhist and Adventist schools too," I said.

"What did you think about them?"

"They were good. If they discriminated against me they wouldn't have invited me to teach in their schools. It's clear that I'm not a Catholic."

"Did you sympathize with the Catholics?"

"I sympathize with those people who are kind to me. Maybe they are Catholics. Maybe they are Buddhists, Caodaists, Buddhist Hoa Hao, or Baptists," I said.

"What do you practice meditation for?" he asked.

"To get rid of my daily worries, to forget any hardship, and to develop forgiveness. Every day we take a shower to get rid of the dust from our skin. How can we clean our minds every day without using meditation to keep our mind quiet? Water gets clear after decanting or filtration. Quiet and worriless minds are more easily illuminated. Meditation is my daily static exercise," I said.

The investigator looked at me and smiled. His smile wasn't a wicked one. As an atheist he couldn't share my ideas. But he couldn't accuse me. He went on. "Do you know Nguyen Van Bong and Nguyen Ngoc Huy?"

"Yes, I do," I replied.

"How?"

"Because they were well-known intellectuals in South Vietnam."

"They were two reactionary intellectuals," he said.

I sat quietly and listened to his accusations. But he didn't say anything else. He could have been their student.

One Wednesday afternoon, while waiting for my turn to be investigated, I sat on a bench near a wall covered with thorny plants with dark red flowers. I shut my eyes to have a short nap in front of the police department. Suddenly I heard a Honda stopping by the bench. I opened my eyes and saw a man who, in 1967, was a presidential candidate on the ticket that was trying to defeat General Nguyen Van Thieu and Nguyen Cao Ky. I avoided seeing him by turning to the wall, thinking that he was under investigation like me. I felt horrible when I saw him hugging my investigator with joy as if they had missed each other for a long time.

One evening, the investigator took me to Tran Hung Dao Street. We stood under the shade of a big tree. The investigator returned to me all of my papers, which he had kept for the past five years.

"I know that you weren't happy to see the police in the past years," he said.

"Nobody is happy to be detained or investigated by the police," I said sincerely.

"I know a lot about you. You were my sister's teacher. She said that she liked you very much."

To this day, I don't know who his sister was or what school she attended.

I received my papers, shook hands with him, and rode to Laithieu with fatigue. The sun set in the West but it was still sultry. In the distance, some songs sounded in the air, giving me sorrowful and horrible feelings.

The black clouds of my life were deemed to disappear. Reality wasn't so simple. The Song Be police sought to get some evidence of my past activities to arrest me. They never forgot me. The security and safety of the reeducation detainees after release were uncertain. They could lose their freedom any time. The Communist media incessantly warned Communist cadres and the police of counterrevolutionary activities, which they enlarged and exaggerated to push the police to watch the suspects and reeducation detainees closely.

I had many troubles caused by the Communist police but didn't dare to tell anybody, even my mother, wife, and brothers.

In the reeducation camps in North Vietnam my brother thought a lot about my security. Some mean-minded detainees asked my brother and younger brother whether I was a "menace." My brother bribed them with sugar, salt, and dried food to stop their mean-minded curiosity. My younger brother said that I was in such-and-such reeducation camp.

My brother was moved from Long Thanh (Bien Hoa) to Bac Thai province in North Vietnam. A few years later, he was moved to Thanh Hoa, the cradle of the Le and Nguyen dynasties. From the reeducation camp of Thanh Hoa, he was brought to the South by train. His brainwashing and forced labor continued in Ham Tan. After spending eight years in four reeducation camps in South and North Vietnam he was released. During this critical period he did hard labor without having enough food, heavy clothes, or medicine. Many detainees died of languishment. Some were killed when cutting down trees. Some died for lack of food. Some couldn't resist the severe weather in the remote mountainous areas of North Vietnam. My brother lost eight teeth. He almost died of suffocation due to asthma during his detention in the camps.

Coming home he felt heartbroken to see his house empty and to learn that his children had quit school. His youngest son was three years old when he was sent to the reeducation camp. Now the son didn't recognize his father.

My brother had to redo his life. As for me, I continued to play the boring, tragic comedy unwillingly. The darkest days passed heavily and slowly. Life in my family got more and more boring. It was vivid only on the fifth day of Tet. We celebrated the victory of Dong Da in memory of Emperor Quang Trung on the fifth day of the year of the Rooster (1789). On that day my oldest brother, some of my friends, and some students came to my house to light incense sticks before the altar of Emperor Quang Trung and to have a big lunch with my family. On this occasion we exchanged our life concepts and historic viewpoints. We talked about meditation, Chinese astrology, religions, our present lives, and the role of Emperor Quang Trung in history.

I told my former students whatever they wanted to know. Sooner or later, I would leave my country. I taught my children English, gave them primary orientation on life in America, nourished their ethical and religious lives, and encouraged them to practice meditation and to read the Bible in English.

One day, my professor and I went to Dakao to see a man in his thirties. He was in white. He was surrounded by some ladies. One of them was the wife of a former minister of the economy. My professor introduced me to them. The man was smiling. He looked at me as if I were familiar to him.

"Last night, I had a white night," he said.

"Why?" one of the ladies asked.

"Because of this man," he replied, pointing at me.

In memory of Emperor Quang Trung. My family, friends and former students at my house in Laithieu, commemorating the Dong Da victory on the fifth day of Tet.

"I don't understand what you mean," the lady said.

"Bodhisattva Kwan Yin asked me to repeat a long psalm to remind him of his past lives," the man said.

Then he asked us to record the psalm he would recite. He closed his eyes and began to recite the 630 verses. He was tired and his voice was hoarse after he finished reciting the long psalm. The house owner gave him a cup of tea. We talked to one another. A lady gave me the tape and told me to return it to her after I transcribed the psalm. My professor and I thanked the young man and all the ladies. Then we left.

I needed to listen to the psalm. But I had already sold my cassette recorder. I went to my cousin's house to borrow his. He told me that his cassette recorder was out of order. I blamed myself for putting him in a dilemma. On the way home, I stopped by the house of a friend of mine. I told him that I needed a cassette recorder to listen to a poem.

"My son just sent me a cassette recorder. Take it home for a couple of days," my friend said.

I shook my head and said, "It's impossible. I only need an old cassette recorder. I can't use your new one in this case. I am unlucky these days. I am afraid that something wrong will happen to me."

I shook hands with him and left. An hour later, his son brought me the cassette recorder. My wife, my children, and I stayed home to listen to the psalm that evening. I wrote down the 630 verses in an old quire. This long psalm influenced me a lot. It reflected my past, present, and future. Regarding my past life we had:

You were born in the Holy Land in your early life.
From Jerusalem you were illuminated by the teachings of God.
Your Father in Heaven gave you immense blessings.
You followed the path of the Lord in the Middle Ages.

The following verses related to my present life:

Sometimes your life was stormy.
Sometimes it was quiet, frosty and full of anxieties.
From any earthy jobs you did,
You haven't ever been free in a single day.

About politics we had:

The political path was colorfully embellished.
Walking on it, you felt frigid and lonely.

Some verses explained my suffering:

The [sufferings] were the shields protecting you
So that your afflatus flourished.

Or:

Your earthy life was bitter, sour and broken-hearted.
Traveling around the world,
You were always in the ethical orbit.

The psalm predicted my diaspora:

Due to the primordial causality,
You are going to go West.
It is a divine order
For Amida confides in your innate faith.

Bodhisattva Kwan Yin advised me to live as an eremite like Chang Leang:

Remember Chang Leang
Who, one time, exercised his political apprenticeship.
When everybody knew his honor and fame,
He left for the mountains to live an eremitical life.

At that time, I didn't know anything about this young man. I thanked him for reciting the 630 verses from Bodhisattva Kwan Yin. The psalm moved me and my family. It made us more optimistic and gave us the light of hope in our miserable situation. I couldn't anticipate that God had prepared a big change for me by letting my friend and cousin endanger me and by letting society isolate and abandon me. I had stayed home to educate my children and to help people. I had to have many sufferings in order to witness miracles and the divine force of God and to be aware of the suffering of others due to oppression, injustice, poverty, illness, starvation, and illiteracy.

I continued doing what I could to make myself useful to society. I taught languages to earn my living and to equip my children with some linguistic skills. I practiced acupuncture and studied it incessantly. My oldest brother, one of my Chinese students, and a friend of mine encouraged me to study it profoundly by supplying me with acupuncture and traditional medicine books in Vietnamese and French. Most of my old books had been destroyed. They were replaced by oriental medicine books. I was curious and greedy to know about the herbal medicine used by the highlanders, Tibetans, and Hindus. It was the best and the shortest way of health care during this critical period.

One day, a former student of mine in Saigon came to see me in Laithieu. He asked me, "You are influenced by Western culture. Why are you interested in traditional Vietnamese medicine?"

"Like many young Vietnamese imbued with Western culture, I committed a serious mistake by looking down upon traditional Vietnamese medicine. My insight came from two reasons: (1) our country is rich in medicinal plants while our people suffer from diseases. This period of shortage reminds us of our natural resources for medicine, and (2) the French introduced Western medicine in our country in the nineteenth century. Western medicine is efficacious but it is very expensive. Many Vietnamese can't afford it.

"What happened to our people before the introduction of Western medicine when they fell sick? How did they survive if they didn't have good physicians and efficient medicine? How did they defeat foreign invaders? How did they build up a stable national agricultural economy? How did they carry out their territorial expansion by mastering the mountains, clearing the forests, filling the everglades, and facing various kinds of enemies, wild animals, and illnesses?

"Each people have their own traditional medicine. We have to retain what is simple and efficient and eliminate what isn't," I said.

My student seemed curious to know about many things around me. He looked at the picture of Emperor Quang Trung and asked me, "Are you influenced by scholar Ho Huu Tuong in your worship of Emperor Quang Trung?"

"No, I'm not. It's my personal idea."

"Why do you worship him?"

"We have many national heroes in our history. I admire and adore them all. Our hero Quang Trung Nguyen Hue was predestined to reunify our country and free us from the claws of the two feudal forces. He was an extraordinary hero in our history.

"First, he wasn't a learned man. He was from an ordinary family in the remote hamlet of Tay Son in Qui Nhon province. But he was an excellent organizer and tactician. He entered history with resounding victories. Our people have many things to learn from him.

"Second, he was the youngest general in the world, commanding the army at the age of eighteen without having spent a day in a military academy. He defeated all the famous generals of the Nguyen in the South and of the Trinh in the North. He expelled the Thai and Chinese troops from Vietnam in a few days.

"Third, he was not only a young general but an invincible one. In the course of his military life, he didn't know any defeat. He crushed his enemies on the ground and on the sea as well. In him, we see the images of Napoleon I in the battle of Austerlitz and Admiral Nelson in the naval battle of Trafalgar. But he remained victorious until the end of his life while Napoleon was defeated at Waterloo. He danced safely with death on the battlefields while Nelson died heroically while bringing victory to England.

"Fourth, he was respected not only by his soldiers but by the scholars and by his enemies, the Nguyen, Trinh, and Qing," I replied.

"Who worships Emperor Quang Trung like you?" he asked.

"I don't know for sure."

"Do you hurt the existing beliefs of your family when you worship Emperor Quang Trung?" my student asked.

"Nobody in the Pham family worships him but me. I don't think that I hurt my family's beliefs. Most Vietnamese worship their ancestors. I worship a national hero as our forefather," I replied.

"Can we compare Uncle Ho to Emperor Quang Trung?"

"Such a comparison is difficult. One lived in the eighteenth century. The other lived in the twentieth century. The foreign interference was less important in the eighteenth century than in the twentieth century. However, I will try to show you some of their differences:

"Emperor Quang Trung reunified the country after defeating the two feudal forces (the Nguyen and Trinh), as well as Thai and Chinese troops without receiving foreign aid. As a result, he was very independent.

"President Ho Chi Minh went to Russia, then to China to learn their political experiences in organization and their techniques of stirring mass movements. In 1954 he beat the French thanks to active aid from China, but he had to listen to Beijing and accept the partition of Vietnam. The victory of Dien Bien Phu and the Geneva Accord led to the tragic partition and separation but not to real victory and joy. Emperor Quang Trung reunified the country while President Ho divided it. In the Vietnam War North Vietnam received aid from both China and the Soviet Union. The Vietnamese people struggled for independence only to get economic and political dependence! They expelled the French in order to bow down before the Soviets and Chinese. In the 1970s the Americans left and were replaced by the Soviets. Our country is ruined. Our people are disunited and separated. Did they spill their blood for such an international cause?

"President Ho has a name in history. But we can't compare him to any of our heroes because of his international Communist background. It is undeniable that Nguyen Tat Thanh was a patriot. But Ho Chi Minh was a fervent member of the Comintern.

"In the past our people were happy after expelling the invaders from our country. In our time, after every victory of Ho Chi Minh, people were fearful and thoughtful. They had to leave their native land like your family in 1954 and like now," I said.

Looking at a painting on the wall my student asked me, "Who drew this painting?"

"Which one?" I asked him.

"The five children and the cricket fighting," he replied.

"The painter was a graduate of the Ecole des Beaux Arts of Gia Dinh in the 1940s. He wasn't a famous artist. He joined the resistance and spent nine years in the Plain of Reeds. Now he is tired of politics. He gave me this painting in 1966 as a souvenir of our acquaintance.

"The crickets bite each other. The winner is cocky. The loser runs for its life. A child catches it and spits some saliva on its face to make it stronger and more courageous to fight again. Sometimes the crickets kill each other and lie down on the tray. The five children laugh, throw the dead crickets away, and continue the game," I said.

"Do you plan to leave the country?" my student asked.

"So far, I don't. But it's difficult to predict the future."

It was sunset. I urged my student to ride home for the traffic was unsafe at dark. He said good-bye to me and pedaled slowly on Road 13. I watched him until he disappeared. I went back into my house, which seemed quiet and empty.

Time flew by. My children grew up. My oldest son graduated from high school. My youngest daughter finished elementary school and became a junior high student.

My oldest son wanted to enter college. But it was difficult for him to surpass two thorny barriers: the police and the college student recruitment committee. The police verified and certified his family's background. The recruitment committee recruited students based on that background (social class, revolutionary families, glorious families, members of the Communist party). The students could pass the test and not be admitted. The decisive factor was the curriculum vitae, not the grades.

My oldest son was unhappy, seeing no bright future. I was brokenhearted to see him in his premature hopelessness. I felt dolorous to hear my youngest daughter asking my wife if she had ever eaten grapes in her life.

"You did. You were too young to remember. Before 1975 you all had everything. Your brothers and sister were fat and rosy. They had Dutch milk even when they were six years of age," my wife said.

My youngest daughter looked happy to hear that she had eaten the high quality fruit she dreamed of. She was young but intelligent and curious. One day, she asked her mother, "Is Daddy as educated as my teacher?"

"If your teacher had to go to school, your father would be his teacher," my wife replied.

"Why has Daddy stayed home all this time?" my youngest daughter asked curiously.

My wife kept silent to stop the naïve curiosity of our six-year-old daughter.

One day, she asked my wife why so many people knew me. My wife smiled without satisfying her curiosity.

At times, my wife's younger brother and cousin would come to see my family and bring some agricultural produce. My children felt happy about their concern. They enjoyed good food every time they came.

My wife's cousin was a spinster. She was orphaned in her childhood. My mother-in-law took care of her. She lived in my wife's family as my wife's sister. Unlike most spinsters in celibacy and childlessness, she loved children. She gave herself the right to look after my children when they were in their cradles. My children had attachments to her. She felt sad and brokenhearted every time I punished them. She wouldn't eat anything and would cry silently, hugging them. When I was in a critical situation, she would come to see us and supply us with rice, cassava, sweet potatoes, beans, vegetables, sugar cane, and corn.

She suffered when she saw my oldest son in a dilemma. He neither entered college nor got a job.

"As long as you stay here, your future is dim. If you like, I'll give you gold to escape," she said to my son.

What a big sacrifice! She gave all of her savings to my son to save him from hopelessness. After he left, she missed him but she didn't know how to write to express all of her love for him and his siblings. She cried every time she received our letters from the United States. She asked my wife's younger brother to read and reread them several times and kept the pictures of our family in her pocket as precious gifts.

Two years before I made up my mind to escape by boat, the policeman in charge of political security asked me, "Do you plan to escape?"

This question wasn't new. It had been asked twice in the past eight years. Eight years ago, my answer was "no" on the pretext that I was poor. This time the answer had to be different. If I said that I was poor, the policeman would wonder why I didn't want to leave Vietnam. He might think that I claimed to be poor or that I stayed in Vietnam for a certain political purpose.

I kept my cool temper to choose the best answer to avoid his trap.

"I won't escape by boat. I am going to apply for an exit permit to go to the United States through the ODP [Orderly Departure Program]," I said.

The next day I went to the Tan Thoi People's Committee to have my application notarized before submitting it to the Song Be Police Department. Within an hour many dwellers in the city knew that I applied for an exit permit. I had dissipated the Song Be police's suspicions about my escape. I seemed to be eager to get an exit permit as soon as possible as I contacted the provincial police regularly to follow up on my case.

My daily activities went off normally. Many people came to see me and asked me to translate their affidavits of relationship into Vietnamese from English or French. I was familiar with affidavits of relationship from different countries, especially from the United States, Australia, Canada, and France. I learned a lot from these people. They told me about political prisoners. The rumors were optimistic. But everything was uncertain. The Communist police tried to stop the rumors by arresting some people selling ODP questionnaires and application forms. They searched photocopy shops and watched those people who had typewriters.

In the 1980s copy machine owners made much money after the birth of the ODP in Bangkok. People needed to have copies of their birth certificates and those of their children and grandchildren, marriage certificates, house titles, car titles, diplomas, IDs before and after 1975, household certificates, etc.

Some Saigonese used the names of a judge and a pharmacist to make money, saying that they were representatives of Senator Tran Van Lam, a former ambassador who was helping military men and civil servants of the old regime resettle in Australia with the agreement of both the Australian and Vietnamese governments. The applicants gave the judge and pharmacist symbolic amounts of money to do the paperwork and waited for departure.

Some skeptical people gave some historic details. They said that Tran Van Lam, when ambassador of the Republic of Vietnam to Australia, negotiated with the Australian government to look favorably on the Vietnamese Catholics settling in Australia in case the Communists took over South Vietnam.

Not a few people of the former government "helped" the Communists' victims escape, the reeducation detainees rejoin their families sooner, and the urban residents sell their houses and lands — for gold. They deceived the victims of the Communist regime, their former companions. Some lost their gold. Some became homeless. Some lost their freedom and even their lives! People didn't miss any opportunity to deceive one another. All of them were at the height of misery. They were eager to redo their lives in foreign lands.

One day, one of my cousins came and said to me in a small voice, "I just met a very special man."

"How special is he?" I asked.

"He was a second lieutenant in the army of the Republic of Vietnam. He knows English, French, German, and Latin. He is Mai Chi Tho's nephew. Mai Chi Tho let him know that a foreign boat is coming to Saigon to pick up those who want to go abroad," he said.

"How exciting this news is! How much?" I asked.

"Five hundred thousand old piastres per head."

"I see many absurdities. I wonder, if that man tells the truth, how a boat can pick up uncountable people who wish to go abroad. Be careful! The authenticity of this story is almost nil," I said.

"That is why I wanted to discuss it with you before I gave him any money. Now I want you to go to Saigon to look at the boat anchored at the quay of Bach Dang."

"What for? There are many foreign boats at the quay of Bach Dang."

"I want to know the nationality of the boat."

"I have no idea about your business with the second lieutenant. I am ready to go to Saigon with you to confirm the nationality of the boat only. It is you who will decide your own business," I said.

We rode to Saigon. My cousin showed me the boat and said, "It's that boat, the longest one. Do you see the flag?"

"Yes, I do. That is the flag of the Democratic Republic of Germany," I said.

A boat anchored on the Saigon River had become a method of swindling. It was difficult to distinguish good people from bad ones. The swindlers could be Communists. They could be Nationalists. They took advantage of the thirst for freedom of the South Vietnamese to make money dishonestly. They danced happily on the suffering of their victims.

Dong Nai province was noted for a large number of escapees. Many detainees left Vietnam after their release through this network. Many commissars of the People's Committee of this province were involved in organizing escapes. They were brought to the court. Their intermediary was killed before being sentenced to death.

Escaping was no longer expensive. People could leave Vietnam by sea (boat people), by land (walking people), and by air (immigrants). The number of walking people soared after 1979. Some new *bo doi* sought to walk to the Thai refugee camps after being dispatched to Cambodia.

Since 1976 Vietnam has had a long name: the Socialist Republic of Vietnam. In 1977 Vietnam became a member of the United Nations. The country's name showed that the Vietnamese Communists led by Le Duan were pro–Soviet at the expense of China. Deng Xiao Peng tried to teach Vietnam a "lesson" in 1979 but he faced the heroic resistance from the Vietnamese militia.

Le Duan seriously warned the expansionists that "the East Sea is not a lake of China."

The Vietnam Communist party forced South Vietnam to keep up with socialist North Vietnam. In the 1980s the local governments took control of all economic activities. Restaurants, coffee shops, and even cigarette stands had to be run by the government. The restaurant owners had to fix, repaint, and embellish their restaurants before losing their ownership. They became employees in their own restaurants. Their duty was to keep the activities of the restaurants smooth (getting food, cooking, serving, cleaning). The local government sent cashiers to keep and receive the money from the diners. The former restaurant owners got paid monthly. At the market the police and tax collectors detained and fined clandestine merchants and confiscated their goods.

The state and collective farms ruined production. Farmers were so poor and hungry that they stole the rice, corn, or cassava they had planted in the collective farms. Most farmers were reluctant to work in the collective farms. Some killed their oxen. Some didn't use hoes but shovels to farm. The heads of the collective farms had cozy lives without farming. They sold fertilizer, seeds, and insecticide to black marketeers. They weren't interested in production but in the sale of fertilizer. They used a small quantity of fertilizer for the collective farms and sold the rest. Fertilizer was so misused that it withered plants instead of accelerating their growth. The tragic consequence was that the farmers worked hard without having enough roots to eat. Such a saga was found in the state farms.

One evening, one of my nephews brought me a basket of sweet potatoes.

"Where did you get sweet potatoes?" I asked him.

"From the collective farm. It's what I got after six months of labor there. I brought you some."

"What do you think about the collective farm?"

"It's a scourge, Uncle! I'm going to die of starvation."

Those were the last words I heard from him. In 1989 I learned that he died of tuberculosis from working hard without having enough food. When he fell ill, he was conscious of his slow death. His whole family worked without having enough money to get food and medicine. All of his children had to quit school to face their premature hardship.

I heard many rumors about anti–Communist activities in Di An, Vinh Phu, Phu Van, and Tan Uyen. Many Caodaist followers were arrested and brought to trial in Song Be province. A series of articles about Vo Dai Ton, who was captured by the Laotian militia, appeared in the *Saigon Giai Phong* daily. Some members of an anti–Communist organization led by Le Quoc Tuy, who had returned clandestinely to Vietnam from France, were captured by the Communists. They had connections with different politico-religious sects in South Vietnam. Le Quoc Quan, Tuy's brother, was sentenced to death. So were Tran Van Ba, a son of former representative Tran Van Van, Ho Thai Bach, a Caodaist leader, and Mai Van Hanh, a pilot in France.

A week after this trial, I received a call slip to present myself at the Tan Thoi Police Department. I was investigated by the provincial policeman in charge of political security for six hours. I felt very tired and hungry. It was torrid outside. The policeman asked me about Vo Dai Ton. I said that I neither knew him nor heard of his name. He tried to force me to confess. I insisted that I didn't know him before 1975. After 1975 I lived in Laithieu. How could I have connections with him?

He kept on asking some questions his friends had asked me previously. So it was easy for me to answer. He asked me about the anti–Communist movement aimed at overthrowing the Communist regime. I said that I didn't know anything about that except for the trial in Song Be.

"How do you know it?" he asked.

"I listen to the news broadcast by Song Be radio," I said.

"Do you read newspapers?" he asked.

"Sometimes."

If I had said "no" he would say that I boycotted or disliked Communist newspapers.

If I said "yes" he would ask me why I liked reading or how I had money to subscribe to newspapers while I was poor. I had to choose something neutral.

He got very angry after six hours of investigation without any interesting information.

"Don't lie to the revolution. The revolution knows all of your past and present activities. If you know the reactionaries and don't inform the government, you will be charged with conspiracy. Understand!?" he menaced me.

"I told you everything in my curriculum vitae. I am not lying to you. I don't lie to the revolution. I understand what you said," I said.

He let me go. My shirt was wet with sweat.

The chairman of the Tan Thoi People's Committee was eager to know what had happened to me in the past six hours.

"What is the matter?" he asked.

I didn't answer his questions. "Will you be home this evening?" I asked.

"Yes," he said.

"I would like to see you this evening at 6:00 P.M.," I said.

"You can come any time."

That evening I rode to his house in Dong Ba, less than a mile from the city. He prepared tea. Both of us drank strong tea. I began the conversation, saying, "Today I came here to thank you for our friendship. Maybe you know something about my past. I am afraid that our friendship could endanger you. Today is the last day of our friendship but it remains indelible in my mind. I am responsible for my past. I don't want it to harm your future."

"Don't think that. Our country was at war. Every family was in its paradoxical situation. The North Vietnamese had their relatives in the South. The South Vietnamese had their relatives in the North. When I was in North Vietnam, my family was in the South. My younger brother was an officer of the South Vietnamese army. When I returned, he was in a reeducation camp. I went there to see him after more than twenty years of separation. He refused to see me. Our communication is better now. Our people underwent persistent suffering in a partitioned country at war," he said.

"Thank you for your opinion. Willy-nilly, I think that your acquaintance with me isn't good for you."

"In my opinion, relatives are relatives. Friends are friends. When I arrived in Saigon, I lived in my aunt's house. She was one of the first Vietnamese to leave for France by plane after the liberation. Before her departure she gave me some money.

"During the war I was under the command of Pham Ngoc Thao. Returning to the South I learned that he had an important position in South Vietnam. He deserved it. I respected his personality and admired his talents. The news I just told you doesn't make me change my respect and admiration for him. Society is composed of good and bad people," he said.

I understood what he meant. In the past thirty years he had seen many bad people although they belonged to the same party, believed in the same doctrine, and fought side by side on the same front. They were hateful, despicable, and horrible. I was on the opposite side. But, in his eyes, I was neither a bad man nor a horrible one.

I kept away from him so that he could avoid some troubles. As for him, he never asked me why I planned to leave Vietnam. He understood that I had no choice. He wanted to see me and to converse with me, so he created some more *causeries*.

Vietnam was going to celebrate the 160th birthday of Poet Nguyen Dinh Chieu, or Do Chieu (*sinh do* means high school diploma). Many cultural cadres came to Tan Thoi several times in order to locate the birthplace of the patriotic and blind poet on the map of Song Be province.

Poet Nguyen Dinh Chieu, author of *Luc Van Tien*, was born in Tan Thoi village, Binh Duong district, Tan Binh county, Gia Dinh province. Under President Ngo Dinh Diem, Thudaumot was named Binh Duong. A high school in Bung was named Trinh Hoai Duc for a Vietnamese mandarin of Chinese blood. He was famous for his *Gia Dinh Thanh Thong Chi* (Description of Cochinchina), translated into French by Philastre.

Was Poet Nguyen Dinh Chieu born in Tan Thoi village, Laithieu district, Thudaumot province?

The Tan Thoi People's Committee invited many elderly folks to help these cultural cadres locate the birthplace of the poet. The problem remained unsolved after many meetings. The local government looked for residents whose family name was Truong in the hope of identifying their relationship with the poet's mother, Truong Thi Thiet. But none of them knew who Truong Thi Thiet was. Many villagers in Tan Thoi recited *Luc Van Tien* without knowing its author. *Luc Van Tien* is very popular in South Vietnam. The beggars recite *Luc Van Tien* at the bus station and at the markets. Some verses in *Luc Van Tien* became proverbs. However, few people know Nguyen Dinh Chieu who, influenced by Confucianism, emphasized loyalty, filial piety, patriotism, virginity, and virtue.

The cultural cadres were disappointed. The local government felt ashamed. The problem was in limbo.

A cadre of the Tan Thoi Information and Culture Department said to the chairman of the committee, "I know a man who can give us the answer."

"Who is he?" the chairman asked.

"He has been rigorously watched by the Song Be police," the cadre said.

"Who is he?" the chairman asked.

"He is the man who talked about acupuncture and traditional Vietnamese medicine," the cadre said.

"I like his initiative. Look for him!" the chairman ordered.

The cadre rode to my house and learned that I was at a coffee shop with a Chinese student. He didn't see me in any coffee shops around the market. I rarely had coffee in Tan Thoi village. Usually my student and I had breakfast and coffee about three or four miles from Tan Thoi. The cadre was anxious that he couldn't find me while people were waiting at the auditorium of the village temple.

When he came back to my house one more time, he was happy to see me home. As soon as he saw me, he urged me, "Uncle! Please get dressed and put on clean shoes."

"What happened?" I asked anxiously.

"Please hurry and get dressed. I will tell you a very important thing."

"Let's go right away. I don't have new clothes," I said, not knowing what was happening to me.

"You have to get dressed properly. Today we have many honored guests," the cadre said.

"I have to iron my clothes. I haven't ironed them for a long time. They are wrinkled."

In the past seven years I had gotten used to wearing wrinkled clothes with an old pair of slippers. I felt uneasy getting dressed properly. My feet and shoes seemed to be in conflict. My wife looked at me and said, "You look like yourself in the past!"

The cadre brought me to the Tan Thoi auditorium. Many people waited for me. Some of them were senior residents of Tan Thoi. Some were Communist cadres from Song Be province, Laithieu district, and from neighboring villages. Some weren't familiar to me. Some looked at me with sympathy. Some were surprised.

The cadre showed me to a chair and asked me to sit on it. I was a little hesitant because it was the seat of the reporter.

"It's your seat, Uncle," he said.

I sat on the chair with perplexity. A few days earlier, in this area, I had been questioned by the police, who had made my body wet with sweat and my feet cold on a sultry day. I couldn't believe that a thirteenth-category citizen had become a reporter.

A middle-aged cadre came and shook hands with me. His accent proved that he was from Hue. He told me that he had taught at Van Hanh University before 1975. After 1975 he worked for the new regime in Ho Chi Minh City. After introducing me to all the members of his group he told me about the purpose of their visit to Tan Thoi village. He passed the mike to me.

I summarized poet Nguyen Dinh Chieu's biography. His father was Nguyen Dinh Huy, originally from Phong Dien (Thua Thien). While working for Governor Le Van Duyet in Cochinchina, he got married to Truong Thi Thiet. The latter, a native of Tan Thoi village, Binh Duong district, Tan Binh county, Gia Dinh province, was his second wife. The poet was born in his maternal village. His wife was a native of Can Giuoc. After the French had occupied the three eastern provinces of Cochinchina, his family moved to Ben Tre. Phan Van Hum's wife was poetess Suong Nguyet Anh's granddaughter. Suong Nguyet Anh, or Nguyen Thi Khue, was the fifth daughter of poet Nguyen Dinh Chieu.

I suggested that these cultural cadres visit Hue, Can Giuoc, and Ben Tre and get in touch with Phan Van Hum's wife in Ho Chi Minh City to get some more information about the birthplace of the poet. They told me that they had. But they didn't get anything concrete about the location of Tan Thoi.

"Was it possible that the poet fled to Tan Thoi and stayed there a few days when the French attacked Saigon?" the leader of the group asked.

"I don't think so. When the French attacked Saigon, he moved to his wife's village in Can Giuoc. After the signing of the treaty of 1862 the French occupied Bien Hoa, Gia Dinh, and Dinh Tuong. His family moved to Ben Tre. He went south instead of going north."

"The northern part of Cochinchina had many forests favorable to the guerrillas. In return, it lacked food and its weather was severe. Malaria was horrible. Therefore, all the revolts came from the southern areas of Saigon, such as Can Giuoc, Go Cong, Long An, and Cai Lay," I added.

"Is this Tan Thoi the birthplace of the poet?" a cadre asked.

"Before giving a credible answer to this question, I think that we have to glance at the regional administration during the reign of Gia Long (1802–1819).

I am interested in the regional administration during the reign of Gia Long because our poet was born in 1822. This regional administration was deeply changed by King Minh Mang in 1832.

"Under the reign of Gia Long, Cochinchina had five Tran: Bien Tran (Bien Hoa), Phien Tran (Gia Dinh), Dinh Tran (Dinh Tuong), Vinh Tran (Vinh Long), and Ha Tran (Ha Tien). King Minh Mang changed *Tran* to *Tinh* (province), as in China under the Qing. He created a new province, An Giang. Then, we had Nam Ky Luc Tinh (the six provinces of Cochinchina). They were Bien Hoa, Gia Dinh, Dinh Tuong, Vinh Long, An Giang, and Ha Tien.

"Phien Tran (Gia Dinh) was on the right bank of the Saigon River. It included Saigon, Gia Dinh, Cholon, Long An, and Tay Ninh.

"All the areas stretching along the left bank of the Saigon River belonged to Bien Tran (Bien Hoa). This Tan Thoi was a village of Binh An district (Thudaumot or Binh Duong), Bien Tran.

"After the defeat of the Tay Son, many village names in Gia Dinh province bore the word *Tan* (new) such as Tan Long, Tan Hoi, Tan Thoi, Tan Thuan, Tan Triem, Tan Kien, Tan Dinh, Tan Thoi Nhut, Tan Son Nhut, and Tan Son Nhi. This Tan Thoi was Tan Thoi Dong. In Gia Dinh province there were Tan Thoi Tay, Tan Thoi Trung, Thoi Tam Thon, etc.

"In the early nineteenth century Binh Duong district was inside Ho Chi Minh City but not in Binh Duong province (Thudaumot or Song Be). This name appeared under President Ngo Dinh Diem to replace Thudaumot. Binh Duong province was smaller than Thudaumot province, which, under French rule, included Hon Quan (Binh Long) and Ba Ra (Phuoc Long). For these reasons, I don't think that this Tan Thoi, Laithieu district, was the birthplace of poet Nguyen Dinh Chieu," I said.

"It was written in a number of books that Nguyen Dinh Chieu was born in Tan Khanh, Binh Duong district, Gia Dinh province. Is that Tan Khanh this actual Tan Khanh village in Song Be province?" a cadre asked.

"Tan Khanh is twelve miles from Laithieu. Its true name was Tan Phuoc Khanh. Under the Nguyen dynasty, Thudaumot was only a district of Bien Hoa province. Tan Phuoc Khanh belonged to Bien Hoa province. Cochinchina had twenty-one provinces under French rule. Binh An district became Thudaumot province. Tan Phuoc Khanh wasn't ever a part of Gia Dinh province.

"In our time, Tan Binh and Gia Dinh exist. They are in Ho Chi Minh City. Tan Khanh should be in Ho Chi Minh City. Was *Tan* Thoi annexed to *Khanh* Hoi to become Tan Khanh? Khanh Hoi is on one bank of Ben Nghe Arroyo. Was Tan Thoi on the other bank of this arroyo? In that case Tan Thoi would be in the Second District.

"The poet's mother, Truong Thi Thiet, died and was buried in Tan Triem (Cau Kho). Tan Thoi shouldn't be too far from this place of burial," I concluded.

"Why did the poet move to Ben Tre?" the group leader asked.

"Although blind, our poet was very patriotic. In 1862 the French took control of the three eastern provinces of Cochinchina (Bien Hoa, Gia Dinh, Dinh Tuong). Refusing to accept the French rule, he moved to Ben Tre, Vinh Long province," I said.

The *causerie* won the applause of the audience. The group leader shook hands with me and thanked me. He asked me about the origin of some local city names like Bung and Thudaumot.

"Why is there a rose in this remote village?" he asked.

I didn't say a word. He asked me where my house was. I avoided his question by saying that I spent more time at the farm in Tuy An (An Phu). I tried to calm down so that my words were less sour and ironic.

Once again, I shook hands with him and some of his cadres. Then I walked home. On the way home I thought about poet Nguyen Dinh Chieu's state of mind and mine. What if he had been alive in Ho Chi Minh's era?

In 1984 the Socialist Republic of Vietnam celebrated the thirtieth anniversary of Dien Bien Phu without mentioning General Vo Nguyen Giap, who "braided red flowers to write a chapter of golden history." He was no longer a member of the politburo but was chairman of the Institute of Technology. The cause of this demotion was unclear. General Giap had been the only collegian in the politburo. He had had narrow relations with Ho Chi Minh in World War II and in the Franco-Vietnamese War. He believed strongly in Marxism-Leninism. Maybe, due to his education and his merit, he was inflexible. He was deemed to be pro–Soviet like Le Duan. Was the latter afraid that the Soviet Union would back Giap to replace him?

The Ho Chi Minh City People's Committee decided to exhume graves in Mac Dinh Chi Cemetery and make this cemetery a park.

As soon as the Communists took control of South Vietnam, many military cemeteries were leveled by bulldozers. They successfully punished the military, the civil servants, and the South Vietnamese, alive and dead.

In imitation of Ho Chi Minh City, other cities began to exhume graves in their local cemeteries in the hope of finding gold, jade, and other precious things. They spread the rumor that the reactionaries hid weapons in the graves.

The graves of President Ngo Dinh Diem and his two brothers, Ngo Dinh Nhu and Ngo Dinh Can, were exhumed. Their bones were buried in Thuan An district (new name of Laithieu) near the former base of Song Than. On the tombstones of these new graves there were no real names of the dead, only their baptized names and the dates of their deaths with the words *huynh* (brother) for the grave of President Ngo Dinh Diem and *de* (younger brother) for Ngo Dinh Nhu and Ngo Dinh Can. We can distinguish Ngo Dinh Nhu's grave from Ngo Dinh Can's based on the dates of their deaths. Nhu died in 1963.

Can was executed in Saigon in 1964 while General Nguyen Khanh was president.

Beside these silent graves there is a huge stele with strange words. It is the huge tombstone of the Russian seamen defeated by the Japanese at Tsushima in 1905. They fled to Cam Ranh Bay. Some seamen were seriously sick and were brought to Saigon. They died and were buried in Mac Dinh Chi Cemetery on Massige Street, which was changed to Mac Dinh Chi Street after 1954.

It was an honor for these Russians to rest in peace in the most expensive cemetery in Saigon; France and Russia were allies at that time.

The Vietnamese Communists, after the fall of South Vietnam, were faithful to the Soviet Union. So they paid respect to these dead seamen by building a pretty grave with a huge stele in their memory. They had lost honor, but they were buried twice in Vietnam.

The exhumation created some new lucrative services. The local governments dug up the graves and collected valuable things from the coffins. They sold the coffins to relatives of the dead to rebury the bones of the latter. They threw away or cremated all the bones of the dead whose relatives weren't in Vietnam. People chopped up old coffins to sell as firewood. Some people made money by making paper clothes, cars, houses, bicycles, and motorcycles for the dead in the Yellow Spring. A paper Honda was almost the same price as a real Honda in this period of gas shortages.

Buddhist prayer reciters had a lot of work to do for the number of dead increased due to senility, illness, and even suicide. Many Buddhist monks became secularized or left the country. The Catholic monasteries coped with financial difficulties. The properties of the Catholic church had been requisitioned by the Communist government. Many seminarians returned to their families or sought to leave Vietnam by boat. Some pastors under suspicion were imprisoned. In a Communist society, suspicion is very serious. Such a concept would be strange to American or European lawyers.

The regime encouraged godlessness while sanctifying Marx, Lenin, and Ho Chi Minh. Most of the people have had their own religions. They wouldn't consider Marx, Lenin, or Ho Chi Minh as their god. They turned to the dead to ask for good luck. They went to cemeteries at night to ask the dead to help them win at *De*. Those people who planned to escape came to Thu Duc to pray before the grave of a Catholic priest, Nguyen Minh Dang. The local militia arrested and imprisoned some of them to stop others from visiting this grave. Some people said that they prayed to generals Nguyen Viet Thanh and Do Cao Tri to talk politics.

Many mysterious stories were spread. Of course, they weren't real and believable. They appeared to be a passive reaction against the godless regime and a demonstration of the existence of God, devils, ghosts, and spirits after death. People kept their mouths shut in the totalitarian regime. It was dangerous to tell the truth. They used to speak of devils and ghosts but they meant their leaders. There were many children's songs that ridiculed the unpopular regime and predicted its fall.

While the local government watched and imprisoned many Catholic and Buddhist priests and sorcerers, some Communist cadres with a bizarre disease came to Thu Duc to look for a Buddhist monk who was thought to heal patients with ghost hallucinations. They tried to solicit him, but he refused to help them for fear of being sent to a reeducation camp.

The most horrible event for dwellers in Di An, Thu Duc, and Laithieu occurred in Di An in 1984. A young man killed a hunchback and ate his brain.

He was a strong and quiet man. One day, he touched the shaved head of his mother and said, "I lust for human brains." Thinking that he spoke nonsense, his mother didn't pay attention to his words. The young man said the same thing to others. Everybody had the jimjams and kept away from him. It was rumored that he used to go to the cemetery to dig up the graves to eat the brains of the dead.

One afternoon, seeing a hunchback, who was a carpenter, walking on a deserted road, the young man ran to him and grabbed his shoulders. The hunchback dodged and ran to the coffee shop along the road. The young man pursued him. Nobody was in the coffee shop at lunchtime. The coffee shop owner was eating lunch. He didn't know what was going on in front of his coffee shop. The hunchback fell down at the doorstep of the coffee shop. The young man chopped his skull with a big ice-cutting knife. The victim shook himself, unconsciously, then stayed motionless. The young man chopped his skull and ate his brain.

After lunch the coffee shop owner saw the horrible aftermath. He ran as far as possible, yelling. The police came. The murderer looked fearless and remorseless when the police handcuffed him. He threatened to eat the brain of the policeman in charge of his detention in the prison of Binh Hoa, Song Be province.

The Communist police studied English and Chinese astrology. Some were sent to the Buddhist temples or village temples to be monks or guardians in order to watch the real monks and the people who came to those places to ask for blessings before escaping. They used to go to the Phong Phu temple to draw divination sticks to know whether their departure would be smooth or not before making their final decision. They also went to a Buddhist monk in Phu Nhuan, Ho Chi Minh City. It was said that this monk had a third eye capable of seeing our past and future as if he watched television.

One of my Chinese Vietnamese students had celebrated his wedding ceremony before his wife was approved to leave for Canada. Interviewed by the Canadians she said that she was single. Otherwise, her departure would have been delayed for a long time.

The husband saw off his wife with indescribable suffering. He spent a lot of money to see the Buddhist monk in Phu Nhuan and any fortune-tellers, palm readers, and sorcerers he knew. He wanted to know whether he would rejoin his wife in Canada or not. All of them shook their heads. That disappointed him a lot. A sorcerer asked him to give him a big amount of money and to get plenty of food to offer his "soldiers." He said that my student's case was very complicated. He must dispatch his soldiers to Canada to get information. My student accepted all of his requirements, hoping that the divine force would help him join his wife. The sorcerer received his money and food. A few days later, he let my student know that he hadn't heard anything from his soldiers. "Maybe they got lost in Canada," he said.

My student wrote to his wife once a week. He bribed the Communist cadres working at the central post office to let his letter arrive in Canada as soon as possible. There was a flight from Ho Chi Minh City to Canada on Thursdays. He had to go to Ho Chi Minh City every Wednesday.

He needed my consolation and advice. At one end of the horizon, the husband languished for news of his wife. At the other end of the horizon, the wife was anxious. She didn't know what to tell him. Her long silence gave him a lot of pain. What an adverse circumstance. She had waited for her departure for many years without any positive result. But as soon as they celebrated their wedding ceremony, she got her exit permit and left her husband. Arriving in Canada she couldn't sponsor him because of her "single" marital status. Her husband came to see me every night.

"I am upset. I am a little afraid. Many women, after their resettlement, divorce their husbands," he said.

"It's up to the situation and the personality of each individual," I said, comforting him.

"Do you have any solution for our reunification?"

"You have two choices. First, you escape. Second, you wait until your wife sponsors you. Everything depends on your wife. She has to tell the truth. Why doesn't she sponsor you? Because she told the Canadian interviewers that she was single? Because she doesn't have enough money? We can't solve the problem without having enough data," I said.

"My mother won't let me escape. I tried to escape and was arrested many times. She is very afraid. My parents spent a lot of money to bribe the police when I was in a reeducation camp. I lost gold and freedom. The escape organizers didn't return our gold, saying that the Viet Cong confiscated it. My mother cried every time she came to the camp and saw me working in the sun. I got skinny. My skin got dark brown. Sometimes the Communist cadres hit me with bamboo sticks when they had some trouble or when a prisoner escaped.

"My father was originally from Tai Pou district, South China. He came to Vietnam at the age of eighteen. He has made his fortune here for fifty years. He said that it is easier to do business in Vietnam than anywhere else. One of his friends from Tai Pou district left China for Vietnam with him on the same boat and was co-owner of our pottery kiln in Binh Nham, Laithieu. After 1975 he escaped and resettled in France with many taels of gold while my father decided to stay here. He has an entry-level job in France. He feels unhappy with his life there. His French is poor. He can't drive. He doesn't know how to use the subway. He isn't used to the cold weather and French food. He hopes to return to Vietnam. My father feels that he is right. He never encourages me to escape. I have to wait," my student said.

I wrote a letter and asked his wife to rewrite it and send it to the Canadian government. The letter described on the pitiful situation of a new couple separated from each other a few days after their marriage. About a month later, the student was happy to inform me that he had received an affidavit of relationship from his wife. Three years later, he joined his wife in a city in central Canada.

He began his new life in the frosty land. In the hardest moments of struggle for life, he smiled to himself. In Vietnam he hadn't worked hard. But he was in solitude. In Canada he had his family to take care of. Their first baby was born a year after his family's reunification. The family burden was on the shoulders of the young man, who hadn't worried about food, clothes, or political regimes in Vietnam. This young man became a husband and a father, quitting his past happy days to accept any hardship in the new land in the hope of bringing happiness to his family.

The Communist regime was consolidated in South Vietnam after five years of liberation. The Communist cadres were used to the new commodities. Many Cadres A were sent to the South. It was a favor for the North Vietnamese Communists to be assigned to work in South Vietnam. Their lives improved visibly. They bought watches, radio sets, television sets, refrigerators, expensive bicycles, and Japanese motorcycles. They built houses and brought their families to the South.

They got rich quickly but they had to cover their wealth through their poor appearance, which was symbolized by their sun helmets, Binh Tri Thien sandals, and wrinkled clothes.

Female cadres liked shopping. They bought their first *ao dai* (robe), red sticks, and powder. But they didn't dare to use them. Most of them didn't know how to use them. Some tried to lose weight by taking vinegar as medicine.

The Communist cadres, in spite of their low level of education, were very bossy and bureaucratic. It was difficult for the grassroots to get in touch with them. They were more arrogant, corrupt, bureaucratic, and authoritative than the civil servants of the Saigon government. "He has an important meeting today" was the pretext given by the Communist cadres when they refused to allow somebody to see their superior. To them, working was chatting, eating, drinking, smoking, and talking about prostitution. Many of them died of stomach troubles. Many fell ill from drinking too much foreign brandy and rice alcohol and smoking cigarettes. In the 1980s they didn't smoke local cigarettes but foreign ones. They loved filtered cigarettes made in Thailand, Great Britain, and the United States.

Clandestine brothels mushroomed everywhere. Their protectors were the local governments. The sensualists were mostly Communist cadres. Prostitution seemed official and authorized. Many Communist cadres had gonorrhea and syphilis. But they didn't dare to go to the hospital. They would lose their lucrative jobs if their colleagues knew that they had a venereal disease. Politically speaking, all the Communist members were afraid of hospitalization. They would lose their positions due to their poor health. They would die "legally" if the party wanted to eliminate them. As a result, the role of the South Vietnamese physicians got more important. They were allowed to practice medicine and were protected by the local cadres. In the past many South Vietnamese had thought that French physicians at Hopital Grall or American and Philippine physicians at the Adventist Hospital were better than Vietnamese physicians. Under Communist rule people spoke highly of the South Vietnamese physicians while despising the Communist ones. What we had wasn't precious. What we lost was.

People said that the South Vietnamese teachers were much better and more qualified than teachers from North Vietnam. French medicine was deemed to be more efficient than Soviet medicine.

Foreign tourists arriving in Saigon and Hanoi bore the insignia of their flags to avoid possible assaults from the grassroots with their resentment against the Soviets. The Russians were well protected by the Vietnamese Communist government. The Vietnamese couldn't frequent their residential quarters in the cities or on the beaches. They called them "penniless Americans." They spoke ill of Soviet cigarettes. They preferred Martel, cognac, and Cointreau to vodka. They said that the Soviet tractors were rudimentary, that Soviet commodities were bad, and that American products were the best.

In fact, there were no Soviet products at the flea markets. People saw some Russians buying radio sets in Ho Chi Minh City. The Soviet Union couldn't hide its poverty although it was rich in weapons. It was understood that the South Vietnamese didn't believe the Soviet Union. Even the Vietnamese Communist cadres who visited Moscow recognized that Saigon had more commodities than Moscow and that the standard of living of the Saigonese was higher than the Muscovites'.

Wealthy Communist cadres sought to escape to enjoy the dirty money they had accumulated after the fall of Saigon. Corrupt cadres considered their galloping wealth a symbol of their faith to the party. General Secretary Le Duan promised that, after the fulfillment of the quinquennial plan (1976–

1980), every Vietnamese family would have a tablecloth, a water filter, and some sauce for their meals! All the cadres in the South had radio sets, television sets, refrigerators, motorcycles, and comfortable houses, which showed the brilliant success of the quinquennial plan of the Communist party led by Comrade Le Duan.

Many middle- and high-ranking cadres practiced polygamy clandestinely. Some local commissars lived with their young and beautiful wives from bourgeois or petit bourgeois families and even from the families of reeducation detainees, regardless of party criticism and discipline. People raised many questions about the death of actress Thanh Nga and her husband. Their deaths were deemed to be a result of a tragic game of jealousy with the Communist leaders. From Hanoi to the remote provinces, Communist leaders really changed their lives and aesthetic concepts. They didn't love proletarian and working-class women but bourgeois ones. When they held certain social positions, their concepts were less philosophically Marxist and more realistically capitalist. There was no difference between them and the ones they criticized and overthrew. They were greedy for power, money, honor, food, beer, sex, and other pleasures. They could be brave when fighting. But they weren't above seizing power. Power had been the real purpose of their struggle. Ho Chi Minh had more power than any Communist leader, including Lenin, Stalin, and Mao. He was chief of state, prime minister, chairman and general secretary of the party. In 1946 he had gone to France as a chief of state and diplomat. All the Communist leaders stayed in power until they died or they were forced to resign. None of them resigned because of their age, bad health or inability. Ton Duc Thang was president at the age of eighty-one and died at he age of ninety-two!

In the 1980s revolutionary families and Communist cadres had the right to buy construction materials at special prices. They built big comfortable houses in the countryside and cities. Their houses were well furnished compared to the peasants' slums. They had electricity at night. Their living rooms were full of the certificates of their glorious family and of pictures of Uncle Ho.

Families with children living abroad were distinctive. They had happy lives with fashionable clothes, Laotian slippers, American jeans, Korean ginseng tea, and American cigarettes, soap, and toothpaste. This lifestyle contrasted with the Communist propaganda about the absence of social classes in a Communist society.

Dancing before the suffering of the grassroots, Communist cadres and new arrivistes had big parties at which expensive and rare foods and brandy were served. They sang, shouted, and challenged one another to "bottoms up" every glass of brandy.

For the funerals of their relatives, they bribed the electricians to have light at night. Funerals became noisy and busy with live music. Plenty of food and wine were served.

The wedding ceremonies in the 1980s were fancier, more expensive, and more solemn than before. The brides wore splendid silk *ao dai* and yellow turbans. The grooms put on blue national costumes, black turbans, and black shoes. It reminded us of clothing from the early twentieth century. Firecrackers burst. The sounds of trumpets and drums blared from live bands.

These rich families made a show of their wealth at Christmas and on the eve of the Vietnamese New Year (Tet). On Christmas Eve they made a big noise on the streets by speeding their motorcycles. On the eve of Tet people burst many yards of firecrackers to show off their monetary power. Scared of the deafening noise, many dogs ran so fast and so far that they forgot the way home. The homeless under the bridges, on the sidewalks, at the foot of trees and in the markets felt unhappy with their dark fates. They had worked hard to end up hungry, while some idle people burned money, the smoke dyingd the city gray.

Who were these homeless? Were they wrongdoers? Were they lazy people?

They were urban residents who had been forced to leave the cities for the new economic areas. They were former officers or civil servants who, after their release, lost their shelters in the city and whose wives and children left the country or got married to Communist cadres. They had to cling to the cities in order to have some work to support themselves for the rest of their lives. They were sick, pale, and skinny. Some had to sell their blood to have a meal. They could be victims of the Communist regime. They could be victims of any of the political regimes in our lovely and miserable country. Of them one was a former officer of the army of the Republic of Vietnam and of the Communist People's army. When I heard him saying so, I thought that he made up a story to lie to me. Our man wanted to expose his controversial case. He said, "I was a captain in the army of the Republic of Vietnam. I was captured by 'these gentlemen' [the Viet Cong] in a battle in Quang Tri in early 1975. Then, they needed more soldiers to end the war by force. Therefore, they didn't want to keep war prisoners. They asked me if I would agree to fight for the liberation army as a captain. I agreed."

At this, he stopped a few seconds. Then he continued, "Maybe you think that I agreed because they offered me some favor. That's not true. I didn't think of it. What frightened me was that they could kill me on the spot if I refused for they didn't have time, food, or medicine to take care of prisoners. Their duty was to take over South Vietnam as soon as possible. I would have been sacrificed."

"In what circumstance did you lose an arm?" I asked.

"In a battle in Quang Tri. At that time, I was 'Viet Cong.' A bullet from the South Vietnamese troops hit my arm."

"You are an invalid officer of the people's army. The revolutionary government should take care of you."

"In the first days of liberation, they gave me some sugar, rice, condensed milk, but gradually they forgot me. Now, you see, my old companions-in-arms despise me and keep away from me," he said.

In 1983 many Amerasians, Chinese Vietnamese, and Vietnamese left the country through the Orderly Departure Program. Some reunited their families in Australia, Canada, West Germany, France, and the United States. Most Chinese Vietnamese were settled in English-speaking countries, such as Australia, Canada, and the United States. A few people left for England, Norway, Switzerland, Italy, Greece, Holland, or Belgium.

A few days before their departure, people had big banquets and arranged bus rental in advance to pick up their friends and relatives to take them to Tan Son Nhut Airport to see them off and wish them "bon voyage."

Tan Son Nhut Airport wasn't as busy as it had been before. On the airstrips there were some Soviet-made planes. One of them provided transportation to the immigrants from Ho Chi Minh City to Bangkok. The immigrants stayed there a few days before leaving for the next countries.

The plane was pretty big, but compared with a Boeing it was inferior in size, speed, and comfort. The passengers had to walk to the plane. Some elderly people walked heavily and slowly on the airstrip. From time to time they stopped, trying to look at their relatives and their lovely country for the last time. They continued walking, crying. They waved their hands as if they wanted to say, "Good-bye, Vietnam!"

Tan Son Nhut Airport was an international airport, but its dirty restaurant blackened its name. Eaters used rough bamboo chopsticks. Food was served on inexpensive plates made of clay and mostly chipped. Nobody cleaned the tables, which were dirty and smelled of fish sauce. On the tables there were many remnants of food and traces of tea, coffee, and fish sauce. Flies hovered over the diners.

Separation has been always sorrowful. The stayers feel bitter for continuing to carry their karma until the end of their earthly lives in a country where everybody dreamed of a government for the people. Homesickness and nostalgia invade the departers, who don't know anything about their future in a new land. The stayers and departers wave to one another. Some burst into tears before separation. Some people shout to encourage the departers . Suddenly, a cry for help from the crowd. A man waved his hand to say "bon voyage" to his relatives. In the twinkling of an eye, his watch disappeared. Our unlucky man went home with sorrowful thoughts about society under Communist peace.

10

The Last Days in Vietnam

I lived under the Communist regime for ten years. I tried to dominate my persistent sufferings by accepting and forgetting them.

My daily activities remained boring. My neighbors seemed to have their sterile sentiments. My children didn't have any enthusiasm due to the uncertain situation my family coped with. I had planned to help my oldest son escape, but I hadn't carried out the plan yet.

I felt suffocated by the Communist triumphal hymns as the Communists prepared to celebrate the tenth anniversary of their victory in the South. American reporters came to Ho Chi Minh City to have live pictures of the ceremony after ten years of liberation.

On the first day of Tet of the year of the Buffalo my brother came back to Laithieu to wish me "Happy New Year." I showed him the branch of buttercups on the altar and said, "Look! All of my buttercups have six to eight petals this year. A few blossoms have ten petals. I am sure that something good will happen to us."

"I hope that we will have good luck this new year," my brother said.

"Ten years have passed. We have been in crisis for ten years. Everything is at an impasse. Our children don't have a future. Thinking about that I feel dizzy. However, I believe strongly that God will give us the best solution," I said.

"I think so."

"There will be something special for me this year. If I have a test I will pass it."

"What do you mean by that?"

"If I escape, everything will be smooth."

"How do you know?" my brother asked.

"Based on my horoscope and the psalm," I said.

"What did the psalm say?"

"There will be big changes in my life in the Nham and At years. This year is At Suu," I replied.

My brother seemed excited. After wishing my family "Happy New Year," he was in a hurry to go home.

"I have to get home to see how my branch of buttercups is this year," he said.

A few days later, he came back to Laithieu. He looked optimistic and smiling. As soon as he saw me, he said happily, "I bring you good news. My branch of buttercups has many flowers with six to eight petals like yours."

"It is a good sign. Usually a six-petal blossom is rare while some of ours have eight to ten petals. What a particularity!" I said.

"President Reagan was re-elected. Maybe the fate of the political prisoners will improve," my brother said.

"It is possible. But let's not waste our time looking forward to the departure of the political prisoners. The Vietnamese refugee problem has lasted ten years. It can't last much longer."

"It is very dangerous to escape. We could be arrested by the Viet Cong. We could lose money. We could face many risks. This time, if I am arrested, I will have many troubles," my brother said.

"For that reason we must be careful. Our karma looks like a flame that has disappeared but the ash is still hot. Be patient and pray to be illuminated."

"We will exchange more news and discuss this problem carefully. Now I am going to our uncle's house to get some sugar," my brother said.

He left. A few minutes later, a friend of mine came in.

Strictly speaking, I didn't know anything about him although I had known him for a long time. He wasn't a superman. However, he had many singular characteristics. I knew him in 1966 in a Buddhist school. Twenty years later, I didn't dare to conclude who he was, where he lived, whether he was married or not, even what his real name was. He made acquaintance with anybody. He knew everything and could do everything. He had no ID but he traveled everywhere. Almost all the famous Buddhist monks knew him. So did South Vietnamese politicians in the 1960s and 1970s. Sometimes he lived like a king. Sometimes he slept hungry. He seemed to be generous when he had plenty of money. When he was broke, he would do anything not only to survive but also to please a friend. He would pawn a leather bag to bring a friend to a restaurant for lunch. He would use his friend's name to buy a bottle of beer on credit. He would steal something from somebody not to use it or to sell it but to give it to somebody else. He was kind to me. He used to give my oldest son cake, candy, and chocolate. He often said that he liked me because I was fond of history.

It was wrong to say that he was a bad man. He was born in a sandy and rocky province in Central Vietnam. He was imprisoned in Binh Duong and Saigon in the 1960s. After his release he became the adopted brother of the jailer. He lived in the house of the latter and was considered a member of his family. Even the jailer's family didn't know whether he was married or single.

That showed that he hid his background intelligently and that his social relations were impeccable. I knew the jailer when I was nine years of age. One day, I asked him, "Why was your adopted brother imprisoned?"

"On account of his activities for a political party in Central Vietnam," he said.

It was what he knew about this singular man.

It was wrong to say that he was a good man. All the people who knew him were deceived by him at least once. But nobody detested him. In my eyes, he was particularly rare on this planet. He kept his cool temper when somebody got angry with him or cursed him. His indifference enraged those who cursed him. When their anger was gone, he used to suggest, "Let's go to the coffee shop to have a drink."

Or, he would say, "Stay here and have lunch with me. Mr. Yen's restaurant has some special dishes today."

One day, a senator and lexicographer came to my house and asked me if I had seen my friend. Our respectable senator was a sweet and soft-spoken man. He told me that my friend took the new leather bag he had just bought in France. The next day, he came back to the senator's house during his absence and borrowed his son's motorcycle without bringing it back to his son. He sold it for a price of 39,000 piastres (about $400). Our senator had to pay the buyer 39,000 piastres for the ransom of his son's motorcycle, but he had no complaint about the adventurous acts of this troublesome man.

I was anxious to see him again. Frankly speaking, his enigmatic personality scared me.

"Long time, no see. Were you in jail?" I asked him cynically.

Such cynical words never hurt this man, who used to play adventurous games with the police. I wondered if he was Viet Cong. He was interested in the trial of Vu Ngoc Nha and Huynh Van Trong. I was a little afraid.

As for him, he didn't get angry at my question. He retorted, "How did you know?"

"It's my intuition," I said.

"You are right. I was imprisoned."

"Where?"

"In Ben Tre."

"What were you charged with?"

"Escape."

"How many years in prison?"

"A couple of years," he said vaguely.

He sat on a chair, watching my living room.

"What do you do to make your living?" he asked.

"Farming," I said.

"Oh, no. You can't make your living by farming. You have to leave."

I had no idea.

"If you stay here you must work for the socialist government. You have to choose one of these two ways," he added.

I knew that he was right. But I wondered whether his words were sincere or not. Therefore, I sought to avoid his trap.

"The present situation is fine with me," I said.

"You must leave," he insisted.

"All countries are the same. They are on this planet. Our fates remain the same here or there."

My avoidance made him angry. He stood up and said furiously, "So, stay and live here!" He left without saying good-bye to me.

At present, I don't know whether he gave me sincere advice or if he was trying to discover my true thoughts from my heart and mind. I saw him in anger for the first time.

His capriciousness scared me and made me more careful with him. In reality, he hadn't given me any trouble during the ten years of Communist rule. He didn't give my family any trouble after my escape either.

This enigmatic man spent the last years of his life in misery. He lived with an unknown Buddhist monk in a small village in Song Be province. In the 1960s he had been the monk's benefactor. After 1975 the monk returned to his native village, practicing farming and reciting Buddhist prayers for the dead to earn his living. In 1990 I learned that my friend had passed away. In 1995, by chance, I saw his name in a book on Vu Ngoc Nha, a Communist spy in Saigon in the 1950s and 1960s, who was promoted to general of intelligence after the fall of South Vietnam. I hoped that it wasn't his name but somebody else's.

I didn't trust him. But I paid attention to his advice. It was what my brother and I had been talking about a few minutes before he came. I thought that God was giving me a test to verify whether I wanted to escape or to stay in Vietnam by sending an unreliable person to bring me the message.

My Vietnamese and Chinese students gave me some information about the Southeast Asian refugee camps, sponsorship, the ODP in Bangkok, and some local and international news they heard clandestinely on the VOA and BBC. They told me that the Communist government had stopped accepting applications for exit permits temporarily. It seemed that they pushed me to make my decision as soon as possible.

One Sunday, I rode to Thu Duc to see my dead teacher's family. By chance, I saw a cousin of my sister-in-law.

"Here you are! You look skinny. Why are you still here? One of my cousins just left and arrived in Indonesia safely. I think that you need to leave. You can't live here," she said in a low voice.

"I plan to let my oldest son escape," I said.

"There will be a clandestine departure in a few days. My niece and many of my relatives will escape this time," she said.

It was inconvenient and dangerous to talk on the street. She invited me to stop by her house to discuss our plan in detail. Arriving at her house I put my bicycle against a tree and padlocked it carefully. She cleaned the teapot and prepared special tea for me.

"I haven't sold rice for many years. Now I am selling some inexpensive items clandestinely just to live. It is easy for me because I am single. My sister has many children. I have to share her family burden. Everything is fine with me. But I didn't want to see my nieces in their premature misery," the lady said in a soft voice.

"What do you think about the escape organizers? Can we trust them?" I asked.

"Yes, we can. We need to escape. They need gold. They had the right and duty to arrest the escapees. Now they are escape organizers. We don't have any worry in the area under their control. Their leader is an officer of the police. He fell in love with the daughter of a former major of the army of the Republic of Vietnam. He helped the latter escape after his release. Now the major is in an Indonesian refugee camp. The leader planned to escape after accumulating some gold. He is in Thu Duc right now. Do you want to see him?"

"No, I don't. I need to think about this."

"In my opinion, you had better go with your son. Don't let him go alone," she said.

I left her house, thinking about leaving or staying. I wondered why so many people talked to me about escape. I didn't trust my adventurous friend but I trusted the cousin of my sister-in-law. She was virtuous and sincere.

I paid attention to the virtue of the intermediary for life on a small boat on the immense ocean would be uncertain without the miraculous protection of God. The boat people could be drowned. They could be robbed and killed by the Thai corsairs. They could die of thirst and starvation. It was rare to see a good intermediary in a country full of complications. I had found a rare one. I decided not to miss this good opportunity.

Two months before I made this decision to escape, I saw some significant signs in my dreams.

I saw a herd of goats in a dream. A few days later, I saw two friends of mine, Nguyen Thai Long and Nguyen Thanh Long, in Phuoc Long and Long Thanh, respectively. I saw many boats on an immense river. The people on the boats looked like Indians. I interpreted the dream by myself and felt very optimistic. It was clear that I was going to go abroad. In Sino-Vietnamese *duong* means "goat," and *duong* also means "sea" or "ocean." In the nineteenth century, the Chinese and Vietnamese called the Europeans Tay Duong. Besides, *long* means "dragon," a sacred animal symbolizing strength and prosperity. It is also the symbol of a plane in the air or a boat on the sea. The word *long* also reminded me of Cuu Long (the Mekong).

My interpretation was more or less subjective. In reality, it was quite right. When I escaped, I was on a sampan floating on the Mekong (Cuu Long) all day long (May 27, 1985). The place where the sampan joined the big boat was Long Hoa.

One night while sleeping, I heard a voice repeating, "The golden field of Toledo. The golden field of Toledo."

"Tokaido?" I asked.

The voice went on repeating, "The golden field of Toledo."

"Tolède? I don't have any relation with Spain," I said (Toledo is called Tolède by the French).

The voice repeated some more times and stopped.

The next day I told my wife this story. She smiled, saying that I heard such a voice because I wished to escape earnestly.

I shuttled between Laithieu, Saigon, and Thu Duc over many consecutive days. When somebody looked for me, my wife and children told him that I had gone to Saigon to heal a patient who was my former student's parent.

It wasn't easy to blindfold my friends and neighbors. A friend of mine in Vinh Phu stopped me and gave me a cup of iced sugar cane juice for refreshment.

"I saw you shuttling in this area a couple of times. You have something important to do, don't you?" he asked curiously.

"I went to Saigon to heal my student's parent," I said.

"My life changed terribly after 1975. I worked hard without having enough food for my family. My health is fragile after spending two years in prison. 'They' arrested me, thinking that I am rich and that they will confiscate my house by labeling me 'reactionary.' They said that they found many yellow flags and weapons in my house. They were disappointed when they searched my house and found only some one-piastre bills! How poor I was. However, I was put in detention for two years. I don't know if I can go to France or not for my father was trained in France and died there. My mother received an allowance from the French government regularly," he said.

"Try to contact the French Ministry of Defense to get information about your case."

My suggestion was vague. I knew that. At least, I didn't disappoint my friend.

"I would like you to write a letter for me," he said.

"No problem. But the important thing is that the letter must arrive smoothly in Paris without being censored or destroyed by the local government. I will write it for you whenever you need. Now I must go."

I stood up and shook hands with him, then left.

One night, it was raining cats and dogs. I had to spend the night in my brother's house.

Seeing me going in and out of there many times in the last few days, the neighborhood police had some question marks in their minds. They knocked at the door and searched the house at midnight. How strange it was. They asked all the members of my brother's family to produce their IDs except for me. I lay on the bed, pretending to sleep soundly. My brother showed me to the police and told them about our relationship and the reason why I was spending the night in his house. The police didn't say a word. They left the house silently.

The next day my brother and I went to a house in the First District to give the escape organizers a tael of gold as a down payment for my oldest son. My sister-in-law was there. She asked me, "Why don't you go with your son?" Then she added, "You must go. You play the key role, not your son. If you don't have enough gold, I will tell your brother to lend you some. He just sold his house."

That was May 23, 1985.

The organizers' representative received the down payment for my son. My sister-in-law talked to him about me. "I will give you our decision on the evening of May 25. His son and your brother and nephew will leave Ho Chi Minh City for the Mekong Delta on May 26," he said to my sister-in-law.

My brother was ready to lend me enough gold to escape. Suddenly he said, "I would like to go with you."

I came home to inform my wife that our son was going to leave Laithieu for Ho Chi Minh City on May 25. I was going to escort him to Ho Chi Minh City that day and find out if I could go with him or not. I told my son to leave Laithieu in the afternoon. As for me, I was going to leave at 5:00 P.M.

The last two days in Laithieu were the busiest ones. Learning that I was home, my Chinese Vietnamese students came to my house to take me to the coffee shop. We had coffee and talked with one another as usual. My students guessed that I had some news. But they didn't ask me. Instead, they told me about their difficult lives in Vietnam, about the sudden death of somee Soviet leaders, about bloodshed in Cambodia, and about the death of the Cambodian prime minister in the Soviet Union. They insisted on how bloody and erosive the war was in Cambodia. Many Vietnamese *bo doi* doing their military service there became one-legged veterans because of Chinese mines and grenades. Their companions defected. Other teenagers dodged the draft. Some *bo doi* defectors walked to the Thai refugee camps. Vietnamese Communist troops might have attacked Thailand, which was the stronghold of the three Cambodian warring factions fighting against the Vietnamese-backed government in Phnom Penh. At the Sino-Vietnamese border, smugglers had their activities. People bought the horns and hoofs of oxen and water buffaloes, sweet potatoes, browses, etc., to paralyze the collective farms in North Vietnam.

Sick people came to my house. Students looked happy to see their teacher after some days of absence. I forced my smile, not showing the rising sorrow in my heart. I would only see these familiar people and sites for thirty more hours. I was going to leave the lovely house I had built. I was going to leave my wife, my naïve and innocent children, my mother and relatives, my students, and the people who came to my house every day to witness the vicissitudes of my life. In the Yellow Spring, my father would blame me for not taking care of my old mother and his grave. My young students would ask why I had left the country without saying good-bye to anybody.

A former schoolgirl of mine and her husband, a former officer of the South Vietnamese army, who had just been released, came to see me and gave me a bag of sugar they had made in their sugarmill in Nhi Binh This village, stretching along the right bank of the Saigon River, is a prosperous village with many orchards, fertile rice fields, sugar cane plantations, and sugarmills. It is one of the oldest Catholic villages in South Vietnam, like Binh Nham, Cai Mon, and Ha Tien. The visit of my former student and her husband gave me a good opportunity to wish them good luck on the last day of my stay in Vietnam.

A Chinese Vietnamese businessman in Laithieu brought me a basket of fruit and said good-bye to me.

"Tomorrow my family is going to leave for Toronto. I came to say good-bye to you and wish you good luck," he said.

"I wish you bon voyage and a happy life in your new land," I said.

I felt very happy when thinking of this good sign. I believed that my escape would be successful. Two months later, I saw his brother in Bataan. He shook hands with me and laughed, "You saw me off at Tan Son Nhut. I came here by plane while you were still in Vietnam. Now you are joining me here."

On the evening of May 24 I rode to Binh Nham to read the funeral oration before the coffin of the old man whose deafness had been healed by me in 1982. He had been a journalist working for the *Journal d'Extreme Orient* in Saigon. While a student, he had been involved in the students' demonstration for the amnesty of revolutionary Phan Boi Chau, sentenced to death by the French colonialists in 1925, and in the commemoration of revolutionary Phan Chu Trinh in 1926. Our respected revolutionary died in Saigon just as he returned to Vietnam from France. His funeral was one of the most solemn in history. The Saigonese mourned for him. The Saigonese students wore mourning bands. From Saigon the commemoration was spread throughout the country.

Our old journalist was happy with his normal hearing every time he saw me. He waited for death without any fear. He succumbed to his age burden and broken life. His last wish was to hear a funeral oration written and read by me before his coffin on his last day on the Earth. I tried my best to satisfy his soul in these two busiest days.

This funeral oration was my last writing in Vietnam. It moved all the visitors. They burst into tears when they learned that the quiet man who, over the past thirty years, had lived silently in his wife's native village, had had a vivid past. He traveled to Qui Nhon, Hue, Nghe An, Thanh Hoa, Hanoi, and Saigon from his native land in a southern province of Central Vietnam. After fifty years of struggle the traveler realized that he had been homeless.

I bowed my head to say *adieu* to him when I finished reading the funeral oration. He left the world for God's kingdom. I was going to leave the country and my family to continue the struggle for life in a new land.

I burned the funeral oration and presented my condolences to the family in mourning. Then I went home to prepare for my son's escape and possibly for mine, too.

There was no electricity in the city that night. All the residents seemed to be used to the shortage of light at night. My Chinese student came when I had just finished dinner. We walked to a coffee shop. We drank coffee, smoked British cigarettes, and talked. I advised him to use any way to get an exit permit as soon as possible. I felt vaguely sad, thinking that he would have a lot of worries after my escape.

We left the coffee shop at 10:00 P.M. I walked home in the immense darkness.

As soon as I was ready to go to bed, somebody knocked at the gate.

"Anybody home?"

"Yes, we are home," I said.

I lit the lamp, opened the door, and walked to the gate.

"Your son must go to the People's Committee office to have a health screening for military service tomorrow," the visitor said loudly.

"What time?" I asked.

"Any time. The doctor will be there all day long," he said.

All my children were sleeping except for my oldest son. My wife looked anxious. I tried to keep my cool temper to discuss with her about the "must" and "must not." After analyzing and weighing the problem we told our son to go there before going to Ho Chi Minh City. He would have an exit if his escape was unsuccessful.

"What if he is kept at the People's Committee office?" my wife asked.

"Tell him to bring my curriculum vitae with him when he goes to the People's Committee office. Our son couldn't enter college because of my curriculum vitae. Now he must use it not to be a Communist *bo doi*," I said, comforting my wife.

On the morning of May 25, my son presented himself at the People's Committee office. Nobody knew what he was there for. The neighborhood chief had sent a militia man to my house to give my family some troubles. No young men were there but my son. There was no military service health screening. My son came home happily.

A Chinese young man came to invite me to have breakfast with him.

His father had run a big oriental drugstore in Laithieu in the 1940s, 1950s, and 1960s. He was from Tai Pou, South China. He married a Vietnamese woman. Before 1949 he sent two of his sons to China to live with his father. When the Chinese Communists took over China, he never had any news from his father and his two sons. He died in 1970.

His wife couldn't run the oriental drugstore. She sold almost all of the properties left by her husband. Her son was too young. He was in the South Vietnamese army until the fall of the Republic of Vietnam.

After 1975 the young man was very lonely. His father-in-law returned from North Vietnam. He incited his daughter to divorce the young man because he had been a soldier of the Nationalist government. The young man faced many disadvantages due to this political divorce. Having a permanent headache, he used to see me almost every day.

"I have come here many times without seeing you. It is boring to drink coffee without you," he said.

"I went to Saigon to take care of a patient. He is in recovery. Maybe today I am going to Saigon again," I said.

After breakfast we drank coffee and had a chat until noon.

I had to leave at 5:00 P.M.

At the last minute many people looked for me. They seemed to have the presentiment that I was going to live far away from them.

It was hot that day. My wife prepared a torn shirt for my son based on the instructions of the organizer. It was a new shirt, which my aunt had sent me from Paris. My wife made it dirty, tore it, then mended it with three old pieces of material to turn it really old and dirty. My son put it in a bag. He wore it the day he left Ho Chi Minh City. My daughter sterilized needles and put some cotton balls and alcohol in my acupuncture kit.

At 1:30 P.M. another Chinese student came and invited me to have coffee with him in Cau Ngang. It was a big state-run coffee shop. It was colorful and noisy because of the music and the shouts of the servers. My student told me about the activities of the ODP in Thailand and about the American interviewers in Thu Duc.

This grateful student was an asthmatic. I had helped him recover from his serious asthma. He respected me as his teacher and physician. I liked him as a pious son, a grateful student, and a good man in society.

He was born into a family of twelve children. His brother entered the army and became limbless and blind in 1968. His father was a cheerful, sincere, and sociable merchant. He worked hard to feed his children, including the limbless and blind son, who neither walked nor ate or drank by himself. The father worked so hard that he fell ill and died. All the burden of the family weighed on his second son, my student. The latter looked after his crippled brother, who was rough and nervous, his grandmother with her chronic diabetes, his mother and siblings plus his own family. He wasn't rich but he was pious, compassionate, and sociable. He liked reading and used to give me books. He was a good organizer. He arranged his daily activities in such a way that he spent an hour per day with me. We talked to each other while drinking coffee. He contacted the police to help me get an exit permit. In 1989 his family arrived in Pennsylvania.

Each person has a habit, a hobby, good and bad sides. People having breakfast at Chinese restaurants every morning were addicted not only to the tastes of coffee, cigarettes, and food but also to the warmth of the environment at sunrise, to the good smell of coffee, to exchanging what they saw and heard with their friends. My students had the same addictions. They were addicted to talking to me and to listening to me tell my opinions.

I enjoyed the taste of coffee for the last time in my native province. I felt chilly in torrid May. I felt solitary in a crowded coffee shop with the loud noise of music broadcast by Radio Saigon Giai Phong. I had mixed feelings of melancholy and joy, of union and separation. How sorrowful separation was! I was going to separate from people who loved me and from people who had tried their best to get rid of me as well.

My student dropped me at the gate of my house and rode to the market. I took a shower. Then I lay on the bed to take a rest before riding to Ho Chi Minh City. It was raining. The wind blew strongly. The coconut leaves touched the roof of my house, making an intermittent noise. My daughter was busy arranging some stuff in a small bag for me: sterilized needles, cotton balls, a small bottle of alcohol, and an old shirt.

Suddenly, there was a young man putting his bicycle at the veranda and rushing into my house. He was soaked with water.

"Is Uncle home?" he panted to my wife.

"He is asleep," my wife said.

"My father is seriously ill. He told me to call Uncle to treat him," the young man said.

I got up, sterilized needles, got dressed, and rode to Binh Nham.

The young man's father was a friend of mine. He was fourteen years older than I. He was from a rich family in Laithieu. As a child, he studied in Hue. He spoke French and Japanese fluently. After World War II he had a good job in Saigon. In 1955 he returned to his paternal house in Laithieu and had a petit bourgeois life in a small city although unemployed. His family got poorer and poorer due to his long unemployment. I helped him get a job in Long Khanh, then in Saigon. But he couldn't restore his family from the economic depression. Once again, I helped him get a job in Phuoc Thanh province. I advised him to bring his family there to redo his life.

"Phuoc Thanh is in War Zone D. It is very dangerous," he said.

"I know. But you can make your fortune there. Otherwise, you will die in poverty in this city," I said.

He listened to me. A few years later, Phuoc Thanh province became Phu Giao district of Binh Duong province. Many American soldiers were sent there. In a short time his family got wealthy. He bought two big houses there.

In March 1975 he returned to Laithieu. His old house there had been sold. He had to build a small house in Binh Nham. He told me that Phu Giao was unsafe. When the Communists came, he wasn't there. His family faced a big challenge in the new house. Usually all the members of his family slept hungry. He fell ill. His asthma got more and more serious. Every time I came to his house, I gave them a bag of cassava or sweet potatoes.

As soon as his wife saw me, she forced her smile, saying, "My husband is very ill. He is weak. He refused to go to the hospital because he counts on you. He doesn't trust anybody but you."

"It is sultry. He is suffocating," I said.

I went into his room. He was bony and skinny like a skeleton. He stayed motionless in bed. His eyes were closed. His breathing was spasmodic. When he breathed, his wrinkled skin move slightly.

I began the treatment. A few minutes later, his breathing got regular. He opened his eyes and said, "I could die for lack of food and medicine. My children are impatient with my chronic disease. I wonder what I can do to earn my living in my fifties."

"Do you take your medicine regularly?" I asked.

"I take my medicine irregularly. From time to time the old chief of the Health Department used to come here and give me some medicine for my asthma. He was dismissed by the Viet Cong."

"Why?" I asked.

"Under French rule he was a reserve noncommissioned officer. After 1954 he studied medicine and practiced it until 1975. In his curriculum vitae, instead of writing Tru Bi (reservist), he wrote the abbreviation TB. According to the Viet Cong, TB stands for Tinh Bao (intelligence). He was not only dismissed but also investigated by the Viet Cong for many months," he said.

"Try to take care of yourself in this hard time," I said.

"You know, everybody in this family is sick of my chronic illness. Recently, many of my neighbors died. Some died of illness. Some died of poverty. Some died of despair. One of my children asked me, 'Many people die these days. Why haven't you died yet?' His words reflected not only his state of mind but also that of the other children. I am disgusted," he said, tears in his eyes.

I felt creepy. He had told me the bitter truth of his family. Time had erased the picture of the young student from Pellerin High School in Hue in the 1940s. His comfortable life in the 1940s, 1950s, 1960s, and early 1970s was gone. It had been replaced by a leaky house, awry bamboo poles, cold chicken, fallen beds, and the absence of mattresses and blankets. He was incapable of redressing his family situation. Misery created more misery, destruction, and separation. His wife and children were upset. They didn't pay attention to one another. They were separate from one another even though they lived together in the same house. My skinny patient had to open a martial arts class illegally to have some money to get food and medicine. Some villagers helped him by sending their children to his martial arts class, even though they knew that he had no energy to teach martial arts. Sometimes the students came while their "master" stayed in bed, struggling with his asthma. Everything was in a mess. The torn house seemed to have been abandoned for a long time.

When I was ready to leave, his wife invited me to have a bowl of sugared mung beans.

"I have to go right now," I said.

"Finish it first," she said.

I refused firmly to save time. I waved to her and her husband while I took my bicycle out of his house.

I said good-bye to my wife and children.

"Don't worry if I don't come home. That means I am leaving," I said.

My wife and children looked at me silently. Nobody said a word. All of us tried to control our emotions. Whether the escape was successful or not, my family would have two absent. I didn't tell my plan to my own mother or my mother-in-law. How expensive freedom was!

It was 5:00 P.M. Familiar noisy music was on the air. The announcer talked about the brilliant success of socialist agriculture and economy. Some provinces had surpassed the criteria set by the government. The country remained poor. So did the Vietnamese people.

I rode slowly as if I were enjoying a breath of fresh air. Arriving in Vinh Phu, I heard a man calling me. I stopped. A middle-aged man ran to Road 13. He waved to me and said, "I saw you ride by here a couple of times. But I couldn't call you. I have a delicious jack fruit for you."

I shook hands with him. We walked to his house, talking to each other.

"Where are you going?" he asked.

"I am going to Ho Chi Minh City," I said.

"When will you come back?"

"I have to stay there one or two days. A Saigonese patient needs me."

"Can you carry this jack fruit to Ho Chi Minh City?" he asked.

"It is very inconvenient."

"Pick it up on the way back home. I'll leave it here."

"I don't know how long I'll stay in Ho Chi Minh City. I am afraid that the jack fruit could be rotten. I am not certain that I'll ride on Road 13 on the way back home."

"OK. Let me cut it. You eat a piece and take another piece with you," he said, looking for a knife.

I ate the piece of jack fruit. How sweet it was! I regretted that I didn't have time to enjoy it. I was afraid that I would have a stomachache on the way to the Mekong delta. After I finished eating, I shook hands with him and continued my journey.

I met this man in an interesting circumstance.

One day, one of his friends in Vinh Phu, a clog shop owner, had an acute pain in his stomach and in his back. His two wives looked for the hawker who sold medicine clandestinely in the village to get pain relief medicine for him. But the pain got more and more acute. His face got pale. His body was wet with cold sweat. He said his last words to his wives, who had been his workers. He told them to bury him by his house.

Learning that he was seriously ill, the villagers flowed to his house to visit him. My friend, "the hero of the floating paddy," was among the visitors. The patient told him that I could save his life. He said so because I had healed his backache previously.

"He is my friend. We are very friendly. I can invite him to come here to heal you. But I don't have a motorcycle," my friend said.

A Chinese Vietnamese standing by the door raised his voice, "I have a Mobylette. I can ride to Laithieu to pick him up. But he doesn't know me. I need your letter of introduction."

This man was a former pig breeder. After 1975 he had learned how to make wooden clogs from the sick man.

My friend wrote me some lines. The man put the letter in his pocket and rode his Mobylette to Laithieu, three miles from Vinh Phu village.

When I arrived, I saw a crowd standing around the house of the sick man. There were some men, a few women, and many curious children wishing to get sensational local news. They looked at me with curiosity. They wanted to see what I could do to save the life of this polygamist.

I asked one of his wives to sterilize needles for me. The treatment began. Within ten minutes he felt better. He raised his voice, saying, "I feel better!"

"You feel better, do you?" I asked.

"Much better!" he said.

The crowd broke into laughter. Some applauded. A man shouted, "He isn't dying! Don't worry, you two ladies!"

My friend was proud and happy.

"He told me that only you could save him. He had chronic backache. Nobody healed it but you," he said.

After I pulled out the needles, the patient got up to prepare coffee for me. Everybody there laughed loudly. They asked one another, "Where is this man from? What kind of medicine did he use?"

The middle-aged man who had given me a jack fruit was excited about the whole thing. He came to me and shook hands to make my acquaintance.

"I heard of acupuncture, but this is the first time that I've witnessed its efficacy. Is there medicine in your needles?" he asked.

"No, there isn't."

"What was his trouble?"

"Gas!"

"That is bizarre. What a therapy without medicine," he said.

The villagers left the patient's house except for him and my friend. He invited me to have lunch with his family on Road 13. We became friends on this occasion. Since then, every time he came to Laithieu, he stopped by my house to chat with me. He sent his children to my English class. He was very happy to see their progress. I became a trusted physician in his eyes when I healed his wife of a cough.

My friend in Vinh Phu told me that he was a Communist colonel. Demobilized, he bought a house in Vinh Phu to plant fruit trees and coconut trees and to practice pisciculture. Seeing many dead on the battlefields, probably he was conscious of life's value, of love, and of the meaninglessness of carnage, revenge, and hatred. What if he hadn't been demobilized?

I thanked him for thinking of me and for treating me as a Vietnamese and not a mortal enemy.

I said good-bye to him and rode to Ho Chi Minh City. I arrived there when the lights were on. I went to my brother's house and we went to the place we had gone two days before. My younger brother and my oldest son were there.

The organizer told my son and younger brother what to do on May 26 at the bus station. He said that he couldn't accept my brother and me because there were no vacant places on the boat. I was a little meditative when hearing that. My brother didn't have any reaction. My brother, younger brother, and I went to a coffee shop to have a chat and to wish "bon voyage" to my son and younger brother. My brother invited his friend who lived near there to have coffee with us. This one was a former officer of the South Vietnamese army. His English was impeccable. Besides, he was good at Chinese astrology and the occult sciences. As soon as I saw him, I said, "I had objectively believed that I would escape this year. My prediction was wrong. The escape organizer just said 'no' to us."

He looked at me and said with joy, "Practice meditation right here, at the foot of this tree, and tell me a number. I will give you the answer to your business."

I closed my eyes and concentrated my mind at the foot of a centennial *diphtero carpus* on Phat Diem Street, where the coffee shop owner had placed a small table with four small chairs.

Our friend wrote a number in his palm and asked me to tell mine. When I said, "Number one," he showed the number he had written. The two numbers were the same.

"I don't care what 'they' said. You must go away," he said.

At that moment, my son arrived.

"I looked for you for an hour," my son said to me.

"How did you know that I was here?"

"I rode around this area. By chance, I saw you here."

He said that my sister-in-law wanted to see me urgently.

"What is it about?" I asked.

"I don't know."

Our friend urged us to see my sister-in-law.

"Go right away. It is good news. Good luck to you," he said.

We shook hands with him and left the coffee shop for my sister-in-law's house. She said to a tall man standing in her living room, "These are my husband's brothers. They are in misery. Can you help them escape this time?"

"We have enough escapees. The boat is ten meters long [thirty feet]. It is dangerous to accept more people. If I do, though, I will receive their gold, not the organizer. Don't give it to him!" the man said.

"Well, I will be responsible for that after they get into the boat. Now, please tell them what to do tomorrow," my sister-in-law said.

"Tomorrow you both come here at 3:00 A.M. I will pick you up," the man said to us.

My brother and I went home. My brother called his children and gave them some instructions. Afterward, we went to bed.

As soon as my brother turned off the light, we heard somebody knocking at the door. The neighborhood police searched my brother's house. Like last time, I lay on the bed and pretended to sleep soundly.

The neighborhood police kept their eyes on my brother's house. He was on probation after leaving a reeducation camp. My presence in his house attracted their attention. In addition, my brother's children were in their twenties. Three of his sons were put in reeducation camps after abortive escapes. One of them escaped from the camps four times. Another son escaped from the Song Be camp once. Both of them became illegal citizens. They stayed in a dark attic in the daytime and got out only for a little while at night. They had a lot of time at home to smoke cigarettes, to read books and to study languages. The police were looking for them for they had beat up some militia members. My brother and sister-in-law begged their pardon, saying that my nephews had mental health problems.

The police left the house after the search. We tried to rejoin our sleep vainly. I felt anxious. My mind seemed to be empty. My stomach seemed full although I hadn't had dinner. I couldn't sleep that night. I was afraid that the tall man would leave us if we weren't on time.

It was 3:00 A.M. I woke my brother. All of his children got up to see off both of us in silence. It was drizzling outside. The streets were deserted. We rode silently to our sister-in-law's house. We left our bicycles there and said good-bye to her. The tall man started his black Honda. Three silhouettes moved slowly on the street. Silently I said good-bye to Saigon. The lovely city appeared and disappeared in the rain. I looked at all the trees and apartments along the streets in saying to myself, "Good-bye, Saigon! Good-bye, my lovely city!"

We arrived in Vinh Binh (Tra Vinh) at 11:00 A.M. The guide dropped us at the city limit and told my brother to get a pack of cigarettes but to watch where he turned. As we got off his Honda, he was in a hurry to speed it up. I was a little afraid for this city was unfamiliar to me.

"Why did he drop us here?" I asked.

"He told us to watch where he turned to rejoin him," my brother said.

We made our way toward the alley where he had turned, smoking cigarettes. We walked to the end of the alley without seeing the guide. My brother lost his cool temper.

"Did you really see him turn here?" he asked.

"Yes, I did. I am sure that he turned here," I said.

The residents living along the alley looked at us with curiosity. A lady raised her voice to ask us, "Who are you looking for?"

We didn't answer her question because we didn't know the guide's name. I thought of one of my friends, who was a native of Vinh Binh province. He died of high blood pressure in Ho Chi Minh City. I don't know why I didn't say his name to stop the dangerous curiosity of these people. We tried to control our temper by smoking cigarettes. These curious people were displeased with our silence. They shouted together, "These guys plan to escape!" Their words made us uneasy. We walked slowly in the alley. I saw a man whose face was bony and red. That proved that he drank much beer. He wore a T-shirt that showed his long necklace. His leather slippers were clean. I guessed that he was a policeman. At that time I was anxious, waiting for bad things to happen to us. Suddenly, he ordered us, "Come in!" We obeyed him mechanically. We went into a brick house near there. I saw our guide's black Honda there but the license plate had been removed. I saw an old man at the table. He looked like a rich farmer. It seemed that he was very powerful. He wore a long-sleeved shirt. His hair was well combed. His mustache made him more aggressive.

The table was full of delicious food. But there was only one eater. As soon as we came in, he chastised us, "You are too late for the wedding ceremony. How can we get to Long Hoa by boat at this time?"

We were so dazed that we didn't know how to reply to him. He added, "Well, sit down and have some food. We will solve the problem later."

Our hearts beat quickly. We felt that we were lost in a strange world. Our guide came in. His presence tranquilized us. We knew that we had come to the right place and met with the right man. We ate indifferently although we were hungry and the food was delicious.

Thirty minutes later, the man in the T-shirt brought us to the market. We then walked to a hut, a mile and a half from the market.

My son and younger brother belonged to a group of seven people. Their guide was a lady. Arriving at the bus station in Phu Lam they lined up to get tickets. The peddlers got angry after asking them to buy their stuff unsuccessfully. They shouted, "These guys are escapees!" The seven people in the group were scared. Their feet got cold. Fortunately nothing wrong happened.

While waiting for the ferryboat at My Thuan, they faced the same problem with the peddlers.

The ferryboat brought them to the other bank of the Mekong. There they changed buses, following their guide without talking to her. The lady was very quiet. She behaved as if she were a passenger. All the people in the group pretended not to know one another. The guide got a ticket to Vinh Binh. So did the others.

The bus to Vinh Binh was crowded with women and children. There were some Communist policemen on it. They told one another how they had captured escapees. It happened that these women and children were escapees who had been captured by the police. Men were sent to a reeducation camp. Women and children were released. Captured escapees and hopeful escapees were on the same bus. At 10:00 P.M. the seven people arrived in Vinh Binh They were dispersed to different boats anchored along the river near the hut we were in.

On evening of May 26, the old man with a mustache came to the hut. He greeted us politely.

"Did you have a nap?" he asked.

"Yes, we did," we said.

"I knew you were tired. You needed to take a rest." Looking at us, he said, "You were wrong to wear torn clothes to go to a wedding ceremony. If I were a policeman, I would arrest you."

His words proved that he was an experienced policeman. Looking at our clothing, he could conclude who was the peasant and who was the disguised one.

"Our guide advised us to put on torn clothes," I said.

That evening we had a big dinner with chicken soup, chicken mixed with slaw, and strong rice alcohol. The old man told us what to do on May 27. He advised us not to say anything in case we were arrested by the police.

It drizzled in the early morning of May 27. The old man got up early. He prepared coffee for us. Suddenly, he shouted angrily, "It's time to go to the wedding ceremony. Are you asleep?"

A few minutes later, I saw my son coming to the hut with my sister-in-law's younger brother from the river bank. This one was a teacher of biology and a good acupuncturist.

My son had put on a torn shirt. My sister-in-law's younger brother wore eyeglasses. He looked serious.

That day we heard two different opinions about clothing. The guide told us to wear dirty clothes like the fishermen or farmers. The old man said that we were supposed to get dressed properly to attend the wedding ceremony.

Our boat left Long Hoa, Vinh Binh, on May 27, 1985, and we were rescued by the *Jean Charcot* on the East Sea two days later. The skinny man with the small bag is the author. After the ten-year challenge of the Communist regime, I weighed less than 90 pounds. This photo was taken by Philippe Theard, a French correspondent.

Both opinions were partly right. From the morning until noon the second opinion was right. But from noon until sunset the first opinion was right.

After breakfast we left the hut. The old man wished us "bon voyage." He let us know that we would be on the sampan all day long on the Mekong. We were going to get into the big boat somewhere near the mouth of the Mekong, seventeen miles from Vinh Binh.

We got into the sampan. The boatman was a deaf man. But he talked too much. His loud voice scared us. He said that his son was in the United States. His name was My (*My* means American). He said that he brought escapees to a certain island of Malaysia. After the foreign boats rescued the boat people, he returned to Vinh Binh to organize another escape.

Looking at the four of us he ordered, "Three of you hide yourselves inside. The young man has to wear a shirt. Your skin is bright. You don't look like a rural resident. While I row, you pretend to bail water out of the sampan."

The sampan was clean. There was no water in it. My son had to get water from the Mekong to fill it. Then, he bailed it out of the sampan. The boatman talked while rowing on the immense river. He showed us a Communist boat anchored on the other bank of the river in Ben Tre province and said in a monotone, "Its mission is to arrest escapees. It looks far from us. However, it can approach our sampan in a short time. 'They' have binoculars. When they suspect any boat, 'they' chase it immediately."

He harassed us by saying, "We talk here. But, on the other bank, they can hear."

We kept silent. He added, "We must be careful with the economic controllers. They have a big boat shuttling on this river to check smuggled goods. Sometimes they arrest escapees, too."

The boatman told us a lot of bad things. The sampan moved from one bank to the other, from morning until dark. Approaching our sampan, the other boatmen said, "This sampan carries escapees" or "There is an escape tonight."

We were very anxious. We were afraid of losing our money, freedom, and lives due to typhoons, piracy, or food or water shortage. We had nothing to eat on the sampan all day long. The organizer hadn't allowed us to bring anything bulky. They assured us that the boat had enough gas, food, and fresh water. Anxiety made us full although we had neither lunch nor dinner.

The boatman got tired. He berthed on the bank of Ben Tre province for a rest. It was about 5:00 P.M. The bank was deserted. It was covered with wild *Nipa fruticans*. I didn't see a house there. I felt comfortable breathing fresh air and having a rest after many hours on the Mekong. The sampan anchored. My son went ashore. Suddenly an old woman appeared. She looked mean. She stared at my son and asked, "What are you doing here?" While my son mumbled, she disappeared behind the coconut trees. I called to my son to get back to the sampan and urged the boatman to leave this unsafe place.

The sun disappeared at the horizon. Faded sunlight reflected on the wavy surface of the river like a huge piece of yellow silk. The sampan moved slowly on the immense Mekong, the vital force of the Vietnamese people. In the distance the sea roared as if it were happy to enjoy the moonlight on the birthday of Buddha.

Harmonizing my mind with the clouds and water, I tried to remember my family's daily activities at this time.

11

Good-bye, Dear Vietnam!

We left the sampan for the big boat at 10:00 P.M. on May 27. While getting into the boat, I dropped a slipper in the river.

The bottom of the boat was pretty deep. There were many people there. When I jumped in the boat, I hit a man. He protested violently although we didn't see each other. I apologized to him without seeing him. He continued grumbling. It seemed that he couldn't tolerate my unintentional mistake. It was dark. I didn't know where my brother and son were. I just heard people arguing with one another on the boat. The captain urged them to keep silent.

I felt suffocated for the boat was small and crowded with people. Many of them threw up. Some complained. The children cried. The bottom of the boat became a small hell. It was dark, dirty, smelly, and noisy.

The boat started with a big noise. Gliding along the Mekong, the boat moved to the East Sea in moonlight. The escapees enjoyed neither the moonlight nor fresh air. They stayed motionless in the dark boat. When somebody moved, his neighbor reacted against him. People quarreled with one another without seeing one another.

I listened to the regular explosions of the boat motor. From time to time I heard some noise caused by the friction of the boat along the shoal under water. At dawn some children walked over the escapees to get water. They went back and forth many times to get fresh water. Some people stood up to contemplate the sea at dawn and to breathe some fresh air.

Almost all the people had brought food, medicine, and even heavy clothes. Four of us had nothing.

"Breakfast!" a man shouted.

The rice wasn't well done. I couldn't eat it. I threw up and felt very tired.

Rice and fresh water were almost out after only thirty hours! The fresh water ran out quickly because some children stocked it. My health got worse for not eating anything for two days and for being suffocated on the boat. I remained motionless. My son prayed for me, putting his hand on my heart to check whether it was still beating or not.

On the morning of May 29, my brother said to me, "Water is out. Rice is out. Fuel is almost empty. How will we get to Malaysia?"

I opened my eyes and said in a low voice, "We will be rescued at 11:00 A.M."

"It is 7:00 A.M.," my brother said.

"Four hours more," I said.

The captain asked the escapees to float a white flag for rescue. A boat approached ours. Seeing the boat's name, the *Tien Giang*, the captain ordered everybody to lie down. Nothing wrong happened. The captain of the *Tien Giang* allowed our boat to pass by giving some hand signs. At 11:00 A.M. the *Jean Charcot*, a French boat, rescued forty-one people from our boat. The French, West German, Belgian, and Austrian physicians and journalists thought that I was the captain. They surrounded and interviewed me. Dr. Dominique, vice president of the *Médecins du Monde*, was the first physician to talk to me. After him came the television reporters and journalists. The captain of the *Jean Charcot* came to congratulate the boat people. The seamen came successively and had friendly conversations with us as if they were seeing their old friends again. I introduced them to the true captain of our boat. He was a former major of the cavalry who had spent six years in a reeducation camp.

"We saw your boat last night. It moved slowly," a Frenchman said.

At 11:30 A.M. a Communist cruiser approached the *Jean Charcot*. The captain asked me to tell the boat people to hide themselves in the cabin. The French seamen sank our boat by piercing it with heavy bars of metal. So the Viet Cong didn't see any trace.

"What is happening?" I asked the captain.

"A Viet Cong cruiser is approaching our boat," he said.

I went into the cabin and told the boat people not to make a noise.

The Communist cruiser looked menacing. It was black with a red flag and some machine guns that looked aggressive.

Silence reigned on the *Jean Charcot*, which was as big as an aircraft carrier. The French captain stood on the boat, watching the black cruiser approaching his boat. The machine gun seemed to be ready to open fire on the *Jean Charcot*. The French seamen were indifferent. They did their duties on the boat without paying attention to the Communist cruiser. Some painted the boat. Some washed it. Some carried materials. Others took care of the huge chain. They worked while singing and laughing as if there were nothing dangerous. The Communist cruiser arrived. A Communist cadre raised his voice, asking, "Where are the escapees?"

His question was authoritative and aggressive.

The captain of the *Jean Charcot* shook his head to let him know that he saw nothing.

The Communist cadre asked him to accept an escapee from his cruiser.

The captain refused. He gave him some signs, stating that he was ready to accept all of the crew on the cruiser, but that the cruiser must be sunk after the crew got into the *Jean Charcot.* I didn't know if the Communist cadre understood or not. The cruiser returned to Vietnamese waters.

There were two Vietnamese on the French boat. One was a physician who had studied medicine in France. The other was a lady who had escaped from Vietnam in 1980. She was adopted by a German family. Both of them were volunteers, rescuing the boat people in the East Sea, hoping to see friends or relatives among the rescued. The lady spoke good German, French, and English. My brother knew her father who, according to her, was settled in Canada. Her German adoptive father videotaped some live pictures on the *Jean Charcot,* describing the life of a Vietnamese lady who, having escaped in 1980, participated in the rescue of some boat people five years later and found her father's friend on the French boat.

Journalists and seamen came to talk to us every day. They were curious to know why people escaped, how much they paid, who organized the escape, who escaped, etc. They wanted to know how many escapees were drowned because of typhoons, of piracy, and of other reasons. We said that we didn't know exactly. They told us about cannibalism, rapes, and piracy, the nightmares of the boat people on the East Sea and on the Gulf of Thailand.

Many crew members of the *Jean Charcot* were members of the French Communist party. Some were unfriendly with the boat people. Some were kind and compassionate.

The most fanatic was a seaman originally from Dunkerque. He disliked the boat people and criticized them badly. He didn't know why people escaped after liberation and unity. "Don't they owe a blood debt to their people?" he asked.

He criticized religions violently, saying that the pope was "the richest man in the world."

After many hours of conversation with us, his common sense was hurt by the realization that there were deceptions and illogical things in a Communist society. Without any hesitation he said that he would leave the Communist party when he returned to France. During our stay in Palawan, Philippines, he came to see us many times. He gave us coffee, cakes, butter, cheese, and fruit. He informed us that, on the way to Paris, he was going to go to Singapore from Puerto Princesa Airport. He thanked us for letting him know our personal experiences, those of the honest people punished by the utopian regime he had dreamed of.

Another Communist member, originally from Brest, looked more discreet, calm, sober, and educated than other seamen on the boat. He used to see me at noon after he had accomplished his duties on the boat. I talked to him about what I exchanged with his friend from Dunkerque. I told him about the difference between the Vietnam Communist party and the Communist parties in Western Europe, about armed struggle and political struggle, about dictatorship and democracy.

The Vietnamese Communists heightened armed struggles and despised parliamentary struggles. When they seized power, they dissolved the existing army, the flag, and the country's name and punished all the collaborators of the old government. It would be different if a French Communist were elected president of France. The republic, its army, its flag would still exist.

I told him about the Vietnamese people's patriotism and their disappointment. The cost of independence and liberation was too expensive. Their standard of living was inferior to that of their ancestors during French rule. Their independent government restricted their freedom more rigorously than the foreigners. Nobody risked his life to leave a good regime. And, nobody escaped from a non–Communist country to look for freedom and a happy life in a Communist country.

"If you are an archaeologist or a tourist, you will praise the greatness of the pyramids and the Great Wall of China. If you are forced to do unpaid hard labor to build them, you will react against such great constructions. Beauty and ugliness depend on the positions and situations of the viewers. To be aware of the true Communist society you must be its citizen instead of being an optimistic tourist, making the poverty and suffering of others an artistic beauty," I said.

The seaman nodded his head, agreeing with me. He was curious to know about social evils in Vietnam. He looked meditative when he learned that social evils have been incurable in a poor country in which rich, powerful, and hopeless people enjoyed them. He told me that he was going to move to California. He came to talk to me every day during my one-week stay on the *Jean Charcot*. He gave me a T-shirt bearing the words *Jean Charcot* as a souvenir. I still have this souvenir gift, which reminds me of this turning point of my life.

We talked to different visitors every day from morning until midnight. Dr. Dominique was interested in Vietnamese intellectuals. He wondered if they had left Vietnam or stayed there for different reasons. A French journalist spoke well of the Vietnamese intellectuals in France and Africa. Dr. Dominique and the French journalists wanted us to settle in France.

After ten years of suffering and despair I spent the happiest week on the *Jean Charcot*. I had freedom. I felt that I was already in a new land. The blue and the immensity of the sea reminded me of freedom. I was surrounded by kind and generous people. Their noble actions moved me. They made me think of my unlucky fate and that of many quiet Vietnamese.

Because we spent so much time welcoming visitors, we lost our rations every day. Boat people took our blankets. The seamen brought us bread, meat, and fruit for dinner and gave us blankets.

The children walked to the kitchen to take oranges, apples, and canned food. Some people opened refrigerators to get fresh air for their siesta. Others used fresh water to wash clothes. The seamen asked them to save fresh water, which was rare on the boat, and to use only water they pumped from the sea. They looked disappointed when they faced the unfavorable reactions of these people. The Vietnamese physician coped with the same difficulty when he tried to explain to the boat people about fresh water rarity. He had a headache when hearing rude words from people he loved.

The *Jean Charcot* brought us to Puerto Princesa one evening. On the way to this harbor it was chased by a Soviet cruiser. The chase ended after the French flag was hoisted. I had made a wonderful trip on the Pacific Ocean dotted with islands covered with coconut trees. The insular sites of the Pacific Ocean reminded me of Vietnam with its tropical weather, white sandy beaches, limpid sea water, slender coconut trees, and flocks of seagulls flying with fatigue at sunset. The coconut trees reminded me of Ben Tre, Bong Son, Tam Quan, and An Phu Dong on the right bank of the Saigon River. They made me homesick. I was far from my family and my country. I became stateless.

There were many boats and sampans in Puerto Princesa. The Filipino fishermen waved to the *Jean Charcot*. The boat people got off the boat. Journalists, physicians, and some seamen were at the pier. They shook hands with us and promised to send telegrams to our families in Vietnam and to contact our aunt in Paris.

We got into a military truck full of boat people. Dr. Dominique looked for us. He was happy to see us on the truck, which was ready to start. He shook hands with us and said he hoped to see us in Paris on July 14. The truck moved. He walked slowly, waving to us.

Thirty minutes later, we arrived at the Palawan First Asylum Camp. All the new boat people sat in a long barracks equipped with some bulbs that emitted a flickering light. The barracks was torn, dark, and smelly.

In the flickering light appeared a group of refugees. One of them said, "On behalf of the West Command, we congratulate you on your escape from the Communist hell." A group of boy scouts headed by a young man in his twenties came. This leader asked me about my religion. He left silently when he learned that my religion was different from his. On May 29, if the captain of the *Jean Charcot* had asked forty-one persons on our boat such a question, he would have rescued only one. The other forty people would have waited for rescue from a boat of their religion!

The Palawan First Asylum Camp had approximately 2,500 refugees. It was built along the seashore by the airport of Puerto Princesa. Around the camp there were many houses of local residents. The camp seemed to be flooded when tides were rising. At reflux the boat people could walk more than a mile from the coast. The islanders were poor fishermen and farmers. They had built small sampans to go fishing or shrimping. They were poor but sweet and optimistic. They loved music and dancing. The soldiers looked proud of their uniforms and guns, which were the symbols of power.

Many residents lived in torn slums in the plantations of coconut trees. These slums could collapse in the rainy and windy season. The natives raised pigs and chickens and let them walk around the coconut tree plantations to look for food. At dark, chickens slept on the branches of guava around their slums. Pigs weren't fat. Their meat was tough. At night people lit gas-filled lamps to go fishing.

The Filipinos brought coconuts, mangos, bananas, and custard apples to the refugee camp to sell them or to exchange them for rice. Their exchange was very simple. They sold a coconut at the price of 1.5 pesos. Some boat people went to the plantation of coconut trees and picked coconuts themselves. They paid one peso for ten coconuts.

I saw many children in rags. They didn't go to school. They wandered along the coast all day long, catching fish and clams.

The refugee camp made Puerto Princesa prosperous. The boat people were deemed to be wealthy. In other words, they couldn't be boat people if they had no gold. The refugees bought food, medicine, soft drinks, cigarettes, lighters, matches, clothes, and shoes. They shuttled between the camp and Puerto Princesa City every day. When they moved to another camp and when they were chosen to resettle in their next country, they got a lot of food for their farewell parties. Some Filipinos came to the camp to exchange money, to sell expensive necessities and to buy rice from the refugees. When the exchange was fair and smooth, they said happily, "Salamat. Salamat" (Thank you).

The refugee camp was a Vietnamese village in Palawan. The boat people elected representatives to be in charge of different sections of the camp. The camp needed teachers of languages and translators to work for ICM (Inter-government Commission for Migration), UNHCR, JVA (Joint Voluntary Agencies), etc.

The people in charge of security were authoritative. They gave the refugees many troubles by harassing, menacing, arresting, beating, and jailing them. The camp was noisy and sometimes bloody. The refugees argued with and fought one another. They disagreed with one another on any business. A physician was stabbed by a teenager because of their political divergence. Some boat people abused their proficiency in English to extort those people interviewed by the Americans. Almost all refugees wanted to settle in the United States. Many former officers were denied while some people, who hadn't spent a day in the army, were chosen. How important the role of the translators was. I saw some boat people spending time studying about the carbine, its length, its weight, its bullet size, and its long-range fire — and about military boots.

Some Vietnamese fishermen went fishing in the East Sea. Their boat was dragged by a typhoon to the Philippines. They were deemed by the local government to be Communist spies. Asked by the Filipino officers, they shook their heads for they didn't know English.

"What country are you from?" the investigator asked.

Nobody said a word.

The investigator showed them the flags of different countries in the world and asked them, "Which one is your country's?"

They didn't understand the question. But they recognized the red flag with a yellow star. They pointed to it, saying that they were from the Socialist Republic of Vietnam. The investigator believed firmly that the Communists had sent them to spy on the Philippines. All of these fishermen were put in jail. They were mistreated and tortured by the Filipino prisoners. They did labor like other prisoners. In prison they had to serve the old prisoners. They got skinny. Their skin got dark brown from working outside and inside the prison without eating enough food.

One day, a Filipino came to the camp. He told about the fate of these Vietnamese fishermen. He wondered why they were imprisoned while the other Vietnamese were in the refugee camp. A boat people's representative went to the prison to visit them and to ask them why they were in jail. They said that they were stranded and detained by the Filipinos. The boat people's representative promised to get them out of jail to live in the refugee camp. They asked him to help them return to Phu Qui Island. Their families thought that they were drowned. They didn't want to go abroad. Their hope was to rejoin their families in Phu Qui (Phan Thiet).

The boat people helped them contact their families in Vietnam. They were happy to learn that they were alive and that they were going to be resettled in the United States.

Most boat people in the Palawan refugee camp were from Phu Yen, Nha Trang, and Cam Ranh (South Central Vietnam). They weren't threatened by Thai pirates during their escape. Many of them were fishermen in Vietnam.

Life in the Palawan refugee camp was comfortable. The refugees had enough food, medicine, water, firewood, and light. The ICM took care of their health. Catholic nuns were active in their social and educational activities. The regular activities of the boat people in the camp were to study languages, to get food and water, to cook meals, to clean their residential areas, to watch television, to listen to the radio, to go shopping, and to have weekly parties. Their security was ensured by the Filipino soldiers. Many of them received financial assistance from their relatives and friends in their new countries. Some opened coffee shops, grocery stores, restaurants. They sold instant noodles, beef bowls, beer, Coca-Cola, Pepsi-Cola, cigarettes, ice, fruit, and matches. A fisherman originally from Nha Trang built a sampan and went fishing at night. He sold fish to the local residents and to the boat people in the camp. A refugee made money by grinding rice. Another refugee bought gold to make necklaces, earrings and rings. He sold them to the Filipinos. A Communist major ran a barber shop. A former police officer taught martial arts.

In general, these temporary businesses were lucrative. The boat people needed everything during their stay in the camp. They bought everything at

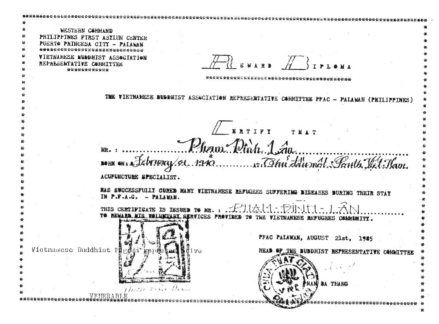

My certification as an acupuncture specialist.

high prices while the refugee "businessmen" didn't pay taxes. They weren't disturbed by gangs. Some long-time stayers had some more babies in the camp. They were good at English; they had studied four hours per day for many years. English, French, and Vietnamese were taught by the boat people, by Catholic nuns, by American and British teachers. Their children spoke good English. Some of them got wealthy by having small businesses in the camp. They weren't interested in resettlement. They wished to stay in the Philippines to practice fishing and farming.

Some long-time stayers became nervous and desperate.

A graduate of the Phu Tho College of Engineering stayed in the camp for many years although his parents had been in the United States since the fall of South Vietnam. For fear of Communist punishments he had served the new regime actively. The Communists trusted him and allowed him to adhere to the Komsomol. He became a trusted engineer in the Communist government. When he arrived at the refugee camp, he faced difficulties rejoining his family in the United States. His case reminded us of Solly, a Jewish teenager in Europe in World War II.

A Communist major escaped with his family. He had been in charge of anti-aircraft defense in North Vietnam during the war. He had shot down some American aircraft. He told accurately the times and places where the aircraft were shot down. His family was accepted by JVA but were denied permission by Immigration and Naturalization Services to be resettled in the United States.

A refugee finally arrived at the camp after trying to escape twenty-three times. Another escaped from a Communist prison in North Vietnam after spending seventeen years there. Two Vietnamese in the camp knew Tagalog. One was a Vietnamese lady whose husband had served in the Filipino civic mission in Vietnam. The other was the Communist major who ran a barber shop in the camp.

A rich lady originally from Vinh Long province escaped with her husband and their two children. The boat was stranded because of the typhoon. People on the boat didn't have enough food to eat. The escape organizers sold it for gold. Some people died for not having gold to get food. Their bodies were thrown into the sea. The escape organizers knew that the lady and her husband were rich. They tortured them and let them be hungry for they wouldn't show the organizers where the had hidden their gold. The two children died of starvation and were thrown into the sea. Their father was badly beaten by the hooligans. Their mother was unconscious from being hungry and from witnessing her children thrown into the sea and their father pitilessly tortured by heartless people.

The boat was rescued by the Filipinos. The lady and her husband were sent to the Palawan First Asylum Camp. Both of them were hospitalized. An hour after their arrival, the husband died. His wife was in a coma. Regaining consciousness, she learned that her husband had died. The bad news made her insensible in the bed. A month later, she left the camp for America by herself.

The cannibals were isolated by the boat people in the camp. They had killed many people on the boat to eat human flesh and drink human blood. They stayed in the camp for a long time. Therefore, their English improved dramatically.

The boat people underwent many nightmares. They had faced dangers and played with death on the immense sea and in the Cambodian jungles, where they could have been killed by mines, Khmer Rouge, Viet Cong, wild animals, or malaria.

One day, a young man came to see me and told me about his worries. He had been born into a rich family in Vietnam. He had escaped with his wife and was rescued by the *Jean Charcot*. He looked anxious and fearful. He feared everything. He was afraid that he couldn't study languages and that he didn't know what to do to make his living after his resettlement in his next country. He looked unhappy when he told me that his wife had integrated into the new lifestyle too fast. He avowed that he was less intelligent than his wife and that he felt awful every time he heard people speaking English.

Some boat people were quarrelsome. They liked fighting. The old boat people fought the new ones. The Nationalists fought the Communists. The long-time stayers quarreled with the lucky refugees. Sometimes they became fanatical, thinking that they conserved Vietnamese traditions and that the others had forgotten their Vietnamese origins.

Leaving the barracks one evening we wandered around the camp without knowing where to go. A group of teenagers invited us to live in their billet near the pagoda, Caodaist temple, Catholic and Baptist churches. Their billet was clean and comfortable.

These teenagers were long-time stayers in the camp. Most boat people were scared of them. Their words were rude. Their hair showed that they were hooligans. But they were polite toward us. They called us "Uncle" with respect and considered themselves members of our family. They were proud of our presence in their billet. They didn't let us do anything. They got water, cooked meals, and lined up to get food for us every day. In the morning they prepared breakfast and coffee for us. They liked to have breakfast, lunch, and dinner with us. They told us about their families in Vietnam and their true hopes. They were rude but frank and helpful. They helped me open an acupuncture room at the Buddhist temple. Listening to my advice, they attended English classes regularly. Their English was satisfactory. I prevented them from fighting the other boat people.

Our life in the camp was cozy. We had coffee, milk, cigarettes, and instant noodles in our billet. Our teenagers and their friends had the pleasure of having coffee, smoking cigarettes, and talking with us. They told us what was going on in the camp.

During our stay in Palawan our security was ensured by them.

They also ensured the life of a refugee who had mental health problems. This unlucky person was a tall man in his thirties. He had come to the camp in 1980. He was active and optimistic. He danced very well.

One day, he left the camp for Manila by boat. Manila is about 500 miles from Puerto Princesa. Our refugee was penniless. Nobody knew how he coul go on board without a ticket. Nobody knew what he went to Manila for.

Manila is the capital of the Philippines. It is a large, busy, and noisy c Our refugee went to the embassy of the Socialist Republic of Vietnam to lo the red flag. His spectacular act put the Philippines in a diplomatic dilem with Hanoi. He wasn't a Filipino but a refugee in the Philippines.

He was hospitalized. After that, he lost his vividness. He became fea unkempt and mute. He was always barebacked. It seemed that he didn' cold or hot. He could sleep anywhere without a mosquito net. He had such a life for five years before I arrived in Palawan. Until today, I don't if he is dead or alive, if he lives in his next country or in the Vietname lage in Palawan.

❖ ❖ ❖

While sleeping on the *Jean Charcot* the first night, I had heard prayers from a church and the pagoda bell ringing. It was 2:00 A.M. I deemed that the French seamen said their prayers before going to bed. The prayers were so loud that I woke up. Everybody was asleep. Lights were on. Some boat people snored noisily. The cold wind blew strongly. The waves hit the boat hull, making monotonous sounds in the moonlight. I lay down to continue my sleep. The prayers resounded in my ears.

I told my brother then that I had heard prayers in French harmonizing with the pagoda bell ringing. According to my interpretation, we were going to live near a Catholic church and a Buddhist temple. My interpretation came true when the long-haired teenagers brought us to their billet, which was surrounded by the pagoda, Caodaist temple, Catholic and Baptist churches.

In the camp I found many great hearts and noble nuns. A Vietnamese nun, Sr. Pascale Le Thi Trieu had an active role in the camp. Sisters Thomasa and Claudita were devoted teachers and social workers. Sister Thomasa opened an elementary school, a junior high, a library, and a Vietnamese class in the refugee camp. She invited me to talk about Vietnam to the Filipino teachers and encouraged me to write by giving me paper and by letting me use her typewriter and copy machine.

"It's your duty," she said.

She said that she had worked in the refugee camp for ten years without knowing a lot about Vietnam.

In the asylum camp one night, I saw in a dream Jesus ascending to the northeast. I saw the word "express" and a colorful bus. People rushed to Jesus while I walked slowly on a path. Four of us were at the rear of the bus.

The next morning I told the dream to my brother to verify it later.

In order to resolve the resettlement of the boat people quickly, UNHCR in Palawan informed us that all the boat people rescued by the *Jean Charcot* would be resettled in France, Canada, Belgium, West Germany, Italy, and Switzerland.

The general consul of France in Manila was a Vietnamese originally from Tra Vinh (Vinh Binh). He came to the camp to visit the boat people rescued by the French boat. Every time he came, he used to converse with my brother. He talked to us about his old memories of his native village during the bloody Autumn Revolution. He missed his ancestors' graves in Tra Vinh and some of his friends, who were my brother's colleagues. He hoped to go back to Vietnam to visit his ancestors' graves and to see his relatives and friends.

The representative of France in the camp was Mr. Bruneau. He taught French and French culture to people who were going to be settled in France. The general consul and Mr. Bruneau promised to help us settle in France as soon as possible. A month after our arrival in Palawan, UNHCR informed us that we were going to leave for Paris in early July. We were going to go to Manila from Puerto Princesa Airport, then to Paris from Manila Airport. The long-time stayers in the camp said that we should be happy to be resettled in such a short time. My son looked upset. He had hoped to go to college in the United States. His studies would be challenging in France because his French was poor. I didn't know what to say to comfort him.

We went shopping in Puerto Princesa to prepare for our settlement in Paris. We had many things to do in a day.

Before going to Puerto Princesa I reminded my brother of my dream concluding that we weren't going to go to France but to the northeast, that is, to Bataan camp. My brother didn't say a word. He didn't believe what I said. It was clear that we were leaving the camp the next day at 8:00 A.M.

Our friends in the camp prepared a big lunch in our honor at noon. They wished us good luck in France. I thanked them, saying, "We're not going to Paris but to Bataan." All of them laughed, thinking that I was joking. My brother, younger brother, and son thought so too.

After lunch we walked home to prepare our luggage. In dismay my brother said, "I have to go to Puerto Princesa again."

"What for?" I asked.

"I need a new pair of shoes," my brother said.

My brother was in a hurry to get to Puerto Princesa. I lay on the bamboo bed to nap. But I couldn't shut my eyes. It was sultry in July in Palawan. There were some signs of thunderstorms. At 3:00 P.M. I heard the loudspeaker calling the four of us to see the UNHCR representative. I was a little anxious. *What's wrong?* I wondered. My younger brother, son, and I went to the UNHCR office to see Mr. Greg. He welcomed us warmly.

"Where is your brother?" he asked.

"He went to Puerto Princesa to buy a new pair of shoes. He will put them on tomorrow when we leave for France," I said.

"You're not going to France. You will stay around here," he said, smiling.

We didn't understand what he meant. Why would we stay in Palawan?

"I just received a phone call from Manila to delay your departure tomorrow," he said, showing me a small piece of paper with his notes.

"How about the other eleven people?"

"They are leaving tomorrow."

"Does ICM know this news?" I asked.

"Not yet. I'll inform them."

Turning to my son he asked, "How old are you?"

"I'm eighteen years old," my son said.

"What are you planning to do in America?" he asked

"I would like to go to college."

"Good! You are young. You need to study," he said.

Leaving the UNHCR office, we walked home. A few days later, we interviewed by JVA and INS officers. We prepared to go to Bataan inste Paris.

Top: The author at the Bataan refugee camp. *Bottom:* In the Bataan refugee camp. From left to right, Pham Dinh Nam Quoc (son), Pham Dinh Lan (author), Bui Thanh Chon (friend) and Pham Dinh Hung (brother).

We went to Manila with 254 boat people by sea. From the Manila dock we went to Bataan, 120 miles from there, by bus. Each bus carried fifty refugees. Everybody got into the five buses while the four of us stood at the dock. When the five buses left, the sixth one arrived to pick up only four people. My son pointed to the bus, saying, "Look! This bus bears the word *express*." All of us laughed happily. Our bus left late but it arrived in Bataan before the other five.

At the welcome center I saw a Chinese friend of mine. He helped the four of us look for a billet in the fifth neighborhood. A few days later, I saw a friend of my oldest brother in the eighth neighborhood. He was pale and skinny. He looked passive although he had a vivid life story.

He was originally from Thuan Giao. His family was the only Catholic family in the village. His father was postmaster.

When a student, he was a turbulent one. He loved the circus and jokes. What he did was adventurous. What he said could be true or imaginary. In 1945 he joined the resistance. In 1953 he left the jungles silently for the city without any explanation. He neither criticized the Communists nor collaborated with the Nationalists. He made his fortune in Laos. In 1955 he returned to Vietnam and ran a joiner's workshop, which brought him much money. But he had to work hard. In the course of his life he changed occupations several times. He was successful in any business he tried although they were new to him. He built a villa near Bien Hoa and had a happy life until 1975.

When the Communists came, he behaved as if he were a Viet Cong in charge of information and culture. Shortly after liberation, some former South Vietnamese Viet Minh in North Vietnam returned to the South. A former Viet Minh recognized him and informed the police that he had killed a Communist commissar during the nine-year war while the latter was asleep. He was sent to a reeducation camp in Song Be on account of this killing. In the re-education camp he suggested that they build a smithy to make hoes. At that time many urban residents became farmers. They needed hoes. So it was easy to sell them. The smithy didn't work regularly for lack of metal. As for him, he learned something new and gained credit with the Communist cadres in the reeducation camp.

He was released after spending five years in the camp. His family was broke. His life became miserable. He was watched and suspected by the local government. He decided to leave Vietnam with his wife and four children. He didn't have gold to escape by boat. He didn't have the money to bribe the *bo doi* in Cambodia to become walking people either.

How could he carry out his dream?

His family consisted of six people. His youngest son was nineteen years old. They went to Chau Doc by bus. They stayed and worked there a few days to get some money. He fixed bicycles. His wife sold vegetables. Their four children helped people carry fish and rice to make their living. The police didn't pay attention to them because they were poor laborers. From Chau Doc, they went to Phnom Penh. This city was ruined under the rule of Pol Pot. Many houses were abandoned. Their owners had been forced to leave the city. Some were killed. Some died of starvation. Some died of languishment. Some died from not being able to stand hardship, torture, or a wandering life. Every family had at least one member missing or killed by the Khmer Rouge.

Phnom Penh was short of electricity and water. Its security was assured by the Vietnamese *bo doi* after the defeat of the Khmer Rouge. Our friend's family was homeless there. In the daytime they earned their living by doing manual labor. The father fixed bicycles. The mother worked for a Chinese restaurant as a dishwasher. The four children were water carriers. In the nighttime they slept in the market.

Silently our friend studied the journey to the West. His family moved slowly to the Thai-Cambodian border. Sometimes they took the train. Sometimes they took buses. They walked in the forests for many days before reaching the Thai border. It took three years to arrive in Thailand. His youngest son died of malaria as soon as they were in Thailand. His family stayed in the Thai refugee camp for two years before leaving for Bataan.

Bataan was a bloody battlefield in World War II. It is mountainous. Sometimes there are earthquakes there. The lands are fertile with many centennial mango trees bearing plenty of fruit. The Filipinos sold vegetables, fruit, and dried food under their shade.

The refugee camp was built in a picturesque valley surrounded by mountains and green meadows. It had 18,000 to 25,000 Southeast Asian refugees who were qualified to be resettled in the United States. Some refugees who had been chosen to settle in Norway lived in the Bataan camp to study Norwegian.

The camp had ten neighborhoods. All the billets were clean and airy. So were the toilets. People could walk from one neighborhood to another. They could take buses. There were two markets in the camp: one for neighborhoods 1, 2, 3, 4, and 5 and one for neighborhoods 6, 7, 8, 9, and 10. Boat people and ODP people (Amerasians and immigrants sponsored by their relatives) lived together in the camp to study ESL (English as a Second Language) and CO (Cultural Orientation) before going to America. Their stay was three months to six months or more. It depended on their level of English, ESL attendance, health, and discipline in the camp.

The Bataan camp was more comfortable than the Palawan camp. The number of refugees breaking the camp regulations was negligible. Boat people in Palawan didn't know their resettlement countries. But the refugees in Bataan did.

The Cambodian and Laotian refugees lived in their own neighborhoods. The Vietnamese built a flagpole and a Buddhist temple. The Cambodian and Laotian refugees built splendid temples in their neighborhoods.

Each neighborhood had its representatives and a Filipino advisor. The camp was headed by a former colonel. He was in Vietnam during the Franco-Vietnamese War and after the partition of Vietnam. He liked Saigon, Hue, and Hanoi. He admired President Magsaysay and Ngo Dinh Diem.

The camp was well organized. It had a big hospital, an ICM office, an ICMC (International Catholic Migration Commission) office, a CMHS (Community Mental Health Service) office, a JVA office, a UNHCR office. The ICM was responsible for health screenings, departure lists, etc. The ICMC was responsible for education and CMHS for family conflicts, mental health problems, etc.

In general, most refugees in Bataan had comfortable lives. Everybody looked optimistic. The springs became romantic dating places. Romantic loves blossomed from ESL classes, coffee shops, and restaurants. The number of newborn babies increased.

Refugees learned many new things. They learned English and the ways of life in America. They learned dancing. They sought to know about life in America, its laws and social assistance. They were curious to learn some strange things, such as the United States of "fifty-two" states or "children, ladies, pets, and men." Women and children were really liberated by the law. Some ladies spoke of divorce. Some teenagers left their families to live with their boyfriends or girlfriends. Polygamists had cold feet. The patriarchal regime seemed to decline. Gender discrimination came to an end. Child and wife abuse must be avoided.

Many Filipino teachers didn't support President Marcos. A few of them supported him passively, saying, "He is smart." A Filipino teacher fell in love with her refugee student. Her family was unfavorable to such an interracial love. She hoped that her boyfriend, after his settlement in America, would write to her and tell her about their marriage. His silence disappointed her. It buried her juvenile love in the mountainous refugee camp. She left Bataan for Manila, trying to forget her short happy time in the refugee camp.

Time flitted by. We were in the Bataan camp for three months. We were waiting for the departure list.

A couple of days before Christmas I told my brother that we would leave for America on January 27. Our destination would be Toledo, the city I saw in a dream before leaving Vietnam.

My brother was surprised.

"Did you see the departure list?" he asked

"No, I didn't," I said.

"How do you know that we are going to leave on January 27?"

I kept silent. I was afraid that my brother thought that I told nonsense.

On New Year's afternoon my son informed me of the new departure list he had seen at ICM, where he worked.

To the United States (January 27, 1986). From left to right, Pham Dinh Nam Quoc (son), Pham Dinh Khuyen (younger brother), Pham Dinh Hung (brother), Bui Kim Tuoi (Chon's sister), Theresa (ESL and CO teacher), and Pham Dinh Lan (author).

"When?" I asked.

"January 27," my son said.

I smiled. Suddenly I felt vaguely sad. I looked at the West, trying to find the image of my country and family behind the gray clouds.

We left Manila Airport on January 27, 1986.

The huge Boeing 747 of Northwest Airlines brought us to Seoul, flew over Japan, crossed the Pacific Ocean, and arrived in the United States on the same day. Frosty snow welcomed us in Washington, Illinois, and Ohio. A new horizon appeared. However, in my mind, there were mixed feelings. I felt happy for having freedom, security, and a stable life in a new land where people were totally different from me. But, the dreary winter of North America made me more homesick. It was frosty outside. Cold winds blew intermittently. They whistled horribly like the sobs in my heart. I missed my country. I missed my family. I missed my mother and blood relatives. I missed the living and the dead as well. I missed my house in Laithieu and my ancestors' graves in Tuy An and Binh Chuan.

The rise of South Korea and American prosperity made me think a lot about our unhappy country. Our people have been a hard-working and studious.

They deforested, dug the mountains and filled up deep everglades
To build up a country with splendid mountains and rivers.

Family reunion. From left to right, Pham Dinh Quoc An (son), Leang Ping (daughter-in-law), Tammy Nguyen Pham (wife), David Lan Pham (author), Wellington Nguyen Pham (son), Elizabeth Lan Pham (daughter), Victoria Chau Pham (youngest daughter) and Albert Quoc Pham (oldest son).

They surmounted multiple hardships and challenges to keep their existence in the world. This people underwent many centuries under foreign rule. They struggled for their country's independence and for their survival in a country permanently threatened by flood, drought, insects, typhoons, and foreign invasions.

Their country became independent. But their lives had no improvement. They were in regression. Their freedom was seriously hurt.

Continual wars tore up their country and disunited the people. The country's prosperity became nebulous and ephemeral. Conscience and ideals became abstract notions.

The leaders didn't love their country or the people but loved power. In return, their people didn't believe them. They became indifferent, passive, and selfish.

The contribution of the intellectuals to the growth and prosperity of the country has been small. Most of them were haughty and bureaucratic. Some were demagogic. Some developed an inferiority complex, thinking that their country had nothing good.

Vietnam hasn't been a poor country. Its plains are fertile. Its natural resources are abundant. Its people are hard-working and creative. Good and capable people have been numerous, but their incapable, greedy, and narrow-minded leaders killed their enthusiasm. Some were forced to retire. Some were imprisoned. Some claimed to have mental health problems. Some had wandering lives in foreign lands. Many people were in adverse situations.

> *Since the end of the war*
> *They have known only their diaspora.*

Many people wept silently for the ups and downs of their country.

> *After years of bloodshed,*
> *Their country is still there.*
> *Their friends are still there.*
> *Everybody remains miserable.*

Many Vietnamese dreamed of good leadership, peace and prosperity in their dear country, waiting for the time when

> *The deep blue sky flower of Freedom,*
> *And the red flower of Happiness*
> *Blossom even on the inanimate rock.*

Many of them prayed for their dear Vietnam to see the dawn after many centuries in darkness.

I was plunged into nostalgia, anxiety and hope. I slept deeply.

It snowed outside.

Index

202, 238, 242, 245, 246, 255, 265, 272, 277
Viet Gian (traitor) 21, 40
Viet Long (cinema) 78, 95
Viet Minh 13, 17, 18, 19, 20, 21, 27, 28, 29, 30, 31, 32, 34, 35, 36, 37, 39, 40, 42, 43, 51, 52, 53, 54, 55, 56, 58, 60, 62, 63, 64, 70, 75, 76, 77, 80, 85, 87, 88, 89, 93, 94, 96, 106, 114, 128, 132, 169, 173, 184, 193, 216, 277
Viet Minh Front 28, 36
Vietnam 6, 9, 11, 16, 17, 19, 24, 28, 32, 36, 40, 49, 54, 55, 67, 68, 69, 71, 72, 74, 75, 76, 77, 84, 85, 87, 90, 91, 92, 94, 95, 96, 106, 108, 111, 112, 113, 114, 116, 118, 119, 120, 121, 123, 124, 127, 134, 137, 141, 143, 144, 145, 149, 150, 152, 154, 155, 160, 169, 173, 178, 181, 183, 184, 188, 189, 196, 203, 204, 205, 211, 224, 227, 228, 229, 231, 236, 238, 239, 243, 244, 247, 250, 251, 252, 264, 266, 267, 268, 270, 272, 273, 274, 277, 279, 281, 282
Vietnam Air Force 75, 105
Viet Nam Dan Xa Dang 88
Vietnamese American Association 111
Vietnam Community Party (Dang Cong San Viet Nam) 175, 185, 191, 193, 229, 266
Vietnamization 122, 139
Viet Nam Nhan Xa Dang 130
Vietnam Navy 75
Viet Nam Phuc Quoc Hoi 88
Viet Nam Phoc Dan Dang (political party) 36, 87, 142, 156
Viet Nam Quoc Tu 107, 110
Vietnam War 96, 100, 104, 114, 119, 122, 126, 127, 132, 139, 150, 191, 198, 199, 224
Vinh Binh (Tra Vinh) 177, 260, 261, 262, 274
Vinh Linh 110
Vinh Long 234, 235, 272
Vinh Phu (near Phu Long) 38, 45, 52, 229, 249, 256, 257, 258
Vinh Phu (near Tuy An) 3
Vinh Tran *see* Vinh Long
Vo Binh Dinh (martial arts) 142
Vo Dai Ton 229, 230
Voice of America (VOA) 104, 144, 161, 247
Vo Ky (Truong Vo Ky) 110

Volkswagen (car) 189
Vo Nguyen Giap 36, 126, 155, 171, 185, 235
Vo Truong Toan 69
Vo Van Kiet 192, 205
Vo Van Ngo 85
Vo Vi Nam (martial arts) 142
Vu Hong Khanh 48
Vu Ngoc Nha 129, 246, 247
Vung Tau (Cap St. Jacques) 68, 73, 86
Vung Tau (Charter) 108
Vuong Van Dong 105
Vuon Lai 71
Vuon Ong Thuong (Vuon Bo Ro) 67
Vu Quoc Thong 40
Vu Van Mau 104, 152, 153

"walking people" 211, 228
War Invalid Day (July 27) 198
War Zone D 20, 53, 254
Washington, George 94
Washington, D.C. 92, 95, 97, 104, 105, 107, 109, 126, 129, 133, 150, 153, 154
Washington State 280
Watergate 140
Waterloo 109, 224
West Berlin 121
West Command (Philippines) 268
Western Europe 213, 267
West Germany 72, 119, 155, 243, 274
White House 134
World War I 66, 113
World War II 9, 10, 14, 17, 42, 46, 69, 84, 92, 95, 113, 131, 134, 142, 155, 157, 168, 179, 203, 235, 254, 271, 278

Xa Cam 4
Xa Cat 4
Xa To *see* To (captain)
Xay Dung (newspaper) 130
Xom Cui 73, 125
Xom Thom 125
Xo Viet Nghe Tinh Street (Hong Thap Tu) 66, 176
Xuan Loc 4, 19, 91

Yen (Mr.) 246
Yugoslavia 120

Zatopek 48